The Profit Box System of Forecasting Stock Prices

The Profit Box System of Forecasting Stock Prices

Wilfred R. George

DOW JONES-IRWIN
Homewood, Illinois 60430

The author is a vice president and account executive with a New York Stock Exchange member firm. The information contained herein, including any expression of opinion, has been obtained from, or is based upon, sources believed to be reliable, but its accuracy or completeness is not guaranteed. The reader must not assume that any chart, theory, or philosophy (including those set forth in this book) can produce profits in the stock market, or that future results in the illustrated securities will equal the performance referred to in this book.

First Printing, October 1976

ISBN 0-87094-129-1
Library of Congress Catalog Card No. 76-15737

Printed in the United States of America

To my professors and associates at
Golden Gate University,
the Technical Securities Analysts of San Francisco,
my wife, and friends
for their help and encouragement.

Preface

If a stock trader wants to be, and stay, successful, he must have a very clear idea of just when it is that the trend of a stock changes. If not, he will give all his profits back in the inevitable bear market, and his financial success is likely to become buried in the financial graveyard along with that of millions of other unfortunate traders.

The purpose of this book is to explore one specific "box" method for defining trend changes, to show how it can provide a practical method to preserve capital and make it grow. I call this method the "Profit Box System" or "PBS." The name may sound commercial but it clearly indicates the objective—profits!

The PBS describes stock trends and trend changes. It is a system designed to "let profits run, and cut losses short," a slogan often heard on Wall Street. The basic concept is not new, but it has not been as well defined as it is in this book. The PBS is but one way to define stock trends. Other ways include moving averages, point and figures, relative strength, accumulation/distribution, and price/volume.

Once you start using the PBS you will find it to be:

Fast (you record prices but once a week).

Simple (neither math nor calculators are required).

A shortcut (it provides early timing signals, especially for those who follow other timing methods).

Anticipatory (it often gives buy or sell signals months before the good or bad news comes out).

Positive (it may give a wrong signal, but it's never an uncertain one).

A relief (it's a relief knowing what direction your stocks are going, when to buy, and when to sell).

Versatile (the PBS can be used with volatile stocks, bonds, options, foreign currency, and other changing economic data to determine trends).

PBS assumes that a time series of stock prices forms trends, which leads to my hypothesis that by using the Profit Box System:

1. *Trends can be defined,*
2. *Trend changes can be defined,*
3. *Worthwhile profits can be made,*
4. *And kept,* in volatile markets over a long period of time.

In this book the PBS is applied to many stocks, over long periods. "After all," you might say, "why not trade just one group of stocks all the time if the system is so good?" The writer recognizes that some judicious selection can dramatically improve a trader's performance. The stocks tested are mostly volatile, and all are listed on the New York Stock Exchange. They are not the most volatile, nor do they necessarily represent an adequate sample. However, the number tested is large enough to challenge the random walk theorists, mostly academicians, who believe that it is impossible to predict the future course of stock prices based on past price fluctuations.

By the time you finish this book you will learn:

How to use the Profit Box System for your own stocks, bonds, and other speculative and economic media.

When to sell, and sell short.

When to buy, and when to cover short sales.

How you can be wrong about 50 percent of the time, yet do very well in the stock market.

How to preserve capital and recognize the forces that are working against you.

Why it may be to your benefit to follow your own stocks and make your own sell decisions—and not rely on your emotions, your broker, and sometimes, even professional advisors.

How to free yourself from the conflicting views of experts.

Successful investing is 60 percent *what* you buy, and 40 percent *when* you buy. This book is devoted to helping you determine the "when."

San Francisco, California
September 1976

WILFRED R. GEORGE

Contents

Chapter 1

Introduction

Recently a client asked me: "What does it take to be a successful stock trader?" I replied that part of the answer lies in the answers to these two questions:

"When does a stock stop going up, and start to come down?"

"When does a stock stop going down, and start to go up?"

Most traders and investors have never really given any serious thought to, or even asked, these basic questions. Therefore, they have never come up with the answers *

Some years ago, I decided these two questions were so terribly important that it would be worth spending a considerable amount of time in finding some answers. In my initial effort I selected a volatile stock to research, Fairchild Camera and Instrument (FCI). I applied four different trend analysis techniques to determine which one produced the best trading results.

The best method, which turned out to be a combination of three trend analysis methods, produced a theoretical gain of 16,720 percent over an 11 year period! Obviously these methods often required exceptionally good judgment, and had the benefit of too much hindsight. In other words, it was doubtful that these methods could have achieved anywhere near this performance in a real situation.

There was, however, one simple method that really surprised me with its results. Once programmed, it required no judgment. It produced clear-cut "buy" and "sell" decisions. I now call it the Profit Box System (PBS).

Over the 11 year period Fairchild Camera would have produced a cumulative 294 percent gain, taking into account both long and short position trading. During this same period the Dow Jones Industrial Averages gained about 38 percent.

Later I extended the PBS research to include International Business

* I use the term "investor," "speculator," and "trader" as one and the same, since each has the same objective but with a different idea on how to achieve it.

Machines (IBM) and Fairchild Camera over longer periods. I found that the PBS, over a 13 year period, would have produced about 50 percent profitable trades and 50 percent loss trades. *The important finding was that the average profitable trade would have been about three times the average loss trade.* These figures were highly significant for several reasons. First, the Profit Box System appeared to *produce outstanding long term performance,* to *preserve capital,* and to *provide a way to cope with unforeseen bull or bear markets, without forecasting.* I marveled at the results, and wondered whether this would be a sound way to trade other stocks.

Here are some results from further research using PBS to define trends and predict trend changes:

1. The PBS gave a buy signal for Fairchild Camera at $47 a share and a subsequent sell signal at $134, the 28th week in 1965 and the 2d week in 1966, respectively, a 185 percent gain before trading costs.
2. The PBS gave a sell (or sell short) signal for Penn Central at $27 a share and a subsequent buy (or buy to cover the short sale) at $7 a share, a 74 percent gain. Or if you did not sell short, it would have protected you from a 74 percent loss!
3. One of the longest and most profitable buy signals came with Skyline Corporation, which signaled a buy at $8³⁄₈ (adjusted for splits) and a sell at $75, from the 26th week of 1967 to the 2d week of 1969, for an 800 percent gain!
4. But the PBS is far from perfect. It also gave a buy signal for Fairchild Camera at $34 a share and a subsequent sell signal at $22 two weeks later in the wild markets of 1974, for a loss of 35 percent.

Before using the PBS for trading be sure to read this book in its entirety with particular attention to the chapters titled, "Is the PBS Really Practical?" which discusses PBS disadvantages and advantages, and "Winners Train." Frankly, I know of no trading formula that will guaranty profitable trading. All examples of PBS trading in this book are hypothetical except where specifically otherwise noted.

What follows in this book is a detailed description of PBS and its applications to securities, timing decisions.

Chapter 2

The Profit Box System — What It Is — How It Works

The Profit Box System (PBS) is a simple method that tells you whether your stock is in an uptrend, a downtrend, or a sideways trend. It also tells you *when* to buy or to sell. Its primary use is for traders. It provides wrong signals all too often, but at no time is it uncertain! The PBS is always very positive in telling you the direction of your stock. It seems to work best on volatile stocks.

This phenomenon is basic to the PBS. Although there can be no assurance that these patterns will always hold, or hold in most cases, the PBS assumes that, in a strong uptrend in the market, a sell signal will not appear until a substantial profit has been realized, while in a down market a sell signal will appear long before the stock has reached its bottom. If you question this basic assumption, *don't use PBS.*

The PBS does not require a multimillion dollar computer system with a huge staff of personnel, all encased in a bombproof skyscraper. All it requires is a newspaper with closing prices for the week, a pad of graph paper (five squares to the inch) from the dime store, and a pencil.

To keep track of your stocks, write down each week's closing prices. You can ask your broker to do this, but don't count on it. After all, your broker has hundreds of accounts with many different objectives, and thousands of different stocks. Further, your broker is paid for executing trades and providing service, not for managing portfolios. This compares with investment advisors who are paid a fee for managing stock portfolios.

PBS DEFINITIONS

The Profit Box System defines trends, and trend changes, as follows:

1. *The trend is "up" as long as each successive lowpoint is higher than the previous lowpoint.* (For stocks and bonds, weekly closing prices are used. Daily prices are not used. See Figure 1.) A lowpoint

Figures 1–6
The Profit Box System

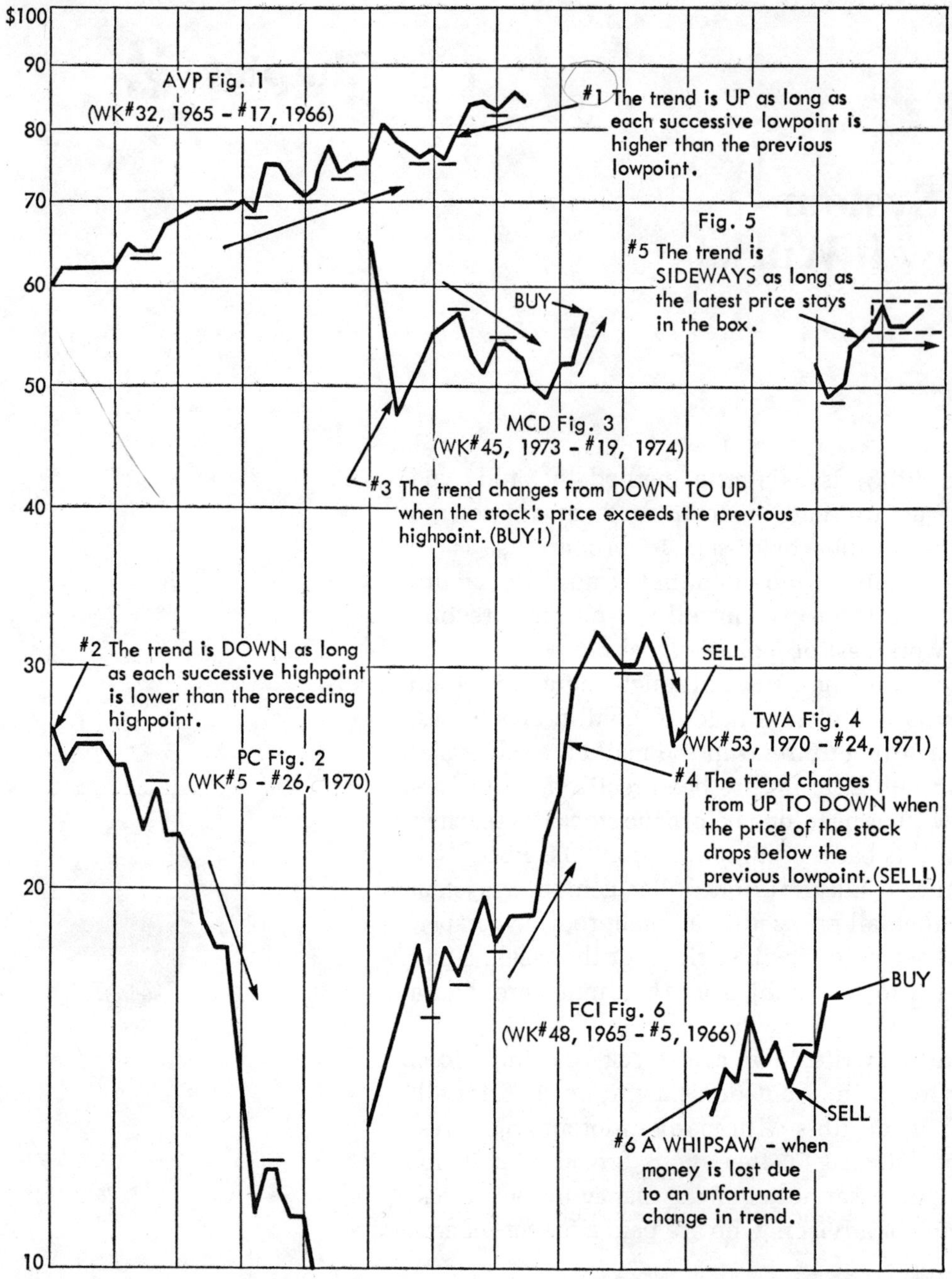

(L) is defined as the price that is lower than both the immediately preceding and following prices, e.g., $35 is the lowpoint in the sequence $36, $35(L), $37. Using a chart, the lowpoint is the bottom point of the "V."

2. *The trend is "down" as long as each successive highpoint is lower than the preceding highpoint.* (See Figure 2.) A highpoint (H) is defined as the price that is higher than both the immediately preceding and following prices, e.g., $18 is the highpoint in the sequence $16, $18(H), $17. On a chart the highpoint is the top point of the pyramid "∧."
3. *The trend changes from down to up when the latest price closes above the previous highpoint.* This is a *Buy* signal. (See Figure 3.)
4. *The trend changes from up to down when the latest price closes below the previous lowpoint.* This is a *Sell* signal. (See Figure 4.)
5. *The trend is "sideways" as long as each succeeding closing price stays within the box,* that is, between the previous highpoint and lowpoint prices. (See Figure 5.)
6. A "whipsaw" occurs when a trade has to be reversed, and money is lost. (See Figure 6.)

The PBS is dynamic, not static. Each new highpoint or lowpoint changes the dimensions of the Profit Box.

As time passes, the lowpoints in an uptrend keep rising until the price makes a lower lowpoint (the sell signal). The highpoints in a downtrend keep declining until the price makes a higher highpoint (the buy signal).

Therefore, a stock is bought, or bought to cover a previous short sale, when the trend changes from "*down*" to "*up*," and is held as long as each successive lowpoint is higher than the previous lowpoint.

When the trend changes from "*up*" to "*down*," the stock is sold (aggressive traders may also wish to sell short). This position (cash or short stock) is held as long as each successive highpoint is lower than the preceding highpoint. Specific steps are given in the Fairchild Camera example in a later chapter.

ONCE UPON A TIME . . .

Several years ago, an investment advisor was interested in buying for his clients a stock called Coastal States Gas (see Figure 7). The stock had dipped down to $42 a share from a high of $56, and he wondered if this were the time to buy it. After checking several previous weekly closing prices, the PBS indicated that Coastal States was in a downtrend, so his answer was, "No, don't buy it yet."

A week or so later the stock had dipped to $37, and the advisor considered it again. The PBS told him, "No, not yet."

The stock continued to drop to $30, then to $25, and the answer continued to be, "No. . . ."

By the time Coastal States Gas had dropped to $20, the bad news had come out: The newspapers reported that the company had a major problem regarding its gas reserves. By now the investment advisor

Figure 7

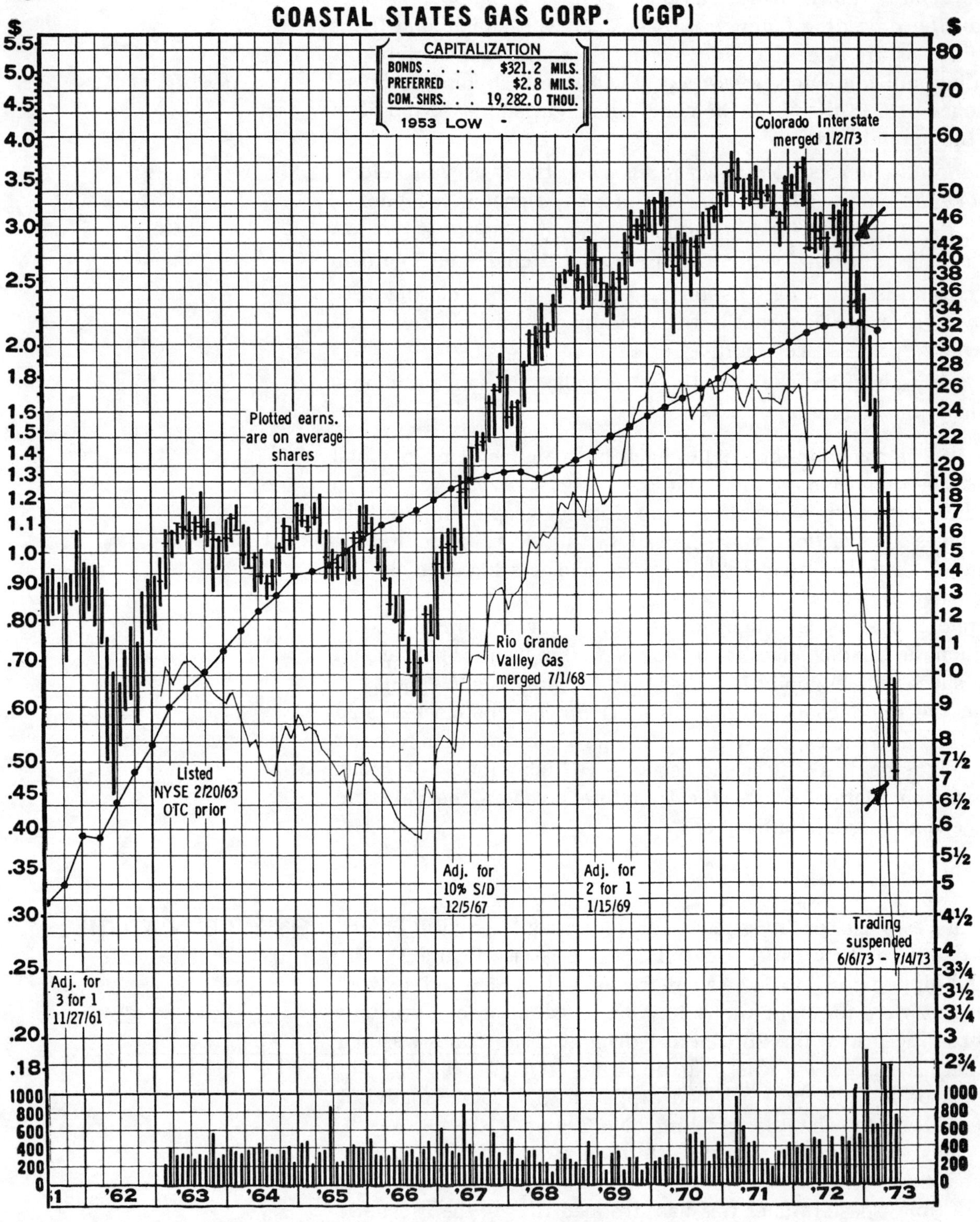

Source: Chart by Securities Research Company, 208 Newbury Street, Boston, Mass. 02116.

Figure 8

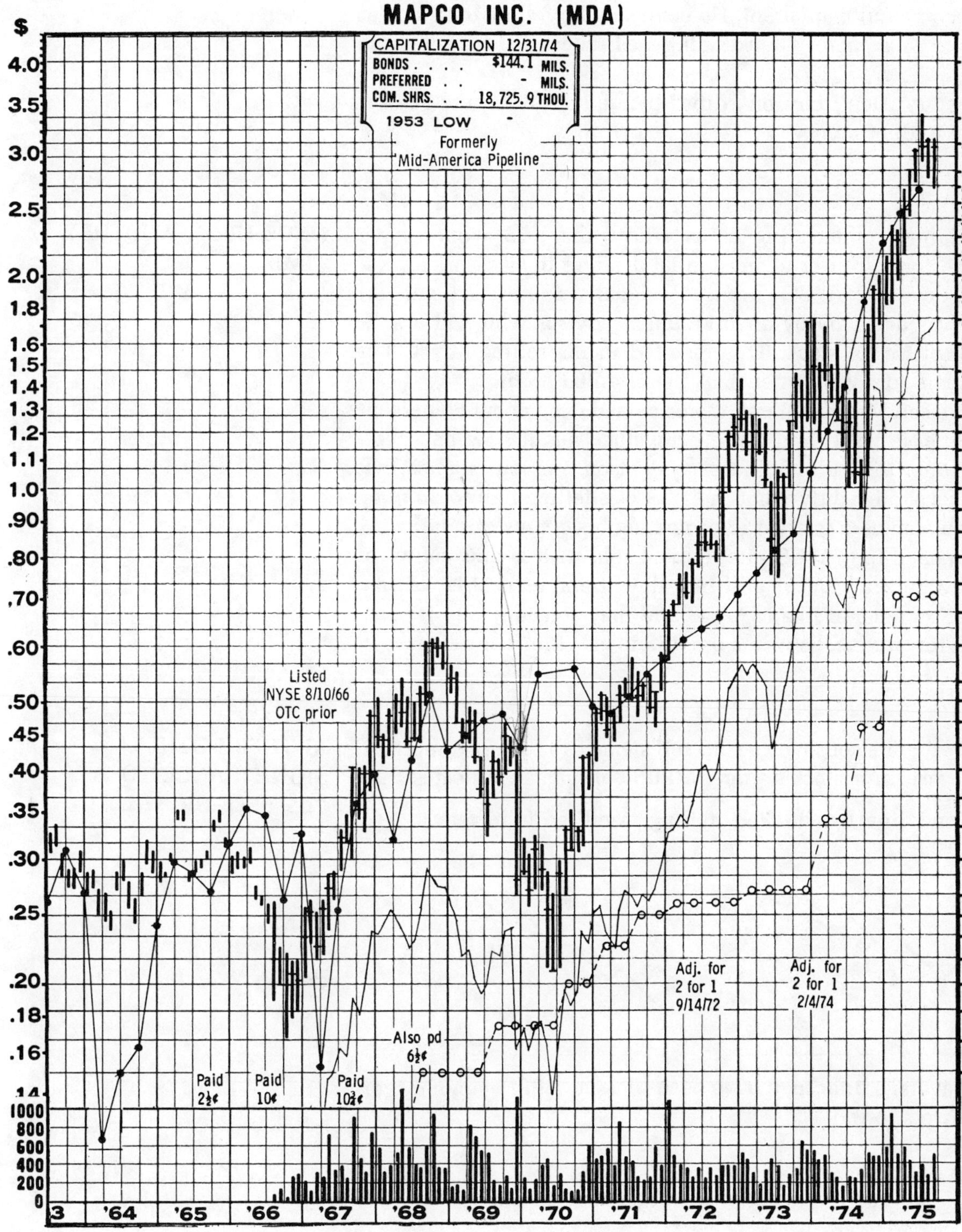

Source: Chart by Securities Research Company, 208 Newbury Street, Boston, Mass. 02116.

had lost all interest in buying the stock, because the company's problems had become quite apparent. He continued to follow the stock as it collapsed to $7 a share. Then trading was suspended (as shown in Figure 7).

Moral of story: Don't buy on "dips" before consulting the PBS! It can save you a lot of money.

ONCE UPON ANOTHER TIME . . .

There are many interesting cases where the PBS would have "tipped" investors off prior to substantial declines in stock prices. Recently a stock called MAPCO gave a sell signal at $44+ (see Figure 8.) This signal was acted on by an investment advisor who had a substantial interest in the stock. This resulted in his selling MAPCO at over $44 a share for all his clients, at a substantial profit.

Why did he sell MAPCO? First, the price had risen about 50 percent from his purchase price, and he felt the stock might now be "overvalued." Second, the PBS had been so right on previous signals that he couldn't pass off lightly what the PBS was telling him to do now. Third, he had a sincere interest in protecting his clients' capital.

What happened to MAPCO after he had sold it? It is now selling at $30, down 32 percent, and is still in a downtrend as of this writing. This advisor happens to like MAPCO and may someday buy it back. When? Well, for starters, he wants the PBS to give him a buy signal . . .

IS THERE OTHER SIGNIFICANCE TO A PBS SELL SIGNAL?

There are other reasons why a PBS sell signal can be very important. After a long rise in a stock's price, a PBS sell signal indicates that:

1. An uptrend line was broken, telling trendline followers to sell.

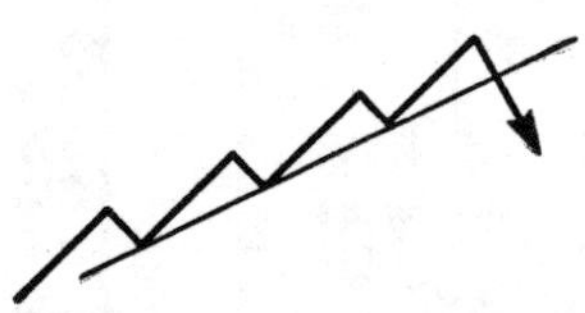

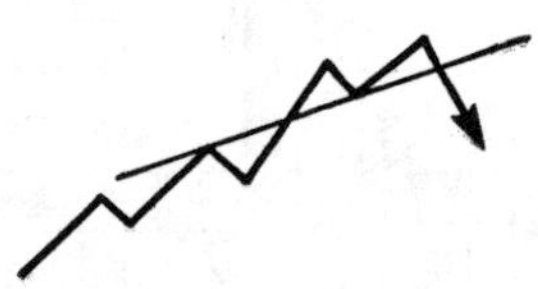

2. Moving average lines may have been broken, telling moving average followers to sell.

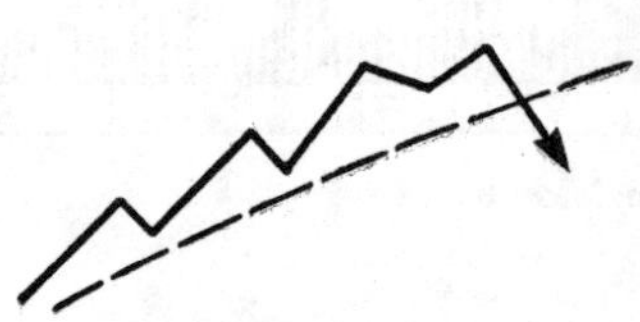

3. Point and figure charts often give concurrent sell signals to their followers.

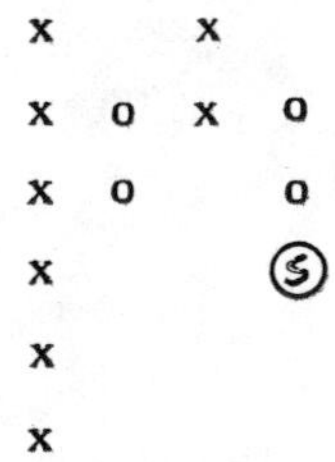

4. Stop orders placed just below the previous lowpoint may be executed.

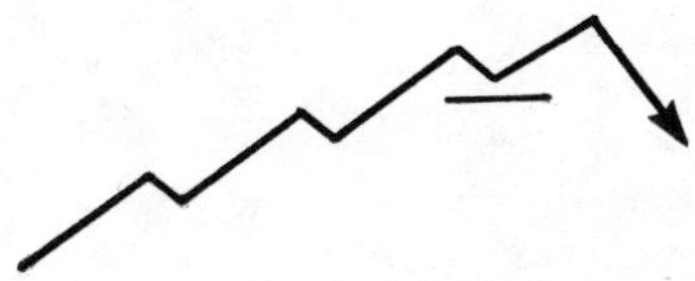

5. The stock may have become "overpriced" when the stock price refuses to push on to new highs and, instead, makes a lower lowpoint.

SOMETIMES A PEBBLE CAN CAUSE AN AVALANCHE

Once the price of a stock is in a "well-defined" downtrend, usually long after the PBS has given its sell signal, other forces tend to add to the momentum:

Other traders are encouraged to sell the stock short.

Financial analysts begin to remove their buy recommendations, or change them to hold, due to "market" or other unforeseen conditions found to be affecting the stock.

The downtrend discourages buyers, encourages sellers.

Investors often sell because the stock is "going down," or they become disillusioned, or they want to establish a tax loss.

Stop orders placed at lower levels are executed.

The momentum gains as margin calls and telegrams go out to undermargined customers telling them to put up more money or collateral. Those who follow the old Wall Street saying, "Never Meet A Margin Call," will sell on the first margin call. Others will deposit more cash and collateral until they can't put up anymore, then they sell. Bankers, who are holding stocks as collateral for loans, get very nervous and request more collateral for their loans. If these requests are not met, the stock is sold to protect their loans. Local newspapers join the growing crowd of bears with such headlines as, "Stock Decline Is Largest In Months!"

A downtrend *can* feed upon itself, and a pebble *can* cause an avalanche.

Chapter 3

For Example . . .

To illustrate how the PBS works, I selected ten stocks to trade, hypothetically, over the ten year period 1965 to 1975, using the Profit Box System. All ten stocks are listed on the New York Stock Exchange, and most represent the largest company in their industry. They represent a wide range of stocks—growth, cyclical, and even the stock of a bankrupt company. An effort was made to select stocks that were above average in volatility. None of the ten stocks could be considered to be an "income stock."

One exception to the above was also tested, American Telephone & Telegraph, to demonstrate why the PBS is not likely to be helpful for nonvolatile stocks.

Any ten year period could have been used for the test, but the further one goes back, the more difficult it is to find the proper statistics. I do suspect that the PBS would have worked as well, for example, for the period 1890 to 1900, or any other previous ten year period.

The 1965 to 1975 period included all kinds of stock markets—bull (up), bear (down), and sideways stock markets. It was a very challenging time for investors and traders. It was easy to make profits during the first part of this period, but few were able to keep their profits during the latter part. Many investors lost huge amounts of money, especially in the bear markets of 1969–70 and 1973–74.

The general trend for this ten year period was not up, as you might suspect, but down. The Dow Jones Industrial Index declined 29 percent, the Dow Jones Utility Index declined 56 percent!

You can see how the stock market indexes performed during the ter year period, 1965 to 1975, in Table 1 on the following page.

These statistics tell a frightening story:

1. The stock market decline reflected many economic problems of this period, perhaps the major one being high inflation (over 10 percent at times), and loss of investor confidence (see Figure 9).
2 The utility index declined 56 percent! It is ironic that this index is made up of "high quality," "conservative" income stocks!

3. Bond yields more than doubled! This meant that long-term bond holders had tremendous losses in their bond portfolios. Yet, high quality bonds were long believed to be very stable and conservative. You may say these losses are only "paper losses," because these bonds will eventually be redeemed at a price near what they originally sold for. But they are *real* losses if one must sell them before maturity.

Table 1

	December 31		Gain or
	1964	*1974*	*Loss (percent)*
Dow Jones Industrial Index	874	616	−30%
Utility Index	155	68	−56%
Transportation	205 (rails)	143 (trans)	−30%
S&P 500 Index	84	68	−19%
Barron's Low Priced Stocks	195	116	−41%
Dow Jones Industrial stock yield	3.63%	6.26%	+ 72%
Dow Jones 40 bond yield	4.59%	9.99%	+117%

Because this ten year period was so difficult, it provided a good—but especially tough—period to test any system for trading stocks.

The end of 1974 proved to be the almost exact bottom of a long two year bear market. As an afterthought, the results for the first six months of 1975 were included to show how PBS performed in a bull market.

Comparisons were made for each stock using three assumptions, as if you had:

1. Bought and held each stock for the entire ten year period, unless otherwise noted.
2. Traded each stock using the PBS, buying and selling.
3. Traded each stock using the PBS in buying the stock, plus buying to cover short sales, and selling the stock plus selling short, i.e., being fully committed at all times.

Due to the tremendous number of statistics used in this book, it is probable that an error might be overlooked, for which I sincerely apologize. If you should find an error, I hope it will be on the positive side—certainly, no harm is intended.

ASSUMPTIONS AND NOTES

When the Profit Box System was used to trade ten stocks, usually for periods of ten or more years, certain assumptions were made:

1. Weekly closing prices were used. The specialists who make the markets in these stocks are assumed to reduce their long or short positions to their lowest point by Friday's close; this lowers their risk and the cost of holding positions over each weekend. Therefore, the last

Figure 9

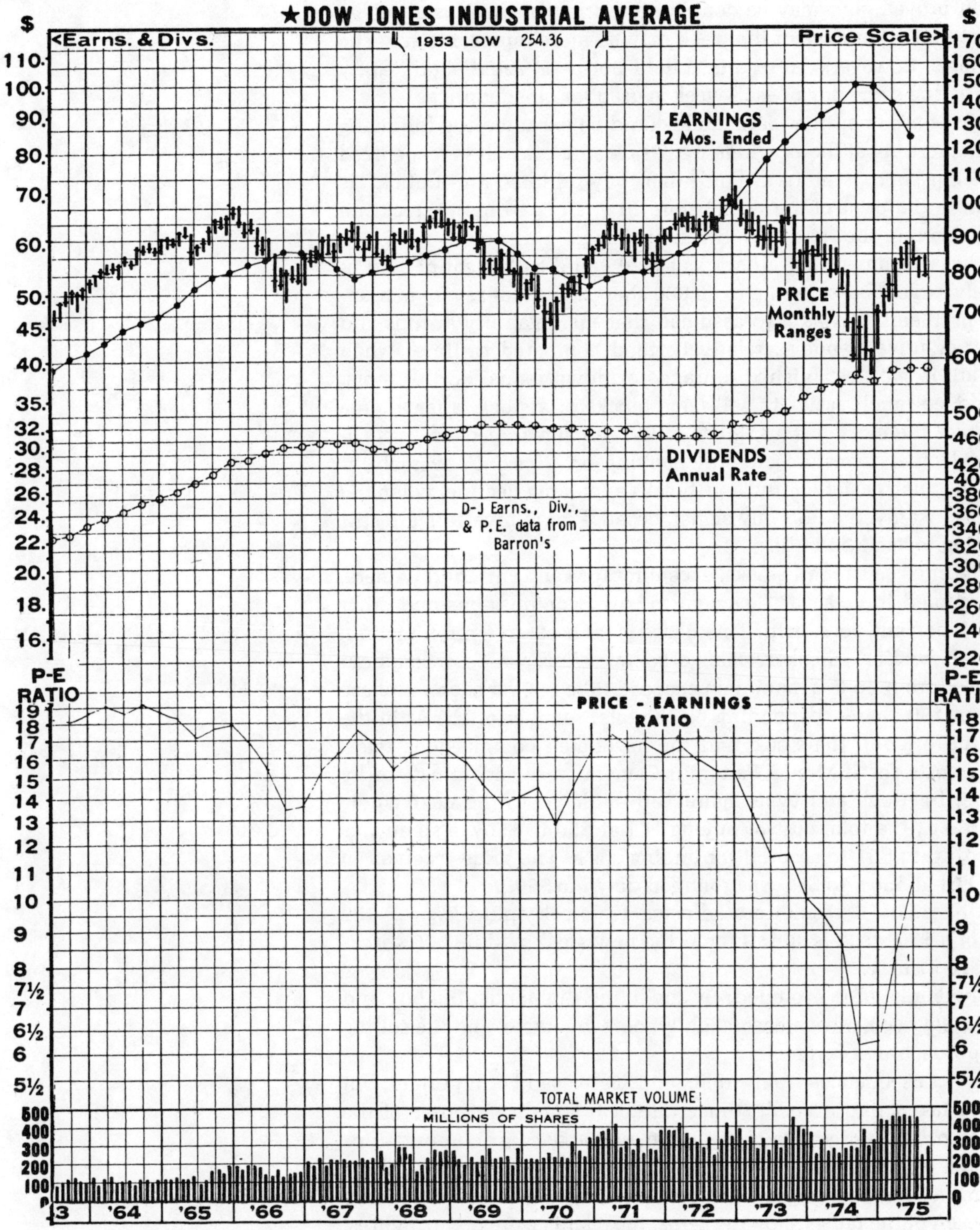

Source: Chart by Securities Research Company, 208 Newbury Street, Boston, Mass. 02116.

price of the week is assumed to be the most representative. This has not been proven, and may be contrary to unproven theories of others who feel that other days of the week may be more representative. The writer feels, however, the results should not be affected significantly as long as the same day of each week is used for closing prices.

2. It was assumed that each trade could be executed the following Monday morning at the previous week's closing price. It is recognized that selling short is more difficult than buying long; an "uptick" is required in the price of the stock before all or any part of the stock can be sold short on the New York Stock Exchange.

3. It was assumed that all stocks tested could be bought or sold in relatively large blocks, say up to 10,000 shares, without severe marketability problems. It was also assumed that marketability at tops and bottoms of price trends is relatively good compared to times when stocks are in well established uptrends or downtrends. For example, it should be much easier to sell large blocks of a stock, after a large rise, where the stock has just given a PBS sell signal, because institutions and other investors are still "buying on dips." Conversely, it should be much easier to buy large blocks after a big decline, when the stock has just given a PBS buy signal, because large investors are still attempting to "sell on rallies."

4. Trading costs for all stocks, except for IBM and Fairchild Camera, were assumed to be a flat 1 percent to cover commissions and other fees, or 2 percent, roundtrip. This figure is, at best, an approximation, because New York Stock Exchange commissions varied throughout this period from up to a maximum cost of $45 to $80 for each purchase or sale of 100 shares, depending on the total number of shares in the order, the price of the stock, and the negotiated commissions rates. Trading costs for IBM and Fairchild Camera were accounted for by rounding fractions and even figures up or down to the next whole number, e.g., the total cost of buying FCI at $50 to $50⅞ a share was rounded up to $51 to account for trading costs. The price received in selling FCI at $50⅛ to $51 was rounded down to $50.

5. All statistical results are adjusted for stock splits, e.g., if 100 shares of a $30 stock is split 3 for 1, the new stock will be 300 shares worth $10 a share.

6. Dividends were excluded. By including dividends, the buy and hold strategy would have been slightly more favorable, and the selling short approach less favorable.

7. Tax consequences from profits and losses can be important, but were not taken into account. Since one of the main purposes of the PBS is to prevent large loss of capital in all markets, tax computations might have obscured this objective. Further, it is assumed that investors *would rather pay taxes on profits than no taxes on losses!* This means that in each of the tables showing gains, the results were pretax figures, and make no allowance for income taxes payable on any of the sales

in trading the securities. Furthermore, it was assumed that the net proceeds (exclusive of the tax bite) from each sale were reinvested at the next buy signal.

8. No margin was used. (Borrowing for margin is not recommended in PBS trading.)

9. No modifications, unless noted, were made to the PBS to improve the results or to eliminate whipsaws.

10. When computing results, all proceeds from each trade were assumed to be committed to each succeeding trade, e.g. The results for buying and selling a stock (without selling short) are shown under Cumulative Results, Long, starting with a unit value of 1.00. Trading costs are deducted in computing these results. The results for selling short and buying to cover the short position are shown under Cumulative Results, Short. The results for being fully committed at all times, that is either owning or being short the stock, are shown under Cumulative Results, Long and Short. In being fully committed, buy signals are used to buy stock as well as to buy to cover any short stock; sell signals are used to sell stock and also to sell stock short.

11. Volume of shares traded was not considered. In the opinion of one highly placed technician who guides multibillion dollar portfolios, "Volume is not important in the stock market, except at major tops or bottoms. *The masses* (including institutions) *buy stocks because their prices have been going up. They sell them because their prices have been going down.*"

12. Valid tests of any mechanical system, such as the PBS, should include the short side, i.e., selling short, and buying to cover the short. There are two reasons for this. First, the short side statistics tell us how good or bad the system is for preserving capital. *Capital can often be preserved by selling before a serious decline,* and rebuying more shares at lower prices. Second, traders can make profits by selling short, i.e., borrowing stock from someone else through their broker, and selling it; then later, buying it back at a lower price in order to return the stock to the owner, and to make a profit.

13. It is assumed that neither the stock market nor stock prices can be forecast to any reliable degree, either in terms of time or magnitude.

14. The PBS should produce better results with stocks that move with wide swings. Although it is difficult, if not impossible, to forecast future price swings reliably, we can establish some characteristics of stocks that should be both active and volatile in the future. Such examples are:

Stocks that have moved with wide swings in the recent past.

Stocks that are being recommended by influential financial services or brokerage houses.

Stocks that have had unexpectedly high increases or decreases in earnings.

Stocks of companies that are considered to be growing rapidly.
Stocks that pay very little or no dividends.
Stocks of companies that have the distinct possibility of going bankrupt.
Stocks that are considered to be special situations.

Stocks selected for hypothetical testing in this book were generally of the largest, or among the largest, corporations in their industry that paid little or no dividends.

15. Selling short should be undertaken only by sophisticated traders or speculators. A short sale is the sale of borrowed stock. The seller expects the stock's price to decline so that he can buy an equal number of shares later at a lower price for return to the lender.

SUMMARY OF STATISTICAL OBSERVATIONS

The PBS was first applied to two actively traded stocks, Fairchild Camera and Instrument and International Business Machines, over 13+ year periods. The simulated results, using the PBS, were outstanding.

If FCI had just been bought and held for the 13+ year period, the loss would have been 70 percent! Trading FCI by the PBS would have resulted in gains of 250 percent; or short only, a gain of 72 percent. Trading FCI, both long and short, resulted in a gain of 502 percent.

If IBM had been bought and held for the 14 year period, the gain would be 96 percent. Trading IBM using the PBS resulted in a gain of 245 percent; short only, a gain of 42 percent. Trading IBM both long and short, that is being fully committed at all times, resulted in a gain of 389 percent.

Whether any one trade is to be profitable appears to be entirely random. However, in the FCI and IBM tests, *the average gain was about three times the average loss*, and this is important.

Whether you can successfully use the PBS depends on your emotional stamina, and your regimen, over a long period. At times, a series of losses must be taken.

The annual turnover was about 2½ times; that is, there were about 2½ buys and 2½ sells each year. This compares with turnover rates of over three times in some aggressive mutual funds.

There were more trades resulting in losses than profits. A total of 74 unprofitable trades were recorded for both FCI and IBM, compared with 62 profitable trades.

Even though the PBS is a trading system, it is possible to achieve long term gains of six months or more. For IBM there were five long term gains, averaging 24 percent each. For FCI there were two long term gains, averaging 122 percent each.

The gain to loss ratios (see Appendix A) indicate that *once a worthwhile trend is established, the PBS locks on it.* The PBS gave good evidence that it does "cut losses short and let profits run."

Once you learn the PBS's limitations, you'll find it to be simple, useful, and dynamic. The results can be excellent when applied to the right trading media. It may turn out to be the best way for you to make and keep wealth, but you may also find that it's like a tight new shoe—you have to wear it awhile before it's comfortable.

(See Appendixes B and C for additional statistical observations.)

PROCEDURAL STEPS

In the next chapter you will find the weekly closing prices for ten stocks for the period 1965 to 1975, unless otherwise noted.

After each weekly closing price was recorded, appropriate notations were made. "H" indicates a highpoint and "L" a lowpoint. These were recorded a week after the high or lowpoint occurred. "B" indicates a buy signal and "S" a sell signal. These signals were recorded as soon as each first higher highpoint or lower lowpoint occurred.

For convenience, the weeks of each year were numbered from 1 to 52, and from 1 to 53 for 1970. (If you wish to convert the week number to the actual date, see Appendix D.)

FAIRCHILD CAMERA AND INSTRUMENT CORPORATION

Let's apply the Profit Box System to Fairchild Camera common stock. (See Figure 10.) FCI was many kinds of stock in the 13+ years, 1961 to 1975. It was at times a growth stock, then a high technology stock, a special situation, a dull stock, a speculative stock, and a cyclical stock. In spite of all these categories, FCI was worth the same price in 1964—$20 a share—as it was ten years later! This is after making all adjustments for splits.

Then how could a trader or an investor make a profit from this kind of stock? The answer is that the "investor" couldn't. The investor who bought FCI at $20 in 1964 collected a few dollars in dividends, and could have done better in a savings bank with a lot less risk.

The trader, however, had a great opportunity to make money in FCI. During this period, FCI wasn't just going sideways—it went from $20 a share up to $140, down to $18, up to $48, down to . . . and on and on.

How well did the PBS work with FCI? Rather well. During my original study of FCI covering 11 years, the cumulative gains from trading both long and short were +294 percent. The later study for

Table 2A
FCI Results—13 Years and 10 Weeks, Ending 1974

DJI Index	−12%
FCI—Bought and Held	−70%
FCI—PBS	+250%
FCI—PBS (including short sales)	+502%

Figure 10

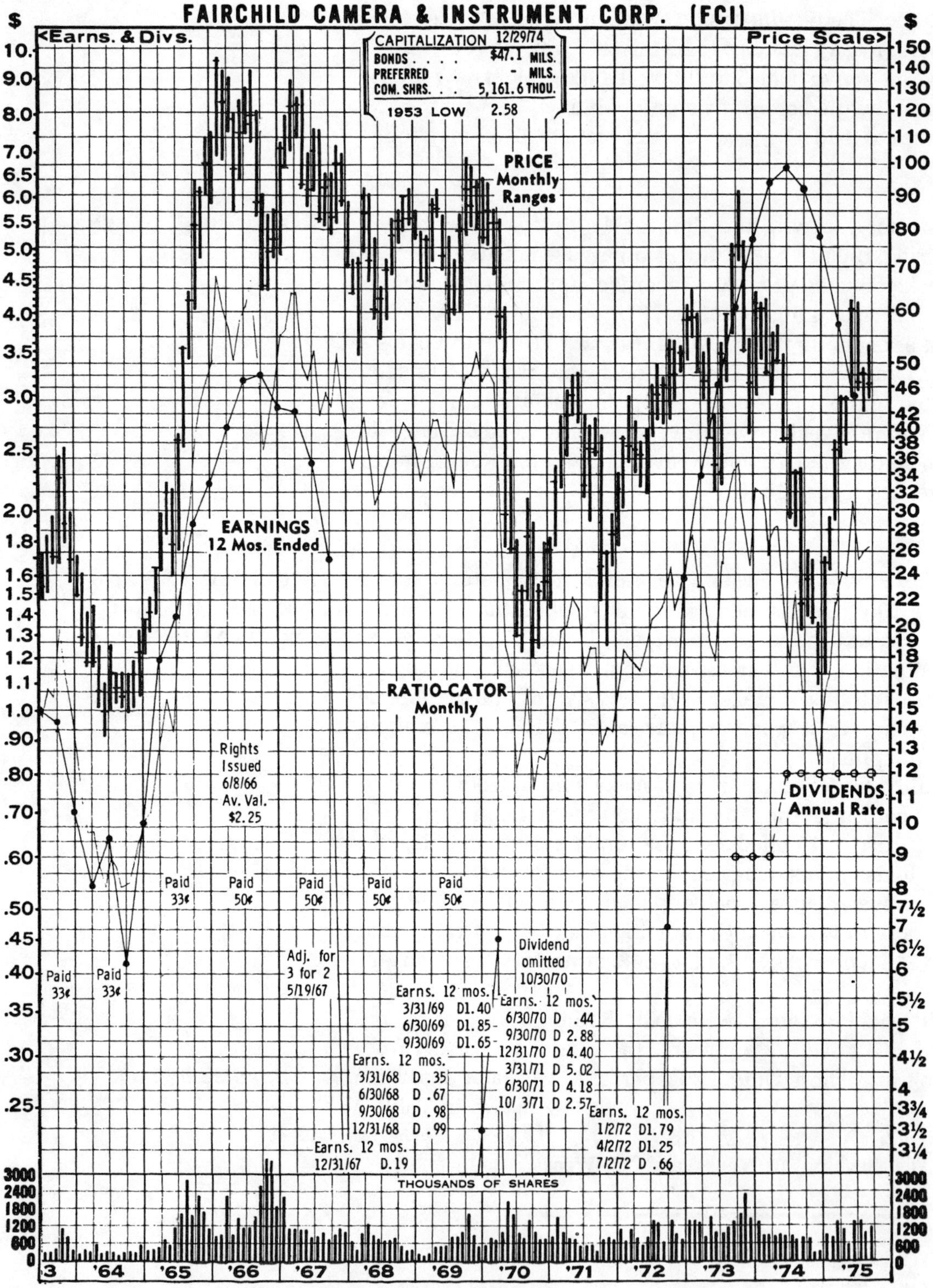

Source: Chart by Securities Research Company, 208 Newbury Street, Boston, Mass. 02116.

13+ years, included in this text, resulted in simulated gains of 502 percent. (See Table 2A.)

Will the PBS results for FCI be the same in the future? I can only answer this with another question: Will FCI continue to fluctuate as it has in the past?

To Repeat

The Profit Box System is defined as follows:

1. *The trend is up* as long as the price at each successive lowpoint is higher than, or the same as, the previous lowpoint.
2. When the price of the stock drops below the previous lowpoint, the trend changes to "down," and this gives a *Sell* signal.
3. *The trend is down* as long as the price at each successive highpoint is lower than, or the same as, the preceding highpoint.
4. Once the price exceeds the previous highpoint, the trend changes to "up," and this gives a *Buy* signal.

See the hypothetical example below.

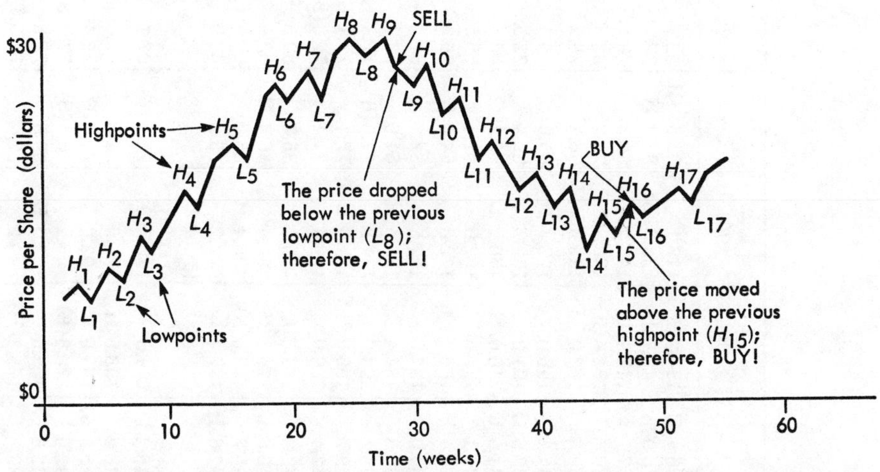

The Profit Box System—A Hypothetical Price Chart of XYZ Corporation

PBS, Step by Step—FCI

If you want to practice using the PBS, let's start back in 1961 and buy and sell FCI. The weekly closing prices are shown in Table 2B. The price per share figures with fractions, i.e., $40⅛, $40¼, $40⅜, and so on, are shown as $40.1, $40.2, $40.3, to minimize paperwork.

Referring to Table 2B, note that FCI made a lowpoint at $66.6 (that is, $66⁶⁄₈ or $66¾ a share after adjusting for the 2 for 1 split), the 47th week of 1961. We didn't know that this was the lowpoint for that move until one week later, when it became obvious that $66.6 was lower than either the week before ($70.6 adjusted for a 2 for 1 split) or the

Table 2B
FCI Weekly Closing Prices

Week	1961	1962	1963	1964	1965	1966	1967	1968	1969	1970	1971	1972	1973	1974
1		58.0 L	47.2	36.2	28.4 H	134.2 (S)	117.1	82.5 (S) L	82.7	95.6 H	21.7 (S) L	30.6 (B) H	56.3 H	47.1
2		59.7	49.3 H	35.4	28.0	148.2 H	138.3	83.7 H	79.1 (S)	89.1	23.1	30.2	53.6 L	49.4
3		63.0 H	48.7	34.6	27.7 L	147.4 L	143.0	80.3	78.5 L	87.0	26.6 (B) H	29.7 L	54.6	53.2
4		58.5 L	48.1	33.7	30.6	164.0 (B)	158.3	74.7	83.3 H	84.7	26.2 L	33.1 H	57.2 H	60.2 H
5		60.4	45.3	33.5 L	30.6	166.0	159.6	68.2	78.2	77.5 (S) L	34.1 H	32.6	55.7 L	57.6
6		62.2	44.0 (S)	35.0 H	31.2	190.0	172.4 H	65.6 L	74.4	81.4	31.6 L	31.3 L	63.3	53.5 L
7		65.4 (B) H	42.4 L	32.6	32.6 H	191.0	169.2	66.4	72.5	86.4	32.0	32.1	64.2 H	56.2
8		63.0 L	42.5 H	32.1	31.6 L	210.0 H	160.2 L	67.1 H	68.1	87.1 H	33.2	34.0	57.6	59.2
9		64.3	39.5	29.0 L	33.1	176.6	162.0	61.5	66.5	85.0	38.5 H	40.7	57.2	60.4 (B) H
10		66.4	39.5	30.5	34.4	166.1	172.0	54.0 L	66.5 L	76.7	38.2 L	42.3 H	56.4 L	57.3
11		70.0 H	39.1	30.6 H	34.0	162.0 L	177.5	57.2	67.6	72.2	39.4	40.4	57.4 H	56.6
12		66.4	37.1	26.5	34.5	184.4	188.6 H	61.6	72.4	70.4 L	39.7	39.2	52.6 (S)	53.1 (S)
13		64.0	34.7	26.5 L	36.7	193.0	184.2	71.0 (B)	77.3 H	77.2 H	40.6 H	37.5 L	48.4	48.3
14		62.0 (S)	34.1 L	29.1	39.7	196.0 H	171.0 L	77.1	73.1 L	72.7	40.5	38.0 H	46.0 L	46.3 L
15		59.5 L	35.5 H	29.6 H	42.4	180.0	178.4	81.4	77.6 (B)	69.7	37.5 (S) L	37.2 (S) L	47.6	49.4
16		62.2 H	34.0 L	28.0	42.6 H	173.6 L	180.2	85.7	80.5	63.7	41.3 (B)	39.2 (B) H	51.6 H	53.3 H
17		56.6	35.2	26.7 L	42.0 L	176.1 H	184.4	86.6 H	85.6	56.5	41.7	37.2	47.0 L	51.6 L
18		56.5	36.7 (B)	28.0 H	45.7	162.0 (S)	185.4 H	85.0	88.3 H	53.2	45.7	33.1 (S) L	49.2 H	52.4
19		48.7	38.0 H	26.7	47.6 H	137.4 L	172.2 (3 for 2 split)	75.2	88.0	39.7	47.4 H	35.5 H	48.7	52.5 H
20		46.5	37.5	26.0	46.2 L	148.6	112.3 (S)	72.2	87.1	36.0	44.4 L	35.3 L	42.3 L	51.6 L
21		42.5	37.1 L	23.5 L	48.0	158.6 H	104.6	71.0 L	85.0 L	29.7	44.7	37.4 (B) H	46.4 H	54.4 (B) H
22		40.6	39.0	24.0 H	45.5 (S)	153.0 L	92.0 L	71.6 H	85.4 H	29.6 L	47.1 H	37.2	38.3 L	50.3 (S) •
23		37.2	42.2 H	22.5	42.0 L	170.6 (B)	95.2	70.5 (S)	77.2 (S)	30.5	46.0	34.3 (S)	41.4 H	44.4 L
24		35.5	40.3 L	20.6 L	42.6 H	175.0	102.0 H	68.5	76.2	32.4 H	42.5 (S)	33.7 L	35.2	45.3 H
25		34.6 L	40.6 H	23.1	39.4 L	175.2 H	99.2	67.4	71.6 L	30.7	41.0	37.2	34.3 L	39.1

26		41.6	37.7(S)	23.3	42.0	172.2 L	91.4 L	60.2 L	73.5	27.4	39.7	39.0(B)	35.1 H	38.4
27		42.5	38.3 H	23.3	47.0(B)	192.0	94.5	62.4 H	77.2 H	23.7 L	38.5	41.0	33.5 L	33.2 L
28		47.1	36.4	27.4(B)H	48.7	193.6 H	108.4(B)H	59.5 L	71.6	24.5	34.5 L	43.2	37.0(B)	35.1 H
29		47.2 H	36.4	26.5 L	52.6	187.1	99.2 L	61.2	68.6	24.6 H	34.6 H	43.5 H	44.5	32.4
30		46.6 L	34.4	26.7 H	57.4	173.0 L	103.0	62.4	59.4 L	23.6	32.5	42.2 L	50.0	30.1
31		48.4(B)	34.1 L	25.6(S)	62.3	178.4	108.3 H	62.4	64.4 H	19.4 L	31.5 L	44.2	52.4 H	28.7 L
32		47.0 L	36.7	24.6 L	71.3 H	202.6 H	98.6(S)	67.0(B)	62.0 L	20.0 H	32.7	49.0 H	52.0	31.3 H
33		49.4	37.4	25.1 H	68.2 L	190.2	91.1	70.4 H	65.0(B)	18.3 L	38.2(B)H	47.2	50.1 L	29.5 L
34		53.2 H	40.3(B)	23.7	73.5	176.4	87.0	67.2 L	71.5 H	20.6(B)	37.7 L	43.6 L	51.0	30.5
35		52.6	41.1	23.3 L	77.6	174.4	83.4	69.2	60.1(S)	22.3	39.7	45.4 H	59.3 H	34.1(B)
36		51.4 L	42.5	23.6	83.5	164.0(S)L	83.2 L	73.1	65.0	25.5 H	39.7	43.2(S)	57.1 L	30.7
37		56.1 H	43.3 H	23.7	88.0	165.0 H	83.7	79.4	76.0(B)	25.3 L	40.0 H	42.0 L	67.1	22.3(S)
38		52.6	41.4	24.0	92.1	147.6	87.1	80.0 H	82.6 H	28.3 H	37.4(S)	43.7	70.6	23.1 H
39		48.4(S)L	38.2 L	24.5	92.1	132.5	92.6	78.3	79.0 L	28.1 L	37.3	46.3(B)H	72.7	21.0 L
40		50.0 H	41.3	24.6 H	105.2	101.2 L	95.6 H	78.1 L	79.6	28.3 H	36.2	45.5 L	84.4	21.3
41		47.4	46.5	24.2 L	122.0	116.0 H	88.2	79.3	83.2	25.0(S)	34.0	46.2	87.2 H	22.4
42		42.4 L	46.7	24.3 H	132.2 H	115.6	80.7 L	79.7	84.2	23.4 L	31.6	47.4	82.4 L	24.4(B)H
43	170.4	43.0	51.4	23.2 L	122.2	102.0 L	86.0 H	83.2 H	95.0 H	24.2 H	24.6	51.5	88.0 H	22.3 L
44	155.2	44.6 H	51.5	23.7	117.3 L	114.2	84.6	81.0	92.0 L	19.1 L	23.4	52.6 H	73.5(S)	23.2
45	141.6	44.0	53.0 H	24.2 H	126.0	114.3 H	83.2 L	80.6 L	97.4 H	20.3 H	22.2	46.6	64.4 L	24.0 H
46	141.4 (2 for 1 split)	42.7 L	51.1	23.2	128.3	102.6	96.4(B)	84.0 H	97.0	19.6	19.4 L	46.5	64.6 H	22.5
47	66.6 L	43.4	40.2 L	23.0 L	132.5	101.0 L	100.3	81.5 L	82.6(S)	19.2 L	22.0	45.6 L	58.2	21.4(S)
48	69.4	46.4(B)	43.2 H	26.0(B)H	144.4 H	108.0	103.7 H	89.4	86.6 H	20.4(B)	26.0	49.6	52.3	20.5
49	69.7 H	48.1 H	40.6	24.6 L	140.6 L	118.2(B)	92.0	91.0 H	84.0 L	24.2	28.3 H	51.2 H	49.2	16.6 L
50	67.6	47.1	36.4(S)	25.0	159.3 H	119.5	90.7	89.6	84.7	24.4 H	26.7 L	50.4	43.7	17.0
51	63.3(S)	45.2 L	35.7 L	27.7	144.6 L	121.7 H	87.5 L	86.5	87.0(B)	23.4	27.2	49.6 L	42.4 L	17.5 H
52	62.4	46.0	38.3 H	29.2 H	150.4 H	116.3 L	87.6 H	83.1	91.7	23.3 L	27.5	51.7	45.4	17.2 L
53				27.4 L						23.4 H				

week after ($69.4). Week #49 turned out to be the next highpoint week at $69.7, which became evident after recording $67.6 for week #50.

Now we have a box—$66.6(L) is the lowpoint or bottom of the box, and $69.7(H) is the highpoint or top. Therefore, as long as the price of the stock fluctuates between these two figures, the stock is going "sideways," as defined by the Profit Box System.

The trend changed during week #51, 1961, when the price broke down through the bottom of the box ($66.6) as it closed at $63.3. This indicates that the trend of the stock is now down; therefore, sell the stock (and sell short if you consider yourself to be a fearless speculator who is comfortable with short sales). Unfortunately, FCI bobbled around for the next few weeks in an uncertain fashion, made a lowpoint at $58.0 on week #1 of 1962, a highpoint at $63.0 on week #3, 1962, all the time staying lower than the previous highpoint at $69.7(H) on week #49, 1961.

Going on, the top and bottom of the box have changed, with $63.0(H) as the top, $58.5(L) as the bottom. Several weeks later FCI closed at $65.4, bursting up through the top of the box ($63.0 for week #3, 1962), indicating the trend has now changed to "up." So far it has been very discouraging. The next signal is to sell at $62, week #14, 1962.

Now, however, we start to see some results. After getting our sell signal for FCI at $62.0, since this is lower than the previous lowpoint, we later get a buy signal at $48.4, resulting in a nice profit on the short side of 21 percent before trading costs. Do you have the gist of it? (The FCI Summary is shown in Table 2C.)

Weekly Closing Prices

If you keep the weekly closing prices of the stocks you follow in this fashion, you will be alerted to trend changes. The part of this chapter that's entitled "P.S. What Happened in the Next Bull Market?" gives a sample format for recording prices.

Drop the Fractions

In the FCI and IBM tests I recorded a buy signal even if the previous highpoint was exceeded by only 0.1 or $1/8th. After more research I found that there is a trade-off. If you only use the whole number digits of stock prices and drop the fractions, i.e., use $46 instead of $46.5, you will get fewer buy and sell signals, and fewer whipsaws (trades resulting in loss of money).

On the other hand, your signals may come later, occasionally, resulting in paying slightly higher prices when buying, and receiving slightly lower prices when selling. It appeared that, on the whole, the whipsaws would cost more than the slightly worse prices. Therefore, I suggest dropping the fractions. All other stocks, except FCI and IBM, were tested by dropping the fractions.

Table 2C
FCI Summary, 1961–1975

Buy Action		*Sell Action*		*Gains*			*Cumulative Results*		
Week/ Year	*Price**	*Week/ Year*	*Price**	*Long Per- cent*	*Short Per- cent*	*Long- Term Gain*	*Long 1.00*	*Short 1.00*	*Long and Short 1.00*
		51/61	$ 63						
7/62	$ 66	14/62	61	−7.6	−4.7		.92	.95	.87
31/62	49	39/62	48	−2.1	+19.6		.90	1.13	1.01
48/62	47	6/63	43	−8.6	+2.0		.82	1.16	.95
18/63	37	26/63	37	0	+13.9		.82	1.32	1.08
34/63	41	50/63	36	−12.2	−10.8		.72	1.18	.84
28/64	28	31/64	25	−10.8	+22.2		.64	1.44	.92
48/64	27	23/65	45	+66.6	−8.0	L.T.	1.07	1.32	1.41
28/65	48	2/66	134	+179.1	−6.6	L.T.	3.01	1.24	3.73
5/66	165	19/66	161	−2.5	−23.1		2.93	.95	2.78
24/66	171	37/66	163	−4.7	−6.2		2.79	.89	2.48
	(3 for 2 split)								
50/66	119	20/67	112	+41.1	+26.9		3.94	1.13	4.45
28/67	109	32/67	98	−10.1	+2.6		3.54	1.16	4.10
46/67	97	1/68	82	−15.5	+1.0		2.99	1.17	3.49
13/68	72	23/68	70	−2.8	+12.1		2.91	1.31	3.81
32/68	68	2/69	79	+16.1	+2.8		3.38	1.35	4.56
15/69	78	23/69	77	−1.3	+1.2		3.34	1.37	4.57
33/69	66	35/69	60	−9.1	+14.2		3.03	1.56	4.72
37/69	77	47/69	82	+6.4	−28.3		3.23	1.12	3.61
51/69	88	5/70	77	−12.5	−7.3		2.82	1.04	2.93
34/70	21	41/70	24	+14.2	+72.7		3.22	1.79	5.76
48/70	21	2/71	21	0	+12.5		3.22	2.02	6.50
4/71	27	16/71	37	+37.0	−28.5		4.42	1.44	6.36
17/71	42	25/71	42	0	−13.5		4.42	1.25	5.52
34/71	39	39/71	37	−5.2	+7.1		4.19	1.34	5.61
1/72	31	15/72	37	+19.3	+16.2		5.00	1.55	7.75
16/72	40	18/72	33	−17.5	−8.1		4.12	1.43	5.89
21/72	38	23/72	34	−10.6	−15.1		3.68	1.21	4.45
26/72	40	36/72	43	+7.5	−17.6		3.96	1.00	3.96
39/72	47	12/73	52	+10.6	−9.3		4.38	.90	3.94
28/73	38	44/73	73	+92.1	+26.9		8.42	1.15	9.68
9/74	61	12/74	53	−13.2	+16.4		7.31	1.34	9.79
21/74	55	22/74	50	−9.1	−3.7		6.64	1.29	8.56
35/74	35	37/74	22	−37.2	+30.0		4.17	1.67	6.96
42/74	25	47/74	21	−16.0	−13.6		3.50	1.45	5.07
(Last)	(17)				+19.0			1.72	6.02

* Prices are adjusted for trading costs.

Low Priced Stocks

What about a low priced stock, less than $10 a share? More research needs to be done in the area of low priced stocks, but so far my work indicates that even here the fractions should be dropped.

Be careful with low priced stocks. Even though they can be more volatile, both the commissions and the spread between the bid and offer prices are usually much higher, in regard to percentage, than for the higher priced stocks. Also, the low price of a stock can be an indication that the stock is out of favor, especially with institutional investors, or that the corporation may have some basic problems that may not be apparent.

INTERNATIONAL BUSINESS MACHINES CORPORATION

IBM is the largest manufacturer of business machines, and it produces over half the world's computer hardware. For years institutions have held more of their investments in IBM stock than in any other stock. IBM has been almost too successful—its gross income passed $12 billion in 1974, and the bigger it gets the more vulnerable it is to antitrust lawsuits. Yet, if you have billions of dollars to invest in stocks, you can't overlook IBM stock as a possible investment.

If you had bought and held IBM from the first of 1961 to 1975, it would have appreciated 96 percent (adjusted for splits and stock dividends). (See Figure 11.) During this period the Dow Jones Industrial Index was up 1 percent, from 610 to 616.

If you had traded IBM via the PBS, your gains would be approximately 245 percent. Going all the way, trading long and short, your gains would be around 389 percent! (See Table 3A.)

Table 3A
IBM Results—14 Years, 1961–1975

DJI Index	+1%
IBM—Bought and held	+96%
IBM—PBS	+245%
IBM—PBS (including short sales)	+389%

The PBS produced five long term trades averaging 24.3 percent each. The average profitable trade was 14.3 percent, and the average loss trade was -4.2 percent. (See Appendixes B and C for a more detailed statistical analysis.)

Those who bought IBM in 1968, 1969, 1970, 1971, 1972, and 1973 all had losses at the end of 1974. Had you traded IBM long and short, using the PBS, the reverse would have been true! (See Tables 3B and 3C.)

Figure 11

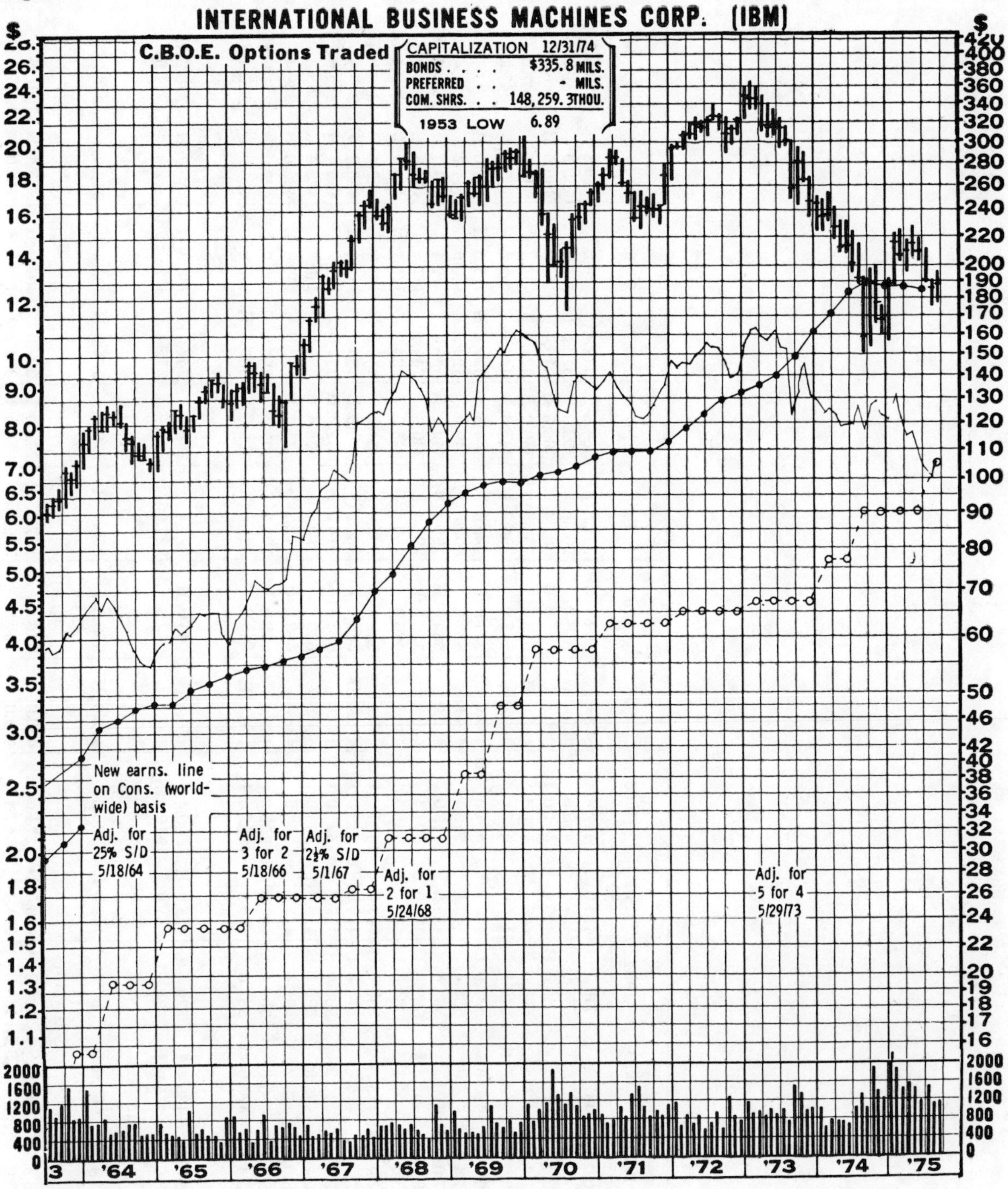

Source: Chart by Securities Research Company, 208 Newbury Street, Boston, Mass. 02116.

Table 3B
IBM Weekly Closing Prices

Week	1961	1962	1963	1964	1965	1966	1967	1968	1969	1970	1971	1972	1973	1974
1	596.4	560.0 L	397.0	510.0	425.0 Ⓑ	497.6	378.0	593.0 L	312.0 Ⓢ	364.6	314.4 Ⓢ	338.6	418.6	230.6 L
2	622.2	564.0 H	407.6	533.0	434.6	496.0	396.4 H	616.0	305.6 L	369.0	310.0 L	350.0	420.0	240.0
3	624.0	553.4	412.4	553.0 H	446.6	491.0 L	390.0 L	621.0 H	307.4 H	369.6 H	316.4	368.2	439.0 H	246.0
4	638.0	541.2 L	418.4	546.0	448.4 H	497.0	401.4 H	618.4	299.6	356.0 Ⓢ	325.4 Ⓑ	368.2	437.6	247.0 H
5	639.4	558.0 H	423.6 H	542.0	445.4	497.4	399.0 L	596.0	296.2 L	335.2 L	336.4	369.6	429.6 L	241.2
6	641.0 H	556.4	420.0	537.0 L	440.7 L	524.6 ⒷH	414.0	571.0 L	298.0	344.6	339.4 H	373.6 H	446.0 H	233.1 L
7	640.0 L	544.4	418.6	555.4	447.4	512.4	424.5	577.0	308.6 ⒷH	349.0	328.2 L	368.6 L	441.2	233.4
8	650.0 Ⓑ	537.0 L	410.2	555.4	455.6 H	512.0	425.0	589.6 H	295.4 Ⓢ	349.4 H	336.4	372.4	433.4 L	236.4 H
9	670.0	548.0	397.2 L	569.0 H	452.0 L	504.4	440.0	577.0 L	293.3 L	340.2	345.4	377.4	442.0 H	236.0 L
10	695.0	553.0 H	408.4	568.0 L	464.4 H	500.0	440.2	579.4	299.6 H	325.2	354.0	378.2 H	439.4 L	240.4 Ⓑ
11	723.0	552.4	413.2	588.4 H	463.0	499.0 L	450.2	589.1 H	295.6 L	324.2	360.5 H	377.0 L	443.4 H	249.2 H
12	695.0	547.0	414.2	574.4 L	449.0 ⓈL	525.0 H	455.4 H	585.4 L	305.4 Ⓑ	319.6 L	358.0	382.6 H	428.0 Ⓢ	243.4
13	695.0	532.6	421.0	588.4	457.4	521.0 L	451.0	612.4 Ⓑ	314.0 H	333.2 H	358.0	382.2 L	431.4 H	235.6 Ⓢ
14	693.4 L	520.4	442.0	598.4 H	470.0 Ⓑ	540.0	446.5 L	630.0	310.6 L	326.4 L	356.6	389.2	423.4 L	233.4
15	716.0 H	518.0 L	446.2	596.6	472.0	553.0	458.4	649.0 H	312.2 H	331.4 H	352.0 L	395.0 H	429.6 H	229.4 L
16	707.4 L	519.0 H	450.0	585.4	480.2	555.0	468.0	636.4 L	308.2 ⓈL	322.4	355.0	385.0 L	429.0	231.5 H
17	714.0 H	485.4 L	470.0 H	583.0	485.0	557.4 H	496.4 H (2½%)	659.0	317.6 Ⓑ	309.0	357.6 H	386.0	405.2 L (5 for 4 split)	225.4 L
18	711.0	486.0 H	465.4 L	579.4 L	485.0 H	530.4	480.4	688.0 H	326.4	296.6	347.0 Ⓢ	388.6 H	340.0 H	226.2 H
19	696.0 Ⓢ (3 for 2 split)	446.0 L	475.0 H	584.4	481.4	519.0 ⓈL (3 for 2 split)	467.4 L	677.6	327.0	290.4	335.4 L	382.0 ⓈL	327.0	224.0
20	452.0 L	451.4 H	467.0	587.4 (5 for 4 split)	469.0 L	360.6	472.0 H	650.0 L (2 for 1 split)	330.4 H	270.6	344.0 H	396.2 Ⓑ	312.0 L	218.2
21	478.0 B	398.4	463.0 ⓈL	491.0 H	478.0 H	371.0 H	470.0	329.4	327.0	248.0 L	327.0	404.0 H	325.4 H	218.6
22	491.4 H	385.0	477.2 ⒷH	480.0	474.4	343.4 L	469.0 L	357.0	319.0	278.0 H	324.2 L	398.4	310.0 L	212.4

23	487.0	371.2	468.2	464.0 L	454.6 (S)L	349.0	486.0	370.0 H	315.0	270.0	324.4 H	391.0 L	324.2 H	229.2 (B)H
24	481.4	333.4	463.2 (S)	472.4	462.4 H	357.0 H	499.4	355.6 L	311.4 L	259.0 L	315.4	398.6 H	318.2	222.6
25	477.0	320.0 L	455.4	479.4 H	446.6 L	355.0	502.0 H	358.2 H	312.2	270.2 H	311.2 L	395.0	316.6 L	213.0 (S)
26	475.4	339.2	436.2 L	478.0 L	464.4 (B)	354.4 L	497.4 L	353.6 (S)L	331.4	257.4	319.0 H	392.0 L	317.0 H	212.6
27	474.4	345.0	445.0 H	484.0 H	469.6	357.2 (B)	501.4	358.0 H	351.2 H	250.6	316.0	404.0 H	300.2 L	205.6 L
28	472.4	376.2 H	431.4	482.4	474.4 H	358.0 H	502.6 H	354.6	331.4	250.2 L	294.4 L	393.2 L	310.0	215.0
29	469.0 L	372.0 L	429.2 L	479.0	466.0 L	354.4	498.4 L	345.0	323.0	259.4 H	298.0 H	396.4	315.0	217.6 H
30	487.0	375.7	431.4	463.6 (S)	479.0	340.6 (S)L	506.4	332.0 L	316.4 L	253.6	291.2	398.0	318.0 (B)H	206.2
31	490.2	385.0 (B)H	432.0	462.0	483.4	342.7	509.4 H	336.0 H	329.4	252.2	285.4 L	416.0	311.4	200.6 L
32	499.4	375.6 L	443.4	449.0	492.4 H	349.4 H	492.0 L	335.0 L	333.4	245.4	295.0	425.4 H	301.2	208.4 H
33	504.2	389.4	452.4 (B)H	447.0	492.0 L	335.4	497.4 H	340.4 (B)H	339.4	229.7 L	309.0 (B)	411.4	300.4	198.4
34	509.4	409.0 H	448.4	439.0	500.4	315.1 L	485.6 L	338.2	350.2 H	249.2	315.4 H	406.0 L	298.2 (S)L	190.0 L
35	522.4	396.2	444.6 L	437.6 L	504.0 H	320.0 H	500.0 (B)	335.0 L	345.0	271.2 (B)	307.6	406.2 H	301.0 H	192.0 H
36	546.4	382.2 L	458.4 H	444.1 H	503.6 L	315.0 L	504.0	340.4 H	338.0 L	272.0 H	305.2	398.6 (S)	296.1 L	179.0
37	549.0 H	388.2 H	455.4 L	425.2 L	514.6 H	329.4 (B)H	511.0	337.4	345.4	268.6 L	300.6 L	397.6 L	298.0 H	152.0 L
38	532.0 L	376.6 (S)	456.4 H	425.4	512.0	319.0	542.4	331.0 (S)L	351.0 H	280.2	304.6	398.2	260.0	171.4 H
39	538.0	353.4 L	448.4 (S)L	438.6 H	507.0 L	317.4	548.2	332.2 H	346.4	288.4	306.0 H	406.4	258.0 L	160.7
40	559.0	360.2 H	461.4 (B)	433.0	515.0	292.5 (S)L	568.0	331.0	344.6 L	299.2 H	304.6 L	401.4	259.4	156.2 L
41	571.0	355.2	469.0	431.0	517.6	316.0	586.0	325.0 L	346.4	296.1	308.6 H	379.0 L	282.0	178.0 (B)
42	585.4	348.1	494.6 H	431.0	529.0	322.0	597.2	327.0 H	351.0	290.6 L	301.5 (S)	387.0 H	291.4 H	184.2 H
43	596.0 H	331.4 L	493.4	421.3	533.0	334.7 (B)	597.4 H	316.6	364.0 H	295.0 H	300.4	378.6 L	285.4	177.2 L
44	583.4 L	357.2	488.4	420.0	536.4	346.4	580.0 L	309.0 L	360.4 L	294.0	300.0	387.6 (B)H	280.2	191.4 H
45	596.0 H	361.2 (B)	484.4 L	418.4 L	538.0	352.0	587.0	315.2	365.0 H	294.0	294.2	372.2 (S)L	278.3 L	190.4
46	594.4	378.4	485.0 H	426.2 H	542.4 H	355.0	616.0 H	327.0	363.0	293.1 L	293.4 L	384.0	284.4 H	180.2
47	576.0 (S)	388.0	465.2 (S)L	425.6	535.4	366.2	614.0 L	327.6 (B)	351.0 (S)L	296.4	298.6	389.0 (B)	272.4	170.4 (S)L
48	579.0 H	398.4 H	485.2 (B)H	416.4 L	506.4 (S)L	367.0	616.0	333.6 H	357.0	308.4	321.0 (B)	398.0	265.0	177.2 H
49	577.0 L	397.4	484.4	417.0 H	518.0 H	376.4 H	644.4 H	326.0	357.0	311.4	324.4	403.0 H	265.0	164.4 L
50	581.4 (B)	389.4	475.2 L	413.2 L	498.4 L	371.2	637.2	316.4 L	359.4	317.0 H	339.0 H	398.1	246.0	167.2
51	573.0 S	385.2 L	483.4	415.0 H	499.0	367.4 L	613.4 (S)L	322.0 H	366.4 (B)H	315.4	336.0 L	390.4 L	240.4 L	169.4 H
52	579.0 H	392.4	493.4	413.4	499.0 H	371.4	627.0 H	319.0	361.0 L	315.0 L	336.4	402.0	249.2 H	162.2 L
53				409.4 L						317.6 H				

Table 3C
IBM Summary, 1961–1975

Buy Action		*Sell Action*		*Gains*			*Cumulative Results*		
Week/ Year	Price*	Week/ Year	Price*	Long Percent	Short Percent	Long Term Gain	Long *1.00*	Short *1.00*	Long and Short *1.00*
8/61 (3 for 2 split)	651	19/61	695	+6.7%			1.06		1.06
21/61	479	47/61	575	+20.0	−3.3%	L.T.	1.28	.96	1.22
50/61	582	51/61	572	−1.8	−1.2		1.25	.95	1.18
31/62	386	38/62	375	−2.9	+32.5		1.22	1.26	1.53
45/62	362	21/63	462	+27.6	+3.4	L.T.	1.55	1.30	2.01
22/63	478	24/63	462	−3.4	−3.4		1.50	1.26	1.89
33/63	453	39/63	445	−1.8	+1.9		1.47	1.28	1.88
40/63	462	47/63 (5 for 4 split)	464	+0.4	−3.8		1.48	1.28	1.89
48/63	486	30/64	462	+18.9	−4.7	L.T.	1.76	1.18	2.07
2/65	426	13/65	448	+5.1	+7.7		1.85	1.27	2.34
15/65	471	24/65	453	−3.9	−5.1		1.78	1.20	2.13
27/65	465	49/65	505	+8.6	−2.6		1.93	1.17	2.25
6/66	525	19/66	518	−1.4	−3.9		1.90	1.13	2.14
27/66 (3 for 2 split)	358	30/66	339	−5.4	−3.6		1.80	1.08	1.94
37/66	330	40/66 (2½%)	291	−11.9	+2.6		1.59	1.11	1.76
44/66	347	32/67	491	+45.0	−19.2	L.T.	2.30	.90	2.07
35/67	501	51/67 (2 for 1 split)	612	+22.1	−2.0		2.81	.88	2.47
13/68	613	26/68	352	+14.8	−0.1		3.23	.88	2.84
33/68	341	38/68	330	−3.3	+3.1		3.12	.91	2.83
47/68	328	1/69	311	−5.2	+0.6		2.96	.91	2.69
7/69	309	8/69	294	−4.9	+0.6		2.81	.92	2.58
12/69	306	16/69	307	+0.3	−4.0		2.82	.88	2.48
17/69	318	47/69	350	+10.0	−3.5	L.T.	3.10	.85	2.63
51/69	367	4/70	355	−3.3	−4.8		3.00	.81	2.43
35/70	272	2/71	313	+15.0	+23.3		3.45	1.00	3.45
5/71	326	19/71	346	+6.1	−4.1		3.66	.96	3.51
34/71	310	43/71	300	−3.3	+10.4		3.54	1.06	3.75
49/71	322	19/72	381	+18.3	−7.3		4.19	.98	4.10
20/72	397	37/72	396	−0.3	−4.1		4.18	.94	3.92
44/72	388	45/72	371	−4.4	+2.0		4.00	.96	3.84
47/72 (5 for 4 split)	390	12/73	427	+9.4	−5.1		4.37	.91	3.97
30/73	319	34/73	297	−6.9	+6.6		4.07	.97	3.94
10/74	241	13/74	234	−3.0	+18.8		3.95	1.15	4.54
23/74	228	25/74	212	−7.9	+1.7		3.64	1.17	4.25
41/74	177			−5.1	+15.5		3.45	1.35	4.65
					+4.7			1.42	4.89

* Prices are adjusted for trading costs.

PENN CENTRAL

What happens if you invest in a company that subsequently goes bankrupt? If there is bad news to come out about a stock, the odds are that it will show up in the PBS with a sell signal, long before the bad news is reported.

Let's look at Penn Central whose Penn Central Transportation Company went into reorganization under the Bankruptcy Act in June 1970. This is a particularly interesting situation because Penn Central, with $2 billion in annual revenues, was at one time considered to be a blue chip investment. As of December 31, 1969, its book value was reported to be $118.33 a share, and six months later it went into bankruptcy! What happened? The answer to this is extremely complex, and is outside the scope of this book. However, the price action of the stock made it excellent for trading.

If one had bought and held Penn Central for ten years, ending 1974, the loss would be about 97 percent—the stock dropped from $37 to $1 a share (see Figure 12). By the time the news about the bankruptcy was reported, the stock had declined from its 1968 high of $86 to around $7, over a 90% drop! Using the PBS, one could have been saved from the slaughter. During the six-year period, 1965 to 1971, the PBS would have been very good to traders. There were mostly small losses, but big gains, including one long term gain of 62 percent when the stock moved from $40 to $65 a share between buy and sell signals. Trading the long side only (that is, not selling short), the PBS would have resulted in approximately 25 percent net gains, versus the whopping 84 percent loss by buying and holding.

Trading the short side only produced approximately 192 percent in gains.

Trading *both* the long and short side, PBS would have produced approximately 265 percent in gains. (See Table 4A.)

Table 4A
Penn Central's Results, 1965–1971 (note: bankruptcy occurred June 1970)

DJI Index	−4%
PC—Bought and held	−84%
PC—PBS	+25%
PC—PBS (including short sales)	+265%
—23 trades, 1 long term gain	
—12 gains, 9 losses, 1 breakeven	

Figure 12

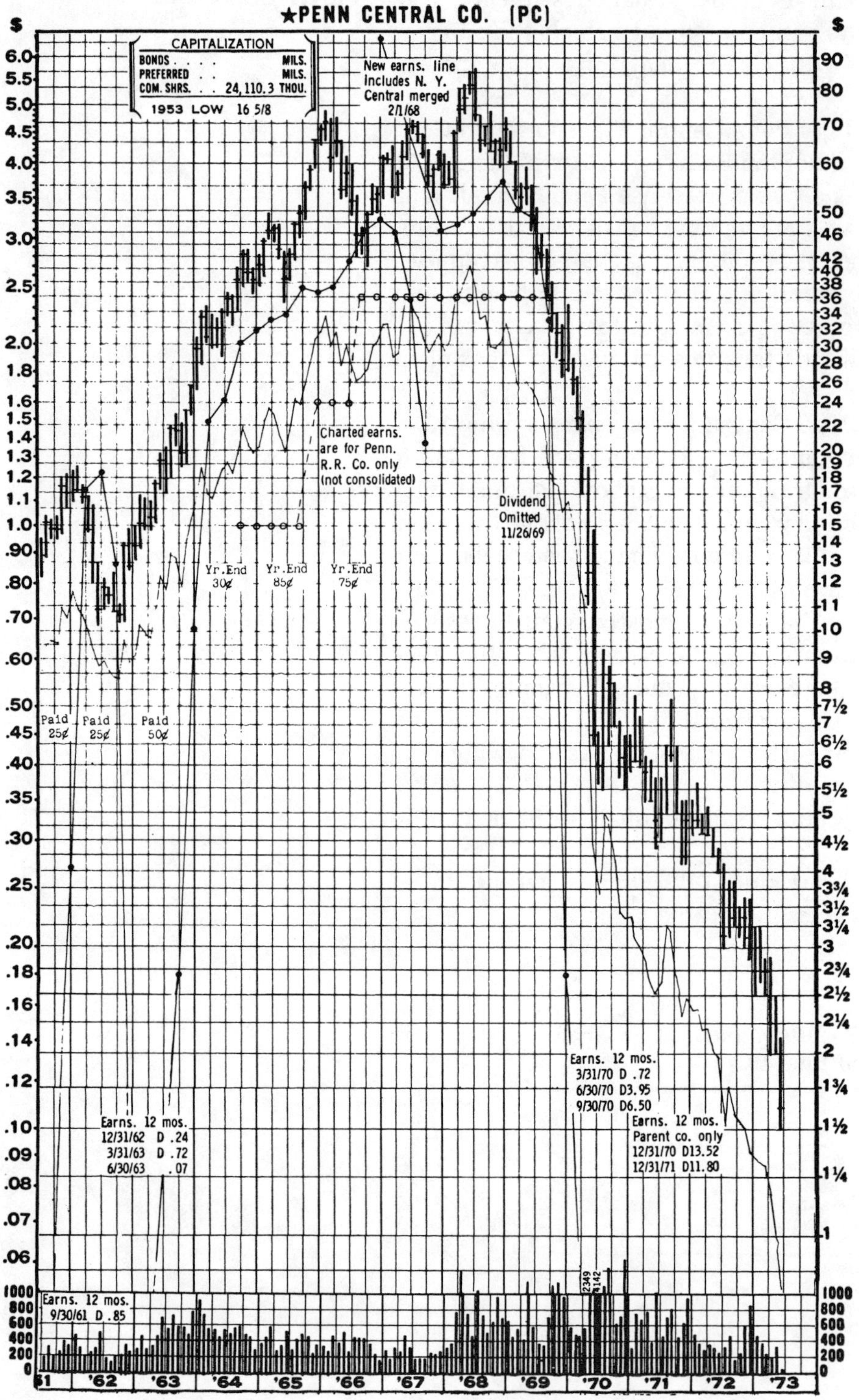

Source: Chart by Securities Research Company, 208 Newbury Street, Boston, Mass. 02116.

Put another way, if $1,000 had been invested in Penn Central the first part of 1964, it would have been worth about $158 six years later. Trading by the PBS, $1,000 would have grown to approximately $3,650! In other words, the PBS results were about 23 times better than that of the buy and hold strategy.

Penn Central results were not computed after the February 5, 1971, buy signal because the bankruptcy news was well known and the stock had dropped below $10 a share. Although I suspect PBS will work on low priced stocks, more work needs to be done in this area. (See Tables 4B and 4C.)

It's ironic—if Penn Central had not gone into bankruptcy, the results may not have been as good.

Table 4B
Penn Central's Weekly Closing Prices

Week	1965	1966	1967	1968	1969	1970	1971	1972	1973	1974
1	$38	$65	$54	$60 (S)	$67 (B) H	$29	$6	$4	$2	$4 H
2	41	69 H	59	58	65 L	29	6 H	4 L	2	3
3	41 H	65 L	59	55 L	67	33 (B)	5 L	5	2	3
4	40	69 H	60	56	70 H	30	6	5	2	3
5	39	67 L	62 H	59 H	68	27 (S)	7	5 H	2 L	3
6	39 L	71 H	61	56 L	66	25 L	7 H	4 L	3	3
7	44 (B)	70	60 L	57	63 (S)	26	6	5 H	3	3
8	44	69	61	59 H	62	26	6 L	4 L	3 H	3
9	46	68	62	55	60	26 H	7 H	5 H	2	3
10	48	65 (S)	64 H	54 L	57	25	6	4 L	2	3
11	49 H	65	63	58	53 L	25	6	5	2	2
12	47	63	58 (S)	63 (B)	56 H	22 L	6	5 H	2	2
13	45 L	63 L	55	67	54	24 H	6	4	2	2
14	46	68	54 L	72	54	22	6	4	2	2
15	46 H	69	56	77 H	54	22	5	4	2	2
16	45 L	69 H	56	73 L	53	21	5	4	2	2
17	46	65	57	75 H	52	19	5	4	2	2
18	46 H	59	57	74 L	52 L	18	5	4	2	2
19	43 (S)	54 L	63	77	53	18	5	4	2	2
20	44 H	56 H	64	77	57 (B)	15	5	4	2	2
21	43	55	65 (B) H	79 H	55	11 L	5	4	2	2
22	41	55 L	64 L	77 L	54	12	5	4	2	2
23	38 L	59 (B)	66	84 H	52	12 H	5	4	1	2
24	39 H	59	68 H	82	50 (S)	11*	4	4	1	2
25	37 L	60 H	65 L	81	48 L	11	4	4	1	2
26	39	57 L	68 H	81 L	49	7	4	4	1	2
27	39	59 H	67 L	84 H	50 H	6	4	4	1	1
28	40 (B) H	53 (S)	69	81	45	6	4 L	4	1 L	1
29	38 L	51	70 H	74 (S)	45	6	5	4	2	1
30	42	51 L	69	72	43 L	6	5	3	2	1
31	42	52 H	69	69	44 H	6	5	3	2	1
32	45	51	69	65 L	43	5	5	3	2	1
33	46	48	67	72 H	42	5 L	5	3	2	1
34	47	45	65 (S) L	66	42	6	6	3	2 H	1
35	48 H	43 L	66	65 L	42	9 H	7 H	3	1	1
36	47	44	67 H	66 H	41	8	6	3	1	1
37	47 L	46 H	64	64 L	40	7	6	3	1	
38	50 H	44 L	62	65	39	7	6	3	1 L	1
39	49 L	45 H	62	68 (B)	37	7 L	6	3	2	1
40	51	41 L	60	72 H	33 L	8 H	5	3	2	1
41	56 H	45	56 L	69 L	37	7	5	3	2	1
42	54	46 (B)	59	71 H	37 H	6 L	5	3	2	1
43	54 L	49	59 H	66 (S)	34	7	5	3	2	1
44	56	50	54 L	64	33	7 H	5	3	2	1
45	57 H	50	56 H	61 L	31	6	4	3	3	1
46	56 L	51	55 L	62	29 L	6	4	3	3	1
47	59	53 H	56	62	32 H	6	4 L	3	3	1
48	63	50 L	59 (B)	65 H	31	6	5 H	3	3	1
49	63	52 H	61	63	29	5 L	4 L	3	3	1
50	64 H	51 L	62 H	62	28	6 H	5 H	3	3	1
51	63 L	54 H	61 L	62 L	28 L	5 L	4	3	3	1
52	64	53 L	62 H	63	29	6	4	3	3	1
53						6				

* Penn Central's transportation subsidiary bankrupt as of June 1970.

Table 4C
Penn Central Summary — 6 + Years from 1965

Date	*Signal to*		*Gains*			*Cumulative Results**		
Week/Year	*Buy*	*Sell*	*Long Percent*	*Short Percent*	*L.T. Gain*	*Long 1.00*	*Short 1.00*	*Long and Short 1.00*
7/65	$44							
19/65		$43	− 2%			.97		
28/65	40			+ 6%			1.05	
10/66		65	+62		L.T.	1.56		
23/66	59			+ 9			1.13	
28/66		53	−10			1.38		
42/66	46			+13			1.27	
12/67		58	+26			1.73		
21/67	65			−12			1.10	
34/67		65	0			1.72		
48/67	59			+ 9			1.19	
1/68		60	+ 1			1.72		
12/68	63			− 5			1.12	
29/68		74	+17			1.99		
39/68	68			+ 8			1.20	
43/68		66	− 2			1.93		
1/69	67			− 1			1.17	
7/69		63	− 5			1.81		
20/69	57			+ 9			1.27	
24/69		50	−14			1.54		
3/70	33			+34			1.68	
5/70		27	−18			1.25		
5/71	7	(Buy to cover short only)†		+74			2.92	3.65

* Trading costs of 1 percent are deducted for each trade.
† Penn Central's transportation subsidiary went into reorganization under Section 77 of the Bankruptcy Act in *June 1970*. Stock was not followed after the 5/71 buy signal due to the bankruptcy and the low price of the stock, which was under $10 a share.

DIGITAL EQUIPMENT CORPORATION

Digital Equipment (DEC), the largest producer of minicomputers, saw its stock move from $10 (adjusted) in 1966 to $124 in 1970. (See Figure 13.) The stock did not exceed this point in the next four years, and closed at $51 in 1974. Since 1970 its revenues kept growing and were up over three times by 1975. DEC's earnings per share were up 2½ times; during this same period DEC dropped 49 percent from its 1970 high!

DEC is one of many stocks over which an investor might lose a lot of sleep—if he didn't have a plan for timing purchases and sales. In this case, PBS could have given a trader more peace of mind than performance.

Hindsight tells us we should have traded DEC using PBS from 1967 through the 10th week of 1970, and walked away with our 526 percent profit. However, PBS shows a very respectable gain of 391 percent by trading the long side, a 45 percent loss on the short side, or a combined gain of 219 percent for the 8+ year period, ending 1974. (See Tables 5B and 5C).

Figure 13

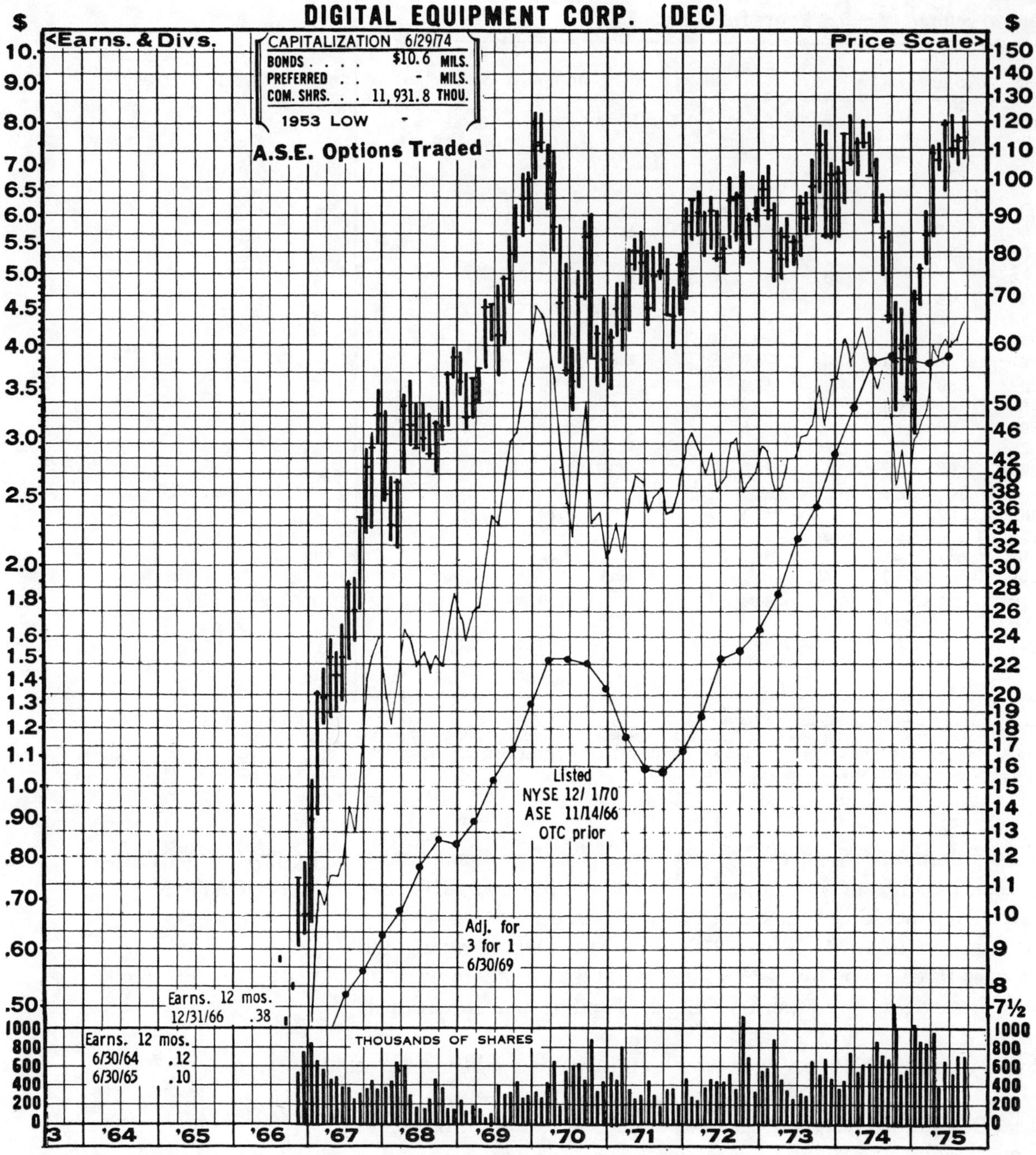

Source: Chart by Securities Research Company, 208 Newbury Street, Boston, MA 02116.

Table 5B
DEC Weekly Closing Prices

Week	1965	1966	1967	1968	1969	1970	1971	1972	1973	1974
1			30 L	124 (S)	173 H	104	53 L	74	93	92
2			33 (B)	122	155 (S) L	107	55	72 L	98 (B)	86 (S) L
3			35	122 L	160	118 H	61	79	98 H	92
4			44	127 H	170 H	117	61	88	97	102 (B) H
5			47 H	106	160 L	112 L	64 (B)	91 H	94 L	100
6			46 L	98 L	163 H	114	72 H	88	100	98
7			51	113 H	161	121 H	66 L	88 L	101 H	98 L
8			57	111	149	119	67	90	93 (S)	108
9			58	102	143 L	112	72 H	95 H	86 L	113
10			62 H	101 L	147	100 (S)	63 (S)	91	87 H	118
11			58	107	151	106 H	62	86 (S)	84	120 H
12			58 L	109	157	97 L	62 L	88	78 L	115
13			59	116 (B)	162 H	102 H	67	90 H	80	105
14			60	132	160	98 L	68	89	82	103 L
15			68	138	157	103 (B)	70	83	82	106
16			68 H	138	155 L	90 (S)	75 (B)	80 L	82 H	110 H
17			67	153	159	84 L	77	85 H	79 L	107 L
18			63	154 H	171 (B)	85 H	78	84	86 (B) H	115 H
19			60 L	141	179	77	81 H	84 L	83	113
20			62	135	185	74	79 L	87 (B)	78 (S) L	113 L
21			67 H	134 L	192	61 L	80	92 H	85 H	117 H
22			63 L	140	198 H	68	83 H	87	81 L	112 (S)
23			70	148 H	192	68	80	84 L	82 H	105 L
24			71 H	138	189	69	78 (S)	86 H	79 L	115 H
25			69	134	189 L	72 H	75 L	83 (S)	81	107
26			67 L	130 (S) L	195 (3 for 1 split)	57	77 H	78 L	83 (B) H	101
27			72	144 H	70 H	55	76	84 H	80 L	97 L
28			78	143	62 (S) L	53	68	81	84	101
29			78	139	65 H	53	66 L	81 L	89	103 H
30			84 H	137	62 L	52 L	67	83	94 H	92
31			83	132 L	63	53	70 H	90 (B)	92	87 L
32			81	143 H	64	56 H	69 L	94	90	90 H
33			79	138	65	55 L	76 (B)	96 H	89	84
33			74 L	137	72 (B)	64 (B)	76	88 L	87 L	77 L
35			80	128	73 H	71	77	93 H	89	84 H
36			81	125	69 L	76 H	79	89	89	83
37			85	125 L	78	71 L	80 H	88	92	73 L
38			87	128	82 H	77	75	87 (S) L	97	74 H
39			104	139	77 L	82	75 L	95 (B)	98	65
40			118 H	149 (B)	82	88 H	76 H	97	100	63
41			110	149 H	82	77	70 (S)	97	106	59
42			109 L	144	85	72	66	99 H	107	57
43			121 H	136 L	86	67 (S)	65 L	85 (S)	115 H	52 L
44			109 L	140	86	57	70 H	85	111 L	58
45		N.A.	112	143	91	56	65	82 L	112 H	65 H
46		31	113	149	98 H	54 L	62 L	86	98 (S)	59
47		33	119	149	91 L	56	64	88	94	59
48		34 H	139	164 H	95 H	59	72 (B)	88	84 L	59
49		30	141	163 L	92 L	67 H	79 H	92	92 H	55
50		30 L	146 H	177 H	93	63	77	94 H	88 L	53
51		31 H	137 L	174	97	53 L	77	90 L	93 (B)	52
52		30	144 H	172 L	97	62 H	77	91	101 H	51
53						57				

Table 5C
Digital Equipment Summary—8 Years 7 Weeks, to 1975

	Signal to		*Gains*			*Cumulative Results**		
Date Week/ Year	Buy	Sell	Long Percent	Short Percent	Long Term Gain	Long 1.00	Short 1.00	Long and Short 1.00
2/67	33							
1/68		124	+275%		L.T.	3.74		
13/68	116			+6			1.05	3.927
26/68		130	+12			4.15		
40/68	149			−14			.89	
2/69		155	+4			4.27		
18/69	171			−10			.93	
	(3 for 1 split)							
28/69		62	+8			4.57		
34/69	72			−16			.77	
10/70		100	+38		L.T.	6.26		
15/70	103			−3			.74	
16/70		90	−12			5.45		
34/70	64			+28			.94	
43/70		67	+4			5.61		
5/71	64			+4			.97	
10/71		63	−1			5.50		
16/71	75			−19			.77	
24/71		78	+4			5.66		
33/71	76			+2			.78	
41/71		70	−7			5.21		
48/71	72			−2			.76	
11/72		86	+19			6.15		
20/72	87			−1			.74	
25/72		83	−4			5.84		
31/72	90			−8			.68	
38/72		87	−3			5.61		
39/72	95			−9			.61	
43/72		85	−10			4.99		
2/73	98			−15			.51	
8/73		93	−5			4.69		
18/73	86			+7			.54	
20/73		78	−9			4.22		
26/73	83			−6			.50	
46/73		98	+18			4.94		
51/73	93			+5			.52	
2/74		86	−7			4.54		
4/74	102			−18			.42	
22/74		112	+9			4.91		
Last	(51)			+54			.65	3.19

* Trading costs of 1 percent are deducted for each trade.

The Dow Jones Industrial Index declined approximately 24 percent during this period. If one had bought and held DEC from the first recorded price in week #46, 1966, his profit would be approximately 390 percent. (See Table 5A.)

Table 5A
DEC Results—8 Years 7 Weeks, to 1975

DJI Index	−24%
DEC—Bought and held	+390%
DEC—PBS	+391%
DEC—PBS (including short sales)	+219%

—38 trades, 2 long term gains, 17 gains, 21 losses.

As with all PBS examples, the stop limit order is not used. However, stop limit orders (discussed in a later chapter) can substantially improve the PBS results from volatile stocks.

KAUFMAN AND BROAD

Kaufman and Broad (KB), one of the largest builders of medium priced housing, saw its stock make a giant pyramid within a decade. Its stock climbed from about $1 (adjusted) a share in 1965 to $52 in 1972, then back down to $2 in 1974! (See Figure 14.)

The buy and hold investor for the ten year period would have seen his investment rise from $1.25 (adjusted) to $2, a 60 percent gain.

The PBS trader should have realized a gain of 279 percent on the long side, a 65 percent loss on the short side, or a combined gain of 32 percent. (See Table 6A.) Note that KB was a treacherous stock to sell short up until 1972, on Tables 6B and 6C.

Table 6A
Kaufman & Broad Results, 1965–1975

DJI Index	−29%
KB—Bought and held	+60%
KB—PBS	+279%
KB—PBS (including short sales)	+32%

—34 trades, 3 long term gains, 12 gains, 20 losses, 2 breakevens.

In early 1973 housing starts fell apart. Then the short side produced good gains, +46 percent from week #2 to #23 in 1973, +38% from week #42 in 1973 to week #10 in 1974, and +77% from week #17, 1974, to the end of 1974!

In this book I attempt to apply the PBS as a pure and simple technical tool. However, if you also look at the fundamentals, that is, what is going on in the housing industry, I suggest that PBS can be extremely

Figure 14

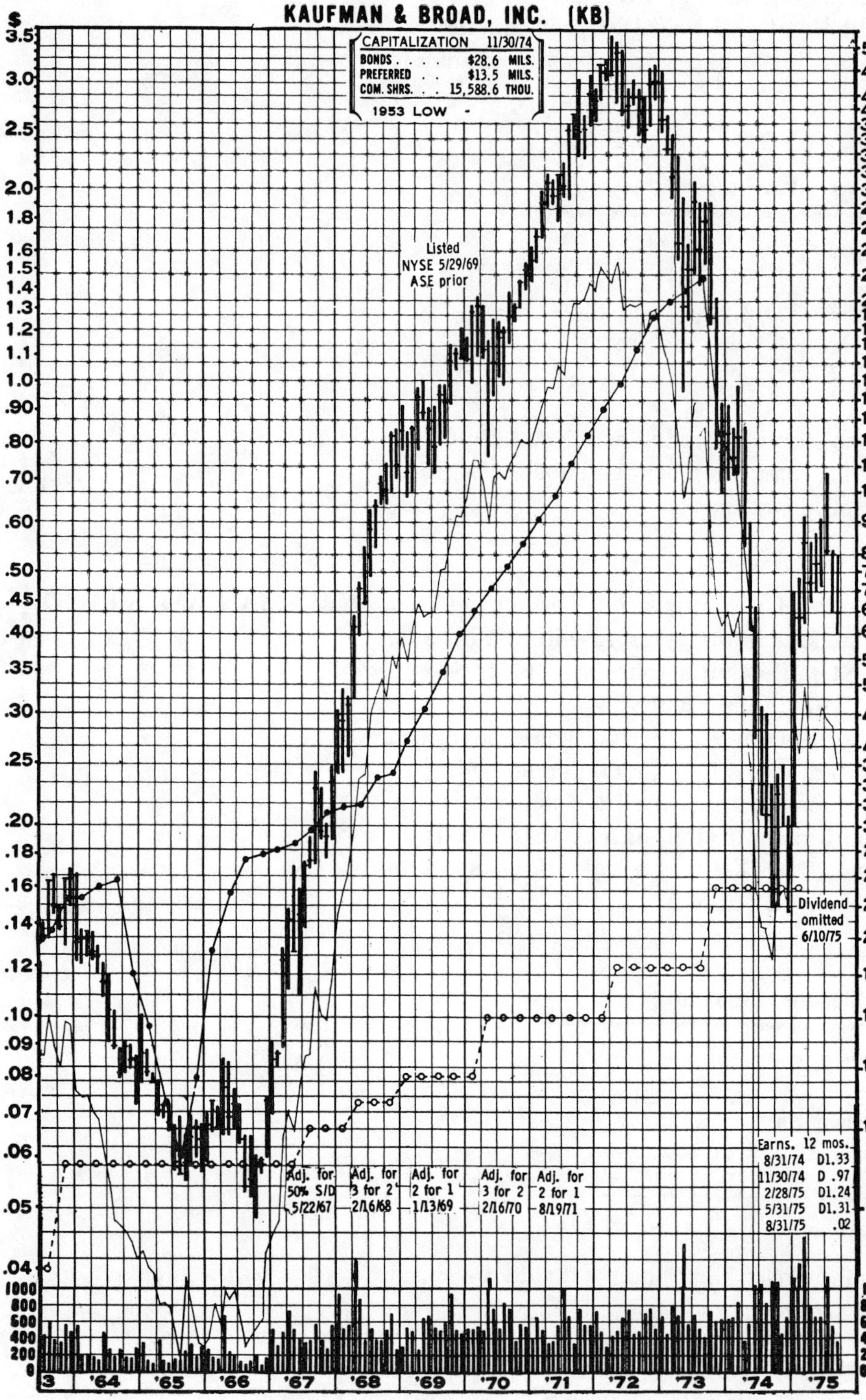

Source: Chart by Securities Research Company, 208 Newbury Street, Boston, MA 02116.

Table 6B
Kaufman and Broad Weekly Closing Prices

Week	1965	1966	1967	1968	1969	1970	1971	1972	1973	1974
1	17	13 H	14	34	71 H	48	44	40	44	11
2	17 H	12 L	16	36	70 L (2 for 1 split)	48	47	40	41(S)	10 L
3	16 L	13	16	40 H	40(B)H	48 L	48 H	40 L	40	11
4	17	13	18 H	39	38	51 H	46 L	41	37 L	12
5	17 H	13	17	38	37	48	48	44 H	38 H	12 H
6	16	14(B)	17	35 L (3 for 2 split)	35 L	45(S)L	52 H	42 L	36	11
7	16	14	17	24	36 H	53(B) (3 for 2 split)	49 L	44	35	11
8	16	15 H	17 L	28 H	31(S)	36	50	45	34	11
9	16	14	18	25	32	38 H	54	46	34	10 L
10	16	13	18	24 L	32 H	36	55	47	34	13(B)H
11	16	13	19 H	25 H	30 L	35	58 H	47 H	32	12
12	15	13	18 L	23(S)L	32	35 L	56	46	29 L	12
13	15	13 L	24 H	28(B)	37(B)	38	56 L	45 L	31	12
14	15	16 H	22 L	29	36 L	38 H	57	49	31	11
15	15	15 L	25	34 H	38 H	36	59	50 H	33 H	10 L
16	14	16 H	28	33 L	37 L	34(S)L	62 H	47	32	11 H
17	14	15	29	36	38	35 H	61	45	24 L	9(S)
18	14	15	35 H	39	41	34	60	43(S)L	27 H	8
19	14	14(S)	32	40	41	33	60	44	26	7
20	14	13	31 L (3 for 2 split)	42 H	42 H	28	58	49	16 L	6 L
21	14	13 L	18 H	40 L	41	24 L	58 L	50 H	21 H	7 H
22	14	14	17 L	42	40	28	60	47	19 L	6
23	13	15	18	48 H	37	30	60 H	43	22 B	6
24	13	15 H	20	44	34(S)L	30	57(S)L	42	23 H	4
25	13	14	20 H	44	36	35 H	58	42	22	4
26	13	14	19 L	40 L	36	32	63(B)H	40	22 L	4
27	12 L	14	20 H	46	40 H	32 L	62	39	23	3
28	13 H	13	19	48	38	34	62	38 L	23	3 L
29	12	13	19 L	53	37	36(B)	62	39	28	4 H
30	12 L	13	22	56 H	36	36 H	60	40	29 H	3
31	14(B)H	13	25 H	49 L	36 L	35	58 L	42	28	3 L
32	13	12	24	53	39	33	62 (2 for 1 split)	42	22 L	4
33	13	12	24	58 H	43(B)	30(S)L	35	44 H	23	4 H
34	12	11	23 L	56 L	43 H	32	37	41 L	24	3
35	12	10 L	24	57	42	35	37	42 H	24 H	3
36	12	11	28	60	38	35	38	39	23	3
37	12	12	30 H	61	38 L	37(B)	38	38 L	23 L	2
38	11(S)L	13 H	29 L	61	43 H	38	38	41	28 H	2
39	12	11	30	63	41 L	39 H	40	41 H	26	2
40	12	10 L	30 H	65 H	42	38	43 H	37	25 L	2 L
41	12	11	29	59	42	37 L	39	35 L	27 H	3 H
42	13	11	28(S)	59 L	47	38	39	38 H	21(S)	2 L
43	13 H	11	26	62 H	49 H	39	37 L	36 L	20	3
44	12 L	11	26	60	48 L	39	39 H	38	17 L	3
45	13 H	11	26	60 L	49 H	40 H	36(S)	40(B)	19 H	3
46	12 L	11	26	63	47(S)L	39	36	43	17	3
47	13	12	25 L	70	48	39 L	35 L	44 H	14	3
48	13 H	12	27	73	49	40	40(B)	43 L	12	3 H
49	12	12	27 H	74 H	49	43	40	46	12	2
50	12	13	26 L	73 L	50(B)	44	44	47 H	11	2
51	11 L	14(B)	33(B)H	74 H	50 H	45 H	44 H	45	11	2
52	13	14	31 L	69(S)	49	43 L	42	44	11	2 L
53						44				

Table 6C
Kaufman and Broad Summary, 1965–1975

Date Week/ Year	Signal To Buy	Sell	Gain (Loss) Long Percent	Short Percent	Long Term Gain	Cumulative Results* Long 1.00	Short 1.00	Long and Short 1.00
(/64)		(25)						
31/65	14							
38/65		11	−21			.78		
6/66	14			−27			.72	
19/66		14	0			.77		
51/66	14			0			.71	
	(3 for 2 split)							
42/67		28	+200		L.T.	2.30		
51/67	33			−17			.58	
	(3 for 2 split)							
12/68		23	+4			2.37		
13/68	28			−21			.45	
52/68		69	+146		L.T.	5.82		
	(2 for 1 split)							
3/69	40			−15			.38	
8/69		31	−22			4.48		
13/69	37			−19			.30	
24/69		34	−8			4.08		
33/69	43			−26			.22	
46/69		47	+9			4.40		
50/69	50			−6			.20	
6/70		45	−10			3.92		
7/70	53			−17			.17	
	(3 for 2 split)							
16/70		34	−3			3.76		
29/70	36			−5			.16	
33/70		30	−16			3.12		
37/70	37			−23			.12	
24/71		57	+54		L.T.	4.78		
26/71	63			−10			.10	
	(2 for 1 split)							
45/71		36	+14			5.40		
48/71	40			−11			.09	
18/72		43	+7			5.73		
45/72	40			+6			.10	
2/73		41	+2			5.78		
23/73	22			+46			.14	
42/73		21	−4			5.49		
10/74	13			+38			.19	
17/74		9	−30			3.79		
(Last)	(2)			+77			.35	1.32

* Trading costs of 1 percent are deducted for each trade.

profitable in helping you time your decisions. If you feel the housing industry is in for a big increase, then PBS can tell you when to buy and, later, when to sell—stay away from the short side if you are bullish on the industry. If, however, you feel the housing industry is in for a big decline, e.g., due to higher interest rates, PBS can tell you when to sell short and, later, when to cover—and you stay away from the long side.

McDONALD'S CORPORATION

McDonald's Corporation (MCD), the rapid hamburger assembler and dominant force in fast-food restaurants, has become a well-known name in the United States and abroad. It's not nice to sell short such an all-American company—and the PBS statistics show it. Hindsight shows that MCD's earnings did not stumble once in this period, and, as you might expect, the big gains were made on the long side.

In buying and holding MCD for the 8½ year period (sorry, ten years of statistics weren't available), the price appreciated from $2.75 (adjusted) to $28, or about 918 percent. (See Figure 15). The PBS produced 420 percent on the long side, and a 77 percent loss on the short side, or a combined gain of 19 percent. (See Table 7A.)

Table 7A
MCD Results—8½ Years, Mid-1966 to 1975

DJI Index	−29%
MCD—Bought and held	918%
MCD—PBS	420%
MCD—PBS (including short sales)	19%

—38 trades, 5 long term gains, 12 gains, 24 losses, 2 breakevens.

Now will everyone who bought MCD at $2.75 (adjusted) and held it for 8½ years, please raise your hands? Not very many hands!

When MCD came on the market, it was regarded, by many, as another highly speculative restaurant chain. After all, the turnover in the restaurant business is known to be extremely high. If you had been presented with the opportunity to buy MCD in 1966, you might have turned it down because MCD had just dropped from $33 down to $19 from week #27 to week #40, 1966, and furthermore, you had no idea about when to sell such a speculative stock. So you missed the whole show! (Refer to Tables 7B and 7C.)

It's not likely that one can pick a stock that will appreciate 918 percent in 7½ years. However, using the PBS to assist you, you may become brave enough to buy such "speculative" stocks in the future, because you now have a tool to let you know when to buy and, even more important, when to sell!

Figure 15

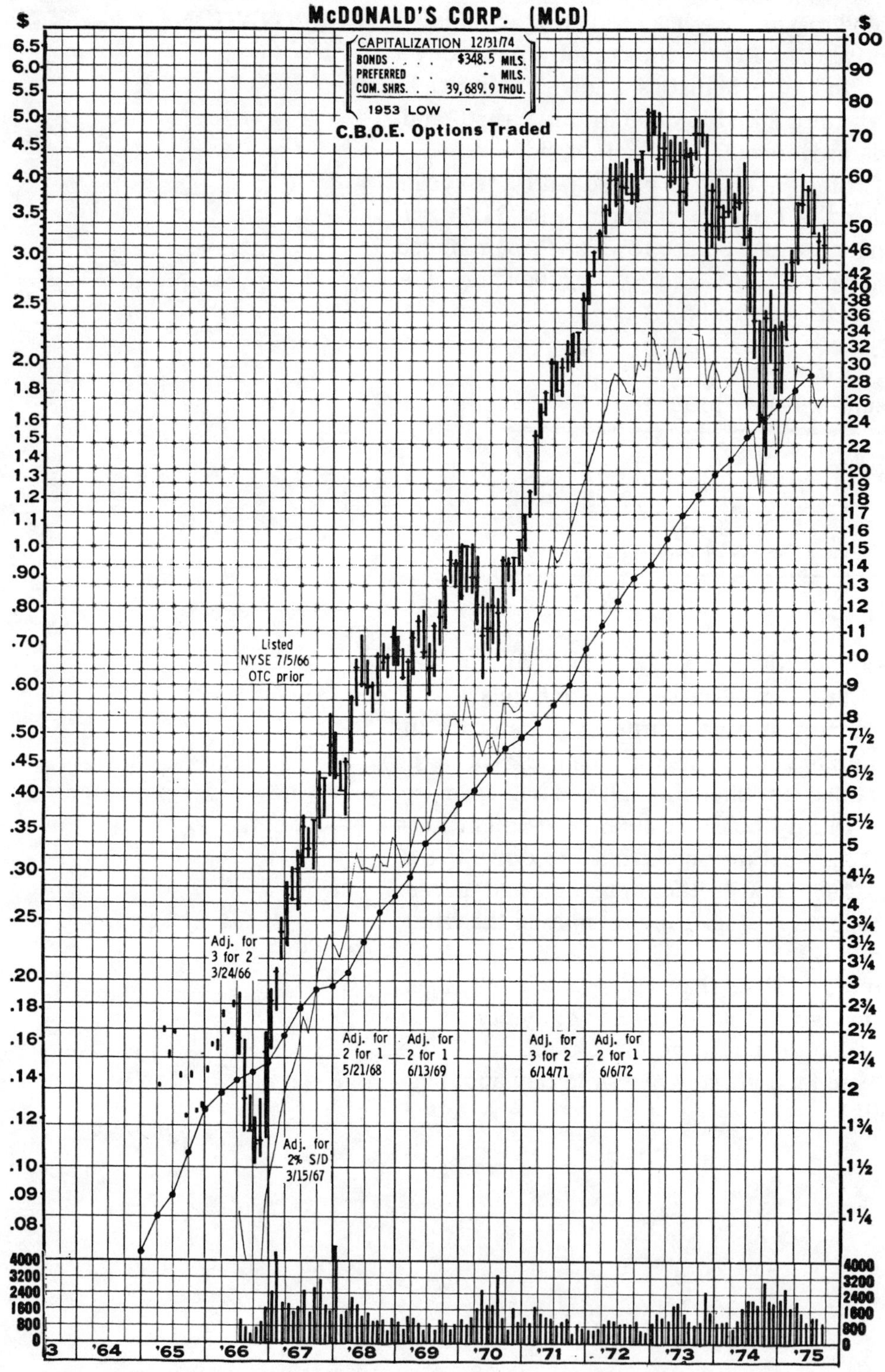

Source: Chart by Securities Research Company, 208 Newbury Street, Boston, Mass. 02116.

Table 7B
MCD Weekly Closing Prices

Week	1965	1966	1967	1968	1969	1970	1971	1972	1973	1974
1			29	82	63	44 H	44(S)L	77 H	73	53
2			33	82 L	60 L	43	46	75	73	51 L
3			33	87 H	61	40	49(B)	75 L	73	54
4			34	82	62 H	39(S)	51	79	72	54 H
5			36	80 S	61	37 L	53	85	66 L	53
6			37	78	60 L	44 H	53	86	73 H	50
7			37	78 L	62 H	43	53	88 H	70	49 L
8			38	79 H	56(S)	43 L	55	87 L	69	52
9			41	72	55	45(B)H	59	92 H	67 L	52
10			43	70 L	51	43	61	91 L	68	57(B)
11			44 H	76 H	51 L	40(S)	65	92	68 H	57
12			41 L	74 L	55	38 L	66	94	62(S)	55
13			43	81 B	58	41 H	69	96	66	52
14			44	87	58	40	70	100	68 H	52
15			46	87	59	37	72	102	65	51 L
16			50 H	90	60	34 L	72	102	65	54 H
17			49 L	98	63(B)	35	75	106	59 L	52 L
18			53 H	110 H	65	37 H	75	110 H	66 H	53
19			50 L	101 L	65	34	79 H	105 L	63	56 H
20			52 H	106 (2 for 1 split)	69	31	77 L	110	61 L	55 L
21			51	57	69 H	28 L	79	122 H	68(B)	58 H
22			49(S)	67 H	68	32	83 H	113 (2 for 1 split)	63 L	54(S)L
23			53(B)	63	68 (2 for 1 split)	34 H	82 L (3 for 2 split)	56 L	65 H	59(B)
24			56	63	32	32 L	55	62 H	59(S)	61 H
25			57 H	57	32	35(B)	58	59	56 L	55
26			54 L	54	30	32 L	59	59 L	57 H	47(S)
27		33	56	53 L	30	33	59 H	60 H	55 L	47
28		32	61	58 H	30	34	56	57(S)	60(B)	42 L
29		30	61	54	28	37	56	57	66 H	43 H
30		29	65 H	53	27 L	37 H	54(S)L	56	64	41
31		29	63	50 S	28	36	55	56 L	63	38 L
32		28	61	50 L	30	33	57	62(B)H	63	41 H
33		25	57	53	31	30(S)L	58	61	62 L	37
34		24	57 L	53	33	34	58	57 L	64	31 L
35		23	59 H	54	33	36	62(B)	59 H	65 H	35 H
36		22 L	58 L	54 H	33	37	64	58	64 L	30
37		23 H	59	52 L	34	40(B)	64 H	56(S)	66	27 L
38		22	59	56 B	34	41	60 L	55 L	72 H	29 H
39		21	65	58	35(B)	41	62	56	70	25
40		19 L	70 H	58	35	43 H	66 H	57	68 L	21 L
41		21	68 L	58	37	40 L	62	57	72 H	28
42		21 H	69	61	39	42	61 L	58	69 L	32(B)
43		19	77 H	62 H	39	43 H	62	61(B)	72 H	32
44		19 L	68 L	57 L	39	42	64 H	64 H	69	35
45		20	72	58	43 H	40	62	61 L	65(S)	38 H
46		22(B)H	72	59 H	40 L	39(S)	60(S)L	62	59	33
47		20 L	74	57 L	41	39 L	62	62	47 L	32 L
48		22	79	59	43 H	41	68(B)	67	50	33 H
49		23	85	62	41	44(B)H	72	70	53	30(S)
50		29 H	93 H	66 H	40 L	43 L	74	70	55	32 H
51		28	91	65	42 H	46 H	74	74	56	26 L
52		28 L	86	63	40 L	45 L	75	76 H	57 H	28
53						46 H				

Table 7C
McDonald's Summary, 8½ Years to 1975

Date Week/ Year	Signal to Buy	Signal to Sell	Gains Long Percent	Gains Short Percent	Long Term Gain	Cumulative Results* Long 1.00	Cumulative Results* Short 1.00	Cumulative Results* Long and Short 1.00
46/66	22							
22/67		49	+122		L.T.	2.21		
23/67	53			−8			.91	
5/68		80	+50		L.T.	3.29		
13/68	81			−1			.89	
	(2 for 1 split)							
31/68		50	+23			4.01		
38/68	56			−12			.77	
8/69		56	-0-			3.97		
17/69	63			−12			.67	
	(2 for 1 split)							
4/70		39	+23		L.T.	4.85		
9/70	45			−15			.56	
11/70		40	−11			4.26		
25/70	35			+12			.62	
33/70		30	−14			3.62		
37/70	40			−33			.41	
46/70		39	−2			3.52		
49/70	44			−12			.36	
1/71		44	-0-			3.48		
3/71	49			−11			.31	
	(3 for 2 split)							
30/71		54	+65		L.T.	5.71		
35/71	62			−14			.27	
46/71		60	−3			5.48		
48/71	68			−13			.23	
	(2 for 1 split)							
28/72		57	+67		L.T.	9.10		
32/72	62			−8			.21	
37/72		56	−9			8.19		
43/72	61			−8			.19	
12/73		62	+1			8.19		
21/73	68			−9			.17	
24/73		59	−13			7.05		
28/73	60			−1			.16	
45/73		65	+8			7.54		
10/74	57			+12			.18	
22/74		54	−5			7.09		
23/74	59			−9			.16	
26/74		47	−20			5.60		
42/74	32			+31			.22	
49/74		30	−6			5.20		
(Last)	28			+6			.23	1.19

* Trading costs of 1 percent are deducted for each trade.

SKYLINE CORPORATION

Skyline Corporation (SKY), the largest producer of mobile homes, was an outstanding PBS performer. SKY's sales grew from $67 million in 1965 to a peak of $300 million in 1973, then dropped to $179 million in 1974, a net increase of about 260 percent for the ten year period ending 1974. Earnings per share rose from 19¢ (adjusted) in 1965 to $1.76 in 1971, then dropped to 25¢ in 1974, a net gain of about 31 percent for this period.

The investors who bought this stock at $24 a share during the first of 1965 (or $2.67 adjusted for splits), had a paper profit of 461 percent at the end of 1974, a very respectable gain. (See Figure 16.) There may have been some loss of investor sleep, though, since SKY was as low as $1 3/8 (adjusted) and as high as $74 during this period.

A trader using PBS might have realized a substantial gain of over 1,216 percent on the long side, or a gain of 33 percent on the short side, or a combined gain from trading both long and short of 1,650 percent. (See Table 8A.)

Table 8A
SKY Results, 1965–1975

DJI	−29%
SKY—Bought and held	+461%
SKY—PBS	+1,216%
SKY—PBS (including short sales)	+1,650%

—27 trades, 4 long term gains
—13 gains, 11 losses, 2 breakevens

Especially impressive was the gain of 800 percent from week #26 in 1967 to week #2, 1969—from $8.33 (adjusted) to $75 a share! (Refer to Tables 8B and 8C.) Gains of this size and this time period (over 1½ years) are extremely rare. I mention this because the PBS is primarily a short term trading technique, yet *the PBS will "tell" the trader to hold onto his stock as long as it is in an uptrend.* Theoretically, a stock *could* go up forever, but, as much as we'd like to believe this, we know that no stock goes to the sky, including SKY.

Figure 16

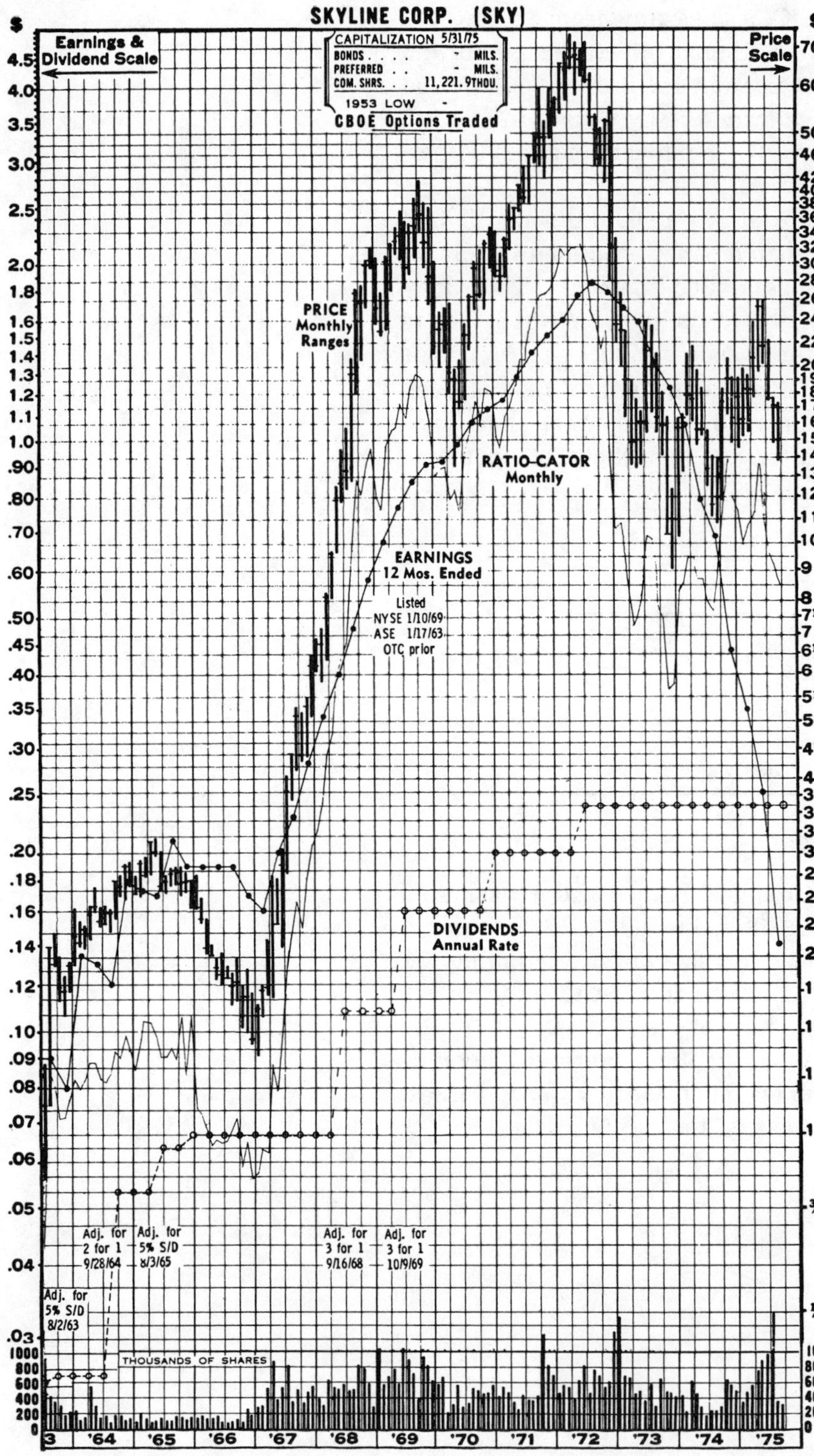

Source: Chart by Securities Research Company, 208 Newbury Street, Boston, Mass. 02116.

Table 8B: SKY Weekly Closing Prices

Week	*1965*	*1966*	*1967*	*1968*	*1969*	*1970*	*1971*	*1972*	*1973*	*1974*
1	24	22	13	55 L	90	28 H	31	55	28	12
2	24 L	22 L	13	60	75 (S) L	26	31	56 H	25 L	12
3	25 H	23 H	12 L	60 H	83	25	29 (S)	55 L	26 H	13
4	24	22	14	58	83 H	22	29	56	23	15
5	24	22	14	55	75 L	21 L	29 L	56	22 L	15 H
6	24 L	22	15	55 L	77 H	23 H	30 H	56	23	14 L
7	26	22	15	56	75	21 L	28	62	24 H	15
8	27	21	15	62 H	73	22	28 L	64	20 L	15
9	27	20	17	60 L	69 L	23	30	66 H	21	17 (B)
10	27	19	18 (B) H	61	71	24 (B) H	30	65	21 H	19 H
11	27 H	18	17	67	73	22	32 (B)	64	19	18
12	26	18	15 L	67	84 (B)	22 L	32	61 L	18 L	17
13	26 L	18	16	73	90 H	23	32	64	19 H	17 L
14	27 H	18	16	74	89 L	25 H	32	70	17	18
15	26	18	18	82 H	90 H	24	33	72 H	17	19
16	26 L	18	22	81 L	87 (S)	21 (S)	34	68	16	19 H
17	29	18	23	87	86 L	20	35	67	14 L	17 L
18	29 H	17	23 H	94	96 (B)	19	35	62 L	15	18 H
19	28 L	17	22 L	96 H	96	18	36 H	65	15 H	17
20	29 H	17	23 H	95 L	101 H	15	35 L	69	14 L	16 (S)
21	28	17	21 (S)	109	100	15 L	37	70 H	15 H	16
22	28	17	20	107	98 L	19 H	39	69	14	15 L
23	28	16 L	20 L	111	105 H	17 L	39 H	65	14	17 H
24	25 (S)	18 H	22	127 H	98	18	38 L	65	14	16
25	25	17	23	116	94 (S) L	18 H	39	64 L	14 L	15
26	24 L	16 L	25 (B)	114 L	99	17 L	41	67	16 (B)	15
27	26 H	17 H	29	115	105 H	18	42	69 H	16	14
28	25	16 L	31 H	135 H	98	20 (B)	43 H	64	18	14
29	24 L	17 H	30 L	131	93	21	42	64	23 H	14
30	25 H	16	35 H	120	85 L	22	38 L	63 (S)	21 L	13
31	24	16	33 L	118 L	90	22	40	60	22 H	12
32	24	16	34 H	122	92	22 H	41	57	21	12
33	24	16	33 L	147	99	21 L	44	56	17 (S) L	11
34	24	16	35	152	102	23	44	54	18	11
35	24	16	39 H	175	102 H	26	47 H	53	20 H	11 L
36	24 L	15	37 L	185 H	96 L	26	45 L	48 L	19	13 H
37	25	15 L	41	182 L (3 for 1 split)	104 (B)	26	47	49	17 L	11 L
38	25	17 H	41	61	113 H	27	48	49	19 H	12
39	25 H	16	45	77 H	104 L	27	53	50 H	16 L	12
40	24	15	45 H	70	109 (3 for 1 split)	30	58 H	46	17 H	13
41	23	15	43	69	38 H	30 H	55	46	15	15 (B)
42	23 L	15	40 L	67 L	36 L	28	52	46	15	17 H
43	24	14	43 H	71	37 H	28	49 L	45	14 L	16 L
44	24	14	42 L	77	36 L	26	50 H	42	16 H	17
45	24 H	14	44	80	37 H	26	48 (S)	41 L	14	19 H
46	23	14 L	44	90 H	34 (S)	26 L	47	46	13	18 L
47	23	17 H	45	85 L	31 L	27	46 L	50	12	19
48	23	15	46	89 H	32 H	30	51 (B)	54 (B) H	10	19 H
49	23	14	48	88 L	31	33 H	55	51	10	15 (S) L
50	22	13	52	89	30	31 L	58	50	10	16
51	22 L	13	58 H	95 H	28	32 H	58 H	47	10 L	16 H
52	24 H	13	56	94	26 L	31 L	53 L	32 (S)	11	15
53						33 H				

Table 8C
SKY Summary, 1965–1975

Date Week/ Year	Signal to Buy	Signal to Sell	Gains Long Percent	Gains Short Percent	Long Term Gain	Cumulative Results Long* 1.00	Cumulative Results Short* 1.00	Cumulative Results Long and Short* 1.00
(1964)	(24)							
24/65		$25						
10/67	$18			+28			1.27	
21/67		21	+16			1.15		
26/67	25			−19			1.01	
	(3 for 1 split)							
2/69		75	+800		L.T.	10.33		
12/69	84			−12			.88	
16/69		87	+3			10.54		
18/69	96			−10			.78	
25/69		94	−2			10.22		
37/69	104			−10			.70	
	(3 for 1 split)							
46/69		34	−1			10.02		
10/70	24			+29			.89	
16/70		21	−12			8.72		
28/70	20			+4			.92	
3/71		29	+45		L.T.	12.55		
11/71	32			−10			.82	
45/71		48	+50		L.T.	18.71		
48/71	51			−6			.76	
30/72		63	+23		L.T.	22.82		
48/72	54			+14			.86	
52/72		32	−40			13.46		
26/73	16			+50			1.28	
33/73		17	+6			14.14		
9/74	17			0			1.27	
20/74		16	−5			13.29		
41/74	15			+6			1.33	
49/74		15	0			13.16		17.50
(Last)	(15)							

* Trading costs of 1 percent are deducted from each trade.

TRANS WORLD AIRLINES, INCORPORATED

Trans World Airlines (TWA) is the only airline authorized to operate a scheduled passenger and cargo service both domestically and internationally. TWA's stock had a rough flight over a ten year period. It ranged from *$101 a share in 1966 down to $4.75 in 1974, in spite of its revenues growing every year* for these ten years! Unfortunately, TWA's earnings were extremely cyclical, ranging from a profit of $5.74 in 1965 to a loss of $6.39 a share in 1970.

Why trade TWA? Because it's a volatile stock. The investor who bought TWA at $48, at the first of 1965, would have had a loss of almost 90 percent, at $5.25 a share, ten years later! (See Figure 17.)

The trader, using the PBS, might have a loss of 24 percent on the long side, a gain of 99 percent on the short side, or a combined gain of 51 percent. (See Table 9A and Tables 9B and 9C.)

Figure 17

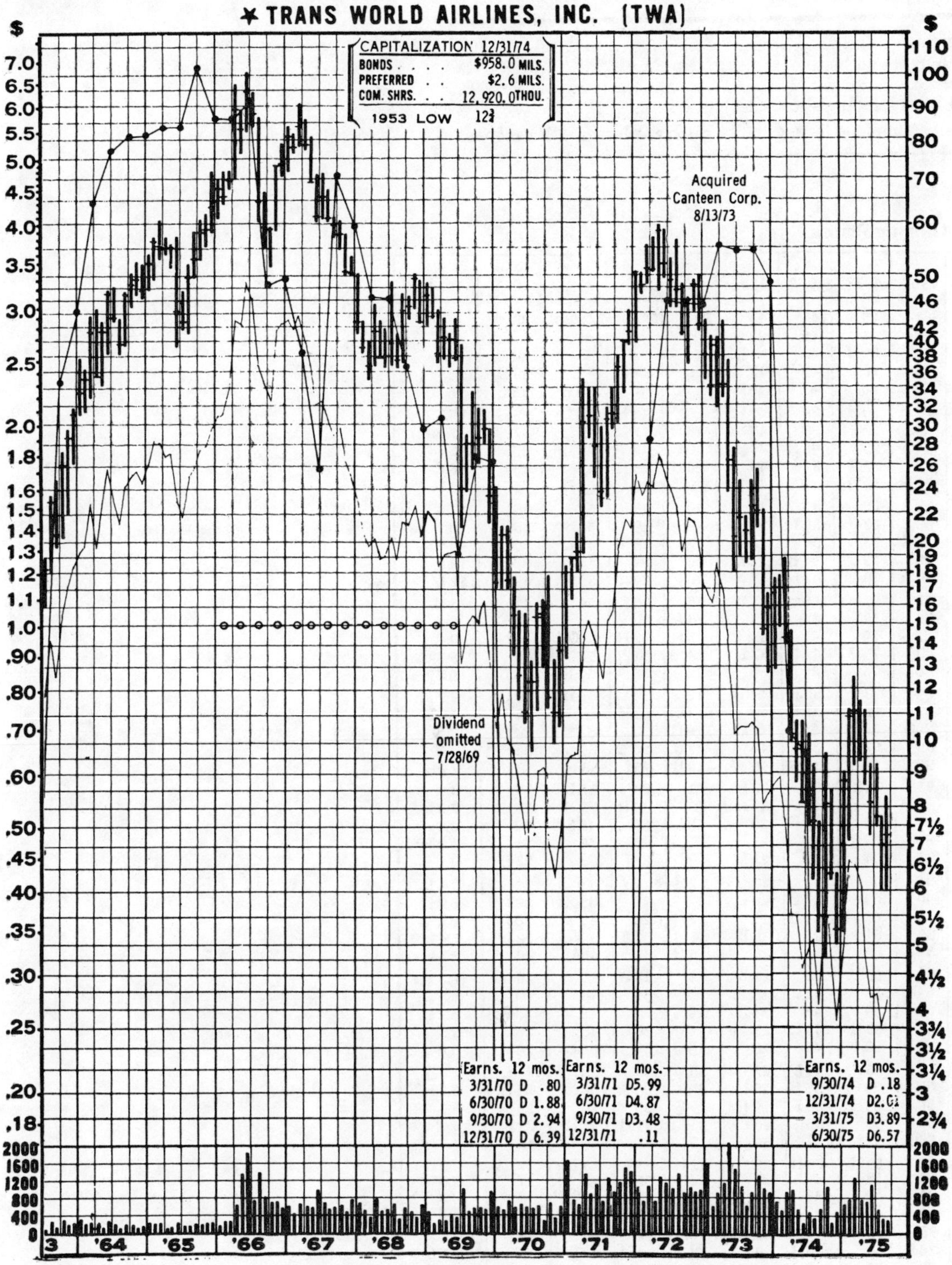

Source: Chart by Securities Research Company, 208 Newbury Street, Boston, Mass. 02116.

Table 9A
TWA Results, 1965–1975

DJI Index	−29%
TWA—Bought and held	−89%
TWA—PBS	−24%
TWA—PBS (including short sales)	+51%

—41 trades, one long term gain, 15 gains, 24 losses, 2 breakevens

Table 9B
TWA Weekly Closing Prices

Week	1965	1966	1967	1968	1969	1970	1971	1972	1973	1974
1	$48	$61 L	$75	$45	$43	$23	$14	$42	$38	$16 H
2	51Ⓑ	63	81	45	43 L	23	15	45	35 L	13 L
3	53 H	64	81 H	45	48ⒷH	21	16	45	39	15
4	52	68 H	78 L	42	47	20	18 H	49	39 H	16
5	51 L	65 L	80	41	46 L	17 L	16 L	49 H	36 L	16 H
6	53	70 H	80 H	39	47 H	18	18 H	48 L	39 H	15 L
7	55	68	77ⓈL	38 L	46	20 H	17 L	49 H	37	17ⒷH
8	56	64Ⓢ	78	41 H	44Ⓢ	18 L	18	48 L	36	16
9	58	63	85Ⓑ	37 L	43	20 H	20 H	51	33 L	16 L
10	59 H	61 L	89 H	38 H	41	19	18 L	53 H	35	18 H
11	56	62	88	37	39	18	19	51	35	17
12	53 L	68	83	35 L	39	18	19	51	35	16
13	55	73Ⓑ	83	36	38	17	19	51 L	39 H	14 S
14	56 H	80	79 L	41 B	38 L	16	22	56 H	38L	12
15	54	90 H	80	43 H	41	16	24	55	42ⒷH	12 L
16	53 L	87 L	82 H	42	42 H	15	29	54	41	13 H
17	55 H	88 H	78Ⓢ	42	39	13 L	30	51	33ⓈL	10
18	54	82Ⓢ	77 L	41 L	39	15 H	32 H	49ⓈL	36 H	10
19	54	80	78 H	42 H	37 L	14	31	54	30	8.6 L
20	52ⓈL	80 L	75	41	39	13	30	57Ⓑ	25 L	9.5
21	55	84	72	39Ⓢ	39	12	30 L	59 H	29 H	9.7 H
22	55 H	87	70	37 L	40	12L	32 H	56	26	9.6 L
23	49	93Ⓑ	66 L	41 H	42 H	14 H	30	52	24	10Ⓑ
24	48	96	67 H	38	40	12 L	26Ⓢ	51 L	23	10 H
25	44	96 H	65	36 L	40	13 H	25L	53 H	18 L	9.2 S
26	43 L	91 L	61 L	38	37 L	11	27	52 L	20	8.1
27	45	94 H	67 H	41	39 H	10	29 H	53 H	20	7.7 L
28	46 H	91	64	48Ⓑ	30	10 L	26	48 S L	20	8.2
29	44	88Ⓢ	63 L	42	27	11 H	25	50	21	9.4 H
30	42 L	87	64	41	21 L	10 L	23 L	50	23 H	9.1
31	43	81	66 H	38	25 H	12Ⓑ	24	53	21	8.4 L
32	47ⒷH	80	65	37 L	24 L	12	26	55ⒷH	19 L	8.7 H
33	46 L	76	62	38 H	25	13	29	48	20 H	8.2
34	50	62	61	37	28Ⓑ	13	31Ⓑ	45ⓈL	19 L	7.4 L
35	52 H	57 L	60	37 L	28	15 H	32	48 H	20	7.5 H
36	50 L	61	58 L	38	27 L	14	32 H	45	20	7.3
37	51	64 H	59	41	29	13 L	30	44	20	5.5 L
38	57 H	60	59	45	31 H	14	30	43	23ⒷH	6.2 H
39	54 L	59	59 H	45 H	28	14	30 L	40	22 L	5.5
40	57 H	52 L	58	43	28	16 H	32	38 L	24 H	5.0 L
41	56	57	55 L	43 L	27	15	33	39	23 L	7.5Ⓑ
42	56 L	57	58	45 H	27 L	13	36	40	24 H	8.5 H
43	58	59	59 H	44 L	29 H	12Ⓢ	36	44	23	8.3
44	61 H	63	56	45	28 L	11 L	37 H	47 H	21Ⓢ	8.0
45	58	66Ⓑ	55 L	47	31 H	12	35	45	19	7.5
46	56 L	68	56 H	50 H	30	12 H	35 L	44 L	17	7.0
47	60	71	54	47 L	29	10	36	47	17	6.5
48	61	71	50	49 H	29	10 L	40	48ⒷH	14	6.3
49	64	75	50 L	45Ⓢ	27Ⓢ	12	42	47	14	5.6
50	70 H	75	51 H	45 L	23	12	42	44	14 L	5.4
51	66	76 H	50	46 H	23 L	12	44 H	42Ⓢ	15	5.1 L
52	63	73 L	50	43	24 H	12	41 L	42	15	5.2
53						13Ⓑ				

Table 9C
TWA Summary, 1965–1975

Date Week/ Year	Signal to Buy	Signal to Sell	Gains: Long Per- cent	Gains: Short Per- cent	Long- Term Gain	Cumulative Results*: Long 1.00	Cumulative Results*: Short 1.00	Cumulative Results*: Long and Short 1.00
2/65	$51							
20/65		$52	+1			1.00		
32/65	47			+9			1.08	
8/66		64	+36			1.35		
13/66	73			−14			.91	
18/66		82	+12			1.49		
23/66	93			−13			.78	
29/66		88	−5			1.40		
45/66	66			+25			.97	
7/67		77	+16			1.61		
9/67	85			−10			.87	
17/67		78	−8			1.47		
14/68	41			+47			1.27	
21/68		39	−4			1.40		
28/68	48			−23			.96	
49/68		45	−6			1.30		
3/69	48			−6			.89	
8/69		44	−8			1.18		
34/69	28			+36			1.21	
49/69		27	−3			1.13		
31/70	12			+55			1.86	
43/70		12	0			1.12		
53/70	13			−8			1.70	
24/71		26	+100			2.24		
34/71	31			−19			1.36	
18/72		49	+58		L.T.	3.51		
20/72	57			−16			1.12	
28/72		48	−15			2.95		
32/72	55			−14			.96	
34/72		45	−18			2.39		
48/72	48			−6			.89	
51/72		42	−12			2.08		
14/73	42			0			.88	
17/73		33	−21			1.62		
38/73	23			+30			1.14	
44/73		21	−8			1.47		
7/74	17			+19			1.34	
13/74		14	−17			1.21		
22/74	10			+28			1.70	
25/74		9.2	−8			1.10		
41/74	7.5			+18			1.99	
(Last)		(5.2)	−30			.76		1.51

* Trading costs of 1 percent are deducted for each trade.

If you follow the airline industry and become convinced its future is good, the PBS can help you to time your purchases and sales. Stay away from the short side because, if you are basically optimistic about the airline industry, you'll feel very uncomfortable being short, regardless of whether you eventually profit or not. And, whether it makes sense or not, it's important that you be comfortable with your investments. We have sufficient neurotics in our great country without adding more because they are committed to positions (long or short) that might make them very nervous, such as being bullish on the airlines, but short the stock.

On the other hand, if your analysis tells you the outlook for the airlines industry, or TWA, is about to change for the worse, the PBS should be quite helpful in telling when to sell, or sell short, and when to cover.

XEROX CORPORATION

Xerox (XRX) is the leading manufacturer and seller of photocopy reproduction machines. Although the large gains in its stock price took place before 1965, XRX's growth stock image lives on, and one wonders how long this multibillion business will continue to grow.

The investor who bought XRX the first of 1965 at $33 (adjusted) had a 48 percent paper profit at $49 ten years later (See Figure 18.)

The PBS trader might have taken two routes. The regular PBS would have produced a 116 percent profit on the long side, a 16 percent loss on the short side, or a combined gain of 81 percent, not much better than buying and holding. (See Table 10A–1 and Tables 10B and 10C–1.)

Table 10A–1
XRX Results, 1965–1975, PBS not Modified

DJI Index	−29%
XRX—Bought and held	+48%
XRX—PBS	+116%
XRX—PBS (including short sales)	+81%

—48 trades, 4 long term gains
—16 gains, 29 losses, 3 breakevens

Figure 18

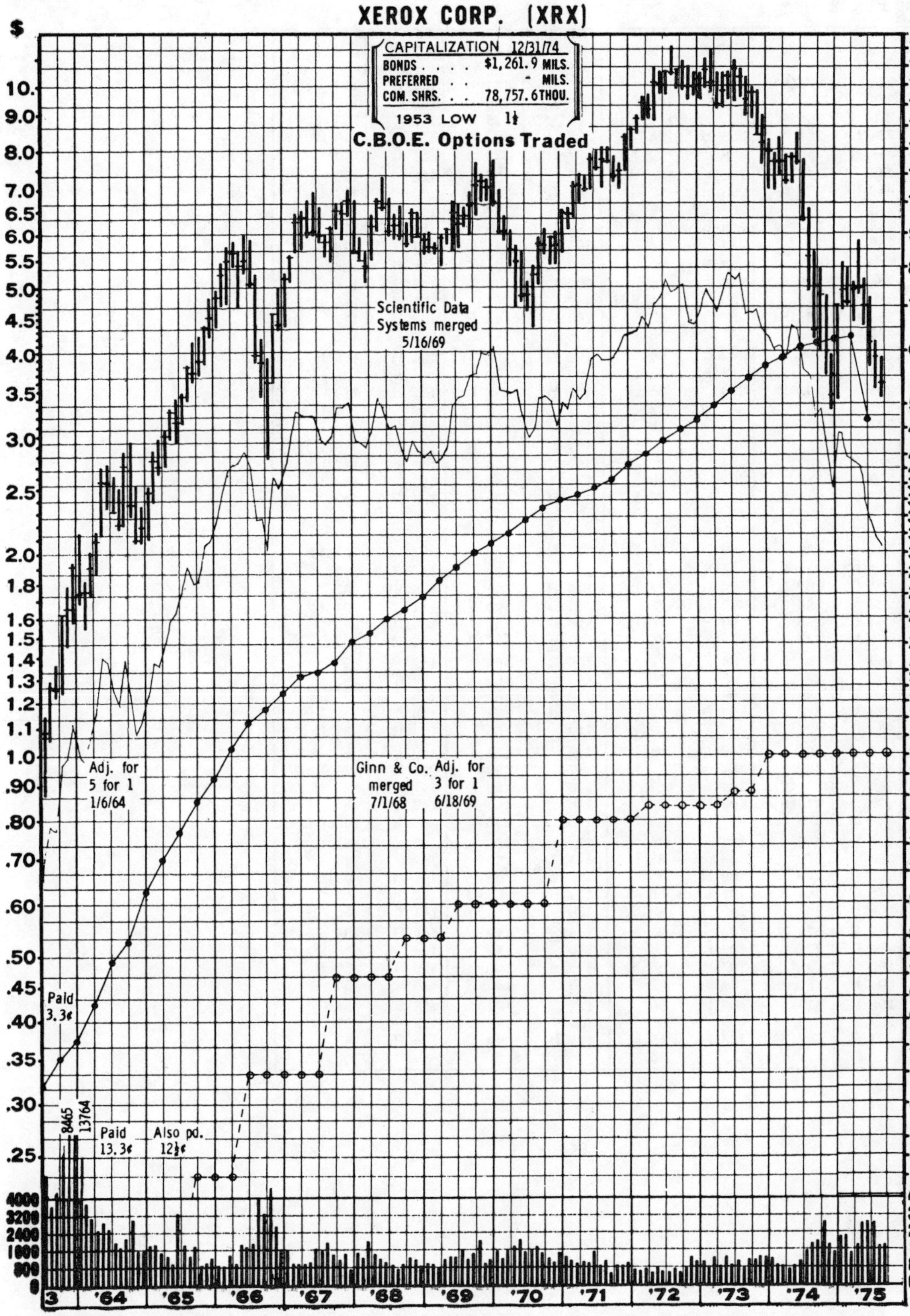

Source: Chart by Securities Research Company, 208 Newbury Street, Boston, Mass. 02116.

Table 10B
XRX Weekly Closing Prices

Week	1965	1966	1967	1968	1969	1970	1971	1972	1973	1974
1	99	198 L	215	279 Ⓢ	264	104	86 H	124	151 H	114
2	102	211	225	277	252 L	106	85 L	120 L	149 L	110 L
3	106 Ⓑ	217	225 H	266	263	111 ⒷH	89	125	151	114
4	111	220	224 L	264	265 H	106	97	129	156 ⒷH	118 H
5	111	223	244 H	256	264 L	100 ⓈL	97 H	129	151 L	115
6	115	239 H	242	255 L	268 Ⓑ	102 H	96	132	156	111
7	122	233	242 L	256 H	268 H	97 L	93 L	133	162	107 L
8	124	231	246	253	256 ⓈL	98 H	96	134	162 H	112
9	124	224 L	265	242	259 H	91 L	99	140	158 L	113
10	128	228	266	241	254 L	93 H	101	141 H	161	118
11	128 H	232	270	237	257 H	90	107 H	138	166 H	124 ⒷH
12	118 L	254 H	284 H	230 L	256	90 L	102 L	137 L	148 ⓈL	116
13	125	246 L	280	241	256	94 ⒷH	107	141	151 H	115
14	128	249	264 L	263 Ⓑ	251	87 Ⓢ	108 H	145 H	148 L	113
15	128	259 H	285	273 H	247	86	105	142	153 Ⓑ	112 L
16	136 H	258	286	266 L	242 L	84	104 L	138	154 H	115 H
17	135 L	252	286	282	258 Ⓑ	83 L	106	138	144 ⓈL	108 ⓈL
18	136	236 Ⓢ	295	292 H	269	85 H	108 H	137 L	152 H	112
19	136	227 L	299 H	285	274 H	82	107	138	149	115 H
20	140	233	297	277 L	272	80	106	147	142 L	113 L
21	146	254 H	282	286	271 L	75 L	104 L	157 H	154 Ⓑ	118 ⒷH
22	152 H	249 L	277 L	302	274 H	82 H	109	156	146 L	117 L
23	143	259 Ⓑ	302	318	269 Ⓢ	80	111	148 L	152	124 H
24	141	257	305 H	321 H	260 L (3 for 1 split)	76 L	114 H	152 H	153 H	123
25	137 L	257	302	310	89	80 H	111 L	150	152 L	116 Ⓢ
26	145	250 L	273 ⓈL	297 L	98 Ⓑ	72	117	150 L	155 H	115
27	152	258	290 H	301 H	99 H	72 L	118 H	152 H	145 ⓈL	108
28	152 H	260 H	284	296 Ⓢ	92 L	75	115 L	149 ⓈL	151	107 L
29	148 L	236 Ⓢ	264 L	276	93 H	76 H	116 H	152	156 Ⓑ	109 H
30	154	227 L	275 H	272	89 ⓈL	74	112 Ⓢ	157 Ⓑ	161 H	100
31	163	233 H	259 L	267 L	94 Ⓑ	72	109 L	166	157	93
32	166 H	230	262	277	95	70	113	168 H	153	93
33	162 L	193	266 H	286 H	96	67 L	117 Ⓑ	166	149	85
34	169	179	254 L	279	97 H	72	120 H	157	149 L	77 L
35	170	170 L	265 H	278 L	95	79 Ⓑ	119	156	154 H	83 H
36	178	179	255	283	92 L	81 H	119	154	149 L	82
37	184 H	182 H	251 L	289	96	77 L	117	153	151 H	73 L
38	172	177	266 Ⓑ	296 ⒷH	101	81	116	150 L	147 Ⓢ	80 H
39	169 L	174	277	276 ⓈL	102 H	86	116	158 H	143	65
40	177	132 L	286 H	279 H	97 L	88 H	115	156	140 L	60 L
41	186 H	158	276 L	276	101	86	112	152 L	146	75 H
42	176	160 H	289	270	108	85 L	111	157	147	68 L
43	174 L	159 L	296 H	270	109 H	86	109 L	158	147 H	69 H
44	177 H	177 Ⓑ	276	261 L	106 L	86 H	111 H	160 H	146	66
45	176 L	181	276 L	263	109 H	83 Ⓢ	109	143 ⓈL	141 L	66
46	187	184	288 H	273 H	104 Ⓢ	83 L	105 ⓈL	149	143 H	63
47	194	199	286 L	271 L	102 L	84	110	149	134	56 L
48	199	199	298	290 ⒷH	107 H	88 Ⓑ	115 Ⓑ	150	126 L	60 H
49	201	214 H	304 H	275	104 L	89 H	119	155 H	130 H	54
50	211 H	211	295 L	273	107 H	86	121	149	118 L	51
51	205	204	297	273	105	85	125	146 L	120	51
52	202	197 L	303 H	267 Ⓢ	103 L	85 L	125 H	149	124 H	49 L
53						86				

Table 10C-1
Xerox Summary, 1965–1975 (regular PBS)

Date Week/ Year	Signal to Buy	Sell	+Gains, −Losses Long Per-cent	Short Per-cent	Long Term Gain	Cumulative Results* Long 1.00	Short 1.00	Long and Short 1.00
3/65	$106							
18/66		$236	+122		L.T.	2.21		
23/66	259			−9			.90	
29/66		236	−8			2.01		
44/66	177			+25			1.11	
26/67		273	+54		L.T.	3.07		
38/67	266			+2			1.12	
1/68		279	+4			3.16		
14/68	263			+5			1.17	
28/68		296	+12			3.51		
38/68	296			0			1.16	
39/68		276	−6			3.27		
48/68	290			−5			1.09	
52/68		267	−7			3.00		
6/69	268			0			1.07	
8/69		256	−4			2.85		
17/69	258			0			1.06	
23/69		269	+4			2.94		
	(3 for 1 split)							
26/69	98			−9			.96	
30/69		89	−9			2.65		
31/69	94			−5			.90	
46/69		104	+10			2.88		
3/70	111			−6			.84	
5/70		100	−9			2.60		
13/70	94			+6			.88	
14/70		87	−7			2.39		
35/70	79			+9			.95	
45/70		83	+5			2.48		
48/70	88			−6			.88	
30/71		112	+27		L.T.	3.13		
33/71	117			−4			.84	
46/71		105	−10			2.79		
48/71	115			−9			.75	
28/72		149	+29		L.T.	3.57		
30/72	157			−5			.71	
45/72		143	−8			3.24		
4/73	156			−9			.64	
12/73		148	−5			3.05		
15/73	153			−3			.61	
17/73		144	−5			2.87		
21/73	154			−6			.57	
27/73		145	−5			2.69		
29/73	156			−7			.52	
38/73		147	−5			2.53		
11/74	124			+15			.60	
17/74		108	−12			2.20		
21/74	118			−9			.54	
25/74		116	−1			2.16		
Last Price	49			+57			.84	1.81

However, by using a modified PBS for high priced stocks, the results would be 198 percent on the long side, 9 percent on the short side, or a combined result of 224 percent. Table 10A–2 uses only the first two significant figures to determine the high and low points for stocks over $100. For example, if the price is $256 a share, consider it as $250.

Table 10A-2
XRX Results, 1965–1975 (PBS, using first two digits only)

DJI Index	−29%
XRX—Bought and held	+48%
XRX—PBS	+198%
XRX—PBS (including short sales)	+224%

—26 trades, 3 long term gains
—10 gains, 15 losses, 1 break even

Table 10C–2
Xerox Summary, 1965–1975 (modified PBS, first two digits only)

			Gains			Cumulative Results*		
Date Week/ Year	Signal to Buy	Sell	Long Per-cent	Short Per-cent	Long Term Gain	Long 1.00	Short 1.00	Long and Short 1.00
3/65	$106							
18/66		$236	+122		L.T.	2.21		
28/66	260			−10			.89	
29/66		236	−9			1.98		
44/66	177			+25			1.10	
29/67		264	+49		L.T.	2.94		
39/67	277			−4			1.04	
1/68		279	0			2.91		
17/68	282			−1			1.02	
29/68		276	−2			2.82		
38/68	296			−7			.94	
44/68		261	−11			2.48		
19/69	274 (3 for 1 split)			−4			.89	
30/69		89	+2			2.51		
31/69	94			−5			.84	
7/70		97	+3			2.56		
13/70	94			+3			.86	
14/70		87	−7			2.35		
35/70	79			+9			.92	
45/70		83	+5			2.45		
48/70	88			−6			.86	
45/72		143	+62		L.T.	3.94		
7/73	162			−13			.74	
12/73		148	−8			3.59		
30/73	161			−8			.67	
47/73		134	−16			2.98		
(Last)	(49)			+63			1.09	3.24

* Trading costs of 1 percent are deducted from each trade.

In the series, $233, 254 (H), 249, and 259 (B), one gets a buy signal at $254 the regular way. But the modified way, using only the first two digits, or $230, 250, 240, and 250, there would be no buy signal until the price closed at $260 or higher. (See Table 10C–2.)

The first-two significant figure method for high priced stocks results in fewer trades, whipsaws, and commissions, and often better results

AVON PRODUCTS, INCORPORATED

Avon Products (AVP) has had an outstanding long term growth record. It's the largest manufacturer of cosmetics and toiletries in the world, and the largest door to door seller of the same. Yet, if an investor had bought Avon on December 31, 1964, at $26 (adjusted for the split) it would have appreciated to $28 in 10 years, a gain of $2 or 7 percent! (See Figure 19.) If you think this is poor, just compare it with the Dow Jones Industrial Index, which lost 29 percent during this same period.

What happens when the PBS is applied to Avon? Had one traded the long side, using the first-two significant figure method for high priced stocks, the original investment would be up approximately 142 percent. Had one also sold short, the original investment would be slightly higher, 151 percent. (See Table 11A.)

Table 11A
AVP Results, 1965–1975 (PBS using first two digits only)

DJI Index	−29%
AVP—Bought and held	+4%
AVP—PBS	+142%
AVP—PBS (including selling short)	+151%

—23 trades, 5 long term gains
—11 gains, 11 losses

It was very difficult to make money by selling Avon short during this ten year period, except for one notable period. This was in 1973 and 1974, when the stock dropped from $112 to $25 a share between the sell (sell short) and buy (buy to cover short sale) signals. This represented a 77 percent gain from shorting AVP. (Refer to Tables 11B and 11C.)

Figure 19

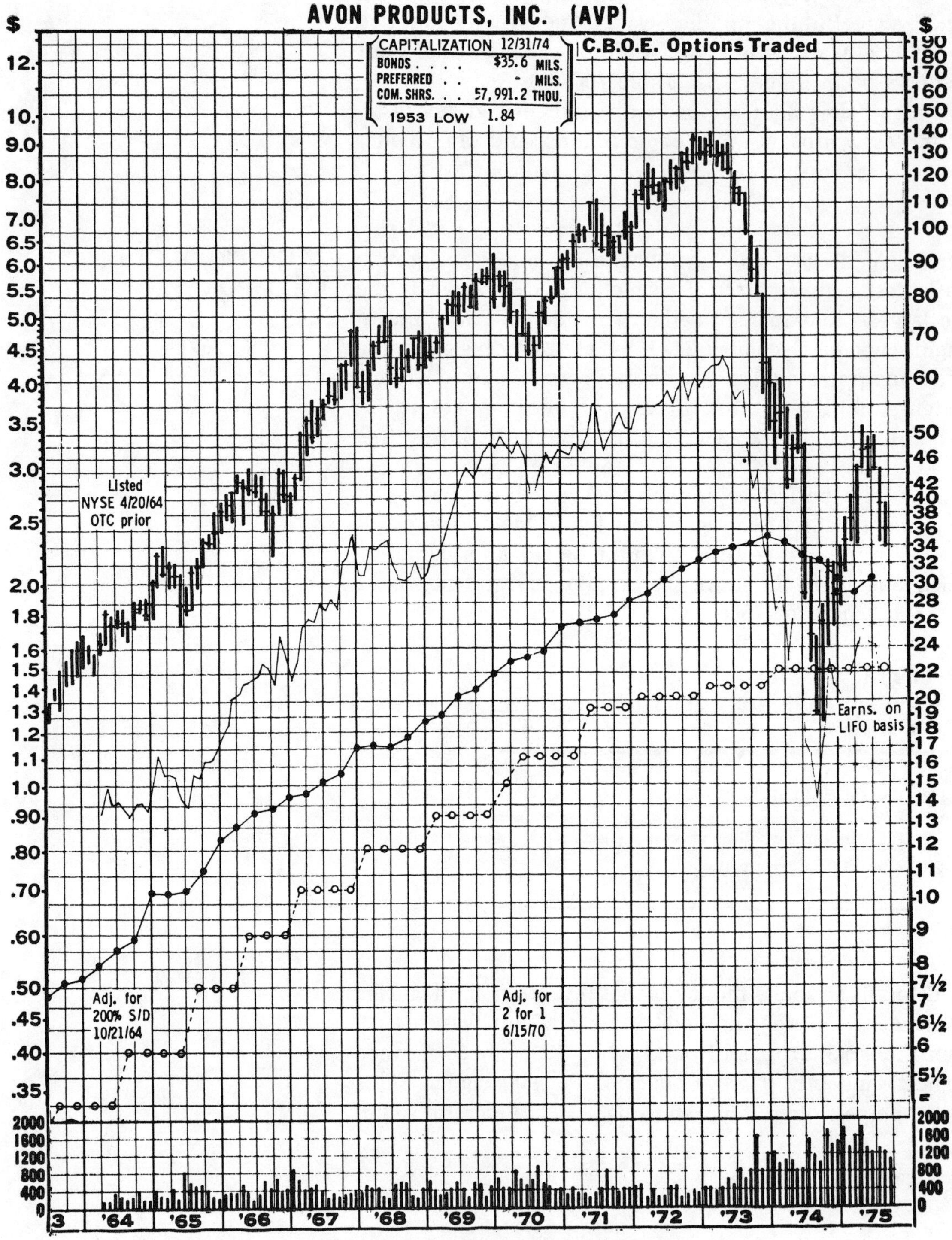

Source: Chart by Securities Research Company, 208 Newbury Street, Boston, Mass. 02116.

Table 11B
AVP Weekly Closing Prices (PBS, first two digits only)

Week	1965	1966	1967	1968	1969	1970	1971	1972	1973	1974
1	53	72	80	130 L	129 H	171 L	85	99	134	57
2	53 L	78 H	79	131 H	128 L	174	83 L	98	132 L	52 L
3	55	74 L	78 L	128	129	181 H	87	96 L	135 H	59
4	60	75	81	125	134 H	165	90	101	130	61 H
5	61 H	75	81	111 L	130 L	158 (S) L	91 H	105	126 L	57
6	59 L	81 H	84 (B)	113	135	166	90	106	131 H	49
7	61	78	85	115	137 H	170 H	88 L	108	130 L	47
8	66 H	77	86	123 H	133	168 L	91	115 H	131	47 L
9	64 L	76 L	90	116 L	132 L	171 H	92	114	133	50
10	65 H	77 H	90	119	134 H	167	94 H	113 L	138 H	55
11	62 (S)	76 L	93	120	132 L	157 L	92 L	118	137	56 H
12	63 H	80	98	120	139 H	160	96	118 H	130 L	54
13	61 L	84	99 H	126	137	164 H	99 H	115 L	134 H	53
14	62	84 H	96 L	126	134 L	162	98 L	119	130 L	52
15	62	83 L	98	132 H	138	157	99 H	122 H	132	49
16	62	85 H	99	131 L	139	155	98	118	132 H	48
17	63 H	84	105	135	145	147 L	98 L	116	129 L	43
18	62	79 (S)	105 H	142 H	148	150 H	100 H	116 L	130 H	43
19	62	76 L	99 L	139	151	147	99 L	119	127	43
20	61	80	101	132 L	158 H	145	100	120 H	126 L	42 L
21	61	85 H	102	138 H	152 L	134 L	100	119	131	48
22	59 L	84 L	102	137 L	155	150 H	108 H	117	127 L	47
23	60 H	85	109 H	140	160 H	145 L	103 L	114	133 H	51
24	57	85	105 L	147 H	154	149 (2 for 1 split)	107	114 L	129 L	51 H
25	53 L	86 (B) H	107 H	143	150 L	77	108	117 H	130 H	48
26	57 H	84 L	105 L	138 L	154	71	110 H	112	123	47
27	56 L	86 H	106	143	161 H	71	107	112 L	112 (S) L	44
28	58 (B) H	84	108	145 H	151 L	69	105	115	115	36
29	56	83 (S)	110	126 (S)	156 H	67 L	99	118	116	35
30	55 (S) L	82 L	110	124 L	149 (S) L	68 H	96	118	117 H	31
31	58	85	119 H	127 H	154	66 L	94 L	123	113	29 L
32	60 (B)	85 H	113	121 L	156	67 H	99	125 H	110 L	30 H
33	62	83	112	127 H	161	61 L	101 H	115 L	111	25
34	62	80	112 L	124	165	66	97	117	112	23 L
35	62	79	113	120 L	165 H	69 (B)	94 L	120 H	113 H	25 H
36	62	77 L	117 H	121	159 L	70	99	118	105 L	23
37	62	79	116 L	125	160	72	99 H	117 L	110 H	19 L
38	65 H	79 H	117 H	133 H	160 H	73	96 L	119	109	22 H
39	64	76	112 L	125 L	154	77 H	98 H	124 H	100	19 L
40	64 L	68 L	117 H	128	153 L	75 L	96	122	92 L	20
41	67	71	116 L	129	159	76 H	93 (S) L	122	95 H	25 (B) H
42	68	73	123	132 H	163	73 (S) L	96	121 L	85 L	24
43	69	75	123 H	129 L	170 (B) H	74	96	129	92 H	22 L
44	69	79	121	131	169 L	78 (B)	96 H	132 H	89	25
45	68	82 (B)	120 L	134	174 H	80 H	94	124 L	89	30 H
46	69	83	123	134	172 L	79	94 L	128 H	87	26 L
47	70 H	88 H	124	136	173 H	79	97 (B)	127	83	28
48	69 L	84 L	128	139	168 L	79 L	101 H	127 L	80	31 H
49	75	87 H	133	141 (B) H	169	84 H	100 L	134	76	28 L
50	75 H	86	133	139	171 H	83	102 H	138 H	62	30 H
51	72	80 (S) L	134	133	169 L	82 L	101	137	61 L	27 (S)
52	71 L	81 H	142 H	126 L	175	83	100	136	65 H	27 L
53						88 H				

Table 11C
Avon Summary, 1965–1975 (first two digits only)

Date Week/ Year	Signal to Buy	Signal to Sell	Gains: Long Percent	Gains: Short Percent	Long Term Gain	Cumulative Results*: Long 1.00	Cumulative Results*: Short 1.00	Cumulative Results*: Long and Short 1.00
(40/64)	($53)							
11/65		$62						
28/65	58			+6%			1.05	
30/65		55	−5%			.94		
32/65	60			−9			.94	
18/66		79	+31		L.T.	1.22		
25/66	86			−8			.85	
29/66		83	−3			1.17		
45/66	82			+1			.85	
51/66		80	−2			1.13		
6/67	84			−5			.80	
29/68		126	+50		L.T.	1.69		
49/68	141			−11			.71	
30/69		149	+5		L.T.	1.76		
43/69	170			−14			.60	
5/70		158	−7			1.62		
	(2 for 1 split)							
35/70	69			+12			.67	
42/70		73	+5			1.68		
44/70	78			−6			.62	
41/71		93	+19		L.T.	1.99		
47/71	97			−4			.59	
27/73		112	+15		L.T.	2.26		
41/74	25			+77			1.04	
51/74		27	+8			2.42		2.51

* Trading costs of 1 percent are deducted from each trade.

P.S. WHAT HAPPENED IN THE NEXT BULL MARKET?

I had planned to cover only the ten year period, January 1965 to 1975. However, the subsequent first six months of 1975 (to the time of this writing) turned out to be a bull market. The Dow Jones Industrial Index rose from 632 to 879, an increase of 39 percent!

So what happens when you use PBS in a bull market? Here's what happened. (See Table 12.)

American Telephone (discussed in a later chapter) gave its buy signal at $44 in week #41 in 1974, and was still in an uptrend at $50 in week #26 in 1975, representing a 13 percent gain.

Avon Products gave a buy signal at $32, a sell at $35, a buy at $42, and was still in an uptrend at $47 as of mid-1975.

Digital Equipment gave a buy signal at $69, a sell at $97, and a buy at $116 in the last week of this six month period.

Fairchild Camera really came to life with a buy at $19.00 (if you use fractions), or $25 (if you drop the fractions), and was still in an uptrend at $61, a paper gain of 221 percent, or 144 percent, respectively,

Table 12
Weekly Closing Prices and PBS Worksheet—First Six Months, 1975

1975 Week	T	AVP	DEC	FCI	IBM*	KB	MCD	PC	TWA	XRX	SKY	D-J 40 Bond Index
1	$46	$30	$ 46 L	$19Ⓑ	$167	$3	$29 H		$ 6	$51	$15 L	10.05% H
2	48 H	32ⒷH	50	19 H	171 H	3	28		6	57 H	16	9.96
3	46 L	31	50	17 L	158 L	4Ⓑ	28 L		6	55 L	16	9.85
4	47	30 L	56	19	162	4	30Ⓑ		6	60Ⓑ	18ⒷH	9.83
5	48	31	69Ⓑ	25Ⓑ	188Ⓑ	6	34		8 H	70	17 L	9.68
6	49	34	71	26	197	6	36		7 L	72	18	9.53
7	50	36 H	75 H	27 H	220 H	6	40		8	76	18 H	9.48
8	50	34	73 L	26 L	218	6	42 H		8	79 H	16Ⓢ	9.38
9	50	34	76	28	215 L	6	40 L		10	74 L	16	9.31 L
10	51 H	37	85	31	217 H	7	43 H		12 H	78	17	9.34 H
11	48	38 H	85	33	215	9 H	42 L		11	78 H	18 H	9.29 L
12	49 H	37 L	86 H	35	209	8	43		10 L	73Ⓢ	17	9.36Ⓤ
13	48	38	85 L	37	207	8	44	(Still	11 H	71	17 L	9.39
14	48	35Ⓢ	87	40 H	198 L	7	47	Bankrupt)	10	67 L	18	9.58
15	48	37 H	98	39 L	205	7	47		10	69	21Ⓑ	9.63
16	48 L	36 L	102	42	209 H	7	48		10	73 H	22 H	9.65
17	50	42Ⓑ	106	42	206 L	7	53		10	71 L	21	9.69
18	51 H	46	108 H	42 H	207	7 L	53		10	78Ⓑ	20 L	9.75 H
19	50	47	107	40 L	214	8 H	54		10	84 H	21	9.69 L
20	49	48	105 L	41	216	7	55 H		10	76	23	9.71 H
21	49	49 H	107 H	44	218 H	7	54		9Ⓢ	76	25	9.63Ⓓ
22	49	47	106 L	44	215	7	54		9	74	25 H	9.62 L
23	48	45	107 H	48	213	7	52		8	70Ⓢ	24	9.64 H
24	48 L	44 L	97Ⓢ	50	206	7	52 L		7	68	22	9.51
25	50	46	104	55	206 L	7 L	54		7 L	67 L	21	9.44
26	50	47	116Ⓑ	61	209	8	57	$1	8	69	21	9.38

* Using the first-two digit method.

depending on whether you use the fractions in determining the higher highpoint.

International Business Machines joined the bull market for the first few weeks only, then went sideways. Using the first-two digit method, IBM gave its buy signal at $188 and was still in a slow uptrend at $209 as of mid-1975. Using the three digits, the PBS buy signal came at $171, sell at $158, buy at $188, sell at $209. This example reinforces the suggestion that only the first two digits be used for stocks selling at over $100 a share, to improve results and reduce whipsaws.

Kaufman and Broad gave its buy signal at $4, and was in an uptrend at $8, a 100 percent unrealized gain, as of mid-1975.

McDonald's, a buy at $30, was still in an uptrend at $57, a 90 percent unrealized gain.

Penn Central was still bankrupt, still trading at $1 a share. May it rest in peace.

Trans World Airlines gave its buy at $7.50 in week #41, 1974; later, a sell at $9, for a small gain. I apologize for using the fractions to buy, dropping the fraction to sell. However, more study needs to be done for stocks selling under $10. A low priced stock, such as TWA below $10, would not normally be a candidate for future PBS trading.

Xerox gave a buy signal at $60, a sell at $73, a buy at $78, a sell at $73, and was in a downtrend at $70 as of mid-1975. Although XRX participated in the bull market, its PBS performance *appears* to be disappointing—however, if you look back you find that the previous sell signal was at $116 in week #25 in 1974, followed by the buy at $60 in week #4 in 1975, representing a 48 percent gain on the short side.

Skyline gave a buy at $18, a sell at $16, a buy at $21, and was in an uptrend in the last week at $21. SKY *was* disappointing for this short period, because it lost a lot of its volatility. However, if you consider SKY's stellar ten year PBS performance of +1,650 percent, it may be telling us that it's a little early for the big expected improvement in mobile home sales.

Reviewing the first six months of 1975, I make these observations:

First, it would have been profitable for a trader, or investor, to use PBS for these stocks as a group.

Second, the PBS signals show that some price trends are much more erratic than others, but that the PBS continued to define trends and trend changes.

Third, although most stocks go up in bull markets, they do so in widely varying degrees. For example, Penn Central did nothing, as might be expected, since it was bankrupt. American Telephone was up 8 percent, IBM up 25 percent, TWA up 33 percent, XRX up 35 percent, SKY up 40 percent, AVP up 56 percent, MCD up 96 percent, DEC up 152 percent, FCI up 221 percent, and KB up 266 percent! These stocks ranged from 0 percent to +266 percent for the first six months of 1975.

Fourth, Table 12 is a suggested format for keeping statistics on your stocks, bonds, or whatever.

AND WHAT HAPPENED TO BONDS?

The Dow Jones 40 Bond Index (discussed in a later chapter) had indicated that bond yields (long term interest rates) were headed down in week #43 in 1974, at 10.14 percent. This meant that bond prices should go up, and should be bought. As of week #12 in 1975, the bond index (see Table 12) indicated that long term interest rates had turned up at 9.36 percent; therefore, the price of bonds was now in a downtrend.

In week #21 in 1975, the index indicated yields had turned down, at 9.63 percent, and were still trending down at 9.38 percent at last recording.

Therefore, while the stock market soared upward, the bond market followed less enthusiastically, and the PBS bond trend changes during this period all proved to be correct.

OVER THE COUNTER STOCKS AND THE PBS

What happens when OTC stocks are traded using the PBS? Take a look at the following charts of volatile stocks supplied by San Francisco Investment Corporation, 576 Sacramento Street, San Francisco, California 94111. (See Figures 20A through 20V.) I have noted the buy (B), and sell (S) signals on these charts to enable you to see the possibilities and limitations of the PBS. Fractions were not dropped as in the previous examples and, therefore, resulted in more whipsaws. Since OTC stocks can't be shorted, for all practical purposes, look at them as stocks to be bought and sold only.

The results for 1974 and 1975 are not likely to be repeated, because these were not typical years in the stock market. But then, when was there ever a typical year?

Figure 20A
American Micro Systems (AMMS—otc)

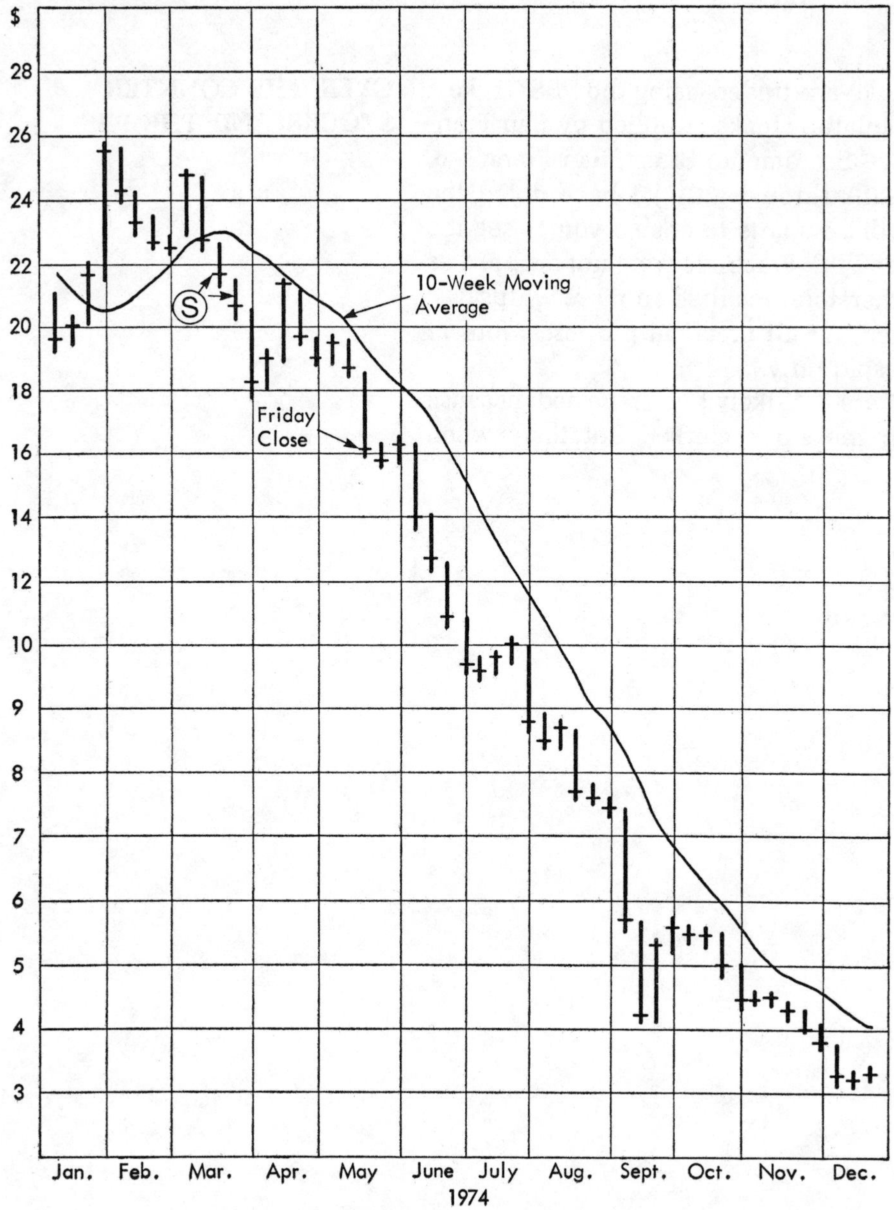

Figure 20B
American Micro Systems (AMMS – otc)

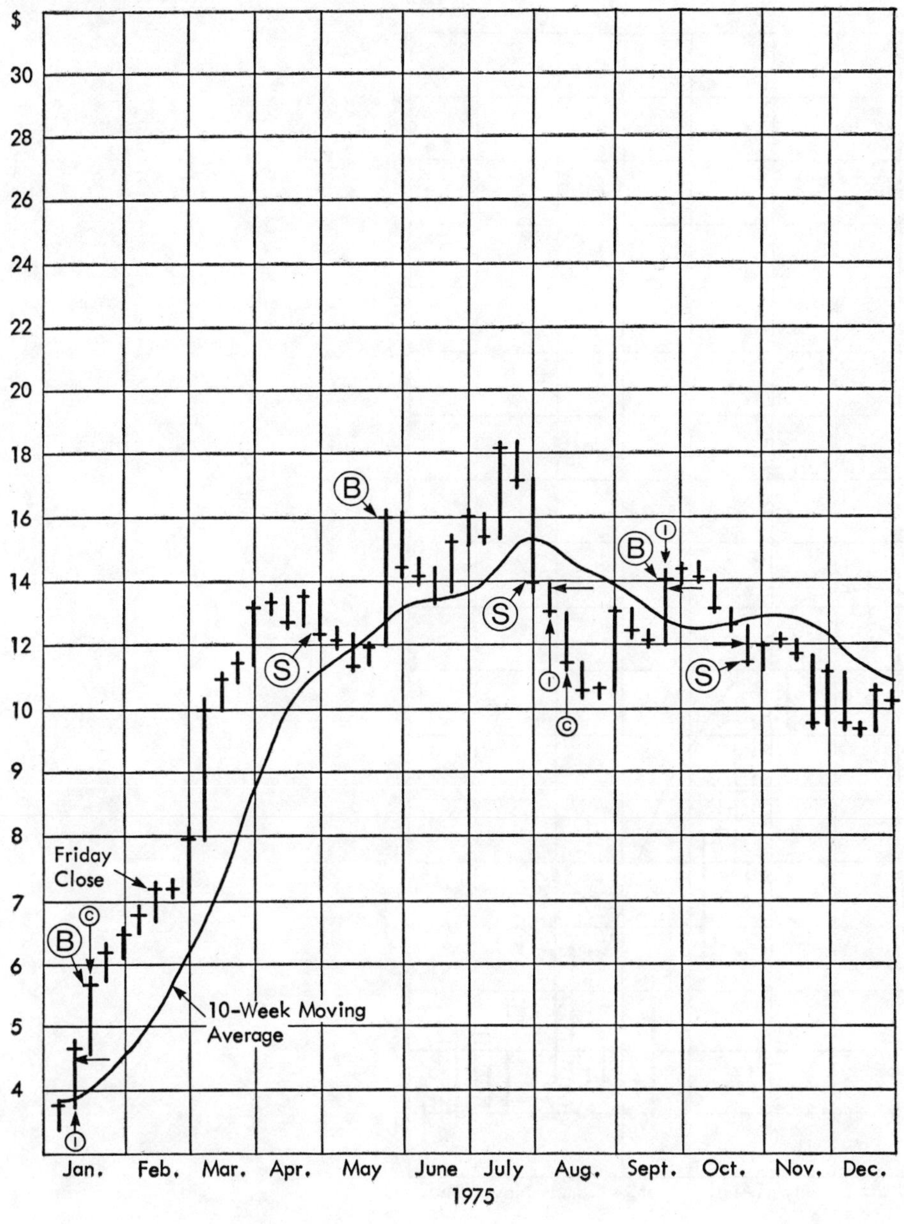

Figure 20C
Coherent Radiation (COHR – otc)

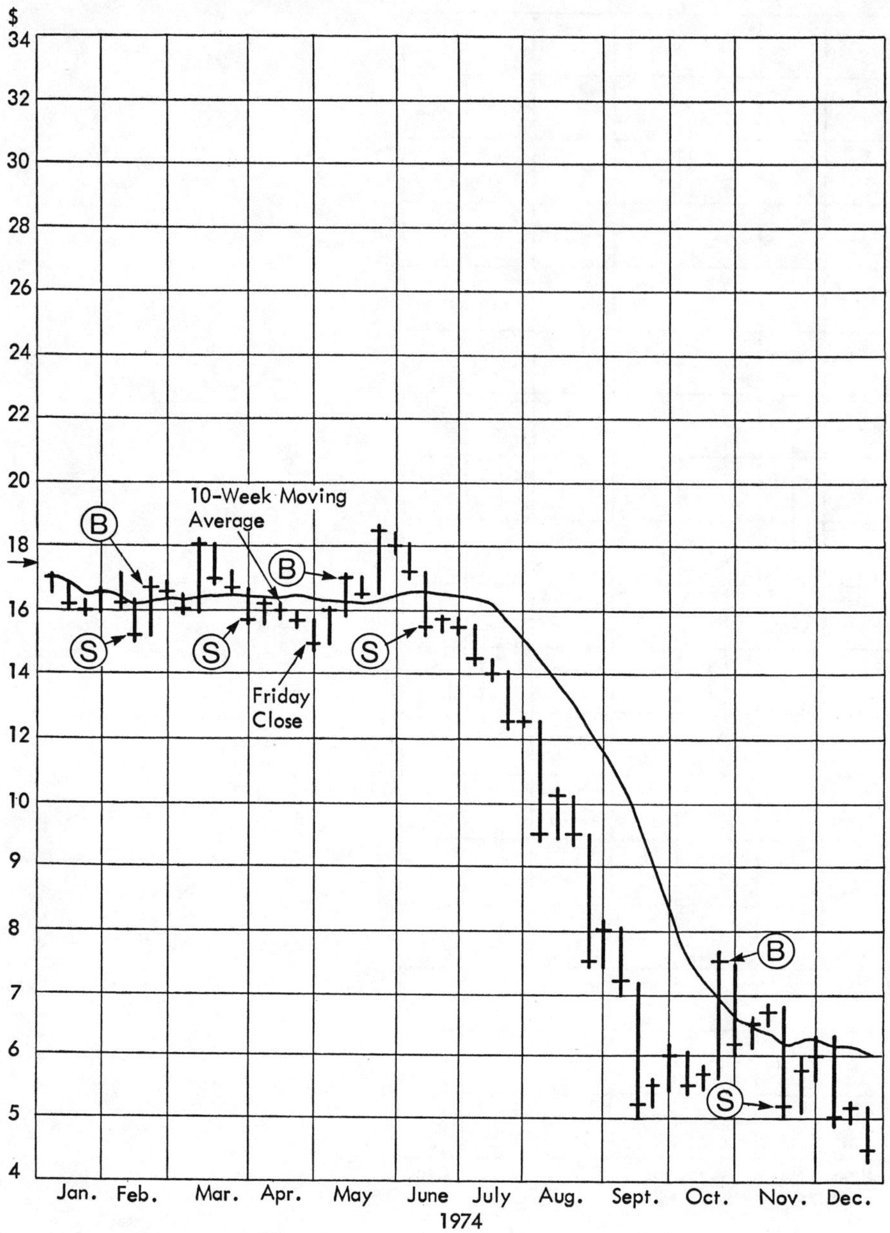

Figure 20D
Coherent Radiation (COHR–otc)

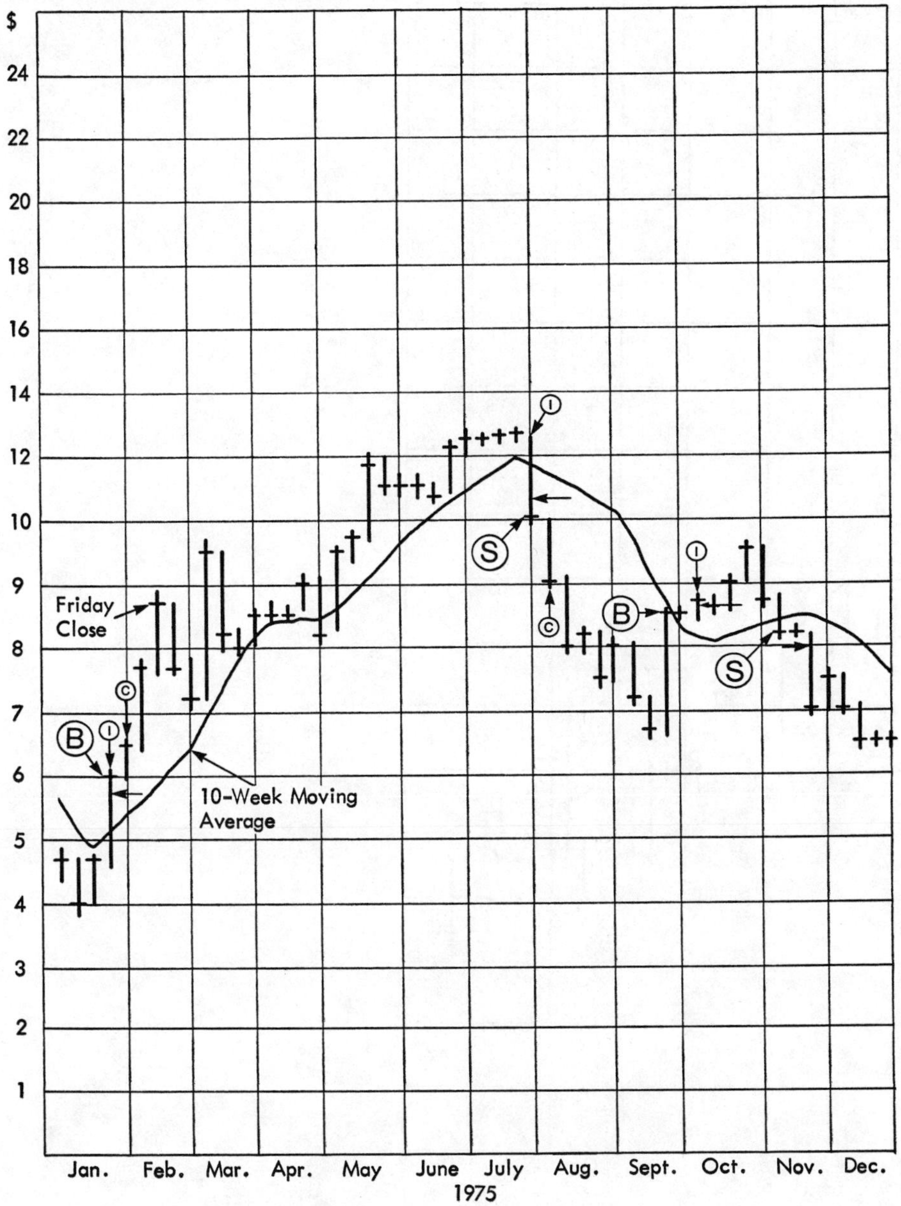

Figure 20E
Data 100 Corporation (DATA—otc)

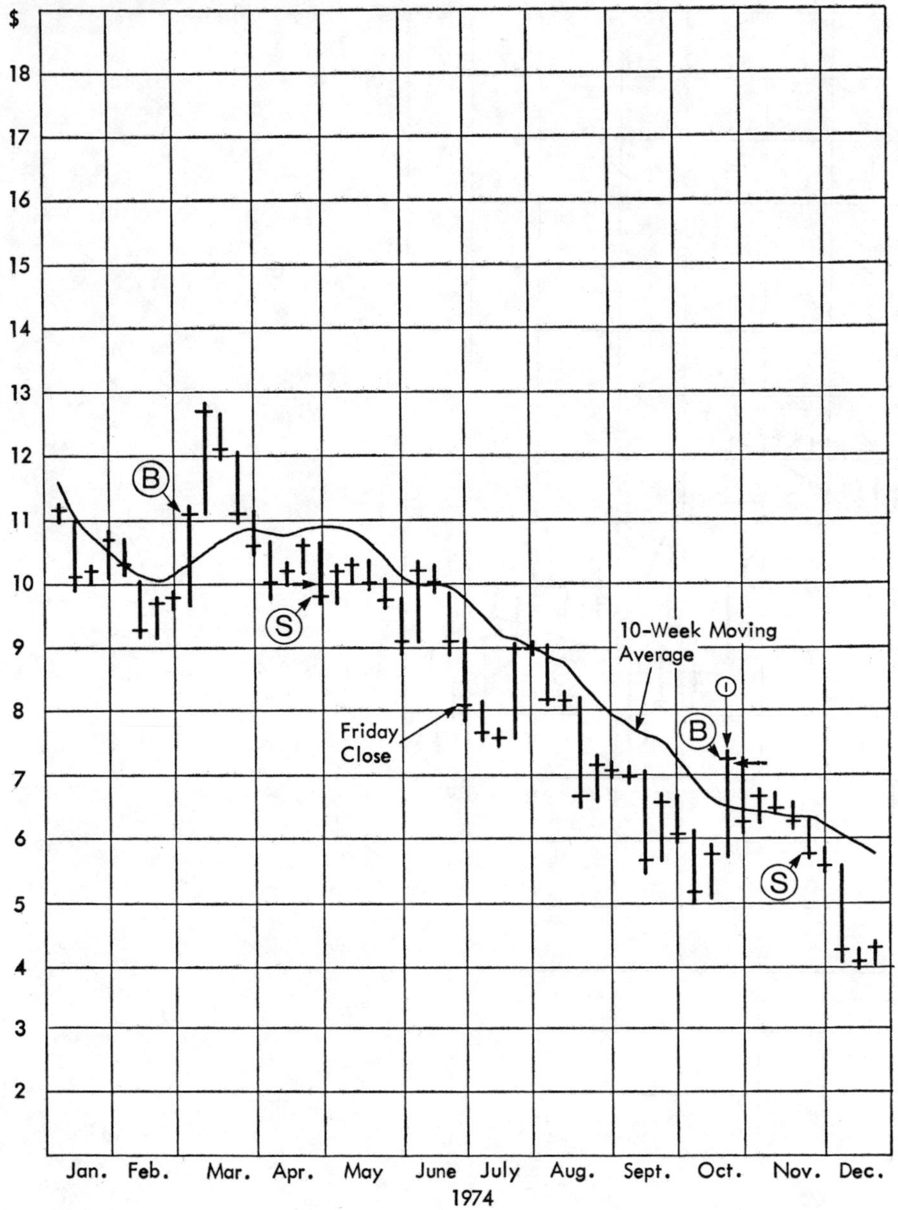

Figure 20F
Data 100 Corporation (DATA—otc)

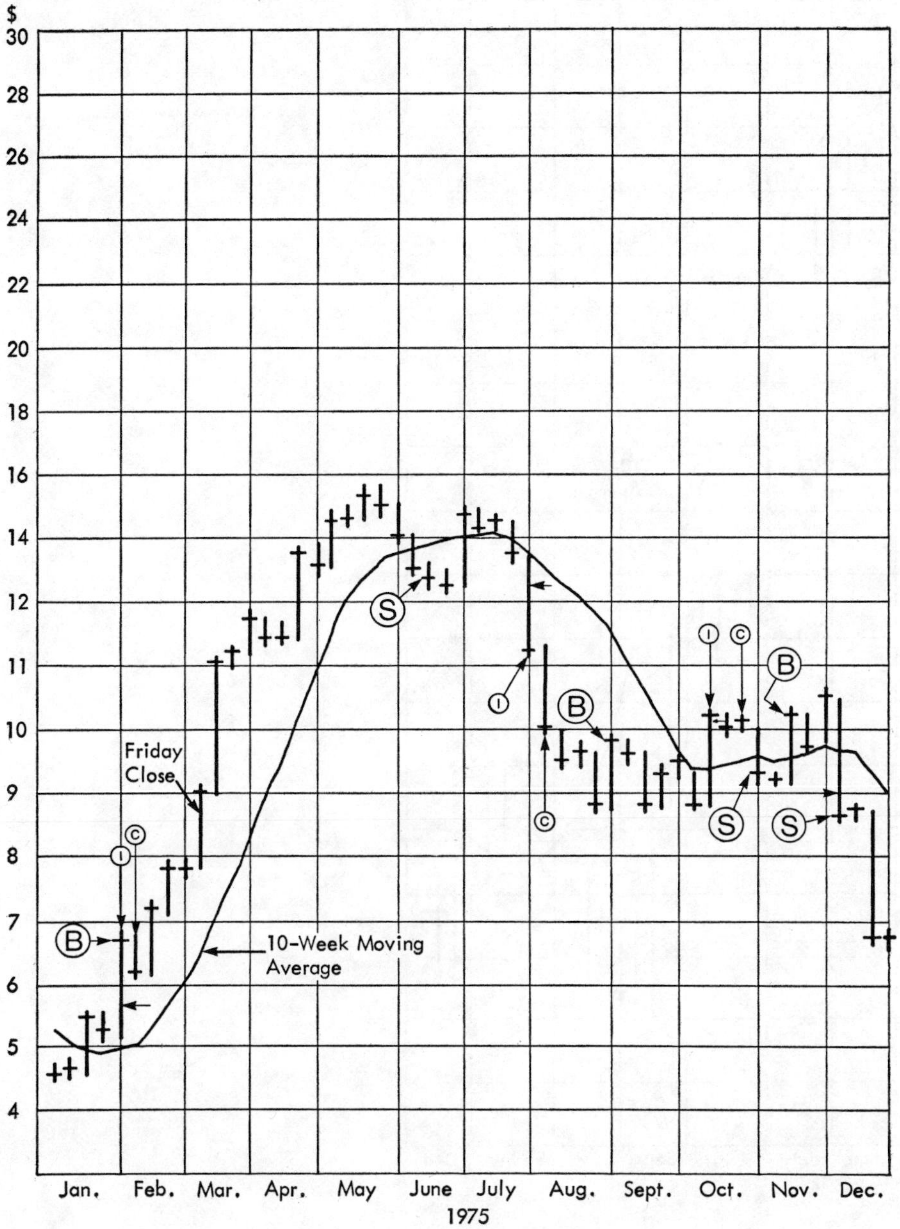

Figure 20G
Intel Corporation (INTC—otc)

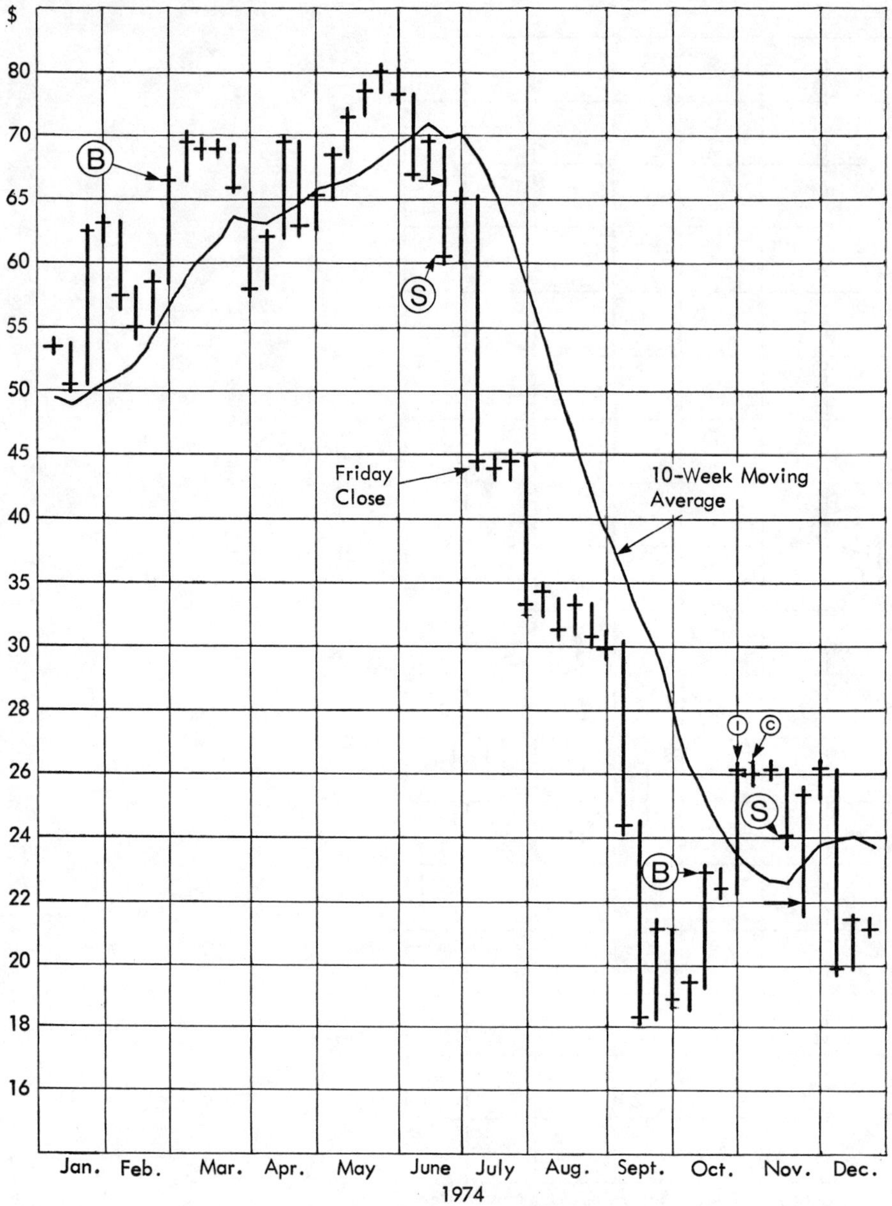

Figure 20H
Intel Corporation (INTC—otc)

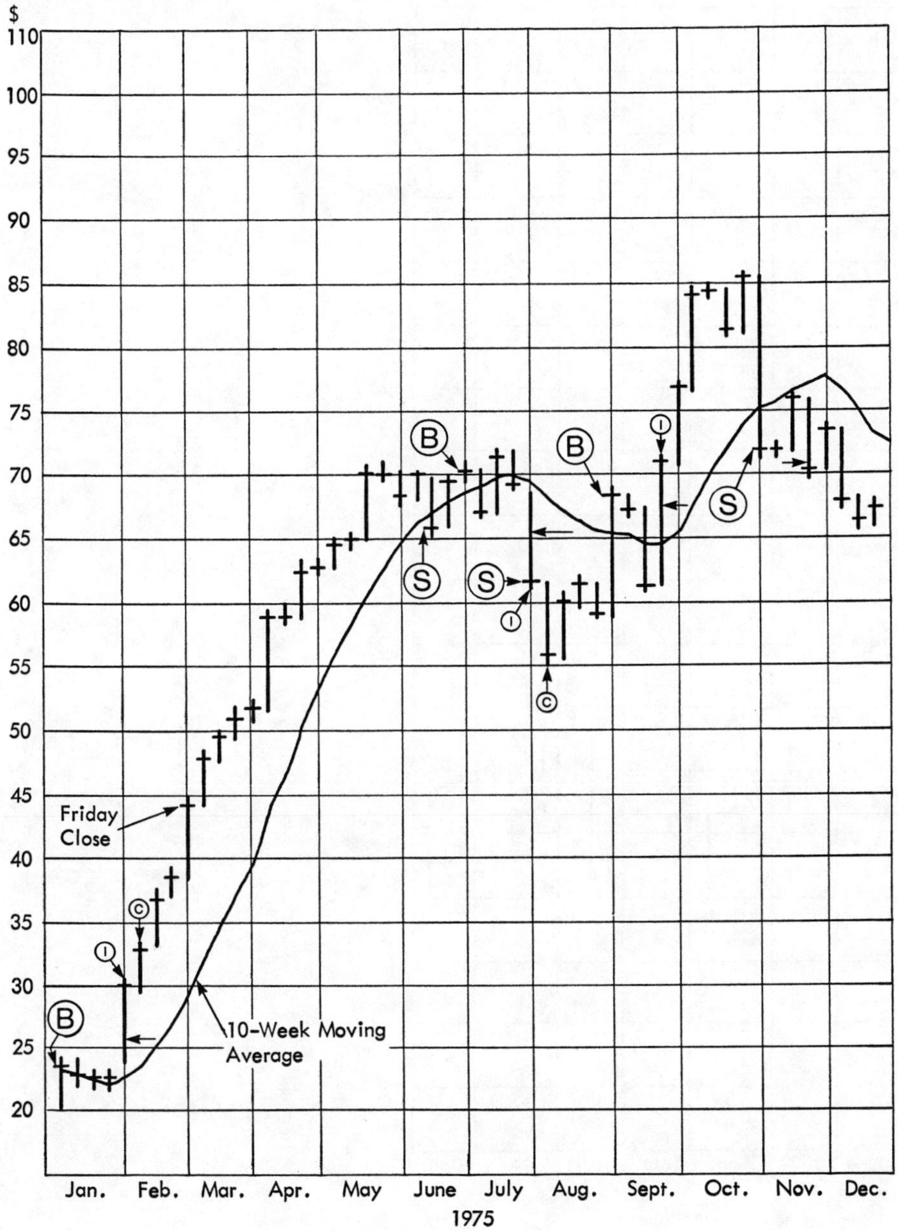

Figure 20I
Measurex Corporation (MSRX—otc)

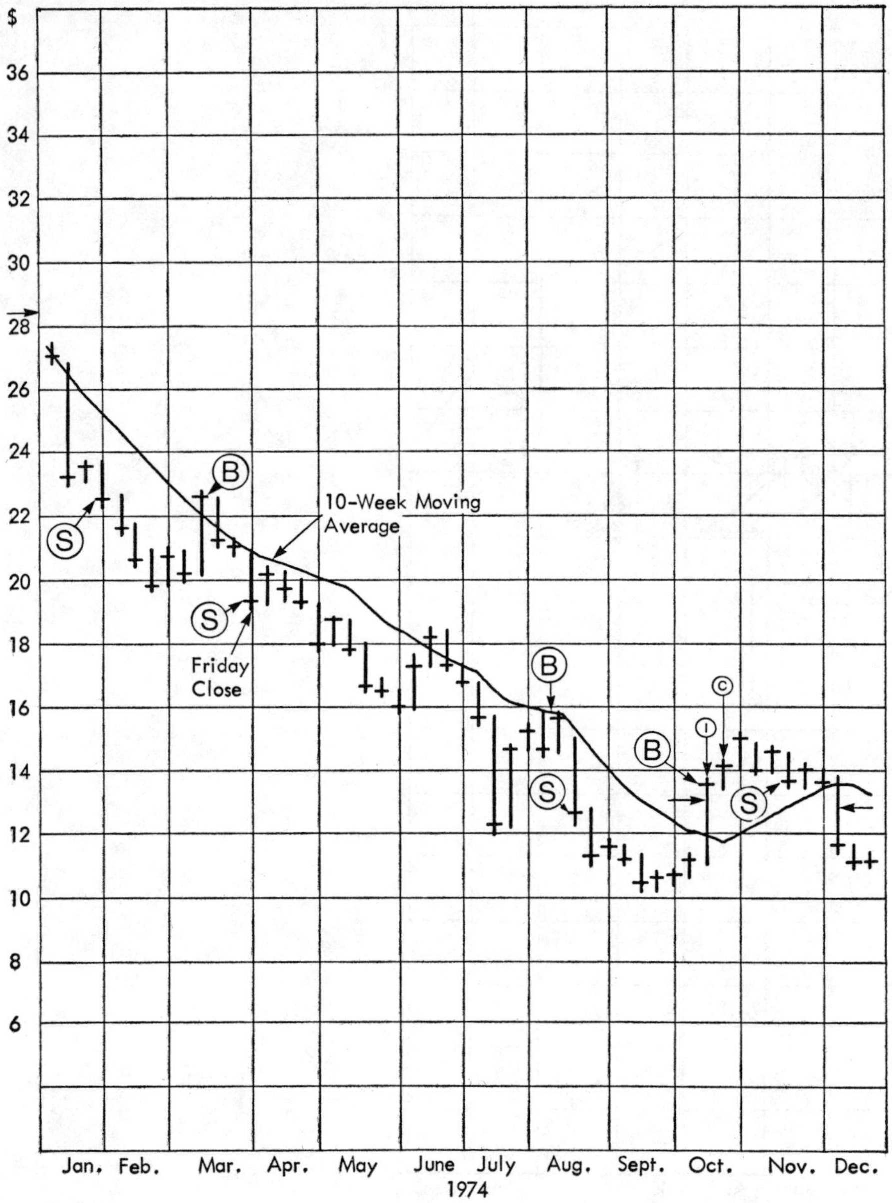

Figure 20J
Measurex Corporation (MSRX—otc)

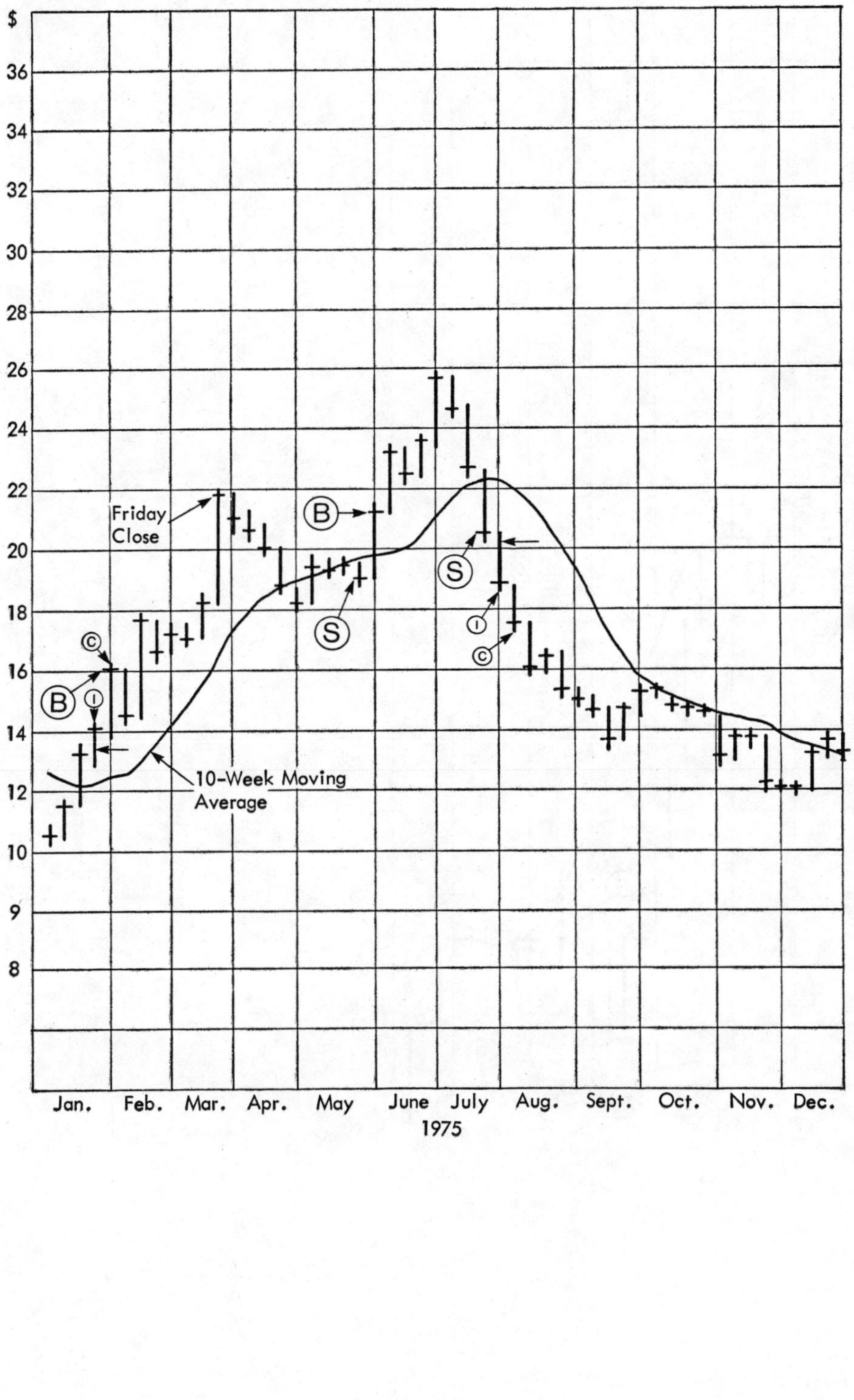

Figure 20K
Mervyn's (MERN—otc)

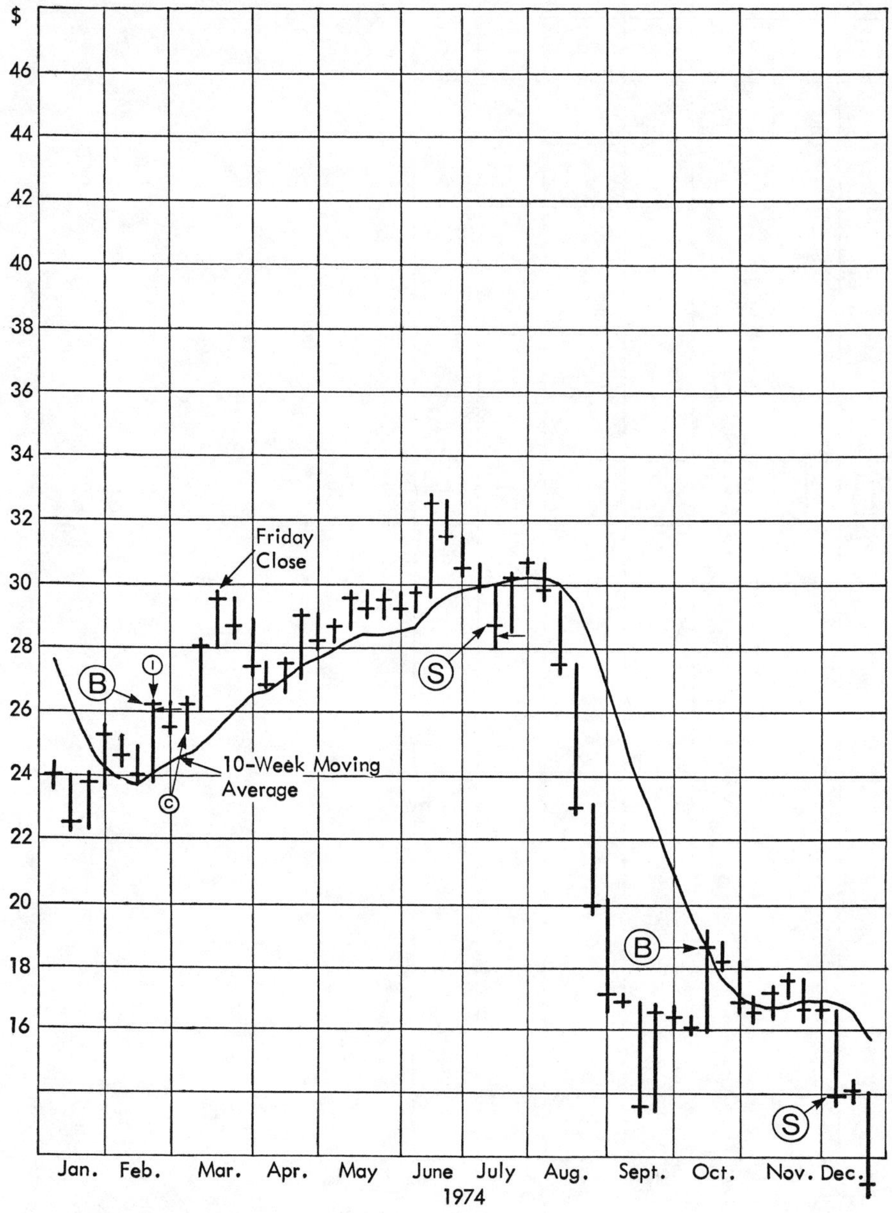

Figure 20L
Mervyn's (MERN–otc)

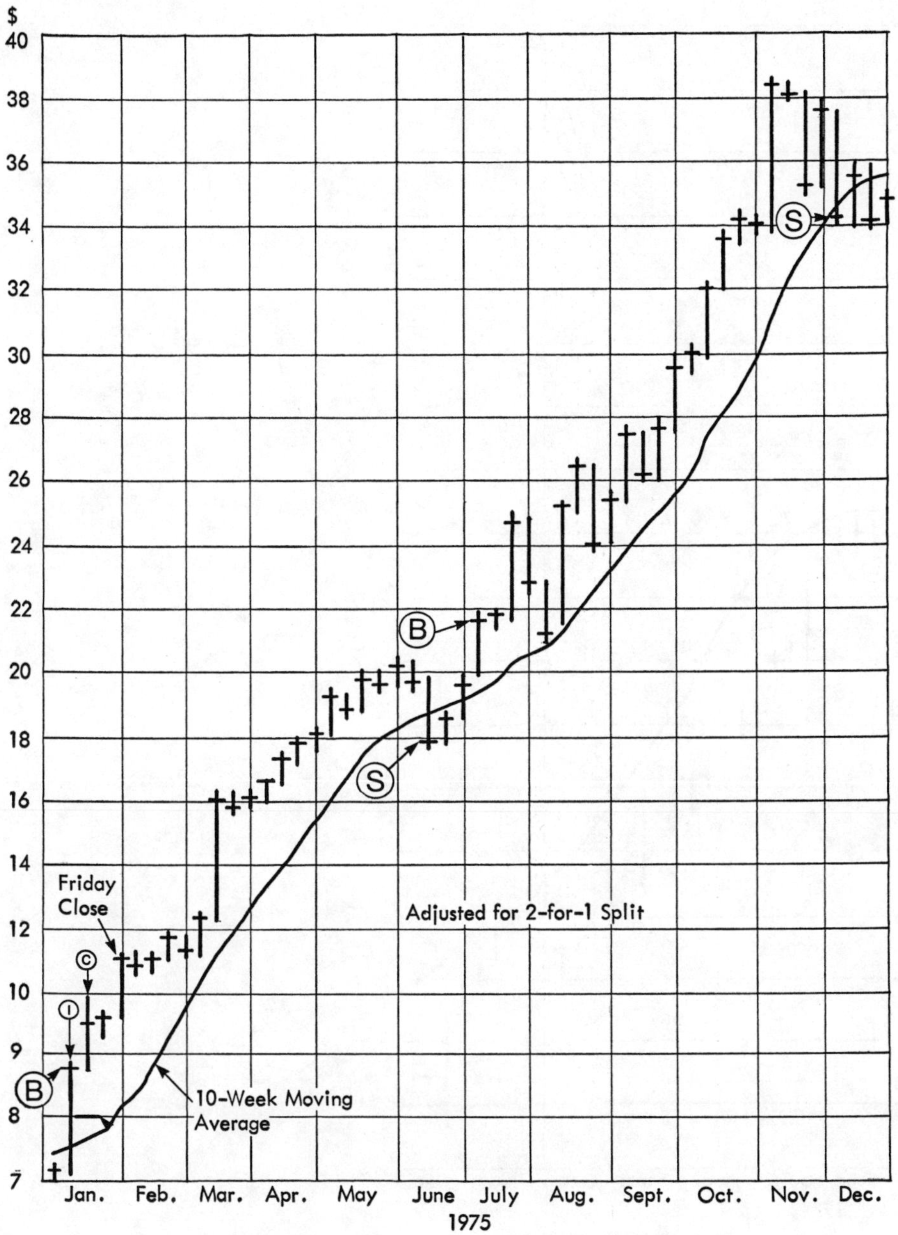

Figure 20M
Modular Computer Systems (MCSS – otc)

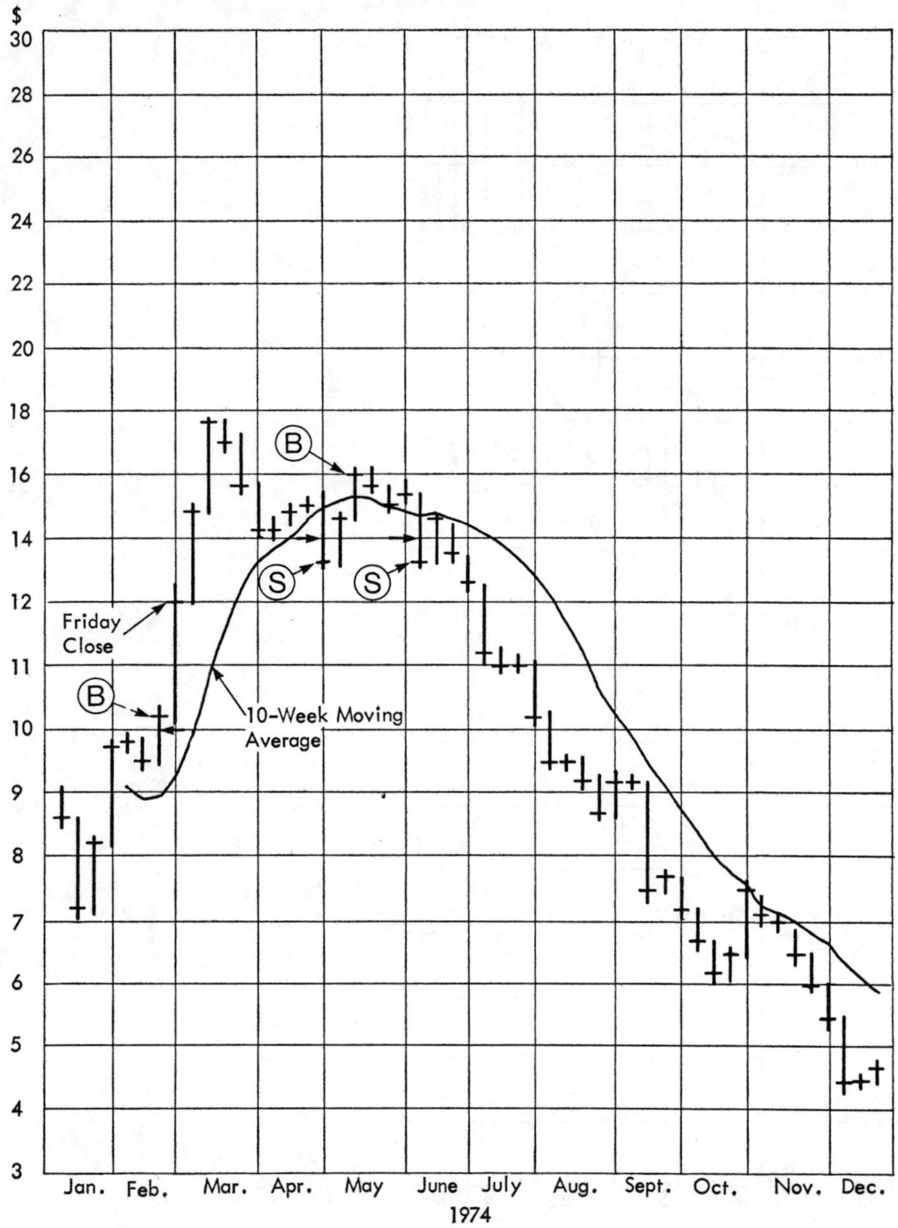

Figure 20N
Modular Computer Systems (MCSS – otc)

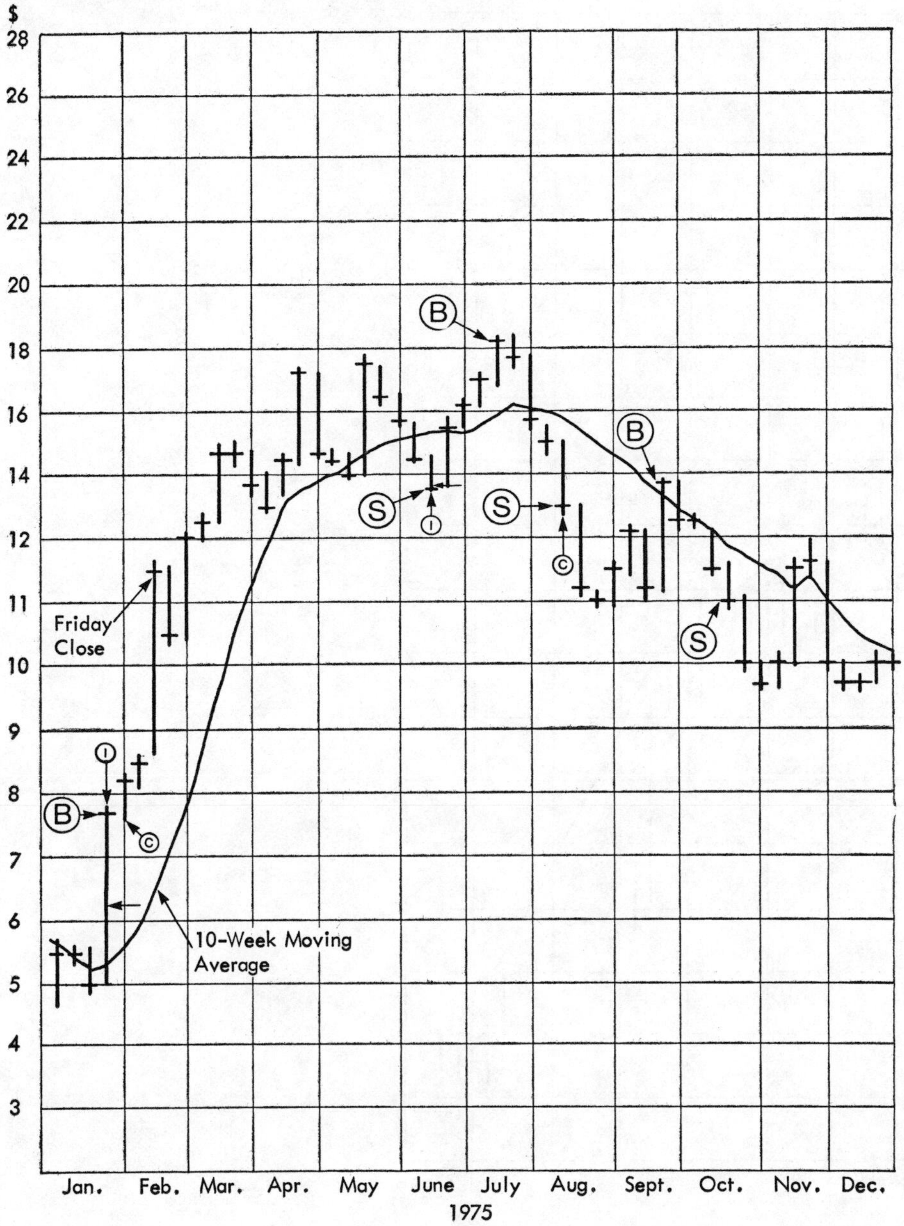

Figure 20O
Spectra–Physics (SPHY – otc)

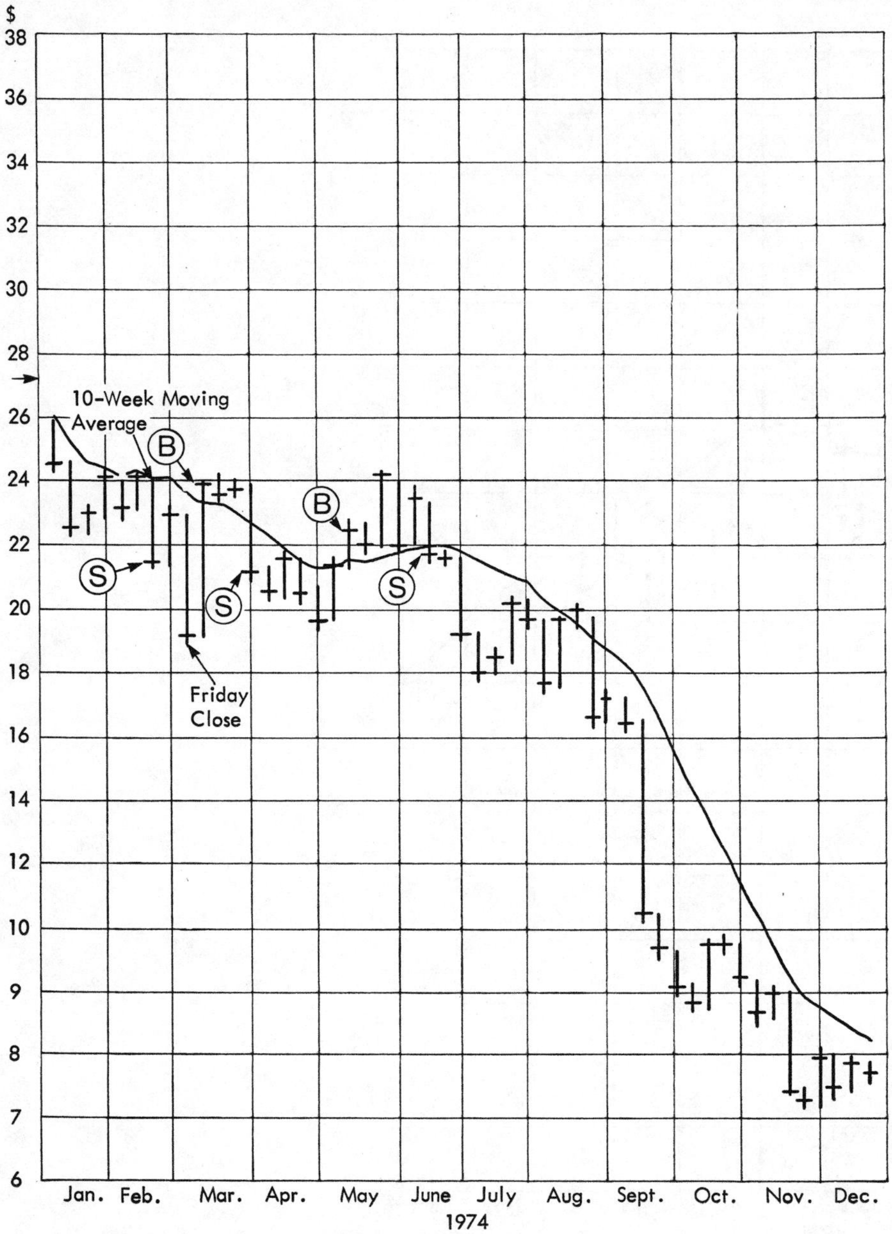

Figure 20P
Spectra-Physics (SPHY—otc)

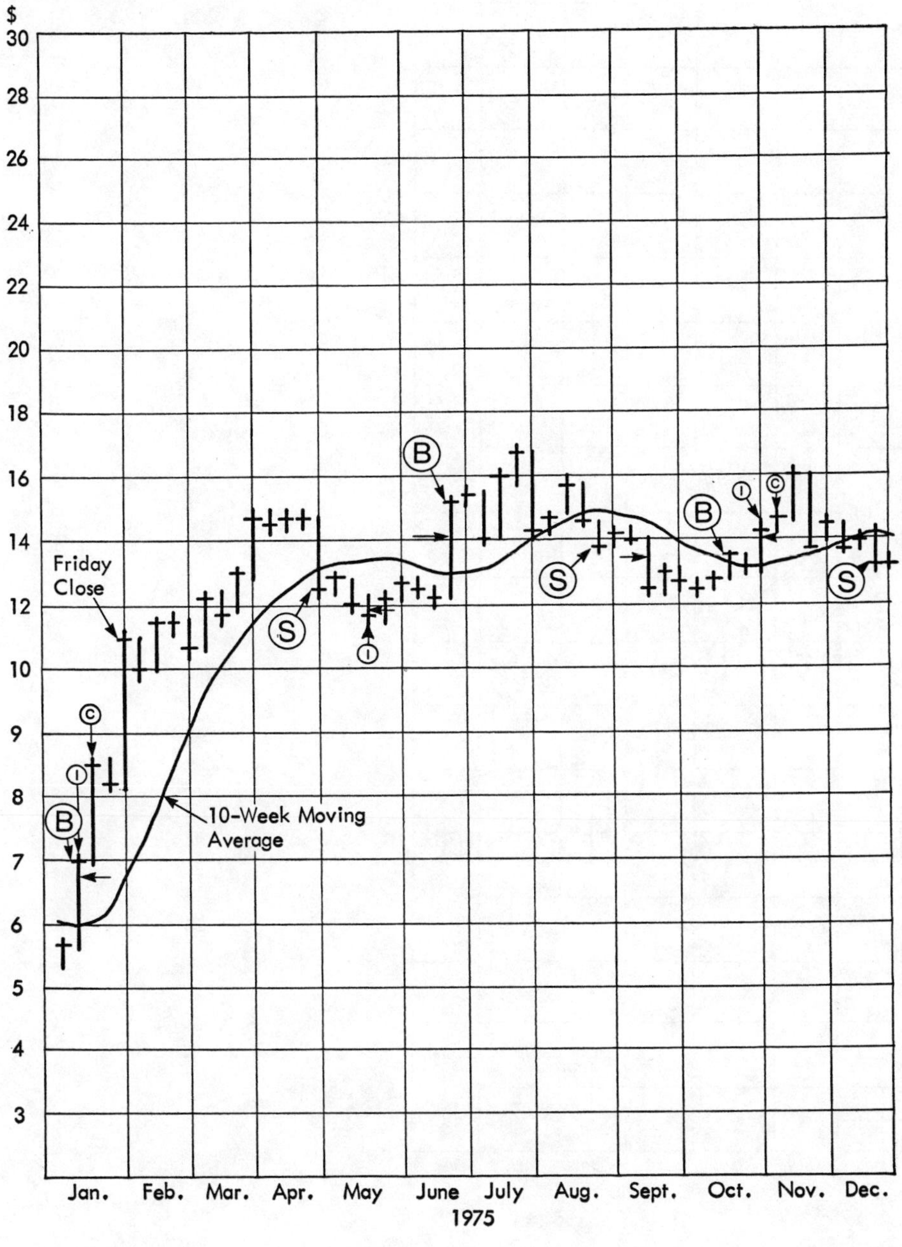

Figure 20Q
Tymshare Incorporated (TSHR—otc)

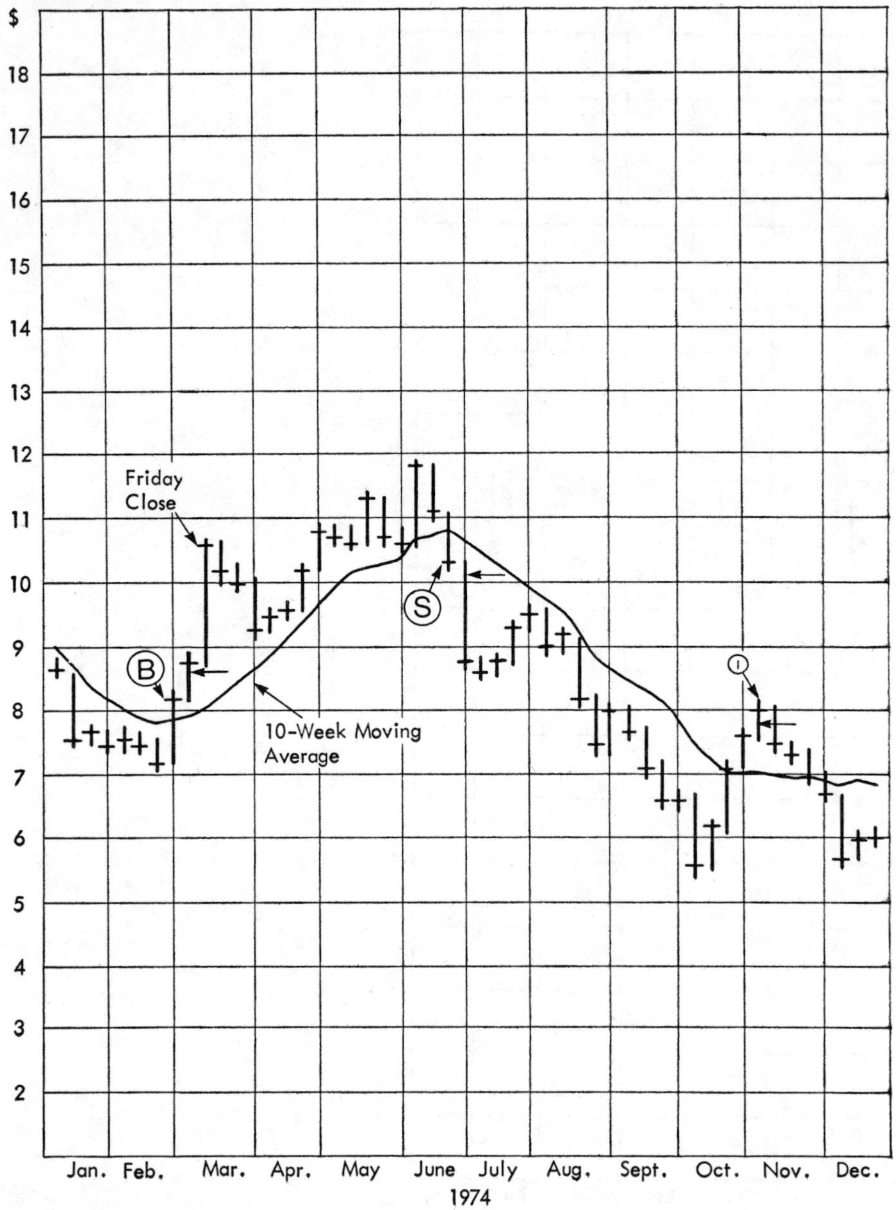

Figure 20R
Tymshare Incorporated (TSHR—otc)

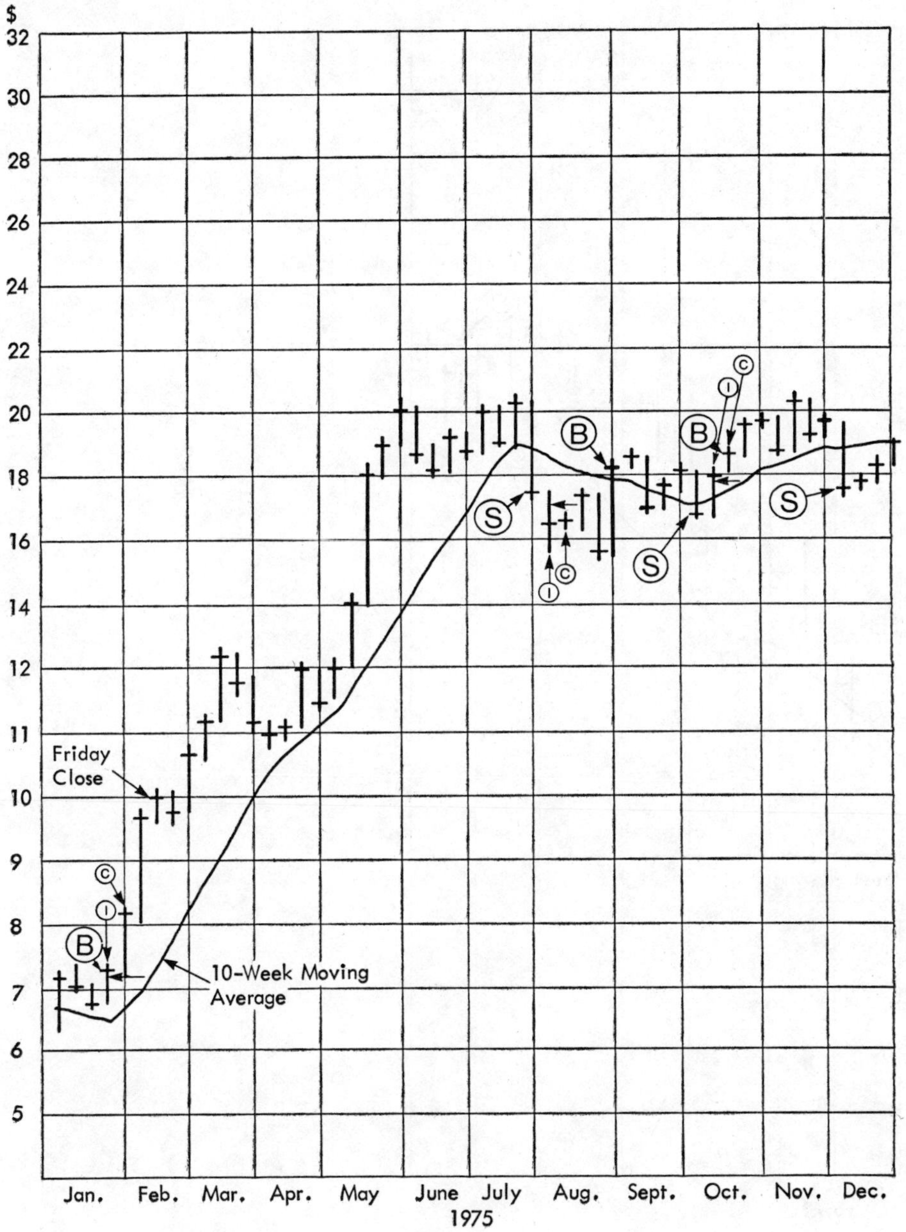

Figure 20S
Fotomat Corporation (FMAT—otc)

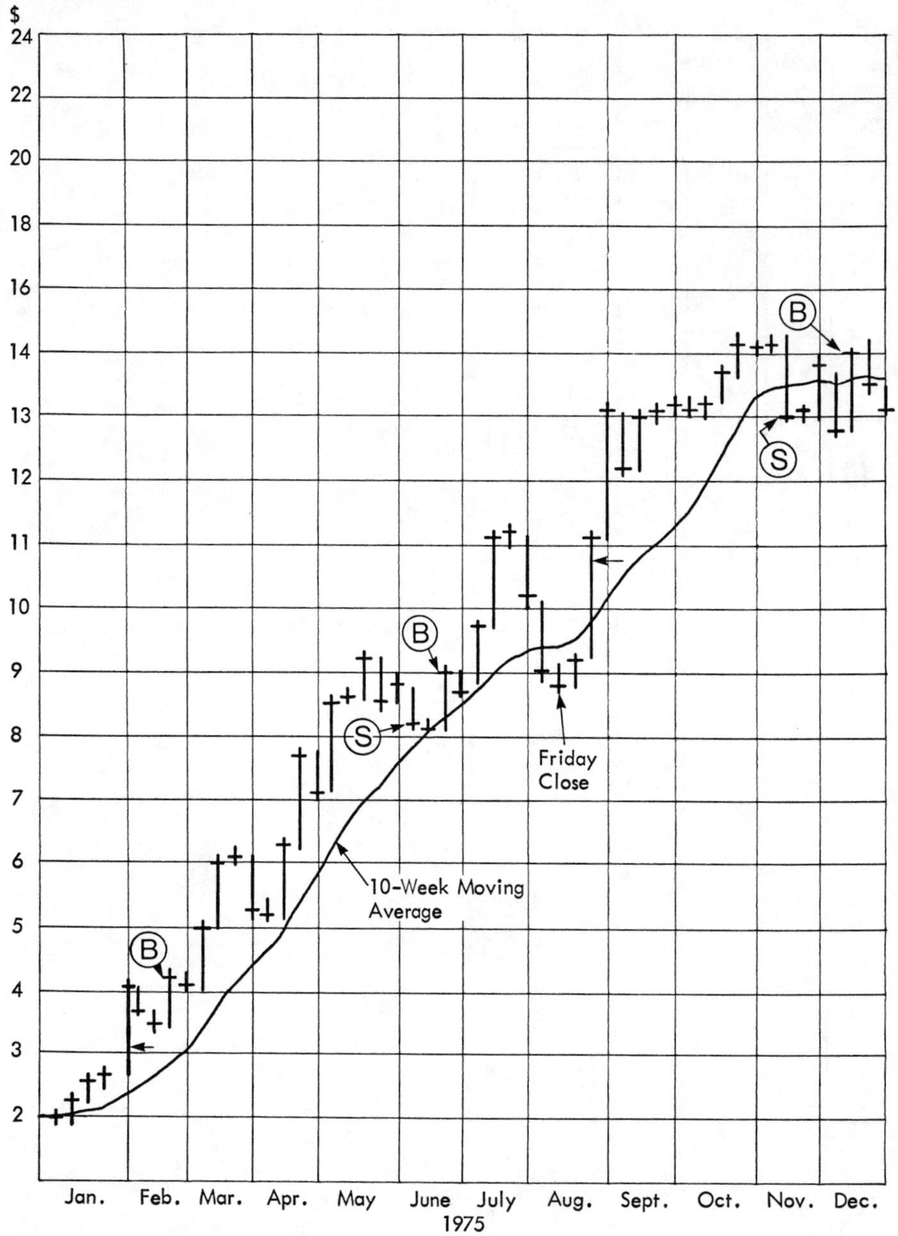

Figure 20T
E. F. Johnson (JHNS—otc)

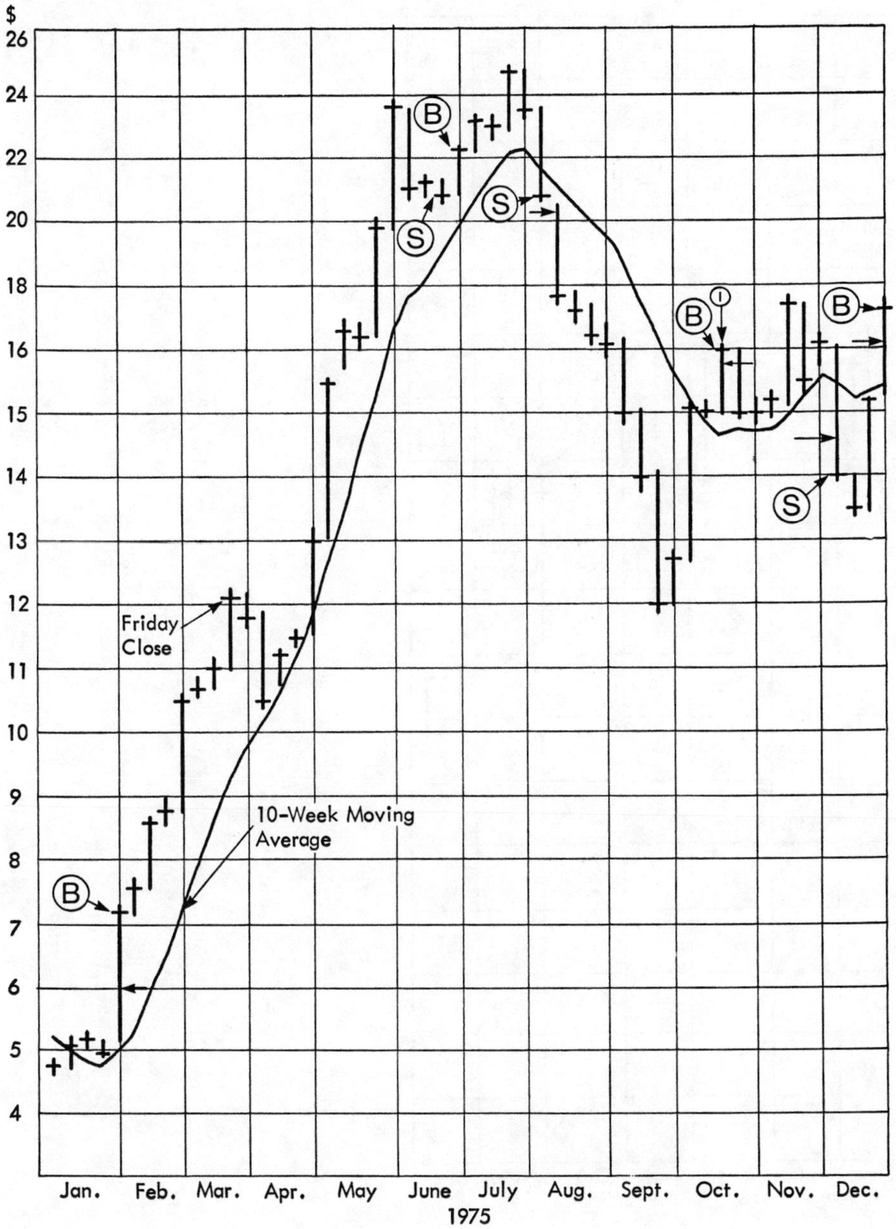

Figure 20U
National Mine Service (NMNE—otc)

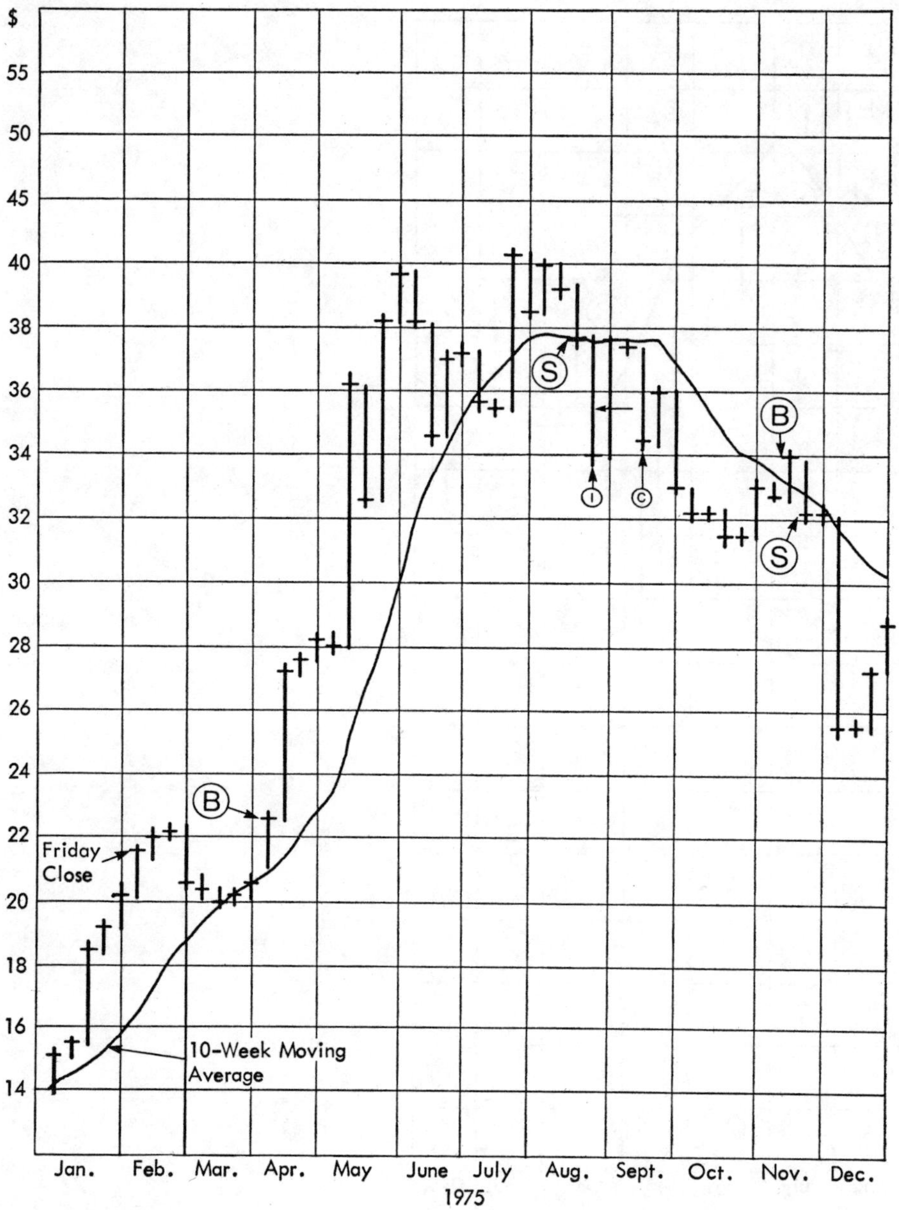

Figure 20V
Taco Bell (TACO—otc)

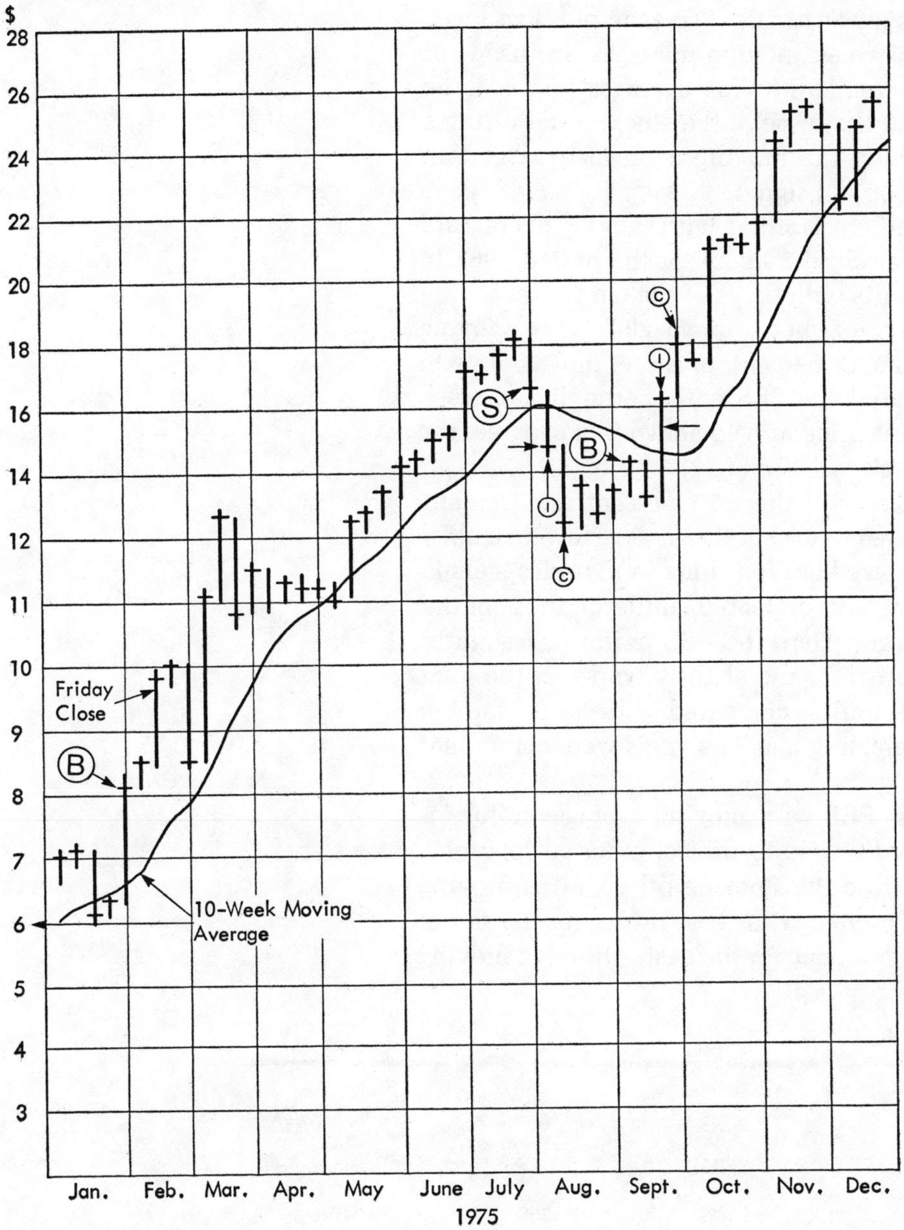

THE PBS COMPARED WITH MOVING AVERAGES

Does the Profit Box System produce better trading results than moving averages? There is no simple answer. Many kinds of moving averages are used to determine stock trends. For example, five week and 10, 17, 20, 26, 30, and 40 week moving averages are used for determining intermediate term trends. Moving averages may also be modified, requiring them to lead the price of the stock; or requiring a price movement above, or below, the moving average by a certain percentage before getting a buy or sell signal.

To partially satisfy those who are familiar with moving averages, I made two comparisons using Fairchild Camera for the period 1961 to 1975. First, I compared PBS results with those of the ten week moving average, requiring a 10 percent, or more, move above the moving average to get a buy signal, and a 10 percent, or more, move below to get a sell signal. Then I compared the PBS with a straight ten week moving average, e.g., if the latest price moved above this average, the stock was a buy, and below, a sell (see Table 13).

The ten-week moving average with the ±10 percent requirement underperformed the PBS in all areas—except that it gave fewer signals, 39 versus 69 for PBS, and it squeezed out four long-term trades, versus two for PBS. However, the PBS results appeared similar to those of the straight ten week moving averages. Here the PBS performed slightly better in trading FCI on the short side, and slightly worse on the long side. The PBS required only 69 trades, compared with 83 for the ten week moving averages. It is interesting that 31 signals were coincident with those of the PBS.

The above comparison of the PBS with moving averages is *for information only*, and should not be used to project other correlations. The results will vary, depending on the stock and the kind of moving average used. Also, the moving average for best future results is not likely to be the same as the optimum one for the past. Although moving

Table 13
FCI—Comparison of Results 1961 to 1975

	PBS	*Ten Week Moving Averages ±10 Percent*	*Ten Week Moving Averages*
FCI—Buying and holding (−70%)			
FCI—Trading long only	+250%	+15%	+315%
FCI—Trading short only	+ 72%	−58%	+ 61%
FCI—Trading long and short	+502%	−52%	+568%
Number of buy and sell signals	69	39	83
Number of long term gains	2	4	2
Number of gains (long and short)	29 (43%)	15 (39%)	31 (38%)
Number of breakeven trades	3 (4%)	1 (3%)	5 (6%)
Number of losses (long and short)	36 (53%)	22 (58%)	46 (56%)
	68 (100%)	38 (100%)	82 (100%)
Number of signals coincident with PBS		5 times*	31 times**

* See Appendix E.
** See Appendix F.

averages are helpful in defining trends, I do not like the extra weekly mathematics and the time they require—along with the possibility of making a mathematical error.

On the bright side, the PBS is easy to remember—with this little rhyming slogan: If the price is a "Higher High, Buy! Lower Low, Go!" ("Go," here, means to sell.)

DEAD STOCKS NEED COFFINS, NOT BOXES

The PBS won't work well with stable stocks. I'm referring to stocks that don't move sufficiently, either up or down, to allow the PBS to work properly. Stable stocks include those that pay high dividends, and they include "safe" stocks that don't drop much in bad markets, or go up much in good markets.

Some investors have very good reasons for buying stable stocks. Usually, these investors are conservative and they want safety and dividends. They may be preparing portfolios for their retirement. However, safe and high yielding stocks tend rather to be "dead" than volatile. ("Dead" is not meant to be derogatory.)

One of the more stable—or "dead"—stocks has been American Telephone. (See Figure 21.) Many very wealthy investors own this stock, and it's generally regarded as a fine blue chip company, upon which the majority of us in the United States depend for our phone service. However, American Telephone is not a good stock to which to apply the PBS. The PBS trader would have realized a loss of 64 percent on the long side, a 26 percent loss on the short side, or a combined loss of 73 percent. (See Table 14.) If you had bought, and held, American Telephone for the ten year period ending in 1974, your results also would have been poor. In January 1965 its price was $69 a share; ten years later it was $44, a loss of $25 a share—a 36 percent drop.

To accommodate a stock like American Telephone, it seemed to make sense to consider a larger box for it. Instead of calling it a box, it was called a "coffin," or a "moving coffin." The top was defined as the highest highpoint in the previous ten weeks, the bottom as low as the lowest lowpoint in the previous ten weeks, and the length of the coffin was, well—ten weeks long. When the price jumped out of the moving coffin, it was time to act. But . . . .

Even applying the ten week moving coffin to American Telephone produced disappointing results. What was the problem? If you look at Figure 21, you will see that American Telephone fits very well into a giant coffin, five years long and 15 points wide. In other words, its entire range for the five year period of 1970 to 1975 was from approximately $40 to $55 a share, a mere $15 range for five years. This is hardly enough movement for a trading stock, especially when there are many more volatile alternatives. In the five year period of 1965 to 1970, American Telephone moved about 20 points, with a low of $50 and a high of $70.

Figure 21

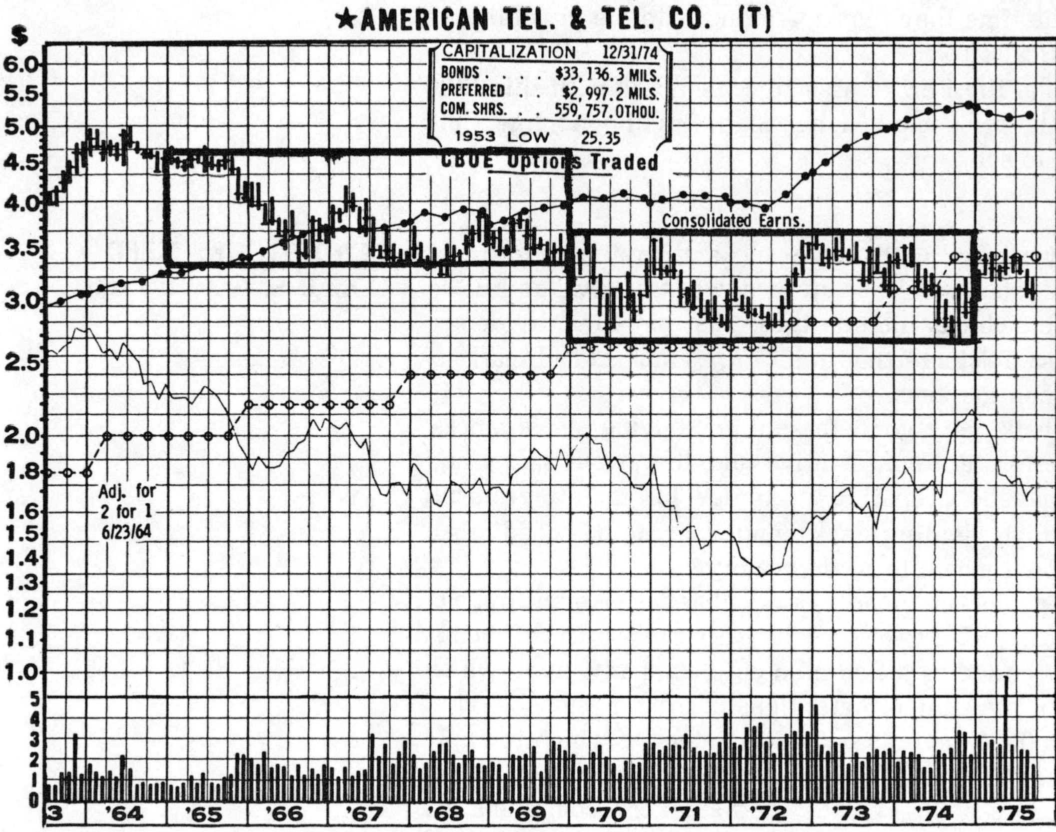

Source: Chart by Securities Research Company, 208 Newbury Street, Boston, Mass. 02116.

It appears that stable stocks may be attractive to investors for one reason only—secure and growing income. Therefore, it would be logical to evaluate stable stocks on the level of income produced. American Telephone might be considered undervalued at $40 a share, slightly undervalued at $45, reasonably valued at $50, and overvalued at $55, all based on the company's growth, dividend yield, and value relative to other income stocks.

If you own income stocks and wish to trade, using this system, be sure to read the chapter entitled "Winners Train!" Then go to your library and gather a minimum of three years of past statistics to see what your trading results would have been. Try to determine whether you have any psychological hangups on selling your stock at the proper time, which is discussed in the chapter entitled "Investors' Enemy #1." If you can't restrain yourself and wish to get going, try the PBS on a small part of your stocks—until you not only get the feel for the PBS but believe in it.

Table 14
AT&T Weekly Closing Prices

Week	1965	1966	1967	1968	1969	1970	1971	1972	1973	1974
1	69	63(B)H	54 L	54(B)	54	49 L	50	46(B)	53	51 H
2	68	61	55	54 H	53(S)L	50 H	51	47 H	53 H	49 L
3	67	60	57	51	54 H	49	52	45	52 L	50
4	67	60 L	58 H	51	52 L	48	53 H	45	53 H	50
5	67	61	56	51	54	47 L	52	45	51(S)	50
6	67	61 H	56 L	50 L	55(B)H	49	52	44	50 L	50
7	67	60	58 H	51 H	54	50	50	44	51 H	51
8	67	60	57 L	50	53	50	49	43	50	52
9	66	58(S)	61	50	51(S)L	51(B)	48	43 L	49 L	52
10	66	58	61	50	52 H	52	48	45 H	50	52
11	66	57	61	50	51 L	52 H	48	44	51 H	52 H
12	66 L	57	61 H	49(S)	52 H	51 L	48	43	50	50
13	67	57 L	60	49 L	51 L	53 H	48 L	43	50	49
14	68	58 H	59	50	52	52	50	43	50 L	48(S)
15	69 H	57	59	51 H	53(B)	50(S)	51 H	43	53(B)	48 L
16	68	57	59	50	54	49	49	43	53 H	49 H
17	68	56	59	50	55	49	48	42(S)	51 L	47 L
18	68 L	56	57	50	56	47	48	42	53	48 H
19	69	55	57	49	57	47	47(S)	42	53 H	47
20	69	55	57	49	57 H	46	46	42 L	52	46
21	69	55	55(S)	48	56	43 L	45	43	51	46
22	69 H	54	55 L	48	56	45 H	44 L	43 H	50(S)L	46 L
23	68	54	56	48 L	55	43	46 H	42	51	48 H
24	68	53 L	57	49	52	41 L	44	42	51	47
25	66 L	55	58 H	52(B)H	52 L	42 H	44 L	41	51	46
26	68 H	56	57	50 L	54	40 L	45	41 L	51	46
27	67	58 H	53	51	54	42	46 H	42 H	51	44
28	67	56	52 L	51 H	54 H	44(B)	45	41 L	51	43
29	66	54	53 H	50 L	53	45	44	42	53 H	43
30	66	54	52	51 H	53	45	43	42	51	43
31	66	53	51	50	52 L	46 H	43	42 H	49	42 L
32	66 L	53	51	50 L	53	45	43	41 L	48	43 H
33	67	52	51	51	53	43 L	43	43(B)	47	42 L
34	67	50 L	51	51	53 H	45	43	44 H	46 L	43 H
35	67	52 H	50	51	52	46	43	43 L	47	42
36	68	50 L	50 L	53 H	51(S)L	47	43	44	49 H	42
37	68 H	52 H	53 H	52	52 H	47 H	42	45	48 L	40 L
38	67	51	51	52	50 L	44	42 L	47 H	51(B)	42
39	67	51	51 L	52 L	51 H	44	43	46 L	52 H	42 H
40	67	50 L	52 H	54	50	44 L	44 H	48 H	51	40 L
41	67	54(B)	51	54	50	45 H	42	47 L	51	44(B)
42	67	55	51	54	50 L	44	42	48	49	45
43	65(S)	56 H	50	55 H	52(B)H	43(S)	42	48	49	45
44	65	55 L	50	54	51 L	43 L	42	49	48	46
45	63	56 H	50 L	54 L	53	44	42	50	48	47
46	63	55	51	56	53 H	45 H	42	51	47(S)L	47 H
47	62	55	51 H	57	52	44	41	53 H	48 H	43
48	61	53(S)L	50	57 H	52	44 L	41	51	46 L	43
49	61	54 H	49	56	50(S)	47(B)	41 L	51 L	48	41 L
50	60 L	53 L	49 L	55	50	47	42	52 H	48	43
51	62 H	54	50	54	49	49	43	51 L	50(B)	44
52	60 L	55(B)H	50	54	49	49 H	44	52	50	44
53						48 L				

As one astute 70 year old investment counselor said, "It takes me ten years to devise a new technique to trade stocks, and another ten years just to believe in it." Allow some time for "training" and for "believing," so you'll know what to expect. But remember—"Dead stocks may need coffins, not boxes."

THE PBS AND STOCK MARKET INDEXES

When I first set up the Profit Box System, I thought I had found a hypothesis that could be applied to "anything that moved"—like the snake medicine that could cure anything, from ingrown toenails to cancer. I applied PBS to volatile stocks, bonds, mutual funds, foreign exchange, economic indexes, and on and on. For the most part the results were pleasing (except for a few disappointments).

The PBS *can* be used with the Dow Jones indexes, the Standard and Poor 500 (see Table 15), and the New York Stock Exchange Composite. However, these indexes were not particularly helpful in determining proper timing for individual stocks. The PBS acknowledges major moves in the market but produces a lot of whipsaws, at times, to reflect directionless markets.

Theoretically, it would seem that if one could determine that the stock market had changed from trending down to trending up, then one should be able to buy a diversified group of stocks and make good profits. However, I don't suggest that the PBS should be used in this way. It is *interesting* to know the direction of the stock market, but it's *much more important to know the direction of the stocks in which your money is actually invested.*

Table 15
S&P Weekly Closing Index

Week	*1965*	*1966*	*1967*	*1968*	*1969*	*1970*	*1971*	*1972*	*1973*	*1974*
1	85	93	82	95 **L**	103	92 **H**	92	102	119	98 **H**
2	86	93	84	96 **H**	100(S)L	91	92	103	119 **H**	93 **L**
3	86	93	86	95	102	89	93	103	118	95
4	87	93	86	93	102	86	94	103	116	96 **H**
5	87 **H**	93	87	92	103	86	95	104	114(S)	95
6	86	93 **H**	87	89	103	86 **L**	96	104	114	92(S)
7	86 **L**	92	87	89 **L**	103 **H**	87	98 **H**	105	114	92 **L**
8	87 **H**	91	87	90 **H**	99	89	96	105	113	95
9	86 **L**	89(S)	88	89	98	90 **H**	96 **L**	106	112 **L**	95
10	87 **H**	88	88	89	98	88	98	107	113	97(B)
11	86	88 **L**	90	89	98 **L**	87 **L**	99	108 **H**	113 **H**	99 **H**
12	86	89	90	88 **L**	99	89	101 **H**	107	108 **L**	97
13	86 **L**	89	90 **H**	90	101 **H**	89	99 **L**	107	111 **H**	93
14	87	91	89 **L**	93(B)	100 **L**	89 **H**	100	107	109 **L**	93
15	88(B)	91	90	96 **H**	101	88	102	107 **L**	112	92 **L**
16	88	92 **H**	92	95 **L**	101	85	103	109	112 **H**	93 **H**
17	89	91	94	97	101	82	104 **H**	109 **H**	107 **L**	90(S)
18	89	87	94 **H**	98	104(B)	81	103	108	111 **H**	91
19	90 **H**	85	93	98 **H**	105	79	102	107	108	91 **H**
20	88	85 **L**	92	96 **L**	105 **H**	76	102	106(S)	103 **L**	88
21	88	87 **H**	90	97	104	72 **L**	100	106 **L**	107 **H**	88
22	87	86	89 **L**	98	103	76	99 **L**	108	103 **L**	87 **L**
23	85(S)	86	91	101	102	76 **H**	101	110(B)H	107 **H**	92(B)H
24	85	86	92 **H**	101 **H**	98(S)	73 **L**	101 **H**	109	105	91
25	83 **L**	86	89	100	96 **L**	77(B)H	98(S)	106 **L**	103 **L**	87
26	85	85 **L**	87(S)L	99 **L**	97	73	97 **L**	108	104 **H**	86(S)
27	85	87	91	100	99 **H**	72(S)L	99	108 **H**	101 **L**	83
28	85 **H**	87	92	102 **H**	95	74	100 **H**	107	104	83
29	84 **L**	85	94(B)	100	94	77	99	107 **L**	107(B)	83
30	85	83 **L**	94	98(S)	92 **L**	77	98	108 **H**	109 **H**	82
31	86(B)	84 **H**	95	96 **L**	93	78(B)H	95	106(S)	106	78 **L**
32	86	83	95 **H**	97	93	77	94 **L**	106 **L**	104	80 **H**
33	86	79	94	98	94	75 **L**	95	107	102	75
34	87	76 **L**	92 **L**	98	95	79	98	110(B)	101 **L**	71 **L**
35	88	77 **H**	93	98	95 **H**	81	100	111	104	72 **H**
36	89	76 **L**	94	101 **H**	93 **L**	82	100	111 **H**	104	71
37	90	79(B)H	96	100 **L**	94	82	100 **H**	110 **L**	104	65 **L**
38	90 **H**	77	97 **H**	101	95 **H**	82	99	111 **H**	107	70 **H**
39	89 **L**	76	96 **L**	102	94	82	98 **L**	110	108	64
40	90	73(S)L	97 **H**	103(B)	93	85	99 **H**	109(S)	109	62 **L**
41	91	76	96	103	93 **L**	85 **H**	97	107 **L**	111 **H**	71(B)
42	91	78	95(S)	104	96(B)	84	95	109	110 **L**	72 **H**
43	92	80(B)	94	104 **H**	98 **H**	83	94	110	111 **H**	70 **L**
44	92	80	91 **L**	103	97 **L**	83 **L**	94	114(B)H	107(S)	73
45	92	81	92	103 **L**	98 **H**	84 **H**	92	113 **L**	105	74 **H**
46	92	81 **H**	92	105	97	83	91	115	103	71
47	92 **H**	80	93	106	94(S)	83 **L**	91 **L**	117	99	68(S)L
48	91	80 **L**	94	108 **H**	93	85	97	117	95 **L**	69 **H**
49	91 **L**	82 **H**	95	107	91	89	97	118	96 **H**	65 **L**
50	92	81	95	107	90 **L**	90	100(B)	118 **H**	93	67 **H**
51	92	81	95	106	91	90	100	115 **L**	93 **L**	66 **L**
52	92	80 **L**	96 **H**	104	91	90	102	118	97 **B**	67
53						92				

Chapter **4**

Investors' Enemy #1—Cognitive Dissonance

Perhaps the most complex problem in managing stocks is in the answer to the question: When to sell? There are technical analytic techniques purportedly 80 percent effective in indicating "when to sell," though no techniques are known to be perfect. Theoretically, an 80 percent effectiveness is great! But then why do these same traders fail so badly in their performance? The most confounding problem turns out to be: *Why didn't the trader sell when his indicators told him to?* or *Why couldn't he bring himself to sell when the trend clearly turned negative?*

I suggest a good part of the answer may have been uncovered by Dr. Leon Festinger, a professor of psychology, in his book, *A Theory of Cognitive Dissonance.* In it he discusses two phenomena:

1. That people tend to reduce the perceived risk of a purchase *after* the purchase has been made.
2. That people seek out information to confirm that their purchase decision was a wise one in a way which reinforces and bolsters the wisdom of their decision.

For example, a person who has just bought an automobile prefers to read ads that favor the auto he just bought, and he will interpret this information to reinforce his decision as being a good one. In other words, *a person who feels that two products are equally attractive before purchase will change—the purchased product increases in attractiveness, the rejected one decreases in attractiveness.* The "dissonance" causes a person to change his opinion or behavior, to exaggerate or overly justify an action in his favor.

This phenomena is called cognitive dissonance. In the securities industry it has long been known as, Falling in Love with a Stock!

What are the implications of cognitive dissonance in buying and selling stocks? There are several:

1. An investor will often prefer to buy, or will have little resistance to buy, more of what he has recently purchased; e.g., a recent owner of IBM stock would be less resistant to buying more IBM than other stocks, regardless of whether the price is lower or higher than his original purchase.

2. *Whereas it is relatively easy for an investor to buy a stock*, e.g., 100 shares of General Motors, *it becomes very difficult for him to sell it because of cognitive dissonance*, which is responsible for silently but firmly building up his stronger liking for the stock *after* he purchases it.

3. Before an investor can sell a stock, he must somehow get rid of all the great fantasies he has built up in his mind about that stock. For example, after buying General Motors, the investor may think that GM is the largest and greatest auto manufacturer in the world. GM is well managed, has good earnings, good dividends, products of high quality, is an undervalued stock, and so on. But before he can sell the stock, he must do two things: First, he must shift to neutral on the stock (a neutral feeling implies that he would just "hold" the stock, not buy or sell it). Second, he must shift from a neutral to a negative feeling towards the stock—, that his selection was wrong, or that the situation has changed drastically. For example, GM is now a stagnant, wallowing giant about to tumble, is poorly managed, its earnings outlook and dividends are questionable, the stock is overpriced, and so on. This represents a 180 degree change in investor perception, and *probably accounts for many investors selling their stocks only after a substantial decline*, rather than close to the optimum selling price.

In buying a stock the advantages to be gained are considered and accentuated. In selling a stock the perceived advantages must not only be destroyed, they must be replaced with perceived risks of holding and with reasons for sale.

I remember one dynamic portfolio manager who "loved" each of the stocks in his portfolio. He would continually try to get other portfolio managers to buy shares of "his" stocks. However, once he sold one of his particular stocks, the love affair was over! He "hated" that stock with a passion. Furthermore, he perceived great risks for those who still held the stock—he was an unknowing victim of cognitive dissonance.

Recently, a research analyst confessed that his own ego was tied up in the recommendation of a certain stock. After he recommended this stock for purchase, he uncovered a whole sea of unfavorable information about this stock, yet he found it extremely difficult to withdraw his recommendation!

Perhaps you can now understand why you, your stockbroker, the research analyst, or the investment advisor, may have a real hang-up when it comes to selling. "When to sell" is often the toughest investment decision to make and to carry out. If there is a hangup in using the PBS, it lies in the mind of the person, not the system.

HOW TO PROTECT YOURSELF FROM INVESTORS' ENEMY #1

Many investors and traders have a problem when it comes to selling their stock, for reasons discussed earlier in this chapter. One solution is to enter a stop order with your broker. This is an automatic instruction to sell your stock at the market, if it drops to a certain price. (A stop order can also be used to buy a stock if its price rises to a certain higher price).

There are several reasons for using stop orders:

You make your decision well in advance. This helps you avoid the emotional stress that often goes into making the decision to sell.

You protect your profits, or minimize your losses, and you keep your capital intact.

If you are away on a long vacation you won't come home to a bad surprise. For example, in 1962 a wealthy investor left for Europe when IBM was selling at $600 a share. Upon his return home several months later, he noticed IBM was then selling at $300. His first question to his broker was, "Did IBM split again?" The answer was, "No, IBM dropped 50 percent!"

Setting limits for stop orders involves judgments, and there is no perfect solution to setting them. In general, stop order limits should be placed just below the previous PBS lowpoint, then moved up as new lowpoints are established. More specifically, I suggest placing the stop order limit 1/8th of a point below the most recent daily lowpoint established during the week of the lowpoint; e.g., if the weekly closing lowpoint is $46½ and the daily lowpoint for that week was $44 5/8, place the stop order at $44 ½. You would tell your broker: "Sell 100 shares of XYZ at $44 ½ stop, good until cancelled."

The reverse would be true for placing a "buy to cover" stop order for a short sale; e.g., if the weekly high point close was $52 ½ and the highpoint during the week was $55 3/8, place the buy to cover order at $55½. Thus, "Buy to cover 100 shares short of XYZ at $55½ stop, good until cancelled."

If you can't sell your stock without becoming emotional, or if you agonize over selling stocks, the stop limit order may be your solution. Remember, it's important to limit losses. If you buy a stock at $100 that later declines to $10, you've lost 90 percent of your capital. To "get even" you now need a 900 percent gain, from $10 to $100 a share, and this is next to impossible. Had you sold your $100 stock at $90, using a stop limit order, you would need only a 11 percent gain to get even.

"Getting back even" is a very dangerous investment philosophy. I know of no one who has ever made money in the stock market who "just wants to get even." This is not consistent with "cutting your losses short and letting your profits run." *"Getting back even" involves just the opposite—limiting your profits, and letting your losses run!* With this concept, I can guarantee you major losses. Mathematically, it is not possible to succeed, simply because many stocks never go back to their former prices—especially the bankrupt ones!

There is another reason for using stop orders with volatile stocks. In certain wild and disorderly stock markets, which may occur only several times in ten years, your stock may drop as much as 50 percent or more in one week. Here a stop order should not only protect your capital, but give you some peace of mind.

Chapter 5

Infallible Forecasting

Trading and investing would be a lot easier if you had a good and reliable forecast of the future. Right? Right. There's only one problem: There just may be *no such thing as a "good and reliable forecast!"*

Donald T. Regan, chairman of Merrill Lynch, remarked before a group of financial analysts that "anyone who has clear and precise ideas about the future is certain to be wrong." (*San Francisco Chronicle*, October 11, 1972.)

Morton Smith, retired senior vice president of the Girard Bank, said: "Having no confidence in my own or anybody else's ability to forecast stock prices over either the short, medium or long term, I tend to place my emphasis on cash dividends." (*San Francisco Chronicle*, April 28, 1975.)

T. Rowe Price, formerly head of a very successful multibillion investment counseling firm, told a *Forbes Magazine* interviewer (October 15, 1975): "I do not try to forecast stock market trends or bond market trends—I learned my lesson in 1931. I learned I don't know anything about what the stock market is going to do—and neither do the others. If they are right, they are right only for a short time."

Please don't get me wrong—forecasting is absolutely necessary. Plans must be made. Our Government is often criticized for lack of needed long range forecasting and planning, e.g., what do we do when our oil resources run out in several decades. However, for a trader or investor to blindly and completely lock in his investments on the basis of one forecast is risky business! Here are some of my personal experiences involving forecasts.

What I Learned from Forecasters

Once when I was sorting out old research reports (the thick detailed reports that are sent to institutional investors), I made a comparison of forecasted earnings per share, which had been made a year earlier, with the actual earnings per share. One very reputable analyst had forecast that a certain recommended company would earn $5 a share—

but the actual results turned out to be a loss of 64¢ a share! Most other forecasted earnings also missed their mark, some by very wide margins.

In one research report, the stock of a large insurance company was recommended for purchase. There was one snag, though—several months later this company went bankrupt!

In another research report, Penn Central had been recommended for purchase, just months before its major problems became apparent. It also went bankrupt!

These forecasts are not examples of frauds. These are examples where sincere and reputable senior research analysts either did not dig deep enough, couldn't get their hands on the right facts, couldn't put the facts together properly, or came to the wrong conclusions. *There were simply too many unknowns and variables*, and *the variables kept changing as time passed.* Where the analyst had forecasted "up," the actual direction turned out to be "down."

Don't fall into the forecasting trap. The evidence is lacking to establish that anyone, or any system, can produce reliable or accurate stock or stock market forecasts in terms of either time or magnitude.

Fortunately, the PBS does not require forecasts other than that the stock you propose to trade will be volatile. It doesn't tell you how far your stock will go up or down, nor does it tell you how long it will take.

There is a saying that "forecasts can be accurate and reliable—as long as they are revised every five minutes!" There's a moral to this, and the PBS applies it—every week the PBS gives you a new forecast.

EXPERTS, OR THE TOWER OF BABEL?

As you use the PBS, you become less dependent on the opinions of experts. The fact is that you have your own PBS tool for judging trends!

Or would you still prefer to listen to the advice of experts? If so, which experts are you going to listen to: The ones who say the market is going up? Those who say the market is going down? Or those who admit they really don't know?

If you've listened to experts on stocks and feel that you're hearing voices straight out of the Tower of Babel, give the PBS a personal test. Then you can still listen to the experts, but you'll find that *you have taken charge in making your own investment decisions*, because you now have some basis for your decision in the definition of a trend change. The chances are that you will be aware of a trend change, using PBS, before you read about experts who have changed their opinions to concur with your own!

If you want to check on "expert opinion," just go to your library and read the back newspaper reports of past major stock market tops and bottoms. You are likely to find that experts often are full of optimism at tops and pessimism at bottoms. Theoretically, if all investors are optimistic (bullish), you can bet on one thing—that investors have all their money invested in stocks. Therefore, no more money is left to buy stocks and push prices up further, which then means there can be only one way to go, and that's down. The PBS at this time will start to flash sell signal alarms.

At major market bottoms, where most investors are pessimistic (bearish), you can bet that investors have sold most of the stocks they are planning to sell, and have a great deal of cash to invest "after the market drops to much lower levels." The PBS will then start to flash its alarm—and this time you can expect to see buy signals.

THE FIRE STATION EFFECT

A successful trader is like a fireman—he's got to be ready for action when the alarm sounds. The alarm may be false, but he can't ignore it!

A fire alarm sounds! Fire trucks rush to the fire. The alarm turns out to be false.

Another alarm is reported. Fire trucks are dispatched again. And again it turns out to be false!

False alarms are frustrating and expensive. So why not close down the fire stations? Ridiculous? We recognize that we must have fire stations, not for the false alarms, but for those alarms that would be disastrous if they weren't answered.

To check on false alarms, I called the San Francisco Fire Department. For its year ending June 1975, over 11,000 out of a total of 31,000 alarms were false! Even many of the "good" alarms included rescuing cats from trees and other menial, if necessary, tasks.

Although we don't like false fire alarms, there is little we can do about them. So we accept them!

The PBS is similar. It does give false alarms—but it also *gets you in early on big moves,* the "barn burners." And more important, it *gets you out early before the big declines,* with very few exceptions.

Is the Answer Better Forecasting?

More about fire stations—if we could forecast when and where fires were going to start, we could simply put a fire truck in that area before the fire started. This would be more efficient. The fire would have a shorter time to burn. Smaller fires are much easier to put out. This would save lots of taxpayer dollars. Make sense? Of course not, because *the time and locations of fires simply cannot be forecast.* Neither can many of the factors that affect stock prices be forecast, at least not to any useful degree of accuracy.

Some general events that affect fires *can* be forecast. For example, we know that in summer the weather will be hot. Therefore, we predict that there will be more fires in summer than in winter. We can also predict that fires are more likely to start in the dryer parts of the country in the summer where there is no rain. But when and where the next fire will start simply can't be forecast, except by the arsonist. Therefore, *it is absolutely necessary to have firemen and fire stations, ready to go, 24 hours a day!*

The PBS provides a trader with his own "fire station." Sure, it will give him false alarms, but it will also give alarms signalling big moves, both up and down. It's up to you, the trader, to be like the fireman—ready for action when the alarm sounds. The alarm may be false, but it can't be ignored, because it may be the big one.

Hopefully, this easy concept (the fire station) will help explain a more difficult concept (the PBS). It is important to understand, because many traders refuse to take small losses in stocks, *so they end up taking large losses!*

Chapter 6

Winners Train!

What would happen if you ran in a ten mile race? If you are like me, you'd probably die of exhaustion! Yet, traders, young and old, enter the stock market race every day expecting to make a killing without proper training. I emphasize "proper" training because I don't consider taking a series of big losses, or losing large amounts of money, to be proper training.

If it were easy to make and keep profits by trading or investing in the stock market, then everyone would be rich!

How does one get properly trained? If you plan to use the PBS, I would suggest you first try the system on paper. Go over the examples given in this book, week by week, for the ten year periods. Get the feel of what can happen. Get a history of weekly prices on your own volatile stocks, if you hold some, to see where you should have sold or bought.

If you train in bull markets only, like the gunslingers of the mid-1960s, you will get slaughtered, as they did, in the following bear market. That's why it is necessary to test stocks over a long period.

A trader who is properly trained should feel as comfortable with a short sale as with buying a stock. This is because he knows exactly what he is going to do, as time goes on.

I often ask this question of myself: *Does a person have to "earn the right" to make, and keep, profits in the stock market?* Perhaps the answer is: *Yes.*

It may be that "fools rush in, where wise men fear to tread." Let's put it another way.

If an investor has not "earned the right" to make and keep profits, he is quite likely to be ambushed and slaughtered either by fear, which causes him to sell his stocks after substantial declines, or by greed, which causes him to buy stocks close to their highs after watching the stocks go up, up, and up! Those who are impatient with their stocks also may not have earned that "right." Some are disappointed in a bull market when their stock moves from, say, $10 to $11, or 10 percent in one week, even though this is a yearly rate of 520 percent! Proper training is the best way I know of for a trader to eliminate fear, greed, and impatience, all of which could otherwise do him in.

You might say that using the PBS is a little like performing an appendectomy—you might want to train a little before doing it!

Part of the purpose of this book is to help the trader make his own decisions. Unfortunately, there are times when the PBS will say "sell" and your gut feeling will say "hold on," and you find yourself in an agonizing dilemma. To break this stalemate, you might try this: Make one-half a decision—sell half and keep half. This way you will be half right, and half wrong. I suggest the "½" decision as a compromise, so you can be at least "½" right!

WHAT IT TAKES TO BE A WINNER

What does it take to be a successful trader? Well . . .

What does it take to become a *baseball* star? Do you have to get to first base every time you're up to bat? No! Even the best baseball players make first base only about 30 percent of the time. In other words, they fail 70 percent of the time, and yet they are champions!

How about *golf?* If the golf course has 18 holes, a perfect record would be 18 strokes for all 18 holes. But the champions take three to four strokes to make one hole. That's an average of only 25 to 33 percent. Or a 67 percent to 75 percent failure rate.

The *weatherman* on TV tells us, "There is an 80 percent chance of rain tomorrow." He won't lose his job if it doesn't rain. We don't stop listening to him even if he's wrong half the time. After all, it's better to carry an umbrella than take a chance on getting soaked. So what if he's 50 percent wrong!

It's the same in investing and trading stocks. Any investor who feels he must make a profit 100 percent of the time is unrealistic. One can make profits on less than half the trades and do very well. How? Here's the secret: The average profit must be much larger than the average loss over some reasonable length of time.

I have met only one person who has never taken a loss. He was a young stockbroker who told me all his clients had profits, no losses. When I asked him how long he had been in business, he said, "Two weeks." Such genius!

Chapter 7

David and Goliath—The Small Investor and the Institutions

Does the small investor have a chance? It has been said that he is "finished," that he can't compete with the institutions. Since the recent average institutional record has been poor, I wonder who would want to compete with the institutions! Yet some institutions have millions invested in computers for fast, accurate information and professional management. According to Mr. Benjamin Graham, co-author of *Security Analysis*, the bible of security analysts, "the institutions have proved as limited as anybody in their intelligence and skill." (*Forbes Magazine*, June 15, 1975).

According to a highly placed technician who guides billions in portfolios, "The biggest amateurs are now the institutions themselves."

You, as an individual, *can* compete with institutions! You have several advantages over them.

First, you have no marketability problem. For example, you tell your broker to sell your 100 shares, and it's done immediately. However, the institution may not be able to sell its 100,000 to 1,000,000 shares of stock because it can't find a buyer for all of it! It may have to offer that block of stock at a substantial discount to sell it. Where you might sell 100 shares at $40 a share, the institution might be able to get only $36 a share for its 100,000 shares.

Second, you can act faster. You don't have to seek approval from the research department, the portfolio supervisor, or an investment committee. You don't have to check on, or seek approval from, numerous clients. You don't have to agonize over and justify your decision to someone else—all this before you can sell your stock. Recently the head of one portfolio management group told me, in confidence, that it would take a very minimum of two months to sell one stock for all his clients *after* the decision had been made to sell!

The individual trader has been intimidated; he has been told repeatedly in the newspaper that he is at a great disadvantage and doesn't

Figure 22

Heard on the Street

By Charles J. Elia

The current bear market is playing havoc with pension-fund assets and showing little respect for investment management reputations. If the latest results at the elite *Morgan Guaranty Trust Co.* are any guide, the next bull market will have to be exceptional, just to make up the past year's losses.

Morgan Guaranty is the nation's largest manager of trust money and at the end of 1973, its purview included a vast pool, *$14.1 billion, of employe-benefit funds.* It managed $2.9 billion, or about 21% of this pension money through 10 commingled, or pooled, funds rather than in separate accounts.

Three of these pooled funds are geared entirely to stock investments. Reports just made available show they

This is the first of two articles on investment results of pooled pension funds managed by Morgan Guaranty Trust Co.

dropped $1 billion, or more than 50%, in value in the funds' fiscal year ended last Sept. 30, exceeding a comparable 39% decline in the market as measured by Standard & Poor's 500-stock index. Results for seven other commingled funds invested in bonds, mortgages, real estate and other sectors were relatively better but fell far short of offsetting the stock funds' losses.

The commingled funds don't necessarily measure how Morgan Guaranty's pension clients fared individually because only a portion of each account is invested in the funds and the accounts have varying investment mixes.

However, the commingled funds do provide a window on the bank's investment experience, and Samuel R. Callaway, executive vice president in charge of investments, concedes that the *past year was "a great disappointment to us in both stocks and bonds."*

The pooled stock funds are Special Situations Equity, invested in small, "emerging" companies; Intermediate, aimed toward medium-sized companies and Common Stock, invested in large companies and dominated by quality growth stocks.

The accompanying table lists results for those three funds in fiscal 1973 and fiscal 1974, as well as total assets in the funds. Performance is measured in "unit value" changes. These are values expressed in terms of portfolio units, similar to the net asset value per share used among mutual funds. The table includes four other pooled funds invested, respectively, in convertible securities; bonds; mortgages and real property, and a special-situation real estate category.

	Assets 9-30-73 ($000,000)	*Assets 9-30-74 ($000,000)*	*Unit Value* (% change fiscal 1973)*	*Unit Value* (% change fiscal 1974)*
Spec. Equity	$748	$327	−17.5%	−55.1%
Intermediate	625	328	− 9.5	−49.7
Common Stock	513	297	un-changed	−44.6
Other funds				
Convertible	417	287	− 5.3	−28.3
Bond	97	82	+ 5.5	− 1.9
Mortgage-Prop.	364	334	+ 4.3	+ 1.7
Spec. Real-Est.	253	152	− 1.5	−36.0
S&P 500 Index (adj. for dividends)			+ 1.0	−39.0

* Results for years ended September 30, 1973, and September 30, 1974, include dividend or interest income added back to fund unit values.

In addition to these seven, the bank has a pooled "reserve" fund that invests mainly in short-term money-market instruments to take advantage of high yields, and two funds started this year. One of the new funds invests in foreign securities; the other is in intermediate-term money-market securities.

An increase of nearly $300 million in the "reserve" fund in the past year reflects the caution that has dominated Morgan Guaranty's approach to investment of new-money inflows. This fund, with $535 million of assets, has provided the best relative return in the past year of the 10 pooled funds—a yield of 9.5% on its portfolio of commercial paper, negotiable certificates of deposit and fixed-income securities.

"We've been committing very little

to stocks," says Mr. Callaway. "Most of our new investment in the past year has been in the short-term, fixed-income area. More recently, we've begun to lengthen the maturity of our yield investments, particularly toward intermediate fixed-income securities." This includes both government issues and recent corporate offerings of six and eight-year notes and bonds.

Morgan Guaranty's new intermediate money-market fund was started last July 1 and has $91 million of its $123 million of assets invested in U.S. government and agency securities. Its indicated current return on Sept. 30 was 9.3%. The international securities fund, started last Jan. 22, had only $4 million of assets on Sept. 30 and 56% of that amount was in cash equivalents. On Sept. 30, unit values of the fund were down 24% since Jan. 31

For the bank's pooled stock funds, the year ended Sept. 30 is the second in a row of disappointing results, particularly in its more aggressive special situations fund.

In the past, the special situations fund has displayed more volatility than the market averages, both in market advances and in declines. Over long period, however, Mr. Callaway notes, the fund has provided an above-average annual rate of return. From inception in 1965 through last Dec. 31, the fund's annual return averaged 11.3%. The common stock fund of larger companies has an average annual return of 9.3% from 1957 through last Dec. 31.

Source: *Wall Street Journal*, December 9, 1974. Italics added.

have a chance. The PBS, plus your own good judgement, should help improve your odds in the stock market.

Sure, you're David, but remember what happened to Goliath?

THE GREAT MYTH—PRESERVATION OF CAPITAL

Most portfolio managers claim that "preservation of capital" is one of their major objectives. A review of the facts, however, indicates that many portfolio managers have been incapable of preserving capital. This became particularly evident in the 1968–74 bear markets, where we saw disastrous results from many prestigious investment managers, including Morgan Guaranty Trust Company.

According to the *Wall Street Journal* (see Figure 22) Morgan's Special Equity Fund lost 55.1 percent per unit in its fiscal year 1974, on top of a loss of 17.5 percent the year before. Morgan's Intermediate Fund lost 49.7 percent, versus a loss of 9.5 percent the year before, and its Common Stock Fund lost 44.6 percent, versus 0 percent the year before. The objectives of these funds may not have been to "preserve capital," but, on the other hand, the objective was certainly not to "lose capital."

Morgan Guaranty held, for example, 100,000 shares of Polaroid, which cost $6.7 million and was later worth $1.5 million, down 78 percent. Apparently there was no other plan to preserve capital than the standard procedure of diversifying into other stocks, such as MGIC Investment, which cost $11.3 million and was later worth $1.8 million, down 84 percent. (See Figure 23.)

Was Morgan's performance unique? No. A review of similar institu-

Figure 23

Heard on the Street

By Charles J. Elia

Morgan Guaranty Trust Co. markedly reduced the trading activity of three stock-oriented pooled funds it uses in managing pension money for its clients in the year ended Sept. 30. The three funds did less than half the buying and selling done the preceding year.

However, the net result was that the funds enlarged their stockholdings somewhat. Consumer-oriented stocks were particularly hard hit and the bank funds continued to have relatively large investment exposure in areas hardest hit by inflation and the economic slowdown—household and consumer product companies.

As reported here yesterday, three pooled stock funds managed by the bank

This is the second of two articles on investment results of pooled pension funds managed by Morgan Guaranty Trust Co.

dropped more than $1 billion, or more than 50%, in value in the year ended Sept. 30. They are the $327 million assets Special Situation Equity fund, invested in small companies, *off 55.1%*; the $328 million-assets Intermediate fund, invested in medium-sized companies, *off 49.7%*; and the $297 million-assets Common Stock fund, invested in large companies, particularly recognized growth stocks, *off 44.6%*. In the period, Standard & Poor's 500-stock index, adjusted for dividends, was off 39%.

The accompanying table summarizes the fiscal 1974 portfolio activity of the three funds, their realized and unrealized losses, and their cash reserves as of Sept. 30. All figures are expressed in millions of dollars.

Fund	Purchases	Sales	Realized Losses	Unrealized Losses	Cash Reserve
Spec. Equity ...	$ 78.7	$60.4	$ 5.9	$420	$32.2
Intermed.........	120.7	55.4	15.1	324	16.1
Common St. ...	54.1	9.1	1.4	262	21.8

Of the three, the aggressive Special Equity fund and the large-company Common Stock fund share most closely a proclivity for consumer-oriented companies. It was in those areas that some of the largest unrealized losses occurred in both portfolios.

The Special fund, for example, had $114 million, or 35%, of its assets in merchandising and household-product companies on Sept. 30. The Common fund, more representative of big bank's liking for established growth stocks, had $121 million, or 41%, of its assets in the consumer-type stocks.

In the Special fund, food and general merchandising stocks carried at a cost of $102 million were worth only $44 million on Sept. 30. Food, beverage and soap stocks that cost $72 million were down to $47 million, and drug stocks that cost $62 million were worth $21 million. Other unusually large declines were recorded in regional bank stocks, carried at a cost of $26 million but worth less than $10 million on Sept. 30.

In the Common fund, a model of most "Favorite Fifty" growth stocks, values were substantially below cost in such glamors as Marriott, McDonald's, Avon Products, Coca-Cola, Bristol-Myers and Richardson-Merrell. The fund's 99,556 shares of *Polaroid* for example, *cost $6.7* million but were *worth only $1.5 million* on Sept. 30. It also owned 170,483 shares of *MGIC Investment*, at a *cost of $11.3 million* and a value of *$1.8 million*.

The Intermediate fund, while it had only 17% of its assets invested in consumer-oriented stocks, had its share of large losers. Holdings of *A. H. Robins, Scholl Inc. and Tampax*, which together cost *$37.4* million, were *worth only $8.5 million* on Sept. 30. *General merchandising stocks acquired at a cost of $42 million dropped in value to $19 million. Insurance stocks carried at a cost of $61 million were worth only $30 million. Information service* stocks, mainly communications companies, *fell to a value of $25 million* from a *cost of $62 million*.

Influenced, perhaps, by the impact of inflation in the consumer areas, Samuel R. Callaway, executive vice president heading Morgan Guaranty's investment division, says the bank won't be inclined to direct much of its new-money inflow into stocks "until we feel that such massive problems as inflation and the overseas dollar glut" are under control.

Here are highlights on some of the stocks bought and sold in the latest fiscal year by the three stock funds:

Special Equity: Biggest purchases were oil-related, including 230,600 shares of Helmerich & Payne, 100,000 of Parker Drilling, 72,900 of Petrolite, and 50,000 of Sabine Royalty. Others: 113,000 Almaden Vineyards, 110,000 of Friona Industries, 66,500 Lance Inc., 77,600 Pioneer Hi-Bred, 50,000 of Pacific Lumber, 70,000 of Intel, 75,000 of A. F. Cross, 74,500 of Leno Inc. and 109,900 of Milton Bradley.

The fund realized a loss of $1 million in selling 141,500 shares of Petrie Stores, a loss of $3.1 million in sale of 65,000 shares of Ponderosa and a loss of $1 million in sale of 17,595 Foster Wheeler Corp. shares. It dispersed 894,182 shares of Marriott into individual pension fund accounts, recording a loss of $2.3 million.

It also sold 101,250 shares of Coca-Cola Bottling of New York at a loss of $1.2 million; the same number of shares showed up as a purchase by the Intermediate fund. Also sold: 181,100 shares of Heck's, 105,000 of Lowe's Companies, 229,800 shares of Colonial Penn and 328,800 shares of Airwick.

Common Stock Fund: Purchases included 104,869 Marriott shares, 38,400 Kresge, 72,900 Richardson-Merrell, 113,000 Warner-Lambert, 80,900 Sterling Drug, 9,918 IBM, 150,600 Marathon Oil, 32,900 Ford, 27,286 General Motors, 140,000 Deere, 191,800 Goodyear, and 12,116 Polaroid. Among the larger sales were 129,600 Middle South Utilities, 39,462 NCR, 20,000 Pfizer, 13,400 Du Pont and 54,300 AMP Inc. shares.

Intermediate Fund: The fund's largest purchases were among regional banks stocks, $17 million; insurance stocks, $16 million; and building-related $22 million. Largest sales included 100,000 shares of Coastal States Gas, 200,000 of Howard Johnson, 63,800 Pillsbury, 67,000 Simplicity Pattern, 10,700 Tampax, 89,000 ABC, 150,900 Williams Cos., 100,000 Maytag, 200,000 Jefferson Pilot, 220,500 Philadelphia Life, and 133,500 ESB.

Within the same year, the fund bought 100,000 shares of Ohio Casualty and sold them at a loss of $1.9 million, bought and sold 93,000 shares of Ryder at a loss of $388,000, and did the same with 75,000 of Barnett Banks, with a gain of $311,000.

Source: *Wall Street Journal*, December 10, 1974. Italics added.

tional portfolios indicates the above to be more typical than the exception.

Many portfolio managers take the following steps in investing in securities: They first determine the future direction of the stock market. Second, they select the industry with the most promising outlook. Third, they select the most promising stocks within the most promising industry group. This approach may sound impressive. A closer look, however, indicates that one dubious forecast is based on other dubious predictions, then further assumes that the portfolio manager can make purchases at prices lower now than they will be in the future.

The answer to the "when-to-sell" decision for many portfolio managers is even more evasive. And it usually assumes that each stock will be sold when the market and the industry group and the stock, or both, become less promising. Just what "less promising" means has always lacked crisp and clear definition.

According to the head of research for a large securities firm, the best trading results come from good fundamental research *and* good timing analysis. Using only one of these approaches, and excluding the other, is a little like milking a cow on a one legged stool—you've got to be awfully good to do it!

BUYING AND HOLDING HIGH QUALITY STOCKS

As an observer of the stock market for over two decades, I have seen many high quality stocks take years to appreciate in price, only to drop down to their former low price in a matter of days or weeks. I have often felt sorry for those portfolio managers and their clients who were left holding the bag in these situations.

I have also become infuriated when I see a friend's assets being managed where there is absolutely no downside protection, or any plan to preserve capital. For example, rather than sell stocks that are in well defined downtrends, some portfolio managers keep buying, and buying, at lower and lower prices, to "average down," e.g., the real estate investment trusts in the 1970s where 90 percent losses and bankruptcies are common.

Chapter 8

Other Boxes . . .

There are many other ways to define "boxes" for trend analysis. Instead of defining the top and bottom of a box as the highpoint and lowpoint . . .

1. The bottom of the box can be defined as a certain percentage below the preceding highpoint, e.g., 20 percent, and the top of the box as a certain percentage above the preceding lowpoint, e.g., 20 percent (the "Percentage Box" System).

2. The top of the box can be defined as the highest point, and the bottom of the box can be the lowest point during a certain preceding time period, say, of 10 weeks (the "Moving Coffin" System).

3. The requirement for a signal can be modified to require a closing price of a certain percentage above the previous highpoint for a "buy" signal, or below the previous lowpoint for, say, a "sell" signal of 10 percent (the "Profit Box Plus 10 Percent" System).

Although there are many ways to define a "box," the basic *Profit Box System* is the simplest to keep and follow.

THE DOW THEORY

Perhaps the best known technique for judging market trends is the Dow Theory. It is used for recognizing turns in a primary bull or bear market. (Leffler, pp. 536–37; *Your Investments,* p. 178; *Encyclopedia of Stock Market Techniques,* pp. 304–72.)

A bull market, according to the Dow Theory, is basically one in which succeeding highs exceed preceding highs, and successive lows are higher than preceding lows. This is similar to the PBS in a very broad sense. The Dow Theory has been helpful in recognizing bull or bear markets, but has often been too late in its signals to be helpful in timing stock trades.

WEEKLY VERSUS DAILY TIME SERIES

Why not use daily rather than weekly closing prices for stocks? I tested the PBS using daily prices for Fairchild Camera and Instrument common stock over the 11½ year period, January 2, 1962, to June 30, 1973. A total of 136 buys and 136 sells were required, with a net gain of less than 1 percent for this period after accounting for commissions. Although modifications to improve results and eliminate whipsaws were not used, the results appeared to make the broker substantially richer than the trader to warrant further research. Also, I suspect that the market makers (the specialists) may play an important part in daily trends, less so in weekly trends.

Chapter 9

Corporate Bonds and the PBS

Whether you are a trader, speculator, or investor, don't overlook the corporate bond market. It's an important market, especially when you can get:

High interest rates.
Capital gains.
Favorable leverage.

There will be capital gains opportunities in corporate bonds as long as our country swings to and from "tight" and "easy" money; as long as we have high Government deficits, and the Federal Reserve continues to open and close the financial spigots; as long as we have major national and international financial crises.

I included this chapter on bond prices for several reasons:

First, to test the PBS in timing bond purchases.

Second, to make the investor/trader aware of bond market trends. (High bond yields tend to draw money out of, and away from, the stock market. The reasoning goes like this: Why invest in relatively risky stocks, when you can get a relatively safe 10 percent yield from bonds?)

Third, to check the speculative aspects of bonds, since they can be leveraged more than stocks. (Currently, it is possible to buy $100,000 worth of U.S. Government bonds with a $10,000 investment, or $100,000 in municipal bonds on a $25,000 investment, or $100,000 of corporate bonds with a $30,000 investment.)

Fourth, to be prepared for possible future shocks in the bond market. (When the prime rate, which is the interest rate paid by blue chip companies, was at 6 percent, it would have been considered nonsense to forecast that the prime rate would subsequently double to 12 percent—but it did! Bond prices were, and will continue to be, greatly affected by this and many other "unforeseen events.")

Table 16
Dow Jones 40 Bond Index—Yields

Week	*1965*	*1966*	*1967*	*1968*	*1969*	*1970*	*1971*	*1972*	*1973*	*1974*
1	4.59%	4.95%	5.75%	6.65% **H**	7.00% **H**	8.24% **L**	8.42% **H**	7.70%	7.78% (U)**H**	8.49% (U)
2	4.59	4.96	5.60 (D)	6.46 (D)	6.99	8.28 **H**	8.18	7.65	7.76	8.41
3	4.58	4.96 **H**	5.48	6.43 **L**	6.93	8.17 (D)	8.03	7.65	7.76 **L**	8.35 **L**
4	4.58	4.93 **L**	5.45	6.45	6.85 **L**	8.22 **H**	7.99	7.62	7.78	8.37 **H**
5	4.56 **L**	4.98	5.44	6.46	6.86 **H**	8.17	7.91	7.61 **L**	7.86	8.34 **D**
6	4.57	5.00	5.44 **L**	6.46	6.85	8.16 **L**	7.81 **L**	7.65 **H**	7.88	8.32 **L**
7	4.58	5.05	5.47	6.46	6.85 **L**	8.18 **H**	7.86	7.63	7.90 **H**	8.33 **H**
8	4.58	5.08	5.50	6.46 **H**	6.86	8.13	7.88	7.63	7.87 **L**	8.30
9	4.59 **H**	5.11	5.51	6.45 **L**	6.91	8.13	7.90 **H**	7.55	7.89	8.29 **L**
10	4.58	5.17	5.52 **H**	6.48 (U)	6.96	8.02 **L**	7.85	7.55 **L**	7.91 **H**	8.33
11	4.58	5.20	5.51	6.53	7.03	8.07 **H**	7.78	7.57	7.86 (D)**L**	8.38 (U)
12	4.58 **L**	5.20	5.47	6.58	7.07	8.06	7.73 **L**	7.59	7.90 **H**	8.40
13	4.60 (U)**H**	5.20	5.46 **L**	6.60	7.12	7.98 **L**	7.80 **H**	7.63	7.87 **L**	8.50
14	4.59	5.22 **H**	5.51 **H**	6.68 **H**	7.21 **H**	8.18 (U)	7.77 **L**	7.73 (U)**H**	8.05 (U)**H**	8.73
15	4.58 **L**	5.20 **L**	5.46 **L**	6.67 **L**	7.15	8.21 **H**	7.78	7.69 **L**	7.98	8.85
16	4.59	5.22	5.47	6.71	7.10	8.18 **L**	7.86 (U)	7.77 **H**	7.96 **L**	8.86
17	4.60 **H**	5.23	5.51	6.73 **H**	7.03 **L**	8.28	7.93 **H**	7.75 **L**	7.97 **H**	9.00
18	4.59 **L**	5.26 **H**	5.56 (U)	6.67	7.05 **H**	8.37	7.91 **L**	7.77 **H**	7.94 (D)	9.05
19	4.60	5.24 **L**	5.60	6.66 (D)**L**	7.03 **L**	8.37	7.99 **H**	7.72 (D)	7.94	9.09
20	4.60	5.27	5.66	6.67	7.04	8.43	7.94 **L**	7.71	7.92 **L**	9.13
21	4.62	5.27 **H**	5.72	6.69	7.12	8.48 **H**	8.01 **H**	7.65	7.93	9.17
22	4.63	5.25 **L**	5.73	6.71 **H**	7.17	8.47	7.98	7.63	7.96	9.18 **H**
23	4.64	5.33	5.78	6.69	7.20	8.46 **L**	7.96 **L**	7.60 **L**	7.97 **H**	9.13
24	4.65 **H**	5.43 **H**	5.79	6.68	7.26	8.63 **H**	8.02	7.61 **H**	7.95 **L**	9.13 **L**
25	4.64 **L**	5.42	5.81	6.65	7.26 **H**	8.61 **L**	8.11	7.60 **L**	7.96	9.17
26	4.66	5.42 **L**	5.84	6.61 **L**	7.24 **L**	8.75	8.22	7.66 (U)	7.98 (U)	9.32
27	4.68 **H**	5.47	5.92	6.70 **H**	7.37	9.16 **H**	8.27 **H**	7.75	8.20	9.59
28	4.67 **L**	5.50	5.92	6.64	7.38 **H**	8.98 **L**	8.22	7.78	8.22	9.65
29	4.68	5.52	5.93	6.62	7.36 **L**	9.06 **H**	8.15 **L**	7.79 **H**	8.33	9.76 **H**
30	4.69 **H**	5.55	5.94 **H**	6.59	7.37	8.95 (D)**L**	8.18	7.78 **L**	8.39	9.67 **L**
31	4.68 **L**	5.58	5.91 **L**	6.51	7.44	8.96	8.20	7.83 **H**	8.52	9.73
32	4.70 **H**	5.61	5.96	6.46	7.44	8.96	8.23 **H**	7.81 **L**	8.56	9.77
33	4.69 **L**	5.67	5.97	6.44	7.47 **H**	9.09 (U)	8.15	7.82 **H**	8.59	9.80
34	4.71	5.76	6.01 **H**	6.43 **L**	7.46 **L**	9.20 **H**	8.12 (D)	7.79 (D)	8.62 **H**	9.80
35	4.72	5.83 **H**	6.00 **L**	6.49 **H**	7.49	9.12	8.05	7.79	8.58	9.97
36	4.72 **H**	5.81	6.01 **H**	6.46	7.52	9.12	7.98 **L**	7.78 **L**	8.51	10.13
37	4.71 **L**	5.76 **L**	5.99 (D)**L**	6.46 **L**	7.55 **H**	9.07	8.01	7.81 **H**	8.49 **L**	10.16
38	4.73	5.79 **H**	6.01	6.49	7.53 **L**	9.01	8.01 **H**	7.80 **L**	8.50 **H**	10.26 **H**
39	4.73	5.76	6.05 (U)	6.50 (U)	7.58	8.90 (D)**L**	8.00 **L**	7.83 (U)	8.38 (D)**L**	10.15 **L**
40	4.76 **H**	5.76	6.15	6.59 **H**	7.82	9.11 **H**	8.03 (U)**H**	7.93 **H**	8.48 **H**	10.38 **H**
41	4.75	5.74 (D)	6.19	6.57 **L**	7.93 **H**	9.09	7.93 (D)**L**	7.87	8.38 **L**	10.36
42	4.75 **L**	5.72	6.25	6.62	7.92	9.07 **L**	7.94 **H**	7.87	8.39	10.23
43	4.76	5.72	6.30	6.65 **H**	7.79	9.10 **H**	7.84 **L**	7.86 **L**	8.42	10.14 (D)
44	4.77	5.72 **L**	6.36	6.63	7.72 **L**	9.07 **L**	7.85 **H**	7.89 **H**	8.45 **H**	10.02
45	4.79	5.75	6.43	6.62 **L**	7.83	9.08 **H**	7.80 **L**	7.84 (D)	8.43	9.93
46	4.81	5.79	6.45	6.67	7.88	8.99	7.84 **H**	7.83	8.41 **L**	9.86
47	4.82	5.84 (U)	6.52	6.68	7.95	8.97	7.82 **L**	7.78	8.43 **H**	9.78 **L**
48	4.83	5.84	6.56	6.71	7.97	8.84	7.85 (U)**H**	7.73 **L**	8.42	9.79
49	4.86	5.85 **H**	6.59	6.74	8.01	8.53	7.83	7.74	8.37 **L**	9.91
50	4.90	5.82	6.61	6.84	8.06	8.50 **L**	7.81 (D)	7.74 **H**	8.42 **H**	9.92
51	4.92	5.80	6.62 **H**	6.88	8.20	8.53 **H**	7.76	7.71 **L**	8.40	9.92
52	4.94	5.76	6.61 **L**	6.93	8.25 **H**	8.51	7.72	7.74	8.35 **L**	9.99
53						8.41 **L**				

Corporate bond prices are much more homogeneous than stocks. That is, bonds issued by General Motors, Exxon, and Xerox are likely to move up together, and down together, depending upon the level of interest rates. At the same time the common stocks of these same companies could move in different directions, i.e., General Motors stock may be moving up, Exxon moving down, and Xerox moving sideways. Rather than apply PBS to each bond you want to follow, try following the Dow Jones 40 Bond Index. (Table 16 shows a ten year history of this bond index.)

Table 17
PBS/Dow Jones 40 Bond Index, 1965–1975 Summary

Date	*PBS Action*	*Yield Percent*	*Dow Jones Bond Index Gain/Loss Percent*
4/26/65	sell bonds	4.60%	
10/14/66	buy	5.74	+24%
11/25/66	sell	5.84	−1
1/13/67	buy	5.60	−4
5/5/67	sell	5.56	0
9/15/67	buy	5.99	+7
9/29/67	sell	6.05	−1
1/12/68	buy	6.46	+6
3/8/68	sell	6.48	0
5/10/68	buy	6.66	+2
9/27/68	sell	6.50	+2
1/16/70	buy	8.17	+25%
4/3/70	sell	8.18	0
7/24/70	buy	8.95	+9
8/14/70	sell	9.09	−1
9/25/70	buy	8.90	−2
4/23/71	sell	7.86	+11
8/27/71	buy	8.12	+3
10/8/71	sell	8.03	+1
10/15/71	buy	7.93	−1
12/3/71	sell	7.85	+1
12/17/71	buy	7.81	0
4/7/72	sell	7.73	+1
5/12/72	buy	7.72	0
6/30/72	sell	7.66	0
8/25/72	buy	7.79	+1
9/29/72	sell	7.83	0
11/10/72	buy	7.84	0
1/5/73	sell	7.78	0
3/16/73	buy	7.86	+1
4/6/73	sell	8.05	−2
5/4/73	buy	7.94	−1
6/29/73	sell	7.98	0
9/28/73	buy	8.38	+5
1/4/74	sell	8.49	−1
2/1/74	buy	8.34	−1
3/15/74	sell	8.38	0
10/25/74	buy	10.14	+21%
	(last)	(9.99)	+1

–38 trades
–17 gains, 10 losses, 11 breakevens

Can the Profit Box System be helpful in timing bond purchases and sales? Yes, but as a tool, not as gospel. Let's look at the ten year record, applying the PBS to the Dow Jones 40 Bond Index. (See Table 16.) Here the weekly yield of this index was used, because historical figures could be gathered conveniently from the *Daily Stock Price Record* listed in the bibliography. Normally, I prefer the basic index of bond values as commonly reported in financial newspapers.

There are three ways to apply the PBS to the bond index—the regular way, the "Moving Coffin" System, and the first-two significant figure method. The method you use will depend on your need. Of these three methods, the Moving Coffin produced the best results.

The regular PBS signaled 38 trend changes in yields in the ten year period ending in 1974. Most of these changes were not worth acting on. However, three times the PBS signals resulted in bond index declines of over 20 percent! (See Table 17.) For the speculator who is leveraging bonds, it is important that he pay off his margin when the PBS indicates yields have turned up, which means bond prices have turned down.

Some investors may feel the PBS is too sensitive to trend changes. In this event I suggest the Moving Coffin, which measures trend changes like this: *Yields*, or interest rates, *turn up when the latest*

Table 18
The "Moving Coffin"/Dow Jones 40 Bond Index, 1965–1975 Summary

Date Week/ Year	Moving Coffin Signals		Gains/Losses (percent)		Cumulative Results		
	Buy	Sell	Long	Short	Long 1.00	Short 1.00	Long and Short
13/65		4.60%					
2/67	5.60%			+18%		1.18	
18/67		5.56	0%		1.00		
25/68	6.65			+17		1.38	
42/68		6.62	0		1.00		
10/70	8.02			+18		1.62	
15/70		8.21	−2		.98		
39/70	8.90			+8		1.75	
17/71		7.93	+12		1.09		
35/71	8.05			+2		1.79	
14/72		7.73	+4		1.14		
23/72	7.60			−1		1.77	
28/72		7.78	−3		1.10		
47/72	7.78			0		1.77	
5/73		7.86	−2		1.08		
49/73	8.37			+7		1.90	
1/74		8.49	−2		1.06		
5/74	8.34			−1		1.88	
13/74		8.50	−2		1.04		
45/74	9.93			+15		2.16	2.24

—20 trades
—9 gains, 7 losses, 3 breakevens

yield is higher than any yield for the previous ten weeks, indicating the direction of bond prices to be down. *The trend turns down when the latest yield drops below any yield figure of the previous ten weeks,* indicating the direction of bond prices to be up.

Table 18 shows the summary for the Moving Coffin with the Dow Jones 40 Bond Index, 1965–75. Out of 20 trend changes, five resulted in magnitudes of 12 percent to 18 percent. This represents basis point moves of 97 to 143, all substantial moves in the bond market.

The third method, using only the first-two significant figures of the bond yield index, will produce even fewer signals. (See Tables 19 and 20.) In all three methods, note how the average gain is large and the average loss is small.

Conservative investors may use the PBS to time their purchases of top quality corporate or government bonds, and there is a great need for this. For example, it's distressing to pay $1,000 for a AAA rated, long term bond, only to find that it could have been purchased later at a much lower price. The only consolation is that most bonds pay interest every six months and will eventually mature at par, say in 20 to 30 years, which offsets some of the frustration of a large price decline.

CAPITAL GAINS AND LEVERAGE

The corporate bond market also offers traders and speculators something—capital gains and leverage possibilities. Let's take several hypothetical examples.

1. If an investor buys an "A" rated, 9 percent coupon bond at $900 a bond, his current yield is 10 percent, i.e., he receives $90 in interest payments each year for each $900 bond he buys.
2. If interest rates decline from 10 percent to 9 percent for "A" rated bonds, this should cause the value of the bond to rise from $900 to $1,000 a bond, thus making a paper profit of about 11 percent for the conservative investor. This is exclusive of the $90 interest he receives each year.
3. If a speculator buys 100 bonds at $900 each with a coupon of 9 percent, he may do so (at least at present) by borrowing 70 percent from his broker at the current rate, say 7 percent, and investing the remaining 30 percent from his own capital. Here's an example:

Total purchase: $100M 9% bonds.	$90,000
Loan from the brokerage firm (70%)	63,000
Speculator's investment (30%)	27,000
Interest income from 100 bonds a year	9,000
Less cost of broker's loan at 7% (7% × $63,000)	4,410
Net annual return from your investment	4,590

$$\text{or } \frac{\$4{,}590}{\$27{,}000} = \underline{\underline{17\%}}$$

Table 19
Dow Jones Bond Index (yields to closest $^1/_{10}$%)

Week	1965	1966	1967	1968	1969	1970	1971	1972	1973	1974
1	4.6%	5.0%	5.8%	6.6%	7.0%	8.2% L	8.4%	7.7%	7.8%	8.5% H
2	4.6	5.0	5.6 (D)	6.5	7.0	8.3 H	8.2	7.7	7.8	8.4
3	4.6	5.0 H	5.5	6.4 L	6.9	8.2	8.0	7.7	7.8	8.4
4	4.6	4.9 L	5.5	6.5	6.6 L	8.2	8.0	7.6	7.8	8.4
5	4.6	5.0	5.4	6.5	6.9	8.2	7.9	7.6 L	7.9	8.3 (D)
6	4.6	5.0	5.4	6.5	6.9	8.2	7.8 L	7.7 H	7.9	8.3
7	4.6	5.1	5.5	6.5	6.9	8.2	7.9	7.6	7.9	8.3
8	4.6	5.1	5.5	6.5	6.9	8.1 (D)	7.9	7.6	7.9	8.3
9	4.6	5.1	5.5	6.5	6.9	8.1	7.9	7.6	7.9	8.3
10	4.6	5.1	5.5	6.5	7.0	8.0 L	7.9 H	7.6	7.9	8.3
11	4.6	5.2	5.5	6.5	7.0	8.1	7.8	7.6	7.9	8.4
12	4.6	5.2	5.5	6.6	7.1	8.1 H	7.7 L	7.6	7.9	8.4
13	4.6	5.2	5.5	6.6	7.1	8.0 L	7.8	7.6 L	7.9	8.5
14	4.6	5.2	5.5	6.7	7.2	8.2 (U)	7.8	7.7	8.1 H	8.7 (U)
15	4.6	5.2	5.5	6.7	7.2 H	8.2	7.8	7.7	8.0	8.9
16	4.6	5.2	5.5	6.7	7.1	8.2	7.9	7.8	8.0	8.9
17	4.6	5.2	5.5 L	6.7	7.0 L	8.3	7.9	7.8	8.0	9.0
18	4.6	5.3 H	5.6	6.7	7.1 H	8.4	7.9	7.8 H	7.9	9.1
19	4.6	5.2 L	5.6	6.7	7.0	8.4	8.0 (U) H	7.7	7.9	9.1
20	4.6	5.3	5.7	6.7	7.0 L	8.4	7.9 L	7.7	7.9	9.1
21	4.6	5.3	5.7	6.7	7.1	8.5	8.0	7.7	7.9 L	9.2
22	4.6	5.3	5.7	6.7	7.2	8.5	8.0	7.6	8.0	9.2 H
23	4.6	5.3	5.8	6.7	7.2	8.5	8.0	7.6	8.0	9.1
24	4.7 H	5.4	5.8	6.7	7.3	8.6	8.0	7.6	8.0	9.1 L
25	4.6 L	5.4	5.8	6.7 H	7.3 H	8.6	8.1	7.6 L	8.0	9.2
26	4.7	5.4	5.8	6.6 L	7.2 L	8.8	8.2	7.7	8.0	9.3
27	4.7	5.5	5.9	6.7	7.4	9.2 H	8.3 H	7.8	8.2	9.6
28	4.7	5.5	5.9	6.7	7.4	9.0 L	8.2	7.8	8.3	9.7
29	4.7	5.5	5.9	6.6	7.4	9.1 H	8.2	7.8	8.4	9.8 H
30	4.7	5.6	5.9	6.6	7.4	9.0	8.2	7.8	8.5	9.7
31	4.7	5.6	5.9	6.5 (D)	7.4	9.0	8.2	7.8	8.6	9.7 L
32	4.7	5.6	6.0 (U)	6.5	7.4	9.0 L	8.2	7.8	8.6	9.8
33	4.7	5.7	6.0	6.4	7.5	9.1	8.2	7.8	8.6	9.8
34	4.7	5.8	6.0	6.4 L	7.5	9.2 H	8.1	7.8	8.6	9.8
35	4.7	5.8	6.0	6.5	7.5	9.1	8.1	7.8	8.6 H	10.0
36	4.7	5.8	6.0	6.5	7.5	9.1	8.0	7.8	8.5	10.1
37	4.7	5.8	6.0	6.5	7.6 H	9.1	8.0	7.8	8.5	10.2
38	4.7	5.8	6.0	6.5	7.5 L	9.0	8.0	7.8	8.5	10.3 H
39	4.7	5.8	6.1	6.5	7.6	8.9 (D)	8.0	7.8	8.4 L	10.2 L
40	4.8 (U)	5.8 H	6.2	6.6	7.8	9.1	8.0	7.9 (U)	8.5 H	10.4
41	4.8	5.7	6.2	6.6	7.9	9.1	7.9	7.9	8.4	10.4 H
42	4.8	5.7	6.3	6.6	7.9 H	9.1	7.9	7.9	8.4	10.2
43	4.8	5.7	6.3	6.7 H	7.8	9.1	7.8 (D) L	7.9	8.4 L	10.1 (D)
44	4.8	5.7 L	6.4	6.6	7.7 L	9.1	7.9 H	7.9 H	8.5 H	10.0
45	4.8	5.8	6.4	6.6 L	7.8	9.1 H	7.8	7.8	8.4	9.9
46	4.8	5.8	6.5	6.7	7.9	9.0	7.8	7.8	8.4	9.9
47	4.8	5.8	6.5	6.7	8.0	9.0	7.8 L	7.8	8.4	9.8
48	4.8	5.8	6.6	6.7	8.0	8.8	7.9 H	7.7	8.4	9.8 L
49	4.9	5.9 H	6.6	6.7	8.0	8.5	7.8	7.7	8.4	9.9
50	4.9	5.8	6.6	6.8 (U)	8.1	8.5	7.8	7.7	8.4	9.9
51	4.9	5.8	6.6	6.9	8.2	8.5	7.8	7.7	8.4	9.9
52	4.9	5.8	6.6	6.9	8.3 H	8.5	7.7	7.7 L	8.4 L	10.0
53						8.4				

Table 20
PBS/Dow Jones 40 Bond Index, 1965–1975 Summary—Yields Are Rounded Off to the Closest $^1/_{10}$ Percent.

Date Week/Year	PBS Action	Dow Jones Bond Index: Yield Percent	Dow Jones Bond Index: Gain/Loss Percent
40/65	sell bonds	4.8%	
2/67	buy	5.6	+15%
32/67	sell	6.0	−7
31/68	buy	6.5	+8
50/68	sell	6.8	−5
8/70	buy	8.1	+17
14/70	sell	8.2	−2
39/70	buy	8.9	+8
19/71	sell	8.0	+11
43/71	buy	7.8	−2
40/72	sell	7.9	−2
5/74	buy	8.3	+5
14/74	sell	8.7	−5
43/74	buy	10.1	+14

—14 trades, 7 gains, 6 losses

4. Now, *if interest yields drop* from 10 percent to 9 percent for "A" rated bonds, the speculator, in paragraph #3 above, benefits as follows:

	Original Purchase	*Value after Interest Rates Decline from 10 to 9 percent*	
Total value of purchase........	$90,000	$100,000	+11%
Less loan from broker..........	63,000	63,000	
Speculators' equity.............	27,000	37,000	+37%

So you can see the possibilities in these investments. The conservative investor receives 10 percent interest. The speculator not only receives 17 percent interest income on his investment but a possible capital gain of $10,000—or an additional 37 percent on his investment, assuming interest rates drop 10 to 9 percent. This example assumes good timing, doesn't take trading costs into account, and assumes the interest on the broker's loan does not increase.

Should yields rise from 10 to 11 percent, almost the reverse should be true—the speculator's equity would drop approximately $9,000, and he is likely to receive a margin call from his broker, unless the interest from his bonds is paid in time to reduce his loan. *If you leverage bonds, you must time both your purchase and sale properly. Poor timing can wipe out your investment, easily!*

REMEMBER WHEN . . .

Do you remember when government, corporate, and municipal bonds were considered to be "stable" investments? If you've followed the bond market since 1965, you know that this is no longer so. Even the "safest" U.S. government bonds are no longer havens from inflation, or loss of capital, due to high interest rates. For example, consider the investors who made the following "conservative" and "stable" investments in the following bonds:

	Original Issue Price	*1974 Low*	*(percent)*
American Telephone deb $3\frac{7}{8}$%, 1990 (rated AAA)	$100	$53	−47%
Chrysler Corp deb 8%, 1998 (rated A)	100	42	−58%
Western Union SF deb 5%, 1992 (rated BBB)	100	30	−70%

Many conservative investors, who have invested in bonds, made one common mistake—they invested all their bond money in long term "safe" bonds to get the highest yields. Sure, 4 percent might have been a good yield in 1965, but recently the yield had to be closer to 10 percent to be considered good. Those 4 percent long term bonds may now sell at roughly one-half their original cost!

Can this problem be avoided? Yes. When investing in bonds, diversify not only by area but by length of maturity; e.g., you might invest 20 percent of your funds in bonds maturing in five years, 20 percent in ten years, 20 percent in 15 years, and so forth. Then if the bond market should decline, your short maturity bonds should drop the least. In this way you always have some bonds with very little loss if you are forced to sell to raise cash. If bond prices rise, your long term bonds should rise the most, your short term bonds the least. This solution is not new—large institutions, such as insurance companies and banks, have been staggering their bond maturities for years!

Chapter 10

Options and the PBS

If the Profit Box System works with stocks, why shouldn't it work as well with options (puts and calls)?

To trade call options, it is important to be aware of these facts and assumptions:

- Options are extremely volatile, and are one of the most speculative forms of investment. A lot can be lost or gained in a relatively short time.
- Options are "wasting" assets, because they are good only for a limited period. The premium you pay for a call will normally decline, day by day, until there is no premium left. Unless the stock moves up, the market value of the call option can decline to nothing by the date it expires.
- Generally speaking, *one can make money by buying call options only when the price of the underlying stock moves up substantially.* You can't make a profit if the stock's price moves up only slightly, stays even, or drops.
- Be sure to read the options prospectus thoroughly. It's available from your broker.
- Buying options is not a game for beginners. Or for those who must preserve capital.

The tables in this chapter show how to use the PBS as a timing tool for both option writers (sellers) and buyers. The tables are not meant to be representative, exhaustive, or adequate samples. Note that daily, not weekly, prices are used when applying the PBS to call options, because of their highly volatile nature.

Table 21
Options Summary

AVP Oct. 40 4/22 to 9/17/75 Signal Price to				IBM Oct. 220 4/22 to 9/17/75 Signal Price to				MCD Oct. 50 4/22 to 9/17/75 Signal Price to				MTC Oct. 50 3/10 to 5/7/75 Signal Price to			MTC Apr. 60 3/10 to 4/25/75 Signal Price to		
Buy	Sell	L	S	Buy	Sell	L	S	Buy	Sell	L	S	Buy	Sell	L	Buy	Sell	L
$ 5.0	$11.2	+		$18.0	$19.0	+		$ 8.4	$8.4	–		$8.7	$19.0	+	$ .6	$8.4	+
12.7	11.0	–	–	13.6	12.0	–	+	10.2	9.5	–	–						
8.0	9.5	+	+	1.3	.7	–	+	8.6	8.3	–	+						
9.3	8.1	–	+					10.0	8.7	–	–						
9.2	7.3	–	–					2.4	15/16	–	+						
4.1	2.4	–	+														
2 15/16	1.7	–	–														

Let's test several call options, which are traded on the Chicago Board of Options Exchange, to get a feel for what can happen. . . . The summary of results is shown in Table 21.

BULL MARKET OBSERVATIONS

Bull markets produce much more dramatic results in trading options. For example, during the test period of March 10, 1975, to May 6, 1975, the Monsanto October 50 calls gave a buy signal at $8⅞, followed by a sell signal at $19, a substantial profit for only 27 trading days!

The Monsanto April 60 calls were much more highly leveraged, and gave a PBS buy signal at $¾, that is, 75¢, and closed at $8½, or $8.50, the last day before they expired—*a gain of over 1,000 percent in only 12 trading days!* During this same period the Dow Jones Industrial Index rose from 776 to 835, up 7 percent; the Monsanto common stock rose from $55 to $68 a share, up 23 percent. This is what can happen to your calls if the underlying stock rises significantly. (See Table 22 and Figure 24.)

BEAR MARKET OBSERVATIONS

When the price of the stock declines, the profits will come from writing (selling) calls naked; that is, selling calls without owning the underlying stock.

For example, the IBM October 220 call gave two very profitable sell signals. One sell signal came at $19, and was followed by a buy-to-cover signal at $13¾, a drop of 28 percent. The second sell signal at $12 was followed by a buy-to-cover signal at $1⅜, that is $1.37½, a drop of 90 percent!

If you had bought this IBM call at $19 and held onto it, you would have lost 100 percent of your cost by the time this call expired! (See Table 23 and Figure 25.)

Table 22

3/10/75 DJI = 776
5/6/75 DJI = 835

Day	*MTC Oct. 50 Price*	*MTC Apr. 60 Price*	*MTC Price*	*DJI Index*
3/10/75	$ 8.3	$1.1	$55	776
	7.6	.7	54	771
	7.1	.6	54	764
	7.0 **L**	.6 **L**	54 **L**	763 **L**
	8.0	15/16	55	773
	8.4 **H**	15/16 **H**	55 **H**	787 **H**
	7.3	11/16	54	779
	6.6	.5	52	769
	6.4	.4	52	764
	6.3	.3	52	763
	5.6 **L**	.2	50 **L**	743 **L**
	6.5	.2 **L**	52	748
	8.1	.4	54	766
	8.7 (B) **H**	9/16 **H**	55	770 **H**
	7.7 **L**	.4	55 **H**	768
	8.0	5/16 **L**	54 **L**	762
	8.1 **H**	.3 **H**	55 **H**	761
	8.0	5/16	54 **L**	752
	8.0 **L**	5/16	55	747
	8.3	5/16	55	743 **L**
	8.4	.2 **L**	55	749
	10.4	.6 (B)	58 (B)	768
	11.5	1.2	59	781 (B)
	14.0	2.7	62	790
	16.5 **H**	4.7 **H**	64	807
	16.0	4.3 **L**	64	815
	15.0 **L**	4.6	65	816
	17.2 **H**	5.5	65	819 **H**
	16.5 **L**	6.0	65	808 **L**
	17.3	6.3	66	816 **H**
	17.3	6.3	66	814
	17.6	6.5 **H**	66	802 (S) **L**
	18.2	6.4 **L**	66	804
4/25/75	18.4	8.4 Sell, Last Day	68	812 **H**
	19.6	Expired	68	810
	19.6		68	803 **L**
	21.2 **H**		69	821 (B)
	21.0 **L**		69	831
	21.4		70	848
	21.4 **H**		70 **H**	856 **H**
5/6/75	19.0 (S)		68	835 **L**
			68	836
			67	841
			67	850 **H**
			66	847 **L**
			65 **L**	850
			67	859 **H**
			68	849
			68	838 (S)

Figure 24

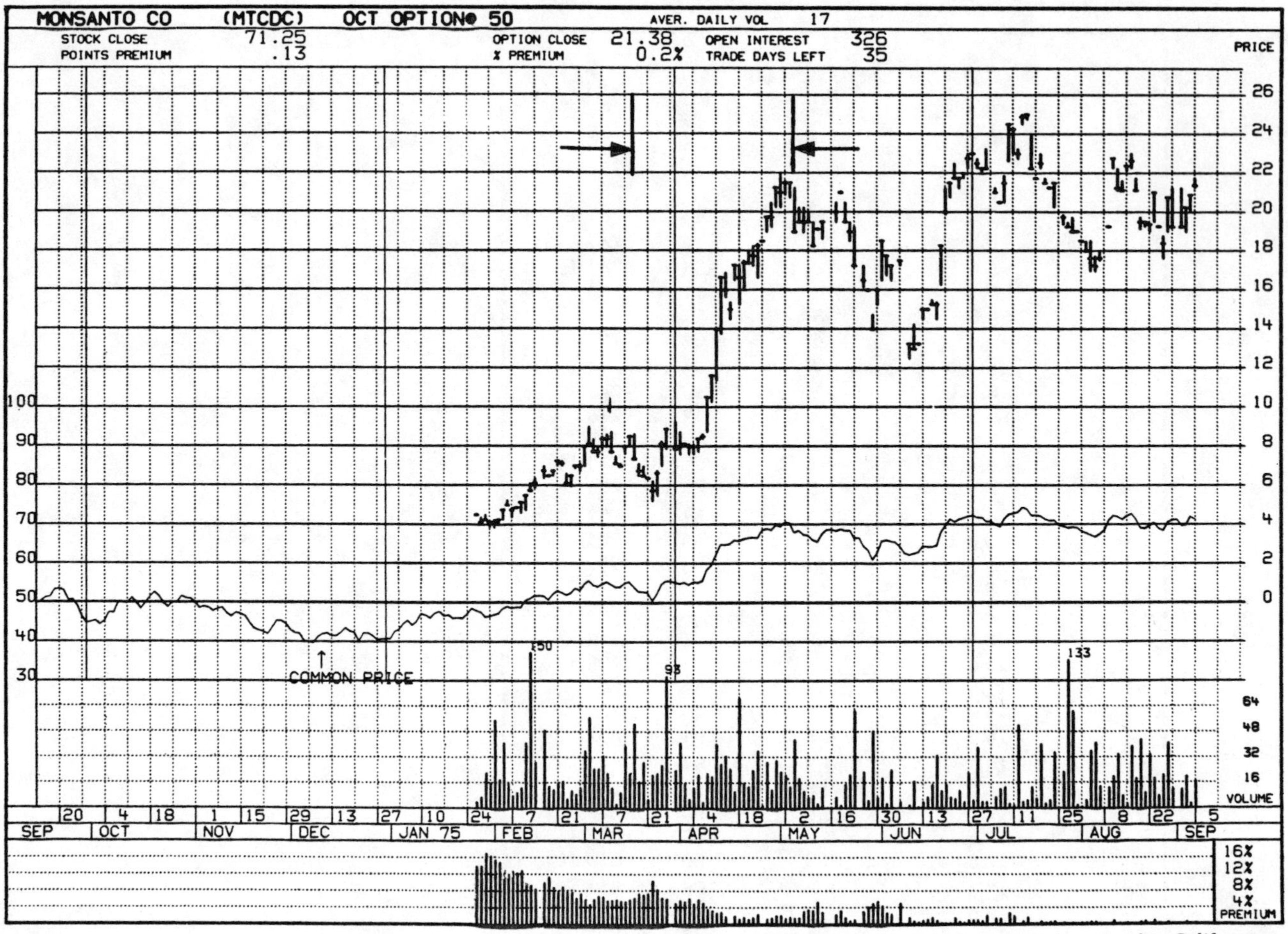

Courtesy of Daily Graphs, P.O. Box 24933, Los Angeles, Calif. 90024.

TRENDLESS MARKET OBSERVATIONS

Unfortunately, many stocks go sideways most of the time. The Avon Products October 40 and the McDonald's October 50 calls are good examples of what happens when stocks go sideways. In these situations, relatively few major profits are there to offset the many smaller losses. Hindsight tells us that these were the calls to stay out of during this period. (See Tables 24 and 25, and Figures 26 and 27.)

Like smoking, options may be dangerous to your financial health. The trading of options is complex, and not for most investors or traders. Although this discussion covers timing, which is, perhaps, the most important factor for successful trading, many other important aspects are not covered here.

Table 23
IBM Oct. 220

Day	Price	Day	Price	Day	Price	Day	Price
4/22/75	$17.3	5/29/75	$19.3 L	7/7/75	$ 9.2 L	8/12/75	$1.6
	16.0		20.4		10.1		1 5/16
	15.6		20.4 H		12.4 H		1.2 L
	15.6		20.2		9.2 L		1.4 H
	15.0		18.6		9.6		1.2
	14.4 L		14.2 L		11.0 H		.7
	17.2 H		16.7 H		9.6		.7 L
	17.0		14.6 L		9.0		1.0
	16.4 L		15.2 H		8.2		1.1
	18.0 (B) H		14.3		7.7		1 3/16 H
	16.4 L		12.4		7.6		1.0 L
	17.5 H		12.3 L		6.7		1.1
	17.4 L		13.1 H		5.1 L		1.3 (B)
	18.6		11.2 L		5.5 H		1.2
	19.5		11.4		4.7		.7 (S)
	23.0		13.6 (B) H		4.6		.7
	24.0 H		12.4 L		4.6 L		.7
	20.2 L		14.0 H		5.1 H		.5 L
	20.6		13.4		4.1		11/16 H
	21.7 H		13.1		3.5		3/16 L
	20.2		12.6		3.0		7/16
	19.0 (S) L		12.5		2 9/16 L		.4
	19.6		12.5		2 11/16 H		.4 H
	21.4 H		12.0 (S)		2.2		7/16
	20.6		11.0		1.7 L		5/16
	19.3		10.6		2.2 H		5/16 L

Figure 25

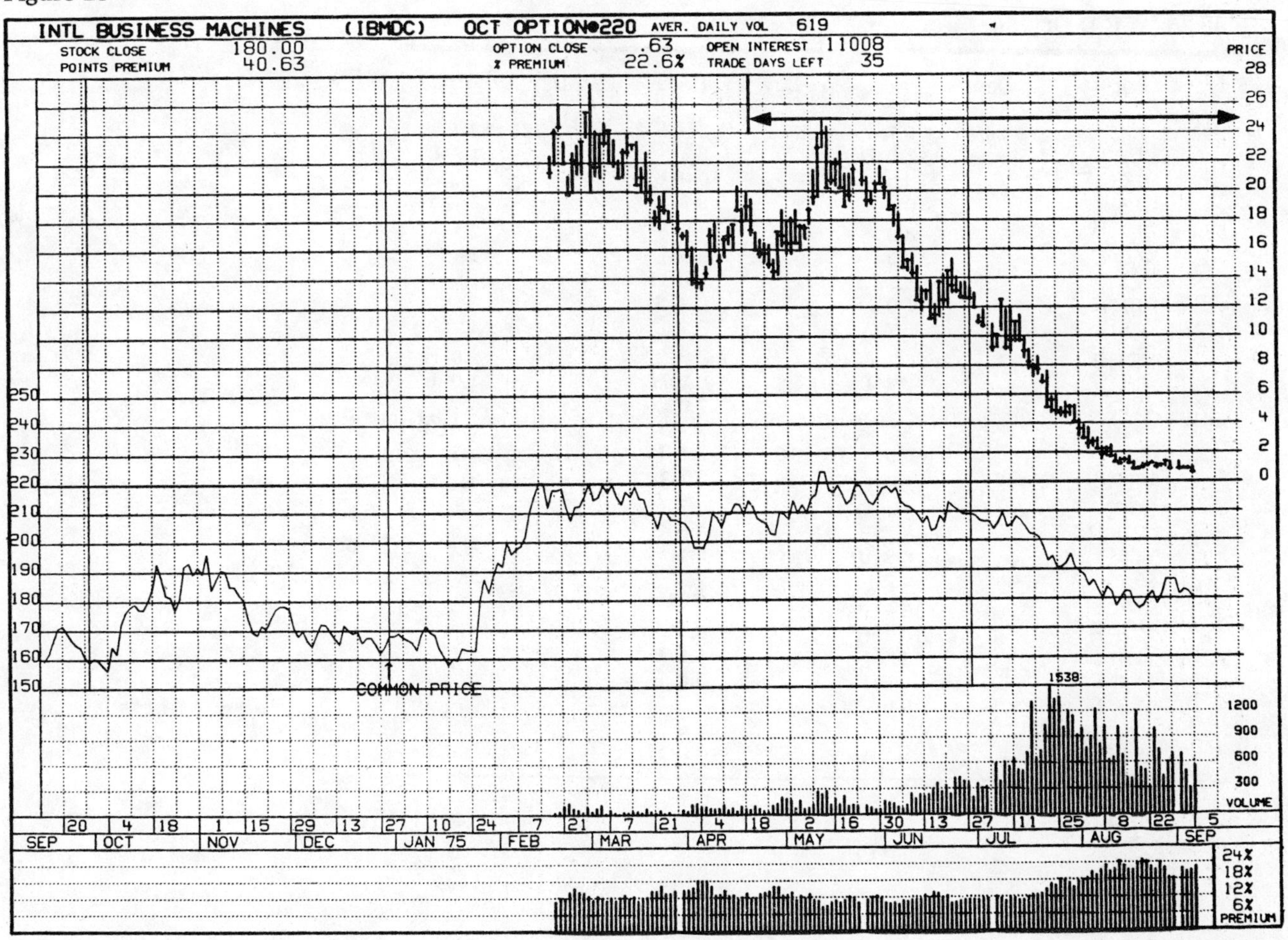

Courtesy of Daily Graphs, P.O. Box 24933, Los Angeles, Calif. 90024.

4/22/75 DJI = 814
9/18/75 DJI = 815

Table 24. AVP Oct. 40

Day	Price	Day	Price	Day	Price	Day	Price
4/22/75	$ 5.0 (B)	5/29/75	$11.0 (S)	7/7/75	$ 8.2	8/11/75	$4.1 H
	5.5		11.0 L		7.6 L		3.3
	6.6		12.0 H		9.3 (B)		2.4 (S) L
	7.3		11.6		9.4 H		3.0 H
	7.6 H		11.4		8.5 L		2.1
	7.4 L		10.6		10.2		1.5
	8.4		10.0		11.1 H		1.4 L
	9.1		8.7		9.6		1 11/16
	9.3 H		8.0		8.1 (S) L		2.1
	9.2		8.0		8.6 H		2.2 H
	8.1 L		7.0 L		8.0 L		1.7 L
	8.3		7.2		9.2 (B) H		2.2
	9.2		7.5 H		8.2		2 15/16 (B) H
	10.0		7.0		8.2		2.7
	10.3		7.0 L		7.3 (S)		2.1 L
	11.2		8.0 (B)		7.2		2.3 H
	12.2 H		9.0		6.6 L		2.1
	11.7 L		9.1		7.5 H		1.7 (S)
	12.1		10.0 H		6.7		1 13/16
	12.1		9.7 L		5.7		1.3
	12.2 H		10.0 H		4.3		1.0
	11.2 (S) L		9.5 (S)		3.1 L		15/16
	12.0		9.4		3.7 H		.7
	12.7 (B) H		9.0		3.6		.5
	12.4		8.2 L		3.1 L		.4 L
	11.2		8.4 H		4.1 (B)		9/16

Table 25. MCD Oct. 50

Day	Price	Day	Price	Day	Price	Day	Price
4/22/75	$ 7.6	5/29/75	$ 9.7	7/7/75	$ 8.3 (S) L	8/11/75	$2.7
	7.2 L		11.0 H		8.5		1.7 L
	8.4 (B)		10.6		10.0 (B) H		2 1/16
	9.1		10.3		9.3 L		2 5/16 H
	9.1 H		8.6		9.6 H		2.1
	8.0 L		8.6		9.5 L		1.4
	9.4		8.3		9.6 H		1 5/16 L
	9.7 H		7.0		8.7 (S)		1.3
	9.0 L		6.7		8.1 L		1.7
	9.3 H		6.7		8.3		2.0 H
	8.4 (S) L		6.4 L		8.3 H		1.3 L
	8.6		7.2		7.6		1 15/16
	9.0		8.6 H		5.4 L		2.4 (B) H
	9.3		8.0		5.5 H		2.1
	10.2 (B)		8.0 L		5.1 L		1.4 L
	11.5		8.4 H		5.3 H		1.5
	12.3 H		8.2 L		4.6 L		1.6 H
	10.6 L		8.6 (B)		5.1 H		1.5
	10.7		9.2		4.1		1 9/16
	11.7		10.6		3.3		15/16 (S) L
	12.0 H		10.7 H		3.3		1.0
	11.4		10.5		3.3 L		1 1/16
	11.1 L		10.5		3.6 H		1 1/16
	11.3 H		9.6		3.2		1 1/16 H
	11.2		9.4 L		2.5 L		.7
	9.5 (S) L		9.5 H		3.2 H		.6 L

Figure 26

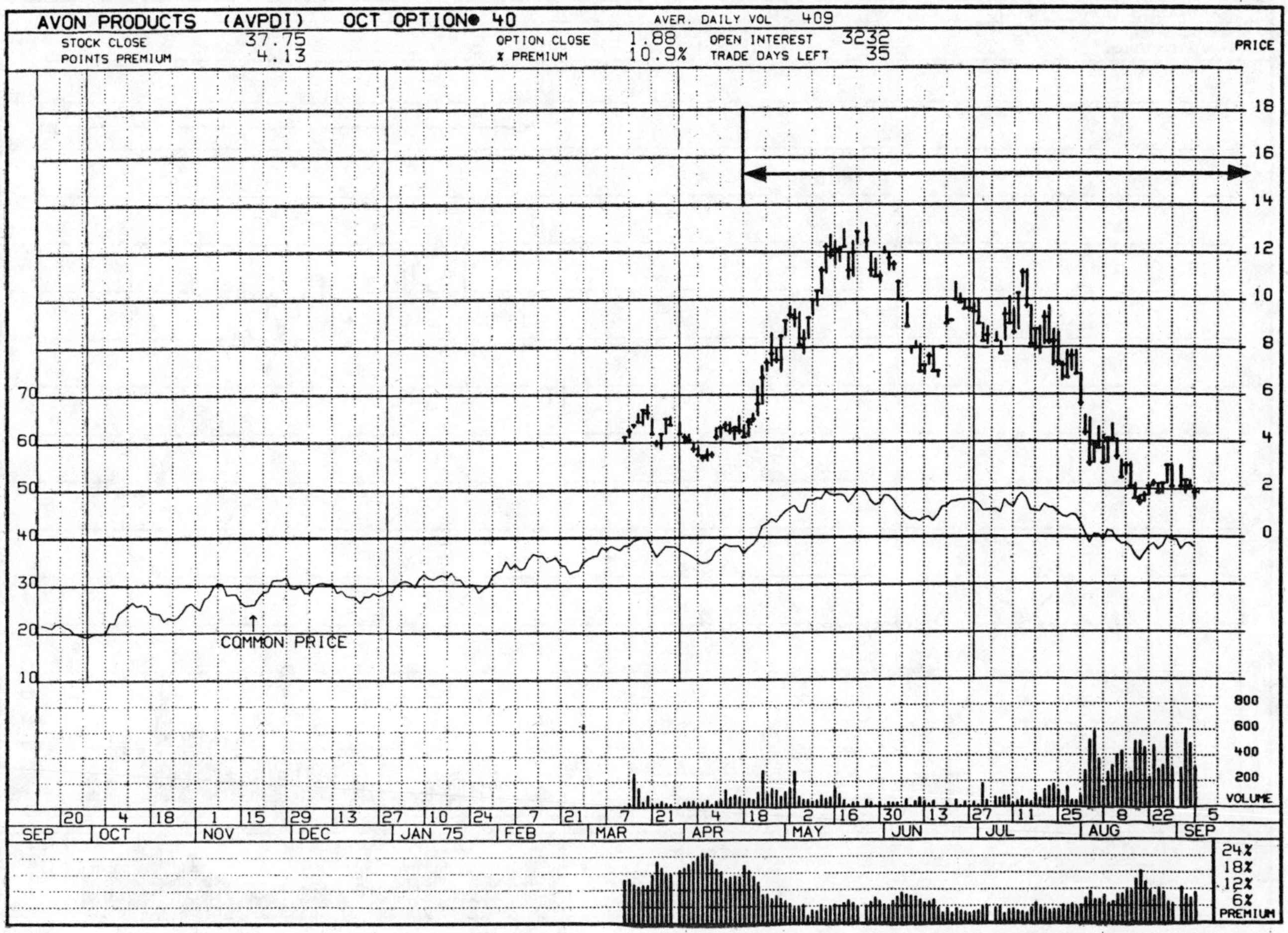

Courtesy of Daily Graphs, P.O. Box 24933, Los Angeles, Calif. 90024.

If I seem to discourage you from trading options, there is a reason. The buyer of options, who is hoping to make a huge profit, rarely does so. He usually loses all or most of his investment. He lets his option expire unused or he sells it before it expires, for much less than he paid. All this, of course, is fairly common knowledge among those in the options industry.

If you recognize the heavy odds against making profits with calls,

Figure 27

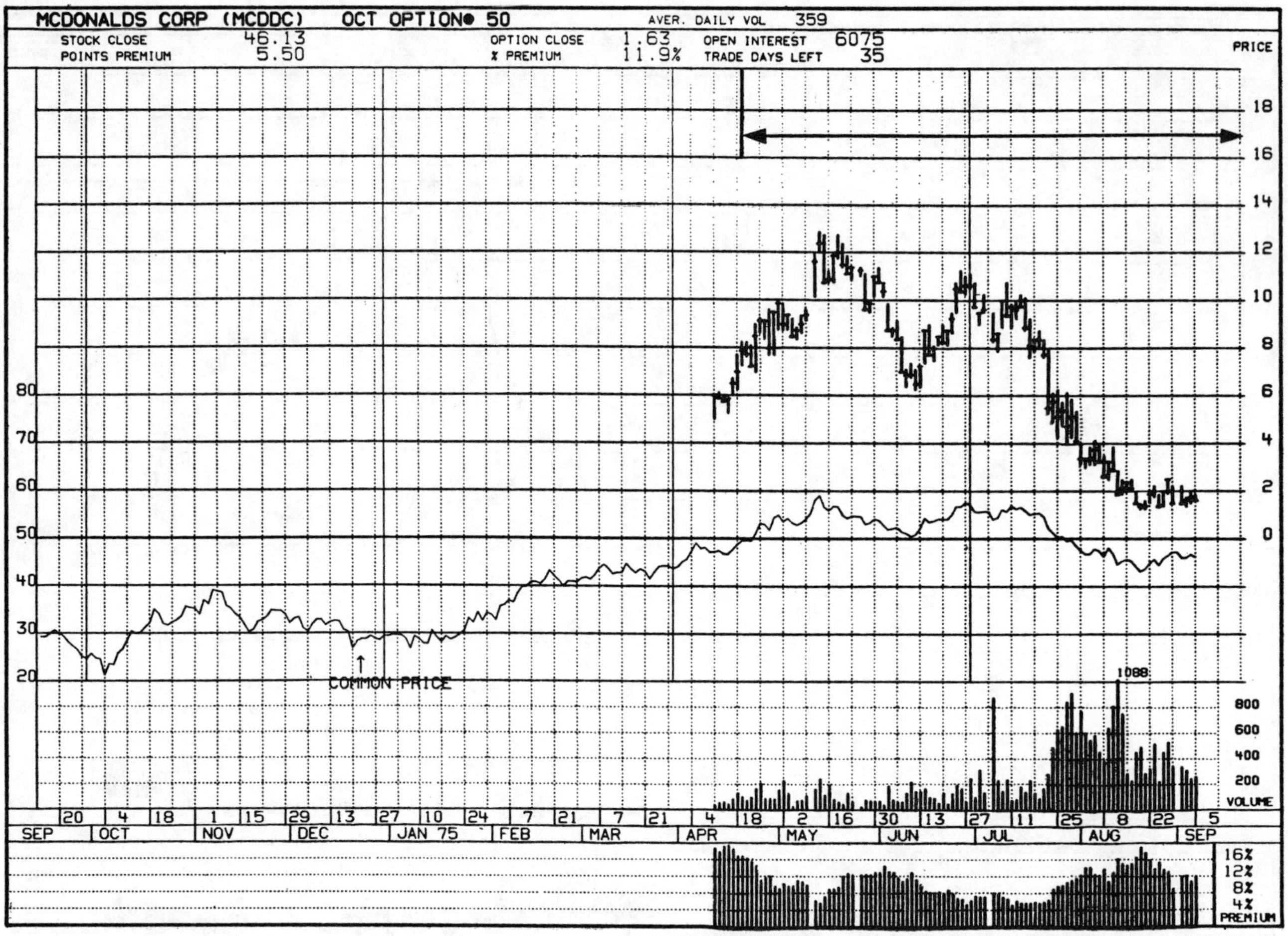

Courtesy of Daily Graphs, P.O. Box 24933, Los Angeles, Calif. 90024.

and you still wish to do so, be sure to have a plan for selling. Although the PBS does not guaranty profits, I've lost money every time I have chosen not to follow the PBS in trading options. I hope you gain from my lessons.

Chapter 11

Foreign Money and the PBS

Recently I learned that a small manufacturer had lost over a million dollars overseas, all because the U.S. dollar lost value relative to certain foreign currencies. After further investigation, I found that U.S. corporations operating overseas have probably lost billions of dollars, due to changes in the U.S. dollar value of the Swiss franc, German mark, British pound, French franc, Italian lira, to name a few. These facts usually are not publicized by corporations because they would reflect poorly on the managements.

Since foreign money does move up, down, and sideways, there is a great need to know the trends of foreign currency relative to the U.S. dollar. Therefore, this chapter illustrates one example of how the PBS might be used with foreign currency, e.g., the German mark.

The German mark, one of the major foreign currencies, was recently valued at 37½ U.S. cents, down from almost 44 U.S. cents six months earlier. This currency was selected for testing using the following premises:

The time period was 1¾ years.

Weekly closing prices were used. (See Table 26 and Figure 28.) (The value of the major foreign currencies in U.S. dollars can be found in most financial newspapers.)

"Up" (U) and "down" (D) signals were used (instead of buy and sell signals) to indicate when the trend of the German mark had changed, as defined by the Profit Box System.

Table 26
German Mark

Date	Value in U.S. Dollars	Date	Value in U.S. Dollars	Date	Value in U.S. Dollars	Date	Value in U.S. Dollars
1/4/74	$.3598 L	14	.3972	22	.4030	5/2	.4198
11	.3605 H	21	.3928 (D)	29	.4044 H	9	.4251 H
18	.3550	28	.3925	12/6	.4030 L	16	.4244 L
25	.3521 L	7/5	.3923	13	.4068	23	.4290 (U)H
2/1	.3611 (U)	12	.3913 L	20	.4108	30	.4267
8	.3620	19	.3920 H	27	.4136	6/6	.4264 L
15	.3669	26	.3903	1/3/75	.4180	13	.4282 H
22	.3762 H	8/2	.3886	10	.4204 H	20	.4271
3/1	.3727 L	9	.3863	17	.4194 L	27	.4252 (D)
8	.3766	16	.3804	24	.4306 H	7/3	.4190
15	.3773	23	.3789	31	.4274	11	.4129
22	.3875	30	.3756	2/7	.4241 L	18	.4003
29	.3948 H	9/6	.3743 L	14	.4298	25	.3960
4/5	.3941	13	.3751	21	.4332	8/1	.3893
12	.3921 L	20	.3757	28	.4391 H	8	.3878 L
19	.3954	27	.3763	3/7	.4293 L	15	.3884
26	.4046	10/4	.3822	14	.4315 H	22	.3891 H
5/3	.4058	11	.3845	21	.4309	29	.3874
10	.4136 H	18	.3877	28	.4265 (D)	9/5	.3871
17	.4098	25	.3886	4/4	.4204	12	.3852
24	.4036	11/1	.3895	11	.4189 L	19	.3794
31	.3964 L	8	.3920	18	.4195	26	.3752
6/7	.4020 H	15	.3987 (U)	25	.4195		

Source: *Bank & Quotation Record, Monthly, Commercial & Financial Chronicle.*

Here are the results from Table 27 below for the period January 4, 1974, through September 26, 1975:

Table 27

Date	Up	Down	Long	Short
2/1/74	$.3611			
6/21/74		$.3928	+8%	
11/15/75	.3987			−1%
3/28/75		.4265	+6%	
5/23/75	.4290			−1%
6/27/75		.4252	−1%	
(last)	.3752			+11%

Note that the average gain is considerably greater than the average loss, or five times, in this case.

If I were managing a corporation heavily involved in foreign currencies, I would use the PBS on each currency—kept by someone within the firm. I would not delegate this important task to any out-

Figure 28
German Mark—Value in U.S. Dollars

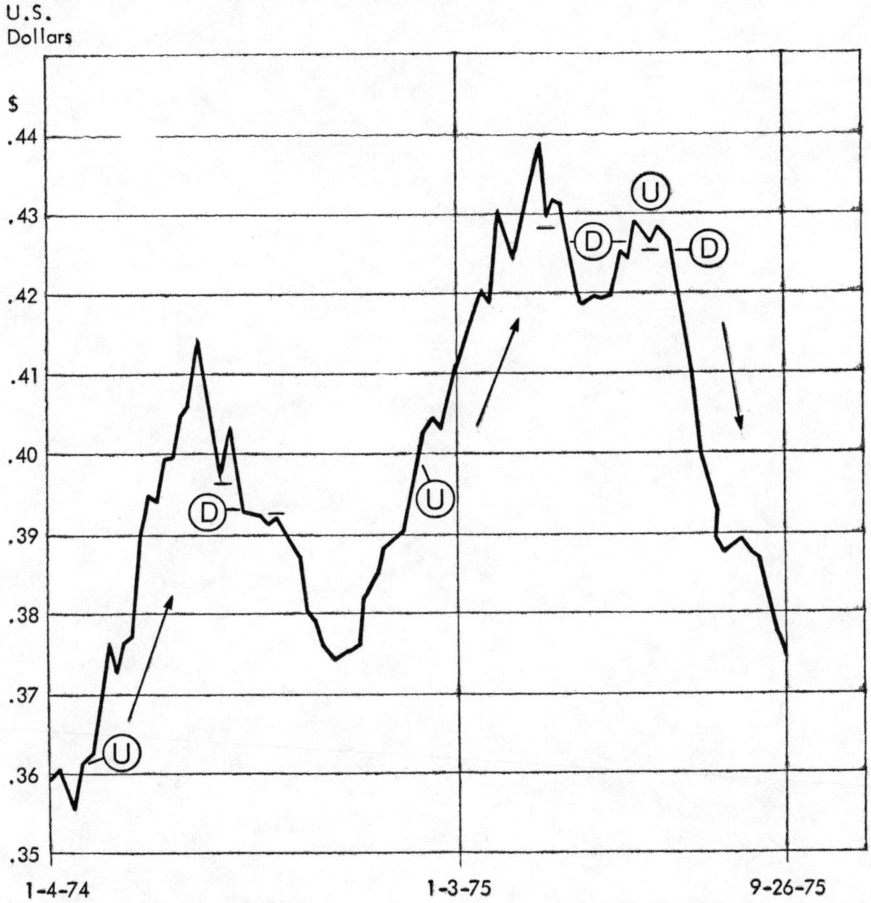

Source: *Bank & Quotation Record.*

sider, including my banker. When one has the capacity for losing or making millions of dollars in foreign currency, he should certainly know what the trends are. It can be a simple matter of corporate life, or death!

Chapter 12

Other Uses for the PBS

Can the concept of The Profit Box System be used for judging other trends? Yes! Any time I see an economic chart in the *Wall Street Journal* or another financial publication, I subconsciously apply the PBS to it, and it works surprisingly well. For example, the PBS gave an indication that housing starts had turned down at 2.15 million the first part of 1973, because this represented a lower lowpoint. (See Figure 29.) Two years later, in the first part of 1975, the PBS indicated that housing starts had turned up at 1.15 million, because it made a higher highpoint. This can be valuable information if your business or investments depend on housing starts.

The PBS has been helpful in determining trend changes directly from charts for other economic indicators. Here are a few:

Unfilled orders (measured in billions of dollars).
New orders (billions of dollars).
Weekly earnings (dollars a week).
Jobless married men (percent of labor force).
Leading indicators (Index: 1967 = 100).
Help wanted advertising (Index: 1967 = 100).
Unemployment rate (percent of labor force).
Industrial production (Index: 1967 = 100).

If I seem obsessed with the PBS, it's because I am fascinated, endlessly, with the PBS's ability to define a change in a trend!

Figure 29
Housing Starts

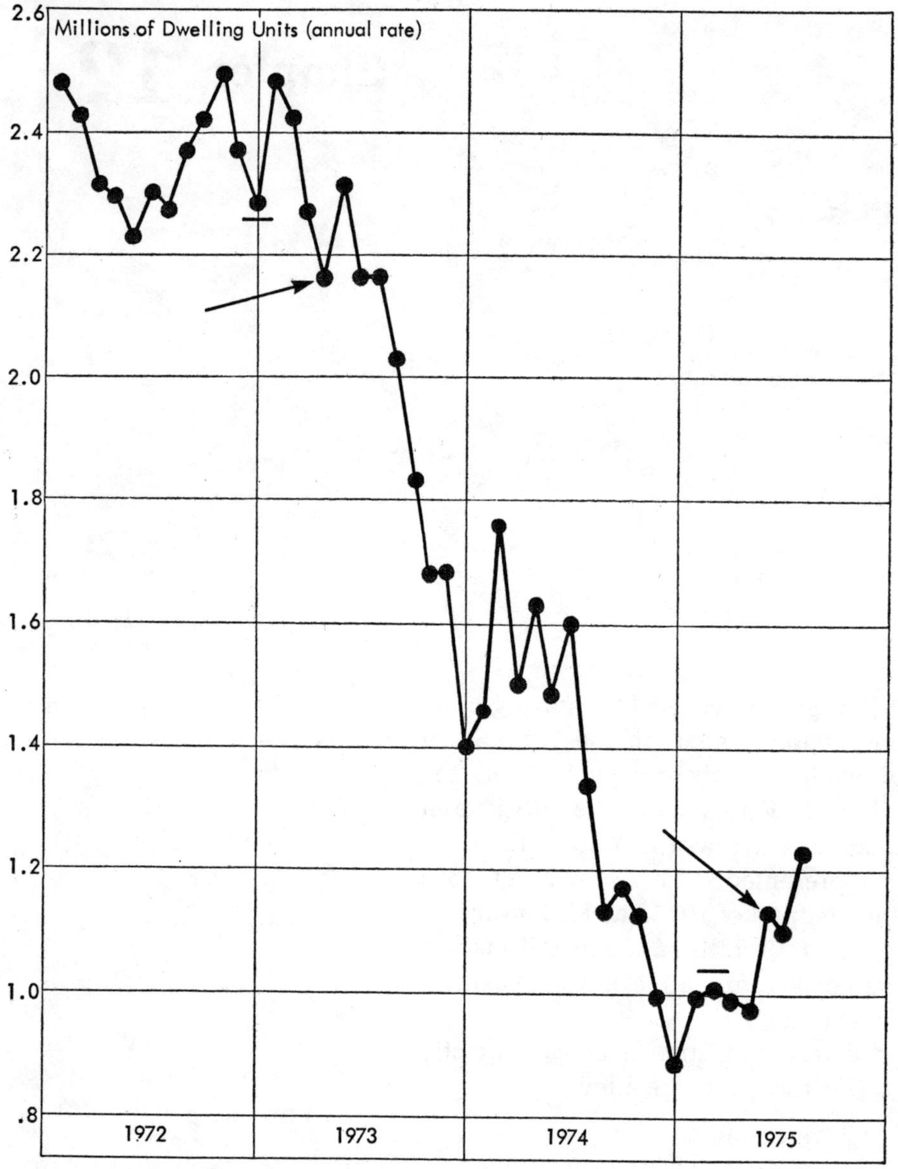

Source: *Wall Street Journal*, August 19, 1975.

Chapter 13

Is the PBS Really Practical?

ADVANTAGES

The PBS is simple. No interpretation is required. It is mechanical. Stock prices are recorded and acted on only once a week. It helps you in the constant struggle to be invested correctly, that is, to be fully invested in an uptrend, and in cash, or short, in a downtrend. It tells you very specifically whether a stock is in an up-, down-, or sideways trend, and when to buy, sell, or sell short.

The PBS can help a long term investor time his purchases or sales. For example, after a stock has had a long profitable run, the PBS can be particularly helpful in pinpointing a good time to sell, to nail down profits.

If you are following an attractive stock that is about to make a major move up, the PBS often gives you a buy signal weeks *before* the market turns up, or *before* the stock is recommended by brokers or financial services. On the other hand, a weak stock that is ready to drop a substantial amount often shows its weakness by giving a PBS sell signal long before the stock market indexes turn down.

The attractive feature in using the PBS is that you are likely to be properly positioned in your stocks *before* the major move in the stock market becomes obvious to most other investors, who lack the tools to tell them whether to buy, sell, or do nothing. Sure, you'll be embarrassed by occasional whipsaws where you buy, say, Xerox at $124 a share, only to find you must sell it six weeks later at $108, a loss of 13 percent. Losses are likely to happen on about half the trades. On the other half of the trades you should find that you purchased early, say, Xerox at $136 and sold it a year later at $236, for a 73 percent gain! If past experience is any guide, the profitable trades should be considerably more profitable, on the average, than the average loss trade! The times I've chosen to ignore the PBS sell signals have proven to be very expensive.

As pointed out by Mr. Gerald Levitz in the *Financial Analysts Journal*, market risk is four times more important than specific risk in reasonably well-diversified portfolios. The PBS makes it unnecessary to forecast the general direction of the stock market. This is important, because *there is lack of evidence to prove that either stocks or stock markets can be profitably forecast, in advance, in either time or magnitude.*

Even if the stock market could be forecast accurately, it is quite possible that a specific stock would not follow the direction of the market, e.g., Fairchild Camera lost ground in the general market rise of 1963 through 1964. The statistics do indicate, however, that more profits are made on the long side, in rising markets (1963–65, 1970–72), and on the short side in declining markets (1962, 1966, 1969–70, 1973–74.)

DISADVANTAGES

The PBS presents a trader with a number of psychological problems. It presents no intellectual challenge, once the decision has been made to use PBS. It requires unswerving discipline to carry out the weekly buy, sell, or hold indications. For some it requires tremendous emotional strength to take losses, and worse yet, to take a series of losses.

The PBS requires fast action. It assumes that no time will be lost seeking committee approval, or in further research, i.e., to determine the reason for a stock's weakness.

There is a human tendency to continually modify the PBS to improve results and eliminate losses and whipsaws. For example, one might modify the PBS by requiring a one point minimum higher high-point before getting a buy signal. Each modification would require more testing to see if the results improved significantly.

In using the PBS, versus buying a stock and holding it, both bookkeeping requirements and commissions are increased. Capital for reinvestment is reduced as taxes take their bite out of net profitable trades in taxable portfolios. (Fortunately, the largest gains using PBS tend to be long term gains, subject to much more favorable tax treatment.)

The PBS tends to work better in a market that is either in a definite uptrend or downtrend. Unfortunately, the market spends a great amount of time going sideways, which tends to produce whipsaws, losses.

Since the PBS is simple and no interpretation is required, it would appear that securities analysts could be eliminated for certain stocks, and that clerks could be substituted to administer purchases, sales, and selling short. This is, in fact, what William O'Neil & Company has done, according to Mr. William O'Neil in a speech before the Technical Securities Analysts of San Francisco. His buy and sell signals come from computer programs, and clerks execute the trades.

There are problems in implementing PBS, in spite of the substantial hypothetical profits for most of the stocks tested. For example, it is a rare trader who can stand, emotionally, to take a series of four loss or no-gain trades, as was the case with FCI on the long side in the 1963–64 period. This is, perhaps, the biggest negative to using the PBS—human inability to take a series of small losses.

Unless one can take a series of small losses, emotionally and financially, one should not attempt to use PBS in its entirety. Ironically, it seems to be easier for traders, emotionally, to take a whopping 50 percent long term loss than it is to take a series of small short term losses, which averaged about 10 percent each for FCI and 4 percent for IBM.

Because the market for the next six months is and always will be difficult to forecast accurately, one must expect to have as many losing as profitable trades, with the possibility of a series of losses, before realizing any gains. This concept of accepting losses applies particularly in the commodity markets, where successful commodity traders expect to lose on seven out of ten trades; however, they expect the average loss to be small and the average gain to be large. The net results are huge gains!

Appendix A

Are PBS Trades Random?

The number of profitable trades compared to loss trades appears to be random, like flipping a coin. For IBM long trades, there were 16 profitable trades, compared with 19 loss trades, a ratio of 16/19; short trades, 16/19; total long and short, 32/38.

For FCI, the profit/loss ratio was 11/20 for long trades; short trades, 19/16; total long and short, 30/36. Had trading cost adjustments been omitted, most ratios would have come closer to 50/50. The ratio of profit to loss trades is psychologically important to traders, but is only one part of the net profit equation.

Because of the almost 50/50 chance of getting a profitable trade before trading costs, it is important that the average profit is large, and the average loss is small. The experience in testing IBM and FCI was approximately 3/1 in favor of profits, e.g., on the long side IBM produced an average profit of 14.3 percent on profitable trades, or 3.4 times the average loss of 4.2 percent on loss trades.

FCI produced an average profit of 44.5 percent on profitable trades, or 4.4 times the average loss of 10.4 percent on loss trades.

On the short side, IBM had an average profit of 1.4 percent on profitable trades, versus an average loss of −4.5 percent on loss trades. FCI had an average profit of 16.8 percent on profitable trades, versus an average loss of 12.6 percent on loss trades.

Appendix B

Additional Statistical Observations

Here are additional statistical observations derived from hypothetical trading of IBM and FCI using the PBS over the 13+ year periods.

The longest series of profitable trades for IBM, trading the long side, was three; trading the short side, it was five; long and short side, it was three.

For FCI the longest series of profitable trades, trading only the long side, was three; trading the short side, it was seven. Being fully committed, long and short, it was three.

To take a series of losses can be emotionally devastating for inexperienced traders, even though the losses are relatively small. The longest series of loss trades for IBM, trading the long side, was four; trading the short side, four; trading both long and short, the longest series of loss trades was four.

For FCI the longest series of loss trades was four when trading the long side; four on the short side; both long and short, five.

Using the PBS with IBM was not significantly better than buying and holding, until the 1973–74 bear market. Thereafter, the PBS results were significantly better than buying and holding.

Trading FCI with the PBS was significantly better than buying and holding in the years of 1962, 1964, 1967, 1968, 1970, 1973, and 1974, but worse in the years of 1969 and 1972.

Appendix C

Statistical Analysis—FCI and IBM

	Applying the PBS to	
	FCI 10/27/61 to 1975	*IBM 1961 to 1975*
Gains, long trades	+250%	+245%
Gains, short trades	+72%	+42%
Gains, long and short trades	+502%	+389%
Number of buys	34	35
Number of sells, short sales	35	34
Total trades	69	69
Completed long trades, profitable	11	16
Completed long trades, loss	20	19
Number of long term gains	2	5
Largest long term profit	+179.1%	+45.0%
Average long term profit	+122.8%	+24.3%
Total long term profits	+245.7%	+121.5%
Average profit per long trade	+9.8%	+4.2%
Average profit per profitable long trade	+44.5%	+14.3%
Average loss per loss long trade	−10.4%	−4.2%
Largest profit trade, long	+179.1%	+45.0%
Largest loss trade, long	−37.2%	−11.9%
Longest series of profitable trades	3	3
Longest series of loss trades, long	4	4
Completed short sales at a profit	19	16
Completed short sales at a loss	16	19
Average profit per short sale	+3.4%	+1.4%
Average profit per profitable short	+16.8%	+8.5%
Average loss per loss short sale	−12.6%	−4.5%
Largest gain, short sale	+72.7%	+32.5%
Largest loss, short sale	−28.5%	−19.2%
Longest series of profitable shorts	7	5
Longest series of loss shorts	4	4

Appendix D

Conversion Table—Week Number versus Dates

Week	*1965*	*1966*	*1967*	*1968*	*1969*	*1970*	*1971*	*1972*	*1973*	*1974*
1	1–8	1–7	1–6	1–5	1–3	1–2	1–8	1–7	1–5	1–4
2	15	14	13	12	10	9	15	14	12	11
3	22	21	20	19	17	16	22	21	19	18
4	29	28	27	26	24	23	29	28	26	25
5	2–5	2–4	2–3	2–2	31	30	2–5	2–4	2–2	2–1
6	12	11	10	9	2–7	2–6	12	11	9	8
7	19	18	17	16	14	13	19	18	16	15
8	26	25	24	23	21	20	25	25	23	22
9	3–5	3–4	3–3	3–1	28	27	3–5	3–3	3–2	3–1
10	12	11	10	8	3–7	3–6	12	10	9	8
11	19	18	17	15	14	13	19	17	16	15
12	26	25	24	22	21	20	26	24	23	22
13	4–2	4–1	31	29	28	27	4–2	30	30	29
14	9	7	4–7	4–5	4–4	4–3	9	4–7	4–6	4–5
15	15	15	14	12	11	10	16	14	13	12
16	23	22	21	19	18	17	23	21	20	19
17	30	29	28	26	25	24	30	28	27	26
18	5–7	5–6	5–5	5–3	5–2	5–1	5–7	5–5	5–4	5–3
19	14	13	12	10	9	8	14	12	11	10
20	21	20	19	17	16	15	21	19	18	17
21	28	27	26	24	23	22	28	26	25	24
22	6–4	6–3	6–2	31	30	29	6–4	6–2	6–1	31
23	11	10	9	6–7	6–6	6–5	11	9	8	6–7
24	18	17	16	14	13	12	18	16	15	14
25	25	24	23	21	20	19	25	23	22	21
26	7–2	7–1	30	28	27	26	7–2	30	29	28
27	9	8	7–7	7–5	7–4	7–3	9	7–7	7–6	7–5
28	16	15	14	12	11	10	16	14	13	12
29	23	22	21	19	18	17	23	21	20	19
30	30	29	28	26	25	24	30	28	27	26
31	8–6	8–5	8–4	8–2	8–1	31	8–6	8–4	8–3	8–2
32	13	12	11	9	8	8–7	13	11	10	9
33	20	19	18	16	15	14	20	18	17	16
34	27	26	25	23	22	21	27	25	24	23
35	9–3	9–2	9–1	30	29	28	9–3	9–1	31	30
36	10	9	8	9–6	9–5	9–4	10	8	9–7	9–6
37	17	16	15	13	12	11	17	15	14	13
38	24	23	22	20	19	18	24	22	21	20
39	10–1	30	29	27	26	25	10–1	29	28	27
40	8	10–7	10–6	10–4	10–3	10–2	8	10–6	10–5	10–4
41	15	14	13	11	10	9	15	13	12	11
42	22	21	20	18	17	16	22	20	19	18
43	29	28	27	25	24	23	29	27	26	25
44	11–5	11–4	11–3	11–1	31	30	11–5	11–3	11–2	11–1
45	12	11	10	8	11–7	11–6	12	10	9	8
46	19	18	17	15	14	13	19	17	16	15
47	26	25	24	22	21	20	26	24	23	22
48	12–3	12–2	12–1	29	28	27	12–3	12–1	30	29
49	10	9	8	12–6	12–5	12–4	10	8	12–7	12–6
50	17	16	18	13	12	11	17	15	14	13
51	23	23	25	20	19	18	24	22	21	20
52	31	30	29	27	26	24	31	29	28	27
53						31				

Appendix E

FCI Summary, 1961–1975, Using 10 Week Moving Averages, Signals of +10 Percent for Buy, −10 Percent for Sell

Buy Action		*Sell Action*		*Gains*			*Cumulative Results*		
Week/ Year	*Price*	*Week/ Year*	*Price*	*Long Per- cent*	*Short Per- cent*	*Long Term Gain*	*Long 1.00*	*Short 1.00*	*Long and Short 1.00*
		51/61	$ 63						
11/62	$ 71	17/62	56	−21.1	−12.6		.78	.87	
28/62	48	42/62	42	−12.5	+14.2		.69	.99	
23/63	43	47/63	40	−6.9	−2.3		.64	.97	
28/64	28	26/65	39	+39.2	+30.0	L.T.	.89	1.26	
30/65	53	20/66	137	+158.4	−35.8	L.T.	2.31	.81	
28/66	193	37/66	163	−15.5	−40.8		1.95	.48	
3/67	139	22/67	104	−25.1	+14.7		1.46	.55	
46/67	97	3/68	80	−17.5	+6.7		1.20	.58	
14/68	78	24/68	68	−12.8	+2.5		1.05	.60	
36/68	74	7/69	72	−2.7	−8.8		1.01	.55	
16/69	81	25/69	71	−12.3	−12.5		.88	.48	
37/69	77	5/70	77	0	−8.4		.88	.44	
36/70	26	44/70	19	−26.9	+66.2		.64	.73	
50/70	25	28/71	38	+52.0	−31.5	L.T.	.98	.50	
36/71	40	43/71	31	−22.5	−5.2		.76	.47	
1/72	28	18/72	33	+17.8	+9.6		.90	.52	
28/72	42	13/73	48	+14.2	−27.2	L.T.	1.02	.38	
29/73	45	45/73	64	+42.2	+6.2		1.46	.40	
4/74	61	13/74	48	−21.3	+4.6		1.15	.42	.48

Appendix F

FCI Summary, 1961–1975, Using 10 Week Moving Average with No Modification (if price moves about 10 W.M.A. by any amount, buy; moves below, sell)

Buy Action		*Sell Action*		*Gains*			*Cumulative Results*		
Week/ Year	Price	Week/ Year	Price	Long Per- cent	Short Per- cent	Long- term Gain	Long 1.00	Short 1.00	Long and Short 1.00
		51/61	$63						
7/62	$66	13/62	63	−4.5	−4.7		.95	.95	
28/62	48	39/62	48	0	+23.8		.95	1.17	
48/62	47	5/63	45	−4.2	+2.0		.91	1.20	
18/63	37	26/63	37	0	+17.7		.91	1.41	
33/63	38	39/63	38	0	−2.7		.91	1.37	
40/63	42	47/63	40	−4.7	−10.5		.87	1.23	
28/64	28	34/64	23	−17.8	+30.0		.71	1.60	
39/64	25	43/64	23	−8.0	−8.6		.65	1.46	
45/64	25	46/64	23	−8.0	−8.6		.60	1.33	
48/64	27	24/65	41	+51.8	−17.3	L.T.	.92	1.10	
28/65	48	2/66	134	+179.1	−17.0	L.T.	2.57	.91	
3/66	149	10/66	176	+18.1	−11.1		3.03	.81	
13/66	185	16/66	179	−3.2	−5.1		2.93	.77	
24/66	171	31/66	172	+0.5	+4.4		2.95	.80	
32/66	179	35/66	176	−1.6	−4.0		2.90	.77	
50/66	119	19/67	172	+44.5	+32.3		4.19	1.02	
(3 for 2 split)									
28/67	109	30/67	99	−9.1	+4.9		3.81	1.07	
31/67	104	32/67	98	−5.7	−5.0		3.59	1.02	
40/67	96	41/67	88	−8.3	+2.0		3.30	1.04	
46/67	97	51/67	87	−10.3	−10.2		2.96	.93	
13/68	72	20/68	72	0	+17.2		2.96	1.10	
32/68	68	52/68	83	+22.0	+5.5		3.61	1.16	
13/69	78	23/69	77	−1.2	+6.0		3.56	1.23	
34/69	72	35/69	60	−16.6	+6.4		2.97	1.30	
37/69	77	47/69	82	+6.4	−28.3		3.16	.93	
52/69	92	2/70	89	−3.2	−12.1		3.06	.82	
8/70	88	9/70	84	−4.5	+1.1		2.92	.83	
36/70	26	42/70	23	−11.5	+69.0		2.59	1.40	
49/70	25	2/71	21	−16.0	−8.6		2.17	1.28	
3/71	24	25/71	42	+75.0	−14.2		3.80	1.10	
34/71	39	41/71	36	−7.6	+7.1		3.51	1.18	
50/71	29	17/72	37	+27.5	+19.4		4.48	1.41	
21/72	38	23/72	34	−10.5	−2.7		4.01	1.37	
25/72	38	37/72	36	−5.2	−11.7		3.80	1.21	
39/72	47	46/72	46	−2.1	−30.5		3.72	.84	
48/72	50	10/73	56	+12.0	−8.6		4.17	.77	
29/73	45	45/73	64	+42.2	+19.6		5.93	.92	
3/74	54	12/74	53	−1.8	+15.6		5.82	1.06	
19/74	53	22/74	50	−5.6	0		5.50	1.06	
35/74	35	36/74	30	−14.2	+30.0		4.72	1.38	
45/74	25	46/74	22	−12.0	+16.6		4.15	1.61	6.68

Bibliography

Allen, Leon B. *A Method for Stock Profits Without Price Forecasting.* Garden City, N.Y.: Doubleday and Company Inc., 1962.

Bank & Quotation Record, monthly, commercial and financial chronicle.

Cootner, Paul H., ed. *The Random Character of Stock Market Prices.* Cambridge, Mass.: The M.I.T. Press, 1964.

Daily Stock Price Record. New York Stock Exchange. N.Y.: Standard and Poor's Corporation, 1961 through 2d quarter 1975, 62 vols.

Darvas, Nicolas. *How I Made $2,000,000 in the Stock Market.* Larchmont, N.Y.: American Research Council, 1960, pp. 47–59.

"The Dow Theory—An Anthology," *Encyclopedia of Stock Market Techniques.* Larchmont, N.Y.: Investors Intelligence, Inc. 1971, pp. 304–72.

Festinger, Leon. "Cognitive Dissonance," *Scientific American,* October 1962, pp. 93–102.

Jiler, William L. *How Charts Can Help You in the Stock Market.* New York: Commodity Research Publications, 1962.

Krow, Harvey A. *Stock Market Behavior—The Technical Approach to Understanding Wall Street.* New York: Random House, 1969.

Levine, Sumner N. *The Financial Analyst's Handbook, vol. I,* Homewood, Ill.: Dow Jones-Irwin, 1975, pp. 944, 988.

Levitz, Gerald. "Market Risk and the Management of Institutional Equity Portfolios," *Financial Analysts Journal,* January/February 1974, p. 53.

Standard N.Y.S.E. Stock Reports. N.Y.: Standard & Poor's Corporation.

"Technical Approaches to Timing Market Shifts," *Your Investments 1969,* Rye, N.Y.: American Research Council, Inc., p. 178.

3-Trend Cycli-Graphs. Boston, Mass.: Securities Research Corp.

Woy, James B. *Investment Information, A Guide to Information Sources,* Detroit, Mich.: Gale Research Co., 1970.

Index

Das Kamasutra

Die Kunst der erotischen Liebe

DK

Inhalt

Vorhergehende Seite: Bereits die Stunden der Vorbereitung, in denen Dienerinnen sie für das nächtliche Liebesabenteuer kleiden und schmücken, sind für die Geliebte ein sinnlicher Genuss.

Gegenüberliegende Seite: Eines der drei wichtigsten Lebensziele für ein Paar ist Kama: Liebe, Lust und Sex in höchster Vollendung.

Einführung

Gegenüberliegende Seite: Eine Frau nähert sich mit verführerischer Absicht ihrem Liebhaber, dessen Gattin im Nebengemach schläft.

Kamasutra – wenn es ein Wort gibt, das unsere erotische Fantasie unmittelbar beflügelt, dann ist es der Titel von Vatsyayanas fast 1800 Jahre altem Lehrbuch über Lust und Liebe. Kein anderes Werk der klassischen erotischen Literatur ist bekannter und populärer. Kein anderes genießt den gleichen Rang und Respekt.

Von Indien nach Europa

Die Entdeckung dieses einzigartigen Meisterwerks der Erotik verdankt die westliche Welt den britischen Indienkennern Sir Richard Francis Burton und Forster Fitzgerald Arbuthnot. Bei ihrer Arbeit am *Ananga Ranga*, einem weiteren berühmten fernöstlichen Handbuch der Liebe, stießen die beiden immer wieder auf Hinweise zum *Kamasutra*. Mit Hilfe zweier indischer Gelehrter gelangten sie schließlich an die Handschriften, die jahrhundertelang in schwer zugänglichen Sanskrit-Bibliotheken verborgen gelegen hatten, und übersetzten den Text aus dem Sanskrit ins Englische – und zwar einschließlich fast

aller als »obszön« geltenden Begriffe. Nur *Lingam* (Penis) und *Yoni* (Vagina) ließen sie in der Sprache des Originals. Das war für die damalige Zeit, Ende des 19. Jahrhunderts, sehr mutig, da alles »Pornografische« der britischen Zensur unterlag. Aber Burton und Arbuthnot zeigten sich gänzlich unbeeindruckt von der Verklemmtheit ihrer viktorianischen Zeitgenossen und veröffentlichten im Jahr 1883 die erste englischsprachige Ausgabe. Seitdem hat das *Kamasutra* unzählige Übersetzungen und Bearbeitungen erfahren, und zum Glück sind die Zeiten längst vorbei, da die »heiklen« Stellen, wie in der ersten deutschen Ausgabe von 1897, ins Lateinische übersetzt wurden, um die Leserschaft nicht allzu sehr zu schockieren.

Oben: Der Mann muss die Frau zu sich heranziehen und ihr versichern, dass er sie liebt und begehrt.

Gegenüberliegende Seite: Der Mann gewinnt eine schüchterne Frau mit gutem Essen, Wein und zärtlichen Schmeicheleien für sich.

Folgende Seiten: Eifersüchtig beobachten Radha und eine Freundin Lord Krishna beim Flirt mit anderen Gopis (Hirtenmädchen).

Liebeskunst als Lebenskunst

Noch heute fasziniert uns am *Kamasutra* sein freizügiger, vollkommen unverkrampfter Umgang mit dem Thema

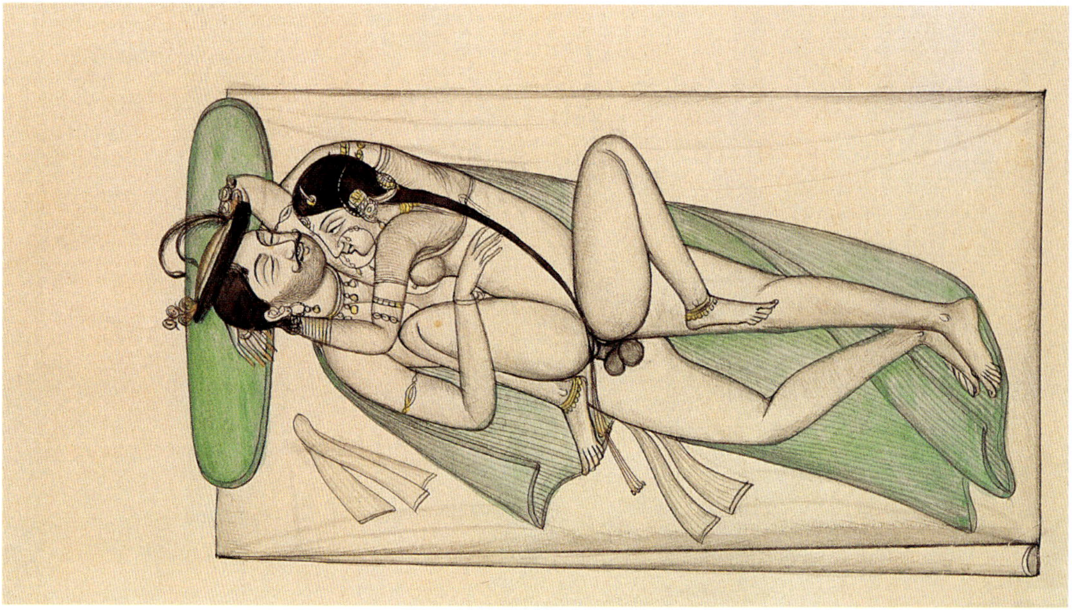

Nur eine Kultur, die Sexualität nicht als etwas Anstößiges empfand, konnte Kunstwerke schaffen, die die körperliche Liebe so offen und gleichzeitig zart, …

Erotik. Der kommt nicht von ungefähr: Dass guter Sex für ein erfülltes Leben mindestens so wichtig ist wie Essen und Trinken, davon waren die Menschen in Indien zur Entstehungszeit des Textes um 250 n. Chr. fest überzeugt.

Für den Autor Mallanaga Vatsyayana, der den Text teils selbst verfasst, teils aus noch älteren Quellen zusammengestellt hat, war es ein heiliges Anliegen, seine Mitmenschen durch seine *Sutra* (Abhandlung) im *Kama Shastra* (der Wissenschaft von Liebe, Lust und Sex) zu unterweisen. So ist der erste Blick ins Original für alle diejenigen, die bisher der Meinung waren, hier gehe es in erster Linie um eine Beschreibung der besten Sexpositionen, zunächst einmal überraschend, denn nur eines von sieben Kapiteln befasst sich mit den berühmten Stellungen. Das *Kamasutra* wollte sehr viel mehr. Für Hindus galten damals drei Lebensziele als erstrebenswert: *Dharma* (Tugendhaftigkeit und religiöser Verdienst), *Artha* (weltlicher Reichtum) und *Kama* (Liebe und sinnliche Lust). Zu den ersten beiden gab es zu Vatsyayanas Zeiten bereits bedeutende Schriften, zum *Kama* noch nicht – das *Kamasutra* schloss diese Lücke und gehört zusammen mit den

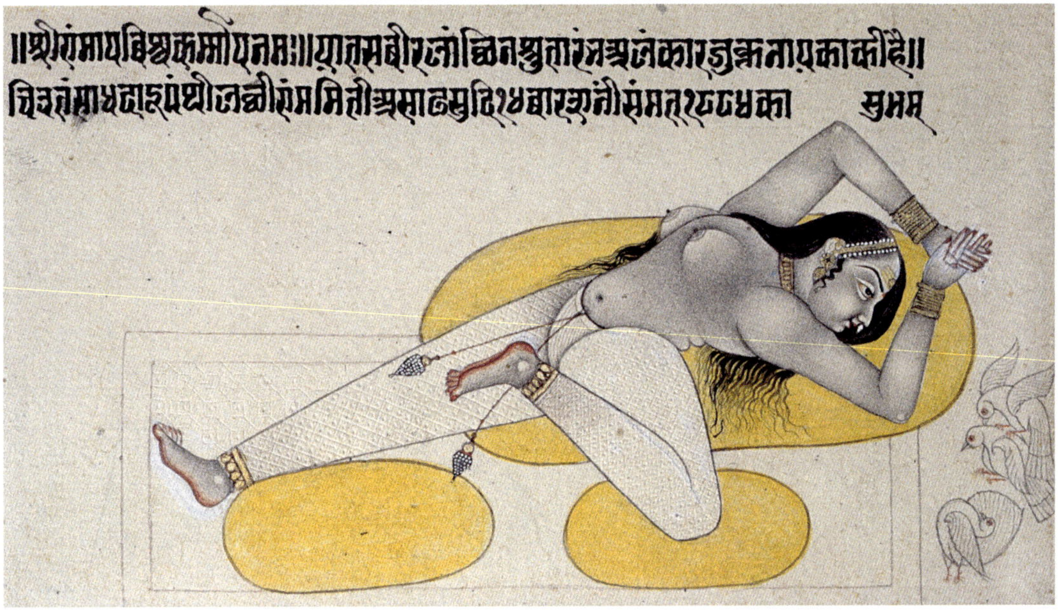

… so freizügig und doch einfühlsam darstellten.

anderen beiden Schriften zu den wichtigsten altindischen »Ratgebern«. Und so verrät uns Vatsyayana nicht nur die erfolgreichsten sexuellen Techniken vom Umarmen, Küssen und Beißen bis zum Oralverkehr, sondern schreibt auch ausführlich über Liebeswerbung, Heirat und Ehe und sogar darüber, wie sich verheiratete Frauen am besten zum Ehebruch verführen lassen. Seiner Leserschaft verspricht er als Lohn für die gewissenhafte Befolgung seiner Liebeslehren: »Eine intelligente und gebildete Person, die ihr *Dharma*, *Artha* und *Kama* beachtet, [...] wird in allem, was sie unternehmen mag, erfolgreich sein.«

Über diese Ausgabe

Wenn Sie mit den Menschen im alten Indien die Auffassung teilen, dass die Liebeskunst ein Teil der Lebenskunst ist, dann wird das *Kamasutra* für Sie ein spannendes und inspirierendes Lesevergnügen sein. Sie werden das vorliegende Buch, das auf der Übersetzung von Burton und Arbuthnot basiert, als eine wunderbare Begegnung mit dem klassischen Text erleben. Natürlich unterscheidet sich unsere Kultur sehr stark von der Lebenswelt des reichen indischen Edelmanns, den Vatsyayana damals, im 3. Jahrhundert n.Chr., ansprechen wollte. Für diese Ausgabe wurden daher die bekanntesten und wichtigsten Abschnitte ausgewählt, um Ihnen einen umfassenden und zugleich unterhaltsamen Einblick in den erotischen Kosmos des berühmtesten Liebeslehrbuchs der Welt zu bieten.

Die prachtvollen Bildtafeln stammen von verschiedenen, meist unbekannten Künstlern aus unterschiedlichen Epochen. Schon früh hat das *Kamasutra* nicht nur die erotische Dichtung Indiens, sondern auch die bildende Kunst inspiriert. Handschriften des *Kamasutra* wurden aufwendig illuminiert, um der Sinnlichkeit des Themas Ausdruck zu verleihen. Die mehr als 200 Malereien in dieser Ausgabe sind zwischen 150 und 500 Jahren alt und waren meist Auftragsarbeiten von Maharadschas, die sich ihre Handschriften von ortsansässigen Künstlern üppig ausstatten ließen. Besonders schön sind die berühmten Bildtafeln von Bikaner, die als die eleganteste Bebilderung des *Kamasutra* gelten (siehe Seite 25, 27, 32, 40 u.ö.) und dem Maler Ruknuddin zugeschrieben werden. Sie entstanden zwischen 1678 und 1698 und gehören heute der Sammlung des Fitzwilliam Museums in Cambridge/Großbritannien.

Gegenüberliegende Seite: Wir staunen heute über die ekstatischen Sexorgien, die es in jahrhundertealten Miniaturen und an über 1000-jährigen Wänden indischer Tempel zu bewundern gibt: vollbusige Schönheiten, aufreizende Posen und kopulierende Paare so weit das Auge reicht.

Das Kamasutra *heute*

Auch fast 1800 Jahre nach ihrer Niederschrift ist die alte indische Liebeskunst immer noch eine wertvolle Quelle für nicht alltägliche sinnliche Erfahrungen. Zweifellos wird Ihnen der eine oder andere Vorschlag kurios und vielleicht sogar lächerlich vorkommen, wie zum Beispiel jene Stellungen, die beim besten Willen nicht lustvoll umzusetzen sind. Folgen Sie einfach

Oben: Um neue Erfahrungen zu sammeln, kann ein Paar beim Liebesspiel auch Yogahaltungen ausprobieren.

Gegenüberliegende Seite: Stellungen, bei denen die Frau oben ist, sind für beide erregend.

Folgende Seite: Sich gegenseitig mit Pan (gewürztem Betelblatt) zu füttern, ist ein altes erotisches Vorspiel zur sexuellen Vereinigung.

der Empfehlung ausgewiesener *Kamasutra*-Kenner und betrachten Sie allzu Gewagtes mit Humor – am besten an einem stimmungsvollen, intimen Abend, gemeinsam mit Ihrem Partner. Lassen Sie sich ein auf Vatsyayanas poetische Sprache mit ihren fantasievollen Begriffen. Als Frau werden Sie begeistert sein, wie ausführlich das *Kamasutra* auf Sextechniken eingeht, bei denen Sie die Initiative übernehmen. Als Mann werden Sie für Ihre Rolle als Liebhaber und Verführer ungeahnte neue Perspektiven entdecken. Tauchen Sie ein in eine große, alte Kultur, deren Liebeskunst noch heute so populär ist, weil sie uns tiefe, zeitlose Einsichten über menschliche Sexualität und Beziehungen vermittelt – und sei es die, dass Leidenschaft letztlich ganz gut ohne weise Lehren auskommt. So heißt es im Kapitel *Vom Umarmen*: »Denn wenn das Rad der Liebe erst in Schwung ist, gibt es kein *Shastra* und keine Regel mehr.«

Teil 1

Über die sexuelle Vereinigung

Vom Studium des Kama Shastra

Männer sollten das *Kamasutra* und die ihm zugeordneten Künste und Wissenschaften studieren, zusätzlich zum Studium der Künste und Wissenschaften, die im *Dharma* und *Artha* enthalten sind. Selbst Jungfrauen sollten dieses *Kamasutra* zusammen mit den Künsten und Wissenschaften vor der Heirat studieren, und danach sollten sie das Studium mit Einwilligung ihres Gatten fortsetzen.

An dieser Stelle widersprechen einige gebildete Männer. Sie sagen, da es Frauen untersagt ist, sich mit Wissenschaft zu befassen, dürfen sie auch das *Kamasutra* nicht lesen. Doch Vatsyayana vertritt die Ansicht, dass dieser Einwand ungerechtfertigt ist, denn die Frauen kennen die Praxis des *Kamasutra* bereits. Und diese Praxis ist abgeleitet vom *Kama Shastra*, d.h. von der Wissenschaft des Kama selbst. Außerdem gibt es viele andere Beispiele dafür, dass das Ausüben einer Wissenschaft allen bekannt ist, obwohl nur ein paar Personen mit den Regeln und Gesetzmäßigkeiten der Wissen-

Gegenüberliegende Seite: Beim farbenfreudigen Fest Holi sind die Schranken von Alter, Kaste und Geschlecht vorübergehend aufgehoben. Die Frauen singen, musizieren und verkleiden sich sogar als Männer.

schaften vertraut sind. So sprechen die Yadnikas (Personen, die ein Opferritual ausführen) die passenden Worte, wenn sie sich an die verschiedenen Gottheiten wenden, obwohl sie weder die Grammatik beherrschen noch deren Schreibweise kennen. Oder Personen erfüllen ihre Verpflichtungen an glückverheißenden Tagen, die von den Astrologen festgesetzt wurden, obwohl sie von der Wissenschaft der Astrologie keine Ahnung haben. Ein weiteres Beispiel: Reiter von Pferden oder Elefanten dressieren diese Tiere, ohne über entsprechende theoretische Kenntnisse zu verfügen. Menschen in den entferntesten Provinzen befolgen die Gesetze des Königreiches, nicht weil sie diese studiert hätten, sondern weil sie aus Gewohnheit den Herrscher respektieren. Und aus Erfahrung kennen wir auch Frauen, beispielsweise Töchter von Prinzen und von Ministern sowie öffentliche Frauen, die im *Kama Shastra* tatsächlich versiert sind.

Eine weibliche Person sollte deshalb das *Kama Shastra*, oder wenigstens Teile daraus, lernen, indem ihr eine Vertraute die Praxis erklärt. Sie sollte im stillen Kämmerlein die vierundsechzig Stellungen studieren, die einen Teil des *Kama Shastra* bilden. Ihre Lehrerin könnte aus folgendem Personenkreis stammen: die verheiratete Tochter einer Amme; eine Freundin, der man völlig vertrauen kann; eine Tante, möglichst die Schwester der Mutter; eine ältere Bedienstete; eine verarmte Bekannte, die früher in der Familie lebte, oder die eigene Schwester, der man stets vertrauen kann.

Zusammen mit dem Studium des *Kamasutra* sollte eine Frau sich mit folgenden Dingen befassen: Gesang, dem Spiel von Musikinstrumenten, Tanz, Schreiben, Malen, Tätowieren. Schmücken der Familiengottheiten mit Blumen und Reis, Blumenarrangements auf Betten und Sofas oder auf dem Boden; Färben der Haare, Nägel

Gegenüberliegende Seite: Je verschlungener die Glieder, desto intensiver die Leidenschaft.

خلوت سلطان خرم ولد جهانگیر
عمل بهیم گجراتی

und Zähne; Bemalen des Körpers; Dekoration der Inneneinrichtung, der Betten, Kissen und Teppiche; Musizieren auf mit Wasser gefüllten Gläsern; Speichern von Wasser in Zisternen und Reservoiren; Anfertigen von Bildern, Rosenkränzen, Girlanden, Kränzen, Schmuckketten und Ohrgehängen; Binden von Turbanen und Haarknoten; Bühnenkunst und Bühnenbild; Zubereitung von Parfüms und Aromen; Anordnen von Schmuck und Kleidung; Zauberei und Hexerei; manueller Geschicklichkeit; Kochkunst; Zubereitung von Limonaden, kalten und alkoholischen Getränken, Obstsäften; Schneidern, Sticken, Nähen und anderen Handarbeiten, Lösen von Rätseln, Üben doppeldeutiger Sprüche und geheimer Zeichen; Kunst des Nachahmens; Lesen; Aufsagen von Reimen, korrekter Aussprache schwieriger Wörter und Sätze; Üben mit dem Schwert, Stock, Pfeil und Bogen; Erkennen von Zusammenhängen, Sinn und Logik; Architektur, Baukunst, Schreinerei; Numismatik; Chemie: Gesteinskunde, besonders Edelsteine und Juwelen; Färben von Edelsteinen und Perlen; Bergbau, Gärtnerei, Pflanzenkunde; Hahnenkampf, Wachtel- und Widderkämpfe; Kunst, Papageien und Starenvögeln das Sprechen beizubringen; Massage mit parfümiertem Balsam; Frisieren und Schmücken des Haares; Verständigung in Geheimschrift oder in einer künstlich veränderten Sprache, bei der Wörter verstellt, ihre Anfänge und Endsilben verändert oder neue hinzugefügt werden; Lernen von Sprachen und regionalen Dialekten; Anfertigen von Blumenständern; Erstellen mystischer Diagramme; Gebrauch von Zaubersprüchen und Amuletten; geistigen Übungen, z. B. unvollständige Verse komplettieren, Gedichte schreiben, mit Wörterbüchern und Nachschlagewerken umgehen. Eine Frau sollte Mittel und Methoden lernen, sich zu verkleiden und das Aussehen von Gegenständen zu verändern, beispielsweise Baumwolle den Schein von Seide zu geben und grobe und

Oben: Sparsame Berührungen an wenigen Körperstellen verdichten und verstärken das Vergnügen.

gewöhnliche Gegenstände als fein und außergewöhnlich erscheinen zu lassen. Sie sollte Methoden des Glücksspiels kennen; die Kunst, durch Mantras (heilige Sprüche) oder durch Verwünschungen den Besitz von anderen zu erlangen; Geschick bei Sport und Spiel haben, gesellschaftliche Regeln kennen, wie man anderen Personen Respekt zollt und Komplimente macht; Kriegskunst; arithmetische Übungen; das Anfertigen

Gegenüberliegende Seite: Durch jahrelange Übung erlangen Liebende eine besondere Körperbeherrschung, ihre Körper werden geschmeidig.

von Kunstblumen und von Figuren und Gegenständen aus Lehm sollte sie beherrschen.

Eine öffentliche Frau, gesegnet mit einem guten Charakter, mit Schönheit und anderen reizenden Eigenschaften und obendrein versiert in den oben aufgezählten Künsten, erhält den Namen Ganika, was öffentliche Frau von hohem Standard bedeutet, sowie einen Ehrenplatz unter der Versammlung von Männern. Mehr noch, sie wird stets vom König geachtet und von den Gelehrten gelobt. Und da alle ihre Gunst suchen, wird sie zum Objekt universaler Achtung. Die Tochter des Königs wie auch die Tochter eines Ministers, erfahren in den genannten Künsten, kann ihren Ehegatten an sich fesseln, selbst wenn dieser Tausende von anderen Frauen haben sollte.

Auch eine von ihrem Gatten getrennte Ehefrau, die in Kummer verfällt, kann sich – selbst in einem fremden Land – trösten und helfen, wenn sie über das Wissen dieser Künste verfügt. Allein deren bloße Kenntnis verleiht einer Frau Attraktivität, auch wenn deren Anwendung nur den konkreten Umständen entsprechend erfolgen kann.

Ein Mann, der sich in diesen Künsten auskennt, der beredt und mit den Feinheiten der Galanterie vertraut ist, gewinnt schnell die Herzen von Frauen, selbst wenn er mit ihnen erst seit kurzem bekannt sein sollte.

Von verschiedenen Formen des Beisammenseins und vom Liebeszwist

Im Vergnügungsraum, der mit Blumen dekoriert und parfümiert ist, von seinen Freunden und Dienern umgeben, empfängt der Herr die Frau, die, gebadet und nett gekleidet, bei ihm eintrifft. Er lädt sie zu Erfrischungen und Getränken ein. Er nimmt an ihrer linken Seite Platz, streicht ihr durchs Haar, berührt den Endknoten ihres Kleidungsstücks und legt zärtlich den rechten Arm um sie. Eine amüsante Unterhaltung über verschiedene Themen folgt. Und suggestiv wird das Gespräch auf Dinge gebracht, die als unanständig gelten und in Gesellschaft eigentlich nicht erwähnt werden. Danach beginnt man, mit oder ohne Gesten, gemeinsam zu singen oder Instrumente zu spielen, über die Kunst zu reden und einander immer wieder zum Trinken zu ermuntern. Wird die Frau schließlich von Liebe und Verlangen übermannt, dann sollte der Mann die anderen Anwesenden mit Blumen, duftenden Salben und Betelblättern beschenken und zum Aufbruch mahnen. Sind die beiden nun allein, so

Gegenüberliegende Seite: Bei einem nächtlichen Ausritt führt das Liebespaar eine vergnügliche Unterhaltung mit Freunden.

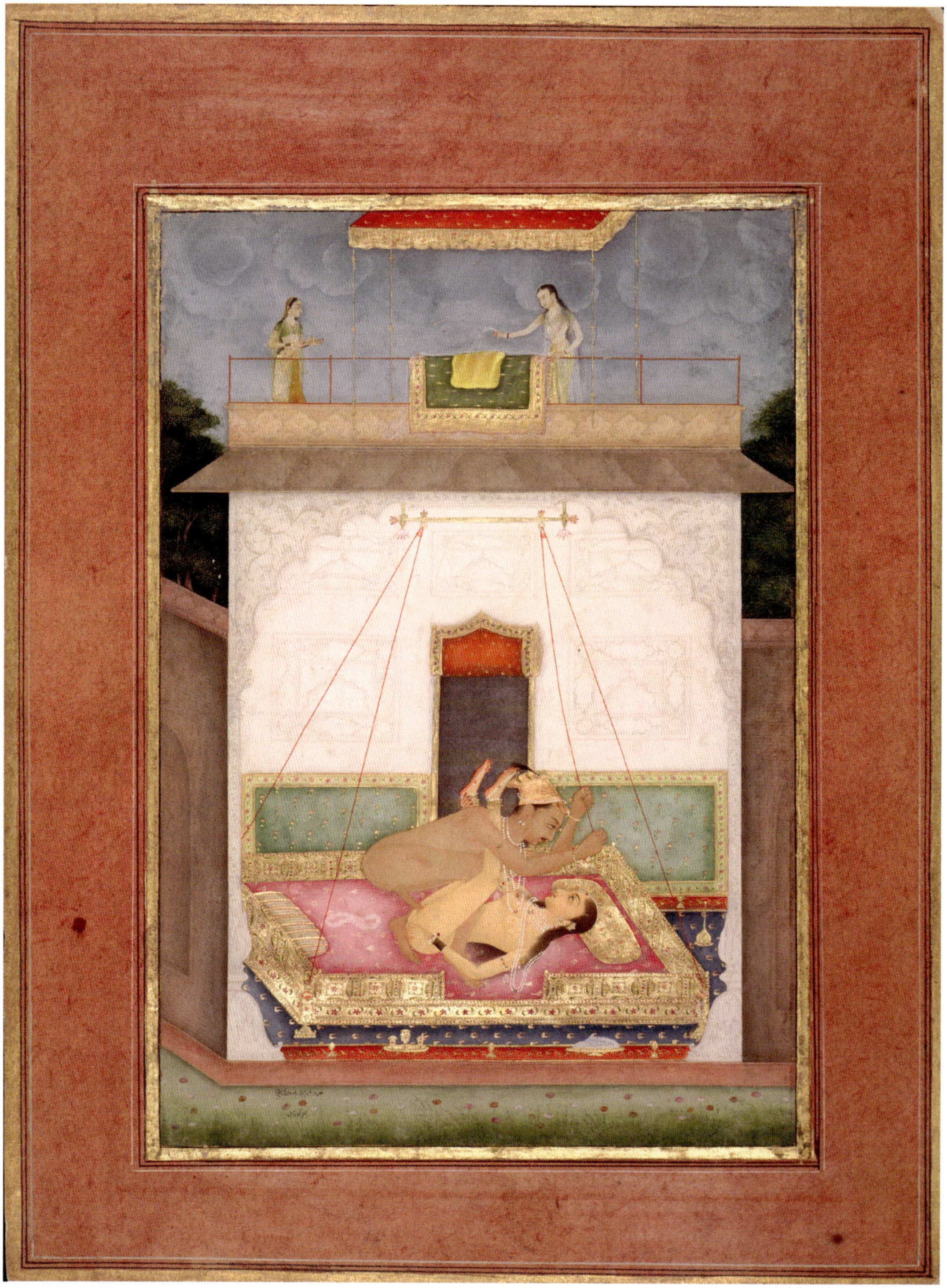

Oben: Der Mann stößt die Schaukel an, auf der die Körper im unbeschwerten Akt der Liebe hin und her schwingen.

Gegenüberliegende Seite: Frauen, die sich dem Drängen des Geliebten zunächst widersetzen und sich spielerisch zieren, gelten als besonders begehrenswert.

sollten sie verfahren, wie es in den folgenden Kapiteln beschrieben wird.

Die sexuelle Vereinigung wird etwa nach der eben dargelegten Art vorbereitet. Am Ende des Beisammenseins sollten die Liebhaber, in Sittsamkeit und ohne aufeinander zu schauen, getrennt ins Bad gehen. Danach, auf ihre jeweiligen Plätze zurückgekehrt, nehmen sie Betel zu sich. Der Mann reibt den Körper der Frau eigenhändig mit ein bisschen reiner Sandelholzpaste oder einer anderen Lotion ein. Er legt seinen linken Arm um sie und fordert sie mit freundlichen Worten auf, aus einem Pokal zu trinken, den er hält. Oder er reicht ihr Wasser zu trinken. Gemeinsam naschen sie Süßigkeiten oder andere Leckereien, die sie mögen. Je nach Wunsch erfrischen sie sich an Fruchtsaft, Sherbet, Mango- oder gesüßtem Zitronensaft oder an anderen Getränken. Auf alle Fälle sollten die Erfrischungsgetränke süß, mild und rein sein. Vielleicht auch nehmen sie Suppe oder Fleischbrühe zu sich. Die Liebenden könnten sich auf die Terrasse setzen, sich am Mondschein ergötzen und romantische Gespräche führen. Während die Frau in seinen Armen liegt, das Gesicht zum Himmel gewandt, erklärt ihr der Mann die Planeten, den Morgenstern, den Polarstern, die Sieben Rishis oder den Großen Bären. All dies schließt sich der sexuellen Vereinigung an.

Das Beisammensein kann auf folgende Arten stattfinden: liebende Vereinigung, Vereinigung mit nachfolgender Liebe, Vereinigung aus künstlicher Liebe, Vereinigung der übertragenen Liebe; Akt, wie der von Eunuchen, falsche Vereinigung, Vereinigung aus spontaner Liebe.

• Wenn ein Mann und eine Frau, die sich seit einiger Zeit lieben, sich nur unter großen Schwierigkeiten treffen können; oder wenn einer von beiden nach einer Reise zurückkehrt oder nach einer Trennung sich aussöhnt, wird das die »liebende Vereinigung« genannt. Sie wird so lange und auf solche Arten ausgeführt, wie es die beiden Partner wünschen.

Gegenüberliegende Seite: Frischvermählte sollten einander zunächst im Gespräch besser kennenlernen, ehe sie sich dem Liebesspiel hingeben.

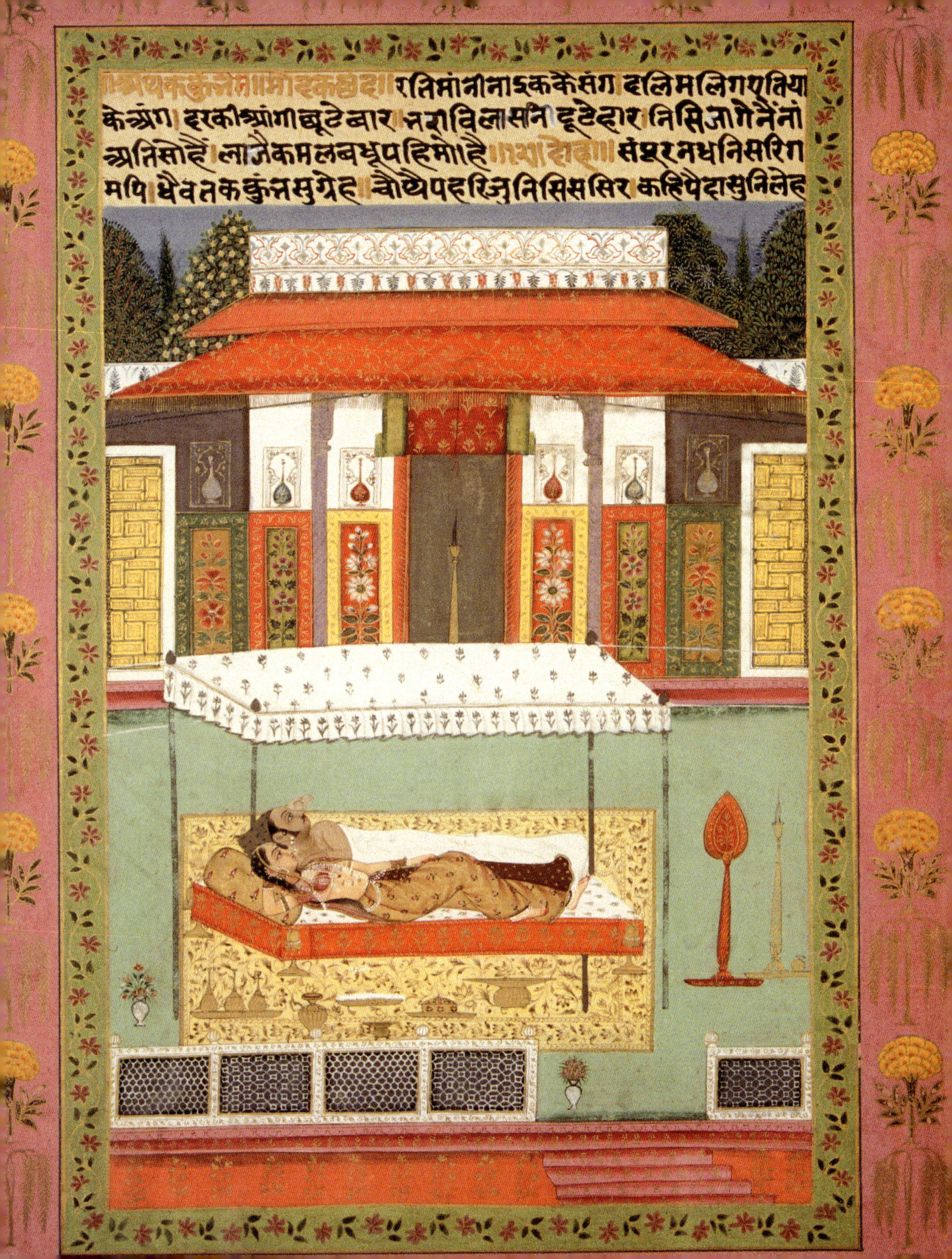
रतिमांनीनाइककेसंग दलिमलिगएतिया
केअंग हरकीअंगीछूटेबार नरा विलासनि टूटेहार निसिजागेनैंनां
अतिसोहैं लाजेकमलबधूपहिमोहै दोहा संपूरनमधनिसरिग
मपि धैवतककुभसुग्रेह चौथेपहरदिननिसिससिर कहिपेदासुनिलेह

• Wenn zwei Menschen zusammenkommen, während ihre Liebe noch im Anfangsstadium ist, nennt man das »Vereinigung mit nachfolgender Liebe«.

• Wenn ein Mann bei der Begegnung sich mittels der vierundsechzig Möglichkeiten erregt oder wenn ein Mann und eine Frau zusammenkommen, heißt das »Vereinigung aus künstlicher Liebe«. Dabei sollten alle Wege und Mittel Anwendung finden, die im *Kama Shastra* Erwähnung finden.

• Wenn ein Mann von Anfang bis Ende der Begegnung, trotz des Kontakts zu der Frau, sich die ganze Zeit über vorstellt, er sei mit einer anderen zusammen, die er liebt, dann ist das »Vereinigung der übertragenen Liebe«.

• Die Vereinigung zwischen einem Mann und einer Wasserträgerin oder einer Dienerin niederer Kaste, die nur bis zur Befriedigung der Lust dauert, wird als »Akt, wie der von Eunuchen« bezeichnet.

• Das Zusammensein einer Kurtisane mit einem Bauern sowie zwischen Bürgerlichen und Frauen aus den Dörfern und Nachbarländern heißt »falsche Vereinigung«.

• Das Beisammensein von zwei Personen, die sich zugetan sind, und das nach ihrem eigenen Geschmack abläuft, wird als »spontane Vereinigung« bezeichnet.

Wir wollen nun zum Liebeszwist kommen. Eine Frau, die sehr in einen Mann verliebt ist, kann es nicht ertragen, den Namen ihrer Rivalin oder ein Gespräch über sie zu hören oder gar versehentlich mit deren Namen angesprochen zu werden. Wenn das passiert, bricht ein Streit vom Zaune, die Frau wird wütend, schreit, rauft sich die Haare, schlägt auf ihren Liebsten ein, fällt vom Bett oder Sitz, schleudert die Girlanden und den Schmuck von sich und wirft sich sogar auf den Boden.

Jetzt muss der Liebhaber sie mit versöhnenden Worten beschwichtigen, sie vorsichtig hochheben und auf ihr Bett legen. Doch sie, nicht auf seine Gesten reagierend, sondern noch erboster, biegt seinen Kopf herunter, zieht ihn an den Haaren, schlägt ihn einmal, zweimal oder dreimal auf seine Arme, den Kopf, die Brust oder den Rücken und begibt sich danach zur Tür. Dattaka meint, sie sollte

Oben: Eine Frau schwelgt in den Erinnerungen an ihren Geliebten, während die Dienerinnen ihr kühle Luft zuwedeln.

Folgende Seiten: Kamadeva, der Gott der erotischen Liebe, macht keine Unterschiede – ob Mann und Frau, wie Krishna und Rhada, oder Mann und Mann: sein Pfeil entfacht bei allen gleichermaßen das Verlangen.

dann ärgerlich an der Tür sitzen, Tränen vergießen, aber das Zimmer nicht verlassen, denn das wäre ein Fehler. Nach einer Weile, wenn sie glaubt, die Versöhnungsbemühungen ihres Liebsten hätten den Höhepunkt erreicht, sollte sie ihn umarmen, in harschen, aber doch werbenden Worten zu ihm sprechen und ihr Begehren nach Vereinigung offenbaren.

Wenn die Frau in ihrem eigenen Haus ist und mit ihrem Liebhaber Streit hat, sollte sie auf ihn zugehen, ihm ihren Ärger zeigen und ihn dann verlassen. Später, nachdem der Herr die Vita, Vidushaka oder Pithamudra nach ihr geschickt hat, um sie zu beruhigen, begleitet sie diese wieder in ihr Haus und verbringt die Nacht mit ihrem Liebhaber. So endet der Liebeszwist.

Ein Mann, der die von Babhravya erwähnten vierundsechzig Varianten anwendet, erreicht sein Ziel und erfreut sich Frauen von erster Güte. Ein Mann ohne andere Kenntnisse, aber versiert in den vierundsechzig Möglichkeiten, wird tonangebend in jeglicher Gesellschaft von Männern und Frauen. Seine eigene Frau schaut in Liebe zu ihm auf, und ebenso betrachten ihn die Frauen anderer sowie Kurtisanen mit Liebe.

कोपरो है स्वभाव इसी ॥ थारा अधर रो अमृत म्हां ए दै ॥ नैं म्हो है जीवाड ॥ कीस भांत ॥
॥ इस सेथ के थारे विषे मन आरोप्यो है ॥ हेरा धेना राय एप्रतें अनुसर ॥

خلوت اکبر بادشاه

Von den Arten der sexuellen Vereinigung

Die Männer werden in drei Kategorien unterteilt, nämlich, entsprechend der Größe ihres *Lingams* (Glied), in den Hasen-Mann, den Bullen-Mann und den Pferde-Mann. Frauen unterteilt man ebenfalls, entsprechend der Tiefe ihrer *Yoni* (Scheide), in folgende drei Kategorien: in Reh, Stute und Elefantenkuh. Daraus resultieren drei gleiche sexuelle Paarungen zwischen den Personen mit zueinander passenden Maßen und sechs ungleiche Paarungen, wenn die Maße nicht übereinstimmen, insgesamt also neun. In diesen ungleichen Paarungen, wenn das männliche Organ das weibliche an Größe übertrifft, wird die Vereinigung mit einer Frau, die ihm in der Größe unmittelbar am nächsten kommt, als hoher Geschlechtsakt bezeichnet. Davon gibt es zwei Arten. Die Vereinigung mit der Frau, die von seiner Größe am weitesten entfernt ist, heißt hingegen der höchste Geschlechtsakt. Und davon gibt es nur eine Art. Andererseits, wenn das weibliche Organ das männliche im Ausmaß übertrifft, nennt man die Vereinigung mit

Gegenüberliegende Seite: Das Kamasutra unterscheidet verschiedene sexuelle Paarungen, z.B. nach der Leidenschaft der Liebenden.

dem Mann, der ihrer Größe am nächsten kommt, den niederen Geschlechtsakt. Davon gibt es wieder zwei Arten. Dagegen ist die Vereinigung mit dem Mann, des ihrer Größe am weitesten entfernt ist, des niederste Geschlechtsakt. Und davon gibt es wieder nur eine Art. Mit anderen Worten: Pferd und Stute, Bulle und Reh vollziehen den hohen Geschlechtsakt, Pferd und Reh den höchsten. Aus der weiblichen Sicht führen die Elefantenkuh und der Bulle sowie die Stute und der Hase niedere Geschlechtsakte aus, die Elefantenkuh und der Hase die niedersten. Somit gibt es entsprechend den Maßen neun Paarungsarten. Unter allen davon sind die gleichen Paarungen die besten, die Superlative, d.h. die höchsten und die niedersten, sind die schlechtesten Paarungen. Der Rest bildet das Mittelmaß, und darunter sind die hohen besser als die niederen.

Gemäß der Stärke der Leidenschaft und der Fleischeslust gibt es ebenfalls neun Arten der Vereinigung. Einem Mann sagt man eine geringe Leidenschaft nach, wenn seine Lust während des Beischlafs nicht stark genug ist, sein Samen nur spärlich kommt und er der warmen Umarmung einer Frau nicht entsprechen kann. Jene, die sich von diesem Temperament unterscheiden, werden Männer mit mittlerer Leidenschaft genannt, während jene mit intensiver Leidenschaft voll von Lust sind. Dementsprechend nimmt man von Frauen an, dass sie ähnliche Abstufungen in ihren Gefühlen haben, wie zuvor beschrieben.

Schließlich gibt es, gemäß der Zeitdauer, drei Typen von Männern und Frauen, nämlich die von kurzer, die von mäßiger und die von langer Dauer. Und davon gibt es neun Arten der Vereinigung. Allerdings bestehen bezüglich der Frauen Meinungsverschiedenheiten, die erwähnt werden sollen:

Auddalika sagt: »Frauen ejakulieren nicht, wie es Männer tun. Die Lust der Männer verebbt danach einfach, während die Frauen aus ihrem Lustempfinden heraus eine gewisse Art von Vergnügen verspüren, die ihnen Befriedigung verschafft. Aber es ist ihnen unmöglich zu

Gegenüberliegende Seite: Berauschende Musik und eine romantische Kulisse gehören zur hohen Kunst der Verführung.

Oben: Frauen bereiten Wein, Leckereien und Musik für zahlreiche sinnliche Genüsse des Mannes vor.

Gegenüberliegende Seite: So wie viele Männer einer Frau beiwohnen können, kann ein Mann vielen Frauen Genuss bereiten.

Gegenüberliegende Seite: Krishna als Spender purer Lebensfreude, dicht umgeben und getragen von einer Gruppe aus Sängerinnen und Musikantinnen.

sagen, was für ein Vergnügen sie denn erleben. Die Tatsache, aus der sich das ableitet, ist, dass Männer nach der Ejakulation sich zurückziehen und befriedigt sind. Aber bei den Frauen ist das nicht so.«

Dieser Ansicht wird widersprochen, denn ist ein Mann beim Koitus der ausdauernde Typ, dann begehrt ihn die Partnerin mehr. Ist er der schnelle Typ, bleibt sie unbefriedigt. Dieser Umstand, meinen einige, würde beweisen, dass Frauen auch ausströmen. Doch es braucht viel Zeit, die Lust einer Frau zu stillen. Dabei erfreut sie sich großen Vergnügens, und wünscht dies fortzusetzen. Zu diesem Thema gibt es einen Merksatz: »Durch die sexuelle Vereinigung mit Männern wird die Lust, das Verlangen, die Leidenschaft der Frauen gestillt. Und das Vergnügen, das aus dieser Kenntnis herrührt, wird ihre Befriedigung genannt.«

Die Anhänger von Babhravya glauben, dass der Samen von Frauen vom Beginn des Koitus bis zu seinem Ende strömt. Zu Beginn des Koitus ist die Leidenschaft der Frau mittelmäßig, und sie kann die Heftigkeit des Liebhabers nicht ertragen. Aber ihre Leidenschaft wächst, bis die Frau aufhört, an ihren Körper zu denken. Schließlich wünscht sie, mit dem Koitus aufzuhören. Gegen diese Auffassung lässt sich nichts einwenden, denn jedes gewöhnliche Ding, das sich kräftig dreht, wie beispielsweise ein Töpferrad, bewegt sich erst langsam, aber allmählich wird es sehr schnell. Ähnlich verhält es sich mit der Leidenschaft der Frau, die sich graduell steigert. Den Wunsch, mit dem Koitus aufzuhören, verspürt sie dann, wenn aller Samen verströmt ist. Und auch dazu gibt es einen Merksatz: »Die Ejakulation des Samens findet beim Mann nur am Ende des Koitus statt, während der Samen der Frau kontinuierlich fließt. Und wenn der Samenfluss beider versiegt ist, dann möchten sie den Koitus beenden.«

Oben: In der sanften Brise des Dschungels ist das heimliche Treffen erfüllt von lieblichem Verlangen.

Gegenüberliegende Seite: Beim Akt schwankt die Frau zwischem dem Zustand der Agonie und der Ekstase.

Schließlich äußert Vatsyayana die Auffassung, dass der Samen der Frau auf gleiche Art fließt wie der des Mannes. Nun fragen gewiss einige: Wenn Männer und Frauen Wesen von gleicher Art sind und dabei sind, das gleiche Resultat hervorzubringen, warum sollten sie dann verschiedene Arbeit verrichten müssen? Vatsyayana erklärt, das sei so, weil die Arten des Zusammenwirkens, bei dem die Männer die handelnden und die Frauen die empfangenden Personen sind, der Natur des Mannes und der Frau entspringen. Sonst würde ja der Handelnde manchmal die empfangende Person sein und umgekehrt. Und

خلوت سلطان خسرو ولد جهانگیر
عمل ننها مصور

aus diesem Unterschied im Zusammenwirken ergibt sich die unterschiedliche Auffassung vom Vergnügen, denn ein Mann denkt: »Diese Frau ist mit mir vereinigt.« Und die Frau denkt. »Ich bin mit diesem Mann vereinigt.« Wenn die Arten im Zusammenwirken von Mann und Frau sich unterscheiden, warum, so könnte man fragen, sollte es dann nicht auch einen Unterschied im Vergnügen geben, das sie dabei empfinden. Dieser Einwand ist gegenstandslos, denn für die agierende und für die empfangende Person, die von verschiedener Art sind, gibt es einen Grund für die unterschiedliche Art ihres Zusammenwirkens. Doch es gibt keinen Grund für einen Unterschied im Vergnügen, das sie spüren, weil sie beide natürlich von dem Geschlechtsakt, den sie ausüben, Vergnügen erlangen.

Da mögen wiederum einige einwenden: Wenn verschiedene Personen dieselbe Tätigkeit verrichten, dann finden wir, erreichen sie dasselbe Ende oder Ziel. Im Gegensatz dazu finden wir, dass im Fall von Mann und Frau jeder sein eigenes Ziel getrennt erreicht, was widersinnig scheint. Aber das ist ein Irrtum, denn wir finden, dass manchmal zwei Sachen zur selben Zeit getan werden. Zum Beispiel beim Kampf der Widder erhalten beide Tiere den Stoß an den Kopf zur selben Zeit. Ebenso ist es, wenn man einen Apfel gegen den anderen wirft, oder beim Ringkampf. Wenn gesagt wird, dass in diesen Fällen die im Spiel befindlichen Dinge dieselben sind, lautet die Antwort, dass auch im Fall von Mann und Frau die Natur der beiden Personen dieselbe ist. Und so wie der Unterschied in der Art ihres Zusammenwirkens nur aus dem Unterschied ihrer Gestaltung entsteht, so folgt, dass Männer dasselbe Vergnügen empfinden wie Frauen.

Der Merksatz zu diesem Thema lautet: »Männer und Frauen von gleicher Wesensart spüren dieselbe Art von Vergnügen. Und deshalb sollte ein Mann eine solche Frau heiraten, denn sie wird ihn ein Leben lang lieben.«

Da nun erwiesen ist, dass Männer und Frauen dasselbe Vergnügen erleben, folgt in Bezug auf die Zeitdauer, dass es neun Arten der sexuellen Vereinigung gibt, genauso wie es neun Arten der Vereinigung in Bezug auf die Leidenschaft gibt. Somit existieren neun Arten der Vereinigung bezüglich der Maße der Organe, der Kraft der Leidenschaft und der Zeitdauer. Kombinationen daraus führen zu zahllosen Möglichkeiten. Deshalb sollten Männer für jede spezielle Form des Beischlafs solche Mittel wählen, die ihnen am passendsten für diese Gelegenheit erscheinen. Beim ersten Beischlaf ist die Leidenschaft des Mannes intensiv, und er kommt schnell. Aber bei weiteren Vereinigungen am selben Tag wird das Gegenteil der Fall sein. Mit der Partnerin ist es genau umgekehrt, denn beim ersten Mal ist ihre Leidenschaft noch schwach, aber dann braucht sie viel Zeit, bis ihr Verlangen befriedigt wird. Männer mit großer Lebenserfahrung vertreten die Meinung, dass es vier Arten von Liebe gibt: die durch dauernde Gewohnheit erworbene Liebe; die aus der Vorstellung resultierende Liebe; die aus dem Glauben abgeleitete Liebe; die von der Vorstellung der Existenz äußerer Objekte stammende Liebe.

• Liebe, die aus konstanter und fortgesetzter Durchführung eines Aktes rührt, heißt durch ständiges Praktizieren und durch Gewohnheit erworbene Liebe. Beispiele sind die Liebe zum Geschlechtsverkehr oder zur Jagd.

• Liebe, die man für etwas empfindet, an das wir nicht gewöhnt sind und das nur in Gedanken besteht, heißt aus der Vorstellung resultierende Liebe. Dazu gehört z. B. die Liebe, die einige Männer und Frauen und Eunuchen für den Auparishtaka, den Oralverkehr, verspüren, sowie die Liebe, die alle für die Umarmung, das Küssen usw. empfinden.

• Die Liebe, die auf Gegenseitigkeit beruht und sich als wahrhaft erweist, bei der einer den anderen als sein Selbst betrachtet, nennen die Erfahrenen aus dem Glauben resultierende Liebe.

• Die Liebe, die aus der Annahme von der Existenz äußerer Objekte resultiert, ist recht evident und der Welt gut bekannt, weil das Vergnügen, das sie bereitet, dem Vergnügen der anderen Formen der Liebe überlegen ist, die nur um ihrer selbst willen existiert.

Vom Umarmen

Dieser Teil des *Kama Shastra*, der die sexuelle Vereinigung behandelt, ist unter dem Namen »Vierundsechzig« – *Chatush-shashti* – bekannt. Einige ältere Autoren sagen, das leite sich aus den vierundsechzig im Werk enthaltenen Kapiteln ab. Andere sind der Meinung, dass der Verfasser dieses Teils Panchala hieß. Und die Person, die den Abschnitt des *Rigveda* rezitierte, der *Dashatapa* genannt wird und vierundsechzig Strophen enthält, hieß ebenfalls Panchala. So habe man diesem Teil des Werkes zu Ehren des *Rigveda* den Namen »vierundsechzig« gegeben. Andererseits behaupten die Anhänger Babhravyas, dass dieser Teil acht Themen enthält, nämlich die Umarmung, das Küssen, Kratzen mit den Fingernägeln, Beißen, Hinlegen, Laute von sich geben, den Teil des Mannes spielen und Oralverkehr. Jedes dieser Themen unterteilt sich in acht Abschnitte. Acht mal acht sind vierundsechzig. Deshalb heißt dieser Teil des *Kama Shastra* eben »vierundsechzig«. Doch Vatsyayana erklärt, dass dieser Name wohl zufällig gegeben wurde, da dieser

Gegenüberliegende Seite: Ein Frau zeigt ihre heftige Leidenschaft bei ihrer Umarmung, wenn sie sich um den Mann legt, wie »eine Ranke sich um einen Baum schlingt«.

Teil des Buches auch die Themen Schlagen, Schreien, die Handlungen des Mannes während der Vereinigung, die verschiedenen Arten des Koitus usw. enthält. Beispielsweise sagen wir doch, dies ist »Saptaparna«, der siebenblättrige Baum. Oder wir sagen: Dieser Reis zum Opfern ist »Panchavarna«, also fünffarbig. Trotzdem wissen wir doch, dass der Baum keine sieben Blätter und der Reis keine fünf Farben hat.

Genug jetzt zur Erklärung der »vierundsechzig«. Wenden wir uns dem ersten Thema zu, dem Umarmen. Es zeigt die gegenseitige Liebe eines Mannes und einer Frau an, die sich treffen. Es besteht aus vier Möglichkeiten, nämlich dem Berühren, dem Anbändeln, dem Reiben und dem Drücken. In jedem einzelnen Fall benennt das Wort, was gemacht wird.

• Wenn ein Mann unter dem einen oder anderen Vorwand neben einer Frau geht und dabei ihren Körper mit dem seinen berührt, dann bezeichnet man das als »berührendes Umarmen«.

• Wenn sich eine Frau an einer abgelegenen Stelle bückt, als ob sie etwas aufheben wollte, und dabei einen sitzenden oder stehenden Mann mit ihren hochgedrückten Brüsten lockt, so dass er nach ihnen greift, dann heißt das »anbändelndes Umarmen«.

Beide Umarmungsformen finden nur zwischen Personen statt, die noch nicht offen miteinander reden.

• Wenn zwei Liebende in der Dunkelheit oder an einem einsamen Ort gemeinsam spazieren und ihre Körper aneinander reiben, dann heißt das »reibendes Umarmen«.

• Wenn bei der eben erwähnten Gelegenheit einer von beiden den Körper des anderen kräftig gegen eine Mauer oder Säule drückt, dann heißt das »drückendes Umarmen« Die beiden letzen Umarmungen sind jenen eigen, die die Absichten des anderen kennen.

Zur Zeit der Begegnung sind die folgenden vier Umarmungen üblich: *Jataveshitaka* oder wie sich eine Ranke windet; *Vrikshadhirudhaka* oder das Erklettern eines Baumes; *Til-tandulaka* oder das Mischen von

Gegenüberliegende Seite: Krischna hält Rhada in der lustvollen Umarmung: der Jaghana.

Sesamsaat und Reis; *Kshiraniraka* oder das Mischen von Milch und Wasser.

• Wenn eine Frau sich so um einen Mann legt, wie sich eine Ranke um den Baum schlingt, seinen Kopf zu sich herunter zieht, um ihn zu küssen und zu liebkosen, dann nennt man das eine Umarmung, die sich wie eine »Ranke windet«.

• Wenn eine Frau einen Fuß auf den ihres Liebhabers gesetzt hat und den anderen auf seinen Oberschenkel, mit einem Arm seinen Rücken umfasst und mit dem anderen seine Schultern, dabei leise singende und gurrende Laute von sich gibt und so tut, als wollte sie den Mann erklimmen, um ihn zu küssen, dann heißt diese Umarmung das »Erklettern eines Baumes«.

Die beiden Umarmungen finden statt, wenn der Liebhaber steht.

• Wenn die Liebenden im Bett liegen und sich einander so eng umschlingen, dass die Arme und Oberschenkel des einen von den Armen und Oberschenkeln des anderen umfangen sind und sich aneinander reiben, dann heißt diese Umarmung das »Mischen von Sesamsaat und Reis«.

• Wenn ein Mann und eine Frau sich sehr lieben und dabei weder an Schmerz noch Verletzung denken, sich einander so umschlingen, als würden sie ineinander eindringen, während die Frau auf dem Schoß des Mannes sitzt, ihr Gesicht ihm zugewandt, dann heißt diese Umarmung eine »Mischung von Milch und Wasser«.

Zu diesen beiden Umarmungen kommt es beim Geschlechtsakt. Derart beschrieb uns Babhravya die zuvor erwähnten acht Arten des Umarmens. Suvarnanabha zeigt uns vier weitere Möglichkeiten, Körperteile zu umfassen: die Umarmung der Oberschenkel; das Umfassen des *Jaghana*, das ist der Teil zwischen Nabel und Oberschenkel; das Umarmen der Brüste und das Berühren der Stirn.

Gegenüberliegende Seite: Umhüllt von seiner zärtlichen Umarmung füttert die Geliebte ihren Liebsten mit süßem Pan.

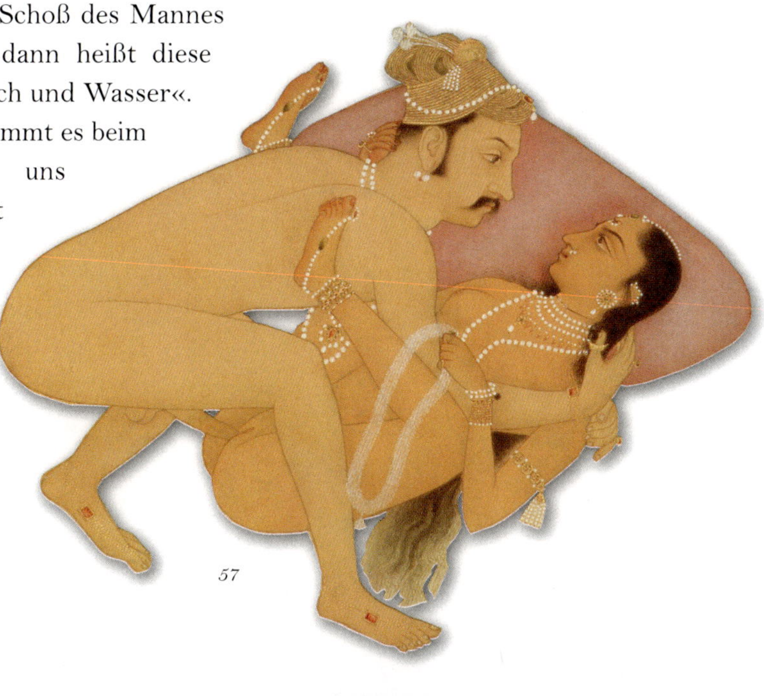

Gegenüberliegende Seite: Zum Auftakt des Liebesspiels verzehren Mann und Frau einander mit sehnsüchtigen Blicken.

• Wenn einer der beiden einen oder beide Oberschenkel des anderen kräftig zwischen seine eigenen presst, dann heißt das »Umarmen der Oberschenkel«.

• Wenn ein Mann den *Jaghana*, also den mittleren Teil des weiblichen Leibes, gegen den seinen drückt und sich auf sie legt, sie mit den Nägeln kratzt oder beißt oder schlägt und küsst, wobei das Haar der Frau offen und wallend ist, dann heißt das die »Umarmung des *Jaghana*«.

• Wenn ein Mann seine Brust auf die Brüste der Frau legt und sie fest an sich drückt, dann heißt das »Umarmen der Brüste«.

• Wenn einer der Liebenden den Mund, die Augen und die Stirn des anderen mit seinem Mund, den Augen oder der Stirn berührt, dann heißt das »Berühren der Stirn«.

Einige Weise sagen, dass selbst das Massieren von Haar und Körper eine Art des Umarmens sei, weil es eine Berührung von Körpern dabei gibt. Doch Vatsyayana denkt, da das Massieren zu einem anderen Zweck und zu anderer Zeit vorgenommen wird und von ganz anderer Art ist, kann man es nicht zum Umarmen zählen.

Dazu gibt es wieder ein paar Merksätze: »Die Thematik des Umarmens ist derart, dass Männer, die Fragen dazu stellen oder die davon sprechen oder davon hören, schon dadurch das Verlangen nach diesem Vergnügen verspüren. Auch jene Umarmungen, die im *Kama Shastra* nicht erwähnt sind, sollte man während der sexuellen Freuden ausüben, sofern sie nur irgendwie dazu beitragen können, die Liebe und die Leidenschaft zu steigern.

Die Richtlinien des *Shastra* finden so lange Anwendung, wie die Leidenschaft mittelmäßig ist. Doch wenn das Rad der Liebe erst in Schwung ist, gibt es kein *Shastra* und keine Regel mehr.«

Vom Küssen

Einige äußern, dass es keinen festen Zeitpunkt und keine Regel gibt für die Umarmung, den Kuss, das Drücken oder das Kratzen mit den Fingernägeln, außer dass das alles vor dem eigentlichen Koitus getan werden sollte, während Schläge und das Äußern von Lauten generell während des Aktes passieren. Vatsyayana hingegen glaubt, dass alles jederzeit Anwendung finden kann, denn Liebe kümmert sich nicht um Zeit und Regeln.

Bei der ersten Vereinigung sollte man mit Küssen und den anderen oben erwähnten Handlungen sparsam umgehen, nicht zu ausgiebig, dafür aber abwechselnd. Bei späteren Gelegenheiten ist keine Mäßigung nötig und keine Zeitbegrenzung. Um die Liebe richtig zu entfachen, mag alles gleichzeitig geschehen.

Die Stirn, die Augen, die Wangen, der Hals, der Busen, die Brüste, die Lippen und das Innere des Mundes – das sind die Stellen für Küsse. Für ein junges Mädchen gibt es drei Sorten von Küssen: den nominalen Kuss; den pochenden Kuss; den Berührungskuss.

Gegenüberliegende Seite: »Oh Radha! Dein hübsches Gesicht ist wie eine Lotusblüte in einem See aus Liebe, deine schwarzen Locken sind wie dunkle Bienen, die um die Blüte tanzen. Wenn ich dich ansehe, spüre ich die Glückseligkeit in Wellen durch meinen Körper fahren.«

Folgende Seiten: Radha versucht ihr Gesicht zu verbergen, als Krishna sie küssen will.

• Wenn ein Mädchen den Mund des Liebhabers nur flüchtig mit dem seinen berührt und sonst nichts weiter macht, dann heißt das der »nominale Kuss«.

• Wenn ein Mädchen, die Schüchternheit ein bisschen ablegend, die Lippe berühren möchte, die sich in ihren Mund schiebt, und deshalb die eigene Unterlippe bewegt – nicht aber die Oberlippe –, dann heißt das der »pochende Kuss«.

• Wenn ein Mädchen die Lippe ihres Liebhabers mit der Zunge berührt, dabei die Augen schließt und seine Hände in die des Partners legt, dann heißt das »Berührungskuss«.

Andere Autoren beschreiben vier Arten von Küssen: den geraden Kuss; den gekrümmten Kuss; den gewendeten Kuss; den gepressten Kuss.

• Wenn die Lippen der beiden Liebhaber in direkten Kontakt miteinander gebracht werden, dann heißt das »gerader Kuss«.

• Wenn die Köpfe beider Partner sich aneinander schmiegen und sie sich so küssen, dann heißt das »gekrümmter Kuss«.

• Wenn einer das Gesicht des anderen zu sich dreht, indem er ihn am Kinn oder Kopf hält und dann küsst, heißt das »gewendeter Kuss«.

• Wenn die Unterlippe mit viel Kraft gedrückt wird, dann heißt das »gepresster Kuss«.

Es gibt noch eine fünfte Art des Kusses – der »stark gepresste Kuss«. Er kommt zustande, indem man die Unterlippe des Partners zwischen zwei Finger klemmt und dann, nach Berührung mit der Zunge, ganz kräftig die eigene Lippe darauf presst.

Was das Küssen anlangt, kann man ein Wettspiel machen, wer wen fangen wird. Verliert die Frau, sollte sie so tun, als ob sie weint, sollte den Liebhaber abwehren, sich von ihm wenden, sich mit ihm streiten und eine neue Wette verlangen. Verliert sie wiederum, sollte sie sich noch verzweifelter geben, und wenn ihr Liebhaber müde wird oder abgelenkt ist, sollte sie sich seine Oberlippe »erobern«, diese zwischen ihren Zähnen festhalten, so

Gegenüberliegende Seite: Wenn die Liebenden mit dem Körper des anderen sehr vertraut sind, können sie sich während des Liebesspiels auch auf ausgefallene Arten küssen.

dass sie nicht wegrutschen kann. Dann sollte sie lachen, ausgelassen Lärm machen, herumtanzen und auf spaßige Art alles sagen, was ihr in den Sinn kommt, mit den Augen rollen und die Augenbrauen hochziehen. So viel zu den Wettspielen und Zwisten ums Küssen. Aber dasselbe kann auch beim Drücken, Beißen, Schlagen oder Kratzen mit den Fingernägeln stattfinden.

Wenn ein Mann die Oberlippe einer Frau küsst, während sie als Antwort seine Unterlippe küsst, dann heißt das »der Kuss der Oberlippe«.

Wenn einer von beiden beide Lippen des anderen zwischen seine eigenen nimmt, dann heißt das »Klammerkuss«. Eine Frau nimmt einen solchen Kuss aber nur von einem Mann an, der keinen Lippenbart trägt.

Und wenn beim Kuss einer die Zähne, die Zunge und den Gaumen des anderen mit seiner Zunge berührt, dann heißt das »Kämpfen der Zungen«.

Küssen kann auf vier Arten erfolgen: gemäßigt, zusammengezogen, gepresst und weich, entsprechend den Körperpartien, die man küssen will, denn verschiedene Arten von Küssen eignen sich für verschiedene Körperteile.

Unten: Fühlen sich die Liebenden miteinander wohl, werden sie sich nach Belieben bewegen.

Wenn eine Frau ihren schlafenden Liebhaber anschaut und sein Gesicht küsst, um ihre Absicht oder ihr Verlangen zu signalisieren, dann heißt das »Kuss, der Liebe entfacht«.

Wenn eine Frau ihren Mann küsst, während der beschäftigt ist oder während er sich mit ihr zankt oder während er sich etwas anderes anschaut, so dass er geistesabwesend ist, dann heißt das »Kuss, der ablenkt«.

Wenn ein Partner spät abends nach Hause kommt und seine schlafende Liebste in ihrem Bett küsst, um ihr sein Verlangen zu zeigen, dann heißt das »Kuss, der munter macht«. Bei dieser Gelegenheit kann die Frau auch vorgeben, bei der Ankunft ihres Liebsten zu schlafen, um so von seinen Absichten zu erfahren.

Wenn eine Person das Bild des Menschen, den sie liebt, im Spiegel, im Wasser oder an der Wand küsst, dann heißt das »Kuss, der die Absicht zeigt.«

Oben: Stellungen, bei denen der Mann seine Partnerin hochhebt, verengen die Yoni – für beide ein besonders erregender Genuss.

Wenn eine Person ein Kind auf ihrem Schoß oder ein Bildnis in Gegenwart der Person küsst, die sie liebt, dann heißt das »übertragener Kuss«.

Wenn nachts bei einer Theatervorstellung oder auf einer Versammlung von Kastenangehörigen sich ein Mann einer Frau nähert, und, wenn sie steht, einen Finger ihrer Hand küsst, oder, wenn sie sitzt, eine ihrer Zehen küsst, oder wenn bei ganz anderer Gelegenheit eine Frau den Körper des Liebsten massiert, dabei ihr Gesicht auf seine Schenkel legt (als wäre sie müde), um seine Leidenschaft zu entfachen, und seine Schenkel oder einen Großzeh küsst, dann heißt das »demonstrativer Kuss«.

Was auch immer ein Liebhaber dem anderen erweist, es sollte vom anderen erwidert werden, d.h. wenn die Frau den Mann küsst, sollte er im Gegenzug sie küssen, wenn sie ihn schlägt, sollte er sie zur Erwiderung ebenfalls schlagen.

Vom Drücken, Markieren oder Kratzen mit den Fingernägeln

Wenn Liebe heftig wird, kann es zum Eindrücken oder Kratzen mit den Fingernägeln kommen – und zwar bei folgenden Gelegenheiten: beim ersten Besuch, bei Vorbereitungen für eine Reise, bei der Rückkehr von einer Reise; wenn ein verärgerter Liebhaber versöhnt wird und schließlich wenn eine Frau berauscht ist. Doch das Eindrücken der Fingernägel gehört zu heftiger Leidenschaft. Es geschieht – bei denen, die es mögen – oft gleichzeitig mit dem Beißen.

Das Eindrücken der Nägel erfolgt auf folgende acht Arten, den Mustern entsprechend, die dabei entstehen: das Geräusch, der Halbmond, der Kreis, die Linie, die Tigerkralle, der Fuß des Pfaus, der Sprung des Hasen, das Blatt des blauen Lotus. Folgende Körperstellen können mit den Nägeln »bearbeitet« werden: die Achselhöhle, der Hals, die Brüste, die Lippen, der Mittelteil des Leibes *Jaghana* und die Schenkel. Gute Fingernägel sollten hell sein, gepflegt, sauber, vollständig, konvex, weich und glänzend.

Gegenüberliegende Seite: Die Liebenden lassen ihren Berührungen freien Lauf und folgen nur ihrem natürlichen Verlangen.

• Wenn eine Person das Kinn, die Brüste, die Unterlippe oder den *Jaghana* des anderen so zart mit den Nägeln überstreicht, dass das keine Spuren hinterlässt, sondern sich nur die Körperhaare durch diese Berührung aufrichten und die Nägel selbst nur ein Geräusch machen, dann heißt das »mit den Nägeln drücken oder ein Geräusch machen«.

Diese Form ist üblich, wenn ein Liebhaber ein junges Mädchen massiert, ihm dabei über den Kopf fährt und ihr ein bisschen Angst machen möchte.

• Die geschwungene Markierung mit den Nägeln, die auf den Nacken oder die Brüste gekratzt wird, nennt man das »Halbmond«.

• Wenn zwei Halbmonde gegenüber eingedrückt werden, entsteht der »Kreis«. Diese Markierung macht man im Allgemeinen am Nabel, an den kleinen Dellen am Gesäß und an den Hüftgelenken.

• Die Markierung in Form einer kleinen Linie, die an jeder Körperpartie »gezeichnet« werden kann, nennt man das »Linie«.

• Dieselbe Linie, wenn sie geschwungen auf der Brust gezogen wird, heißt »Tigerkralle«.

• Wenn eine geschwungene Markierung mit fünf Nägeln auf der Brust gemacht wird, dann heißt das »Pfauenfuß«. Es braucht viel Geschick, ihn richtig zu machen. Und wenn er gelingt, erwartet man dafür Lob.

• Wenn fünf Markierungen dicht nebeneinander nahe der Brustwarzen gesetzt werden, dann heißt das »der Sprung des Hasen«.

• Eine Markierung auf der Brust oder auf den Hüften in Form eines Blattes des blauen Lotus, heißt auch »Blatt des blauen Lotus«.

Wenn eine Person auf Reisen geht und zuvor eine Markierung auf die Schenkel oder die Brust setzt, dann heißt das »Souvenir zur Erinnerung«. Bei dieser Gelegenheit werden drei bis vier Linien dicht beieinander mit den Nägeln gezogen. Es können auch andere als die erwähnten Markierungen mit den Nägeln gemacht werden, denn die alten Autoren sagen, da es unter den Männern

Gegenüberliegende Seite: Auf dem Höhepunkt der Leidenschaft markiert er ihre Brust mit den Nägeln. Das Paar liebt sich in der »lotusähnlichen« Stellung.

unzählige Abstufungen bei den Fertigkeiten gibt, gibt es auch unzählige Möglichkeiten, die Markierungen zu setzen. Und da das Eindrücken von Nägeln oder das Markieren unabhängig ist von der Liebe, kann niemand mit Bestimmtheit sagen, wie viele verschiedene Formen von Markierungen denn tatsächlich existieren.

Gegenüberliegende Seite: Radha und Krishna plaudern in einer Vollmondnacht über Liebe und Verlangen.

Da Verschiedenheit und Abwechslung in der Liebe notwendig sind, sagt Vatsyayana, so wird Liebe auch erzeugt durch das Mittel der Abwechslung. Das ist auch der Grund dafür, dass Kurtisanen, die die verschiedenen Mittel und Methoden kennen, so sehr begehrt sind. Denn Abwechslung wird in allen Künsten, z. B. dem Bogenschießen, und allen Amüsements gesucht und daher erst recht bei dem soeben behandelten Thema.

Markierungen mit den Nägeln sollten nicht bei verheirateten Frauen gesetzt werden. Doch besondere Markierungen könnten zur Erinnerung und Steigerung der Liebe auf ihre intimen Körperteile gemacht werden.

Betrachtet eine Frau die Nagelmarkierungen an intimen Stellen ihres Körpers, selbst wenn sie schon fast verblasst sind, erwacht ihre Liebe erneut. Wenn keine Nagelspuren eine Person an die Stunden der Liebe erinnern, dann flaut die Liebe ebenso ab, als wenn für lange Zeit kein Sex stattfindet. Selbst wenn ein Fremder aus einer gewissen Entfernung eine junge Frau mit Nagelspuren auf der Brust sieht, empfindet er ihr gegenüber Liebe und Achtung.

Ein Mann, der Nagel- und Beißspuren an einigen Stellen seines Körpers trägt, kann ebenfalls die Imagination einer Frau beeinflussen. Alles in allem scheint nichts die Liebe mehr zu steigern als die Effekte der Markierungen von Nägeln und Zähnen.

Von Schlägen und Geräuschen aus Leidenschaft

Der Geschlechtsakt kann angesichts der Gegensätzlichkeiten der Liebe und ihrer Tendenz zum Disput mit einem Zwist verglichen werden. Schläge aus Leidenschaft treffen bestimmte Körperstellen: die Schultern, den Kopf, die Stelle zwischen den Brüsten, den Rücken, den Mittelteil des Leibes *Jaghana*, die Flanken. Es gibt vier Arten des Schlagens: mit dem Handrücken; mit etwas gekrümmten Fingern; mit der Faust; mit der offenen Hand.

Da Schlagen Schmerzen bereitet, führt es auch zu verschiedenen Lauten und Schreien. Es sind die folgenden acht: der Laut des *Hin*, das donnernde Geräusch, das Gurren, das Weinen, der Laut *Phut*, der Laut *Phat*, das Geräusch *Sut* und das Geräusch *Plat*.

Außerdem fallen Wörter wie »Mutter« und jene, die etwas verbieten, die Genughaben, den Wunsch nach Befreiung, Schmerz oder Lob ausdrücken. Dazu noch Geräusche und Laute, wie die der Taube, des Kuckucks, der grünen Taube, des Papageis, der Biene, des Sperlings, des

Gegenüberliegende Seite: Stellungen, bei denen sich die Partner in die Augen sehen, werden als besonders innig und liebevoll empfunden.

Flamingos, der Ente und der Wachtel, die alle gelegentlich geäußert werden.

Schläge mit der Faust sollten auf den Rücken der Frau gemacht werden, während sie auf dem Schoß des Mannes sitzt; und sie sollte die Schläge erwidern, den Mann beschimpfen, als wäre sie ärgerlich, die gurrenden und weinenden Laute von sich geben. Während des Koitus sollte mit dem Handrücken auf die Stelle zwischen den Brüsten der Partnerin geklatscht werden, erst leicht, dann mit sich steigernder Leidenschaft zunehmend bis zum Ende.

Dabei könnten die Laute des *Hin* und andere Laute geäußert werden, abwechselnd je nach Geschmack und Gewohnheit. Wenn der Mann beim Laut *Phat* mit etwas gekrümmten Fingern die Frau leicht auf den Kopf schlägt, heißt das *Prasritaka.* In diesem Fall sind die geeigneten Laute das Gurren, *Phat* sowie *Phut* aus dem Innern des Mundes sowie am Ende des Koitus die seufzenden und weinenden Geräusche. Der Laut *Phat* ist eine Imitation des Geräusches, wenn Bambus gespalten wird, während der Laut *Phut* etwa dem entspricht, wenn etwas ins Wasser fällt. Immer wenn das Küssen und die anderen Handlungen des Vorspiels beginnen, sollte die Frau das mit einem zischenden Geräusch begleiten. Während der Erregung stößt die Frau, die an das Schlagen nicht gewöhnt ist, ständig Wörter der Ablehnung hervor, wie »aufhören« oder »es reicht«, und ebenso Wörter wie »Vater«, »Mutter«, unterbrochen von Seufzern, Schluchzen und aufbrausenden Geräuschen. Gegen Ende des Koitus sollten die Brüste, der *Jaghana* und die Flanken der Frau mit der Handfläche etwas kräftig gedrückt und dabei Geräusche der Wachtel oder der Gans geäußert werden.

Zum Thema zwei Merksätze: »Man sagt, das Wesen der Männlichkeit besteht aus Rohheit und Ungestüm, während dagegen Schwäche, Zärtlichkeit, Sensibilität und eine Abneigung gegen Unangenehmes die bezeichnenden Merkmale der Fraulichkeit sind. Erregung und

Lust sowie persönliche Gewohnheiten und Eigenheiten können mitunter zu einer Umkehr führen; aber das hält nicht lange an, und am Ende wird das natürliche Wesen wiederhergestellt.«

Die Klemme für die Brust, die Schere für den Kopf, das Instrument zum Durchstechen der Wange und die Kneifzange für Brüste und Flanken mag man gemeinsam mit den anderen vier Formen des Schlagens auch in Betracht ziehen. Das ergibt zusammen acht Möglichkeiten. Aber diese vier Arten des Ansetzens von Instrumenten sind den Menschen der südlichen Länder eigen, und die dadurch verursachten Narben sieht man auf den Brüsten der Frauen. Das sind allerdings örtliche Besonderheiten, von denen Vatsyayana jedoch meint, sie sind schmerzhaft und barbarisch und ziemlich unwert, zur Nachahmung empfohlen zu werden.

Örtliche Eigenarten sollten nicht überall übernommen werden. Und selbst dort, wo diese Eigenarten üblich sind, sollte man übermäßigen Gebrauch vermeiden. Ein paar Beispiele mögen zeigen, wie gefährlich ihre Ausübung sein kann: Der König der Panchalas tötete die Kurtisane Madhavasena beim Ansetzen der Zwinge während des Beischlafs. König Shatakarni Shatavahana von Kuntalas nahm seiner großen Königin Malayavati das Leben mit einer Schere, und Naradeva, der eine ver-

krüppelte Hand hatte, blendete ein Tanzmädchen, als ihm das Instrument zum Piercing entglitt.

Die leidenschaftlichen Handlungen und amourösen Gesten, die in der Hitze des Augenblicks und während des Geschlechtsverkehrs entstehen, lassen sich nicht definieren. Sie sind irregulär wie Träume. Ein Pferd, das im Galopp läuft, wird blind vor Tempo, es achtet nicht auf Löcher und andere Hindernisse auf seinem Weg; ähnlich verhält es sich mit einem Liebespaar, das auf dem Höhepunkt der Wollust blind wird und zügellos weitermacht, ohne im geringsten auf ein Übermaß zu achten. Aus diesem Grunde sollte derjenige, welcher in der Wissenschaft der Liebe versiert ist und seine Kraft sowie die Zartheit und das Ungestüm der jungen Frauen kennt, entsprechend handeln. Die verschiedenen Arten der Freude eignen sich nicht für jede Gelegenheit und nicht für jede Person, sondern sie sollten zur passenden Zeit, an den passenden Orten und in den passenden Ländern angewendet werden.

Gegenüberliegende Seite: Die Frau kostet ihre dominante Stellung voll aus, indem sie dem Mann während des Koitus sanfte Schläge versetzt.

Vom Beißen

Alle Stellen, die geküsst werden, sind auch zum Beißen geeignet, außer der Oberlippe, dem Innern des Mundes und den Augen. Gute Zähne lassen sich so beschreiben: Sie sollten ebenmäßig sein, einen gefälligen Glanz haben, sich zum Färben eignen, gute Proportionen aufweisen, unversehrt und mit scharfen Schneiden versehen sein.

Defekte Zähne erkennt man daran, dass sie stumpf sind, aus dem Kiefer nach vorn stehen, rau, weich, groß mit sichtbaren Abständen dazwischen sind.

Die verschiedenen Formen des Beißens sind: der versteckte Biss; der geschwollene Biss; der Punkt; die Linie aus Punkten; die Koralle und das Juwel; das Band der Juwelen; die geborstene Wolke; der Biss des Wildschweins.

• Der Biss, der sich nur durch auffällige Rötung der Haut zeigt, heißt der »versteckte Biss«.

• Wenn die Haut an beiden Seiten heruntergepresst wird, heißt das »geschwollener Biss«.

• Wenn nur ein Stückchen Haut mit beiden Zähnen gebissen wird, heißt das der »Punkt«.

Gegenüberliegende Seite: Angst und Schmerzen als Katalysator der Lust – im Kamasutra sind sie selbstverständlicher Teil des Liebesspiels.

Folgende Seiten: Hingebungsvoll neigt die Frau ihren Körper und präsentiert dem Mann ihre prallen Brüste. Dass er sie in dieser Position nicht küssen kann, steigert die erotische Spannung.

Oben: Der Wagen der Liebe trägt das Paar in das Paradies der Glückseligkeit.

• Wenn solche kleinen Hautabschnitte mit allen Zähnen gebissen werden, heißt das »Linie aus Punkten«.

• Wenn am Biss Zähne und Lippen beteiligt sind, heißt das »die Koralle und das Juwel«.

• Wenn alle Zähne zubeißen, nennt man das »Band der Juwelen«.

• Der Biss, der Ungleichheiten in einem Kreis markiert, was von den Zahnzwischenräumen stammt, heißt »geborstene Wolke«. Er findet sich auf den Brüsten.

• Der Biss, der aus vielen breiten Reihen von Markierungen dicht aneinander besteht und der rote Stellen zwischen ihnen hat, heißt »Biss des Wildschweins«. Er wird auf die Brüste und Schultern gesetzt und gilt als Besonderheit der Personen, die mit intensiver Leidenschaft lieben.

Die Unterlippe ist die Stelle, auf die der »versteckte Biss«, der »geschwollene Biss« und der »Punkt« gesetzt werden. Der »geschwollene Biss« sowie »Koralle und Juwel« werden auf die Wangen gemacht. Küssen, Eindrücken der Fingernägel und Beißen bringen Ornamente für die linke Wange hervor. Wenn das Wort Wange hier fällt, dann ist damit die linke Wange gemeint. Die »Linie aus Punkten« und das »Band der Juwelen« »zeichnet« man auf die Vorderpartie des Halses, die Achselhöhlen und die Hüften, hingegen die »Linie aus Punkten« allein nur auf die Stirn und Schenkel.

Wie ein Tamala-Blatt auf der Stirn, ein Blumenstrauß, ein Betelblatt oder Schmuckstücke auf der Stirn oder am Ohr, die von der geliebten Frau getragen werden, so gehören auch das Markieren der Nägel und das Beißen zu den Zeichen des Verlangens und des Vergnügens. Unter den erwähnten Liebesbekundungen, nämlich Umarmen, Küssen usw., sollten jene zuerst gemacht werden, die die Leidenschaft steigern, während die zum Amüsieren oder zum Variieren später folgen können.

Dazu gibt es wieder ein paar Merksätze: »Wenn ein Mann eine Frau stark beißt, dann sollte sie ärgerlich dasselbe mit doppelter Kraft tun: Also ein »Punkt« muss mit einer »Linie aus Punkten« und eine »Linie aus Punkten« mit einer »geborstenen Wolke« erwidert werden. Und wenn sie so richtig zornig ist, sollte sie plötzlich einen Liebeszwist mit ihm beginnen. Sie könnte ihn bei den Haaren packen, seinen Kopf zu sich biegen, seine Unterlippe küssen, und dann, von der Liebe berauscht, sollte sie die Augen schließen und ihn an verschiedenen Stellen beißen. Auch am Tag und in der Öffentlichkeit, wenn ihr Liebster ihr Markierungen zeigt, die sie auf seinem Körper hinterlassen hat, sollte sie darüber lachen und ein Gesicht aufsetzen, als wollte sie ihn schelten, und ihm dann mit verärgertem Blick die Male auf ihrem Körper zeigen, die von ihm stammen. Darum: Wenn Männer und Frauen so handeln, wie sie es miteinander mögen, dann wird ihre Liebe füreinander selbst in hundert Jahren nicht erkalten.«

Unten: Die Berührung ihres wallenden Haares stimuliert den Liebhaber zusätzlich.

Von verschiedenen Positionen beim Beischlaf

Bei der »hohen Vereinigung« sollte die Rehfrau *(Mrigi)* sich so legen, dass ihre *Yoni* sich weitet, während bei der »niederen Vereinigung« die Elefantenfrau *(Hastini)* sich so legt, dass ihre *Yoni* sich verengt. Bei einer gleichwertigen sexuellen Vereinigung liegt sie in ganz natürlicher Position. Was über die *Mrigi* und *Hastini* gesagt wurde, gilt ebenso für die Stutenfrau *(Vadawa)*. In einer »niederen Vereinigung« kann die Frau zu stimulierenden medizinischen Mitteln greifen, damit ihr Verlangen schnell befriedigt wird.

Die Rehfrau hat drei Möglichkeiten, sich zu legen: die weit geöffnete Stellung; die gähnende Stellung; die Position der Gattin von Indra.

• Wenn sie ihren Kopf nach hinten senkt und den Mittelteil ihres Leibes hebt, dann heißt das die »weit geöffnete Stellung«. Dabei sollte der Mann sich eines Gleitmittels bedienen, um das Eindringen zu erleichtern.

• Wenn sie ihre Schenkel hebt und für den Koitus weit spreizt, dann heißt das die »gähnende Stellung«.

Gegenüberliegende Seite: Indem sie ihn fest mit den Beinen umschlingt, zieht die Frau ihren Partner in der »pressenden Stellung« ganz nah zu sich heran.

• Wenn sie die Schenkel so hochzieht, dass ihre Knie bis an die Achseln stoßen, und sie so zum Koitus bereit ist, dann heißt das die »Stellung von Indrani«. Man lernt sie nur durch Übung.

Die »umfassende Stellung« wird in der »niederen Vereinigung« und in der »niedersten Vereinigung« zusammen mit der »pressenden Stellung«, der »umwindenden Stellung« und der »Stutenposition« bevorzugt.

Wenn die Beine des Mannes und der Frau ganz ausgestreckt aufeinander liegen, heißt das die »umfassende Stellung«. Da gibt es zwei Arten: die Seitenlage sowie die Rückenlage, je nach der Weise, wie die Liebenden liegen. In der Seitenlage sollte der Mann stets auf seiner linken Seite liegen, dementsprechend die Frau auf der rechten Seite.

Wenn nach Beginn des Koitus in der »umfassenden Stellung« die Frau ihren Partner fest mit den Schenkeln drückt, dann heißt das die »pressende Stellung«. Wenn die Frau einen ihrer Schenkel um die Hüfte ihres Partners legt, dann heißt das die »umwindende Stellung«. Wenn die Frau den *Lingam* in ihrer *Yoni* festhält, dann heißt das »Stutenposition«, die man nur durch Übung lernt.

Dies sind die verschiedenen Möglichkeiten zu liegen, wie sie Babhravya erwähnte. Suvarnanabha fügt noch die folgenden hinzu:

Wenn die Frau beide Schenkel gerade hochstreckt, dann heißt das »emporgehobene Position«.

Wenn die Frau beide Schenkel noch höher zieht und die Füße auf die Schultern des Partners stellt oder legt, dann heißt das »gähnende Position«.

Wenn die angewinkelten Beine der Frau vom Liebhaber vor seine Brust gehalten werden, heißt das die »gepresste Stellung«.

Wenn bei der vorigen Stellung eins ihrer Beine ausgestreckt ist, heißt das »halb gepresste Position«.

Wenn die Frau eines ihrer Beine auf die Schulter des Liebhabers legt und das andere ausstreckt, dann das erste ausstreckt und das andere auf die Schulter des

Gegenüberliegende Seite: Die Liebenden gehen bis an ihre Grenzen, um ihre Leidenschaft zu erproben.

Liebsten legt und das abwechselnd tut, dann heißt das »einen Bambus spalten«.

Wenn eins ihrer Beine auf ihrem Kopf ruht und das andere ausgestreckt wird, heißt das »einen Nagel einschlagen«. Die Frau muss sehr gelenkig sein und lernt die Position nur mit viel Übung.

Wenn die Frau beide Beine angewinkelt auf ihren Leib legt, dann heißt das »Krabbenstellung«.

Wenn beide die Schenkel gehoben haben und sie gegeneinander pressen, heißt das die »gepackte Stellung«.

Wenn die Unterschenkel aufeinander gelegt werden, heißt das die »lotusähnliche Position«.

Wenn ein Mann sich während des Geschlechtsaktes dreht und sich dabei nicht von seiner Partnerin trennt, während sie ihn die ganze Zeit über an der Lendenwirbelsäule festhält, dann heißt das die »Wendeposition«. Man lernt sie wiederum nur durch Üben.

Deshalb empfiehlt Suvarnanabha: Diese verschiedenen Möglichkeiten, sich zu legen, zu setzen oder zu stellen, sollten am besten im Wasser praktiziert werden, weil sie sich da einfach durchführen lassen. Doch Vatsyayana meint, dass Geschlechtsverkehr im Wasser unziemlich ist, da religiöse Regeln das verbieten.

Wenn ein Mann und eine Frau ihre Körper gegenseitig abstützen oder sich an eine Wand oder Säule lehnen und so Sex im Stehen machen, dann heißt das »gestützte Vereinigung«. Wenn nur der Mann sich gegen eine Wand lehnt und die Frau – auf seinen gefalteten Händen sitzend und von unten gehalten – ihre Arme um seinen Nacken schlingt und ihre Unterschenkel um seine Hüften, dabei ihren Körper bewegt, weil sich ihre Füße von der Wand abstoßen, an der der Mann lehnt, dann heißt das die »schwebende oder hängende Stellung«.

Wenn eine Frau wie ein Vierfüßler auf Händen und Füßen steht und ihr Partner sie von hinten, wie ein Bulle, begattet, dann heißt das »Begattung einer Kuh«. Dabei kommen dem Rücken und dem Gesäß alle Liebkosungen zu, die sonst normalerweise der Busen erfährt. Auf

Gegenüberliegende Seite: Bei der »Stellung von Indrani« zieht die Frau ihre Schenkel so weit hoch, dass ihre Knie die Achseln berühren.

dieselbe Art kann der Koitus eines Hundes, einer Ziege, eines Rehs, einer Katze, die gewaltsame Paarung mit einer Eselin, der Tigersprung, das Pressen des Elefanten, das Scheuern des Wildschweins und das Bespringen des Pferdes imitiert werden. In allen Fällen kommt es darauf an, die Eigenschaften der verschiedenen Tiere zum Ausdruck zu bringen, indem man den Geschlechtsakt so vollzieht, wie sie sich paaren.

Wenn ein Mann sich zweier Frauen zur gleichen Zeit erfreut, die ihn beide gleichermaßen lieben, dann heißt das »vereinter Koitus«.

Wenn ein Mann mehrere Frauen gleichzeitig beglückt, dann spricht man von einer »Vereinigung mit einer Herde von Kühen«.

Die folgenden sexuellen Vereinigungen, nämlich im Wasser, die Paarung des Elefanten mit vielen Elefantenkühen, die Vereinigung mit einer kleinen Herde von Ziegen, die Vereinigung mit mehreren Rehen, finden statt, indem man diese Tiere nachahmt.

In Gramaneri erfreuen sich junge Männer einer Frau, die mit einem von ihnen verheiratet sein könnte. Diesen Geschlechtsakt können sie nacheinander oder zur gleichen Zeit vollziehen. Einer hält sie, ein anderer begattet sie, ein dritter nutzt ihren Mund, ein vierter umfasst ihren Unterleib. So erfreuen sie sich abwechselnd der Körperpartien der Frau. Dasselbe kann passieren, wenn mehrere Männer sich in Begleitung einer Kurtisane befinden oder wenn eine Kurtisane mit mehreren Männern allein ist.

Die Menschen in den südlichen Ländern praktizieren auch Analverkehr, der »niedere Vereinigung« heißt. Das also zu den Varianten des Beischlafs. Zum Thema gibt es zwei Merksätze: »Eine erfinderische Person sollte die Arten des Sexualaktes durch Anregungen aus der Tier- und Vogelwelt variieren. Denn diese unterschiedlichen Formen der Vereinigung, ausgeübt entsprechend den Gewohnheiten jedes Landes und dem Geschmack jedes einzelnen, wecken Liebe, Freundschaft und Achtung in den Herzen der Frauen.«

Gegenüberliegende Seite: Das Kamasutra kennt keine Tabus. Wenn ein Mann es genießt, seine Ehefrau oder Kurtisane mit anderen zu teilen, so ist auch das erlaubt.

Von vertauschten Rollen

Wenn eine Frau erkennt, dass ihr Liebhaber durch andauernden Sex ermüdet ist, ohne sein Verlangen befriedigt zu haben, dann sollte sie ihn mit seiner Einwilligung auf den Rücken drehen und ihn unterstützen, indem sie seine Rolle übernimmt. Sie kann das auch tun, um die Neugier ihres Partners zu wecken oder seinem Wunsch oder ihrem eigenen Verlangen nach etwas Neuem zu entsprechen.

Es gibt zwei Wege, das zu tun. Der erste ist, wenn sie sich während des Koitus zusammen mit ihrem Liebhaber nach oben dreht, und zwar derart, dass es keine Unterbrechung der Liebesvereinigung gibt. Beim zweiten übernimmt sie die Rolle des Mannes bereits zu Beginn. In beiden Fällen sollte sie mit aufgelöstem Haar, ihr Lächeln von heftigen Atemstößen unterbrochen, ihre Brüste fest auf seinen Brustkorb pressen, den Kopf auf- und abbewegen und dieselben Handlungen vornehmen, die sie von ihm in seiner Rolle gewöhnt ist. Seine Schläge sollte sie erwidern, ihn reizen und sagen: »Ich

Gegenüberliegende Seite: Mit der Zeit lernen die Liebenden, während des Liebesaktes zu entspannen, selbst wenn sie sich dem Höhepunkt nähern.

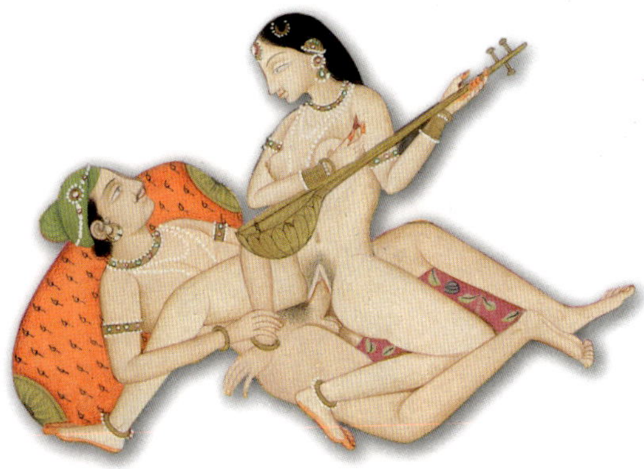

wurde von dir mit hartem Liebesspiel ermüdet. Jetzt werde ich dich ermüden.« Dann muss sie wieder ihre Schüchternheit, ihre Ermattung und ihren Wunsch nach Beendigung des Beischlafs zeigen.

Was ein Mann auch immer zum Vergnügen einer Frau tut, das heißt die Arbeit oder das Werk des Mannes. Das könnte so aussehen: Während die Frau auf seinem Bett liegt und durch seine Unterhaltung abgelenkt wird, sollte er den Knoten ihres Untergewandes lösen. Wenn sie sich deshalb wehren will, überwältigt er sie mit Küssen. Dann, wenn sein *Lingam* steif ist, berührt er sie mit seinen Händen an verschiedenen Körperstellen und streichelt sie zärtlich. Wenn die Frau schüchtern ist und man erstmals zusammen ist, sollte der Mann seine Hände zwischen ihre Schenkel legen, die sie wahrscheinlich geschlossen hält. Wenn sie sehr jung ist, sollte er zunächst eine Hand auf ihre Brust, die sie sicherlich mit ihren Händen bedecken will, dann unter ihre Achsel und auf den Nacken legen. Ist sie allerdings eine erfahrene Frau, kann er alles machen, was beiden gefällt. Danach streichelt er ihr Haar und hebt ihr Kinn, um sie zu küssen. Dabei wird sie schamvoll die Augen schließen, wenn sie noch sehr jung ist. Vom Verhalten der Frau und von ihren Reaktionen sollte er ablesen, welche Dinge ihr vor oder während der Vereinigung gefallen.

Die Zeichen des Vergnügens und der Befriedigung der Frau äußern sich so: Ihr Körper entspannt sich. Sie schließt die Augen. Sie legt alle Scheu und Zurückhaltung ab und deutet wachsende Bereitschaft an, die beiden Organe so eng wie nur möglich miteinander zu vereinen. Andererseits sind die Zeichen ihres Wartens auf sexuelle Freude sowie ausbleibender Befriedigung diese:

Sie schüttelt ihre Hände. Sie lässt den Mann nicht aufstehen, beißt den Mann, stößt ihn und setzt ihre sexuellen Bewegungen fort, nachdem der Mann schon aufgehört hat. In solchen Fällen sollte der Mann beim Vorspiel die *Yoni* der Frau so mit den Fingern reiben und massieren (so wie der Elefant alles mit seinem Rüssel

Gegenüberliegende Seite: Bevor die Kurtisane den Mann oral befriedigt, stimuliert sie ihn nach allen Regeln der Kunst.

Oben: Die Bebilderung des Kamasutra gewährt auch Einblick in das Leben der indischen Oberschicht: hier eine reiche Frau, die sich, umgeben von ihren Dienerinnen, ihren erotischen Fantasien hingibt.

Gegenüberliegende Seite: Für die Frau sind Stellungen mit gehobenem Becken besonders aufregend.

reibt und greift), bis sie feucht wird. Dann kann er seinen *Lingam* in sie einführen.

Was der Mann beim Akt zu machen hat: sich vorwärts bewegen; reiben und rühren; hineinstechen; rubbeln, pressen, zustoßen, den Stoß des Wildschweins und den des Bullen machen, die Spielart des Sperlings anwenden.

• Wenn die Organe direkt und richtig ineinander geführt werden, heißt das »das Organ vorwärts bewegen«.

• Wenn der *Lingam* mit der Hand in der *Yoni* im Kreis bewegt wird, heißt das »Rühren«.

• Wenn die *Yoni* gesenkt wird und der *Lingam* den oberen Teil bearbeitet, dann heißt das »Hineinstechen«.

• Geschieht dasselbe mit dem unteren Teil der Yoni, dann heißt das »Rubbeln«.

• Wenn die *Yoni* lange vom *Lingam* gedrückt wird, dann heißt das »Pressen«.

• Wenn der *Lingam* ein Stück aus der *Yoni* gezogen und dann kräftig wieder hinein geschoben wird, dann heißt das »Zustoßen«.

• Wenn nur ein Teil der *Yoni* vom *Lingam* gerieben wird, dann heißt das »Stoß des Wildschweins«.

• Wird die *Yoni* von zwei Seiten gerieben, dann heißt das der »Stoß des Bullen«.

• Wenn der *Lingam* sich in der *Yoni* schnell auf- und abbewegt, ohne ganz heraus gezogen zu werden, heißt das die »Spielart des Sperlings«.

Wenn eine Frau die Rolle des Mannes übernimmt, kann sie zusätzlich zu den neun genannten Varianten noch die Zange, die Spitze und die Schaukel ausführen.

• Wenn die Frau den *Lingam* in der *Yoni* festhält, ihn zieht und drückt und ihn somit für eine lange Zeit in sich fixiert, dann heißt das die »Zange«.

• Wenn sie sich beim Koitus auf dem Leib des Mannes wie ein Rad dreht, dann heißt das die »Spitze«. Das lernt man nur durch Übung.

• Wenn dabei der Mann den Mittelteil des Körpers hebt und die Frau sich um ihr Mittelteil dreht, dann heißt das die »Schaukel«.

Wenn die Frau müde ist, sollte sie ihre Stirn an die des Partners legen, sich dabei ausruhen, ohne den Koitus der Organe zu stören. Und wenn die Frau etwas ausgeruht hat, sollte der Mann sich wieder drehen und den Akt erneut beginnen.

Die Merksätze lauten: »Obwohl sich eine Frau reserviert gibt und ihre Gefühle nicht offen zeigt, so lässt sie doch erkennen, wenn sie sich auf den Mann legt, wie stark ihre Liebe und ihr Verlangen sind. Ein Mann sollte vom Verhalten der Frau ableiten, was sie im Schilde führt und auf welche Art sie befriedigt werden möchte. Eine Frau während der Menses, eine Frau, die erst kurz zuvor entbunden hat, und eine dicke Frau sollten nicht die Rolle des Mannes übernehmen.«

Gegenüberliegende Seite: Die Frau ergreift im Sturm der Leidenschaft heftig Besitz von ihrem Liebhaber.

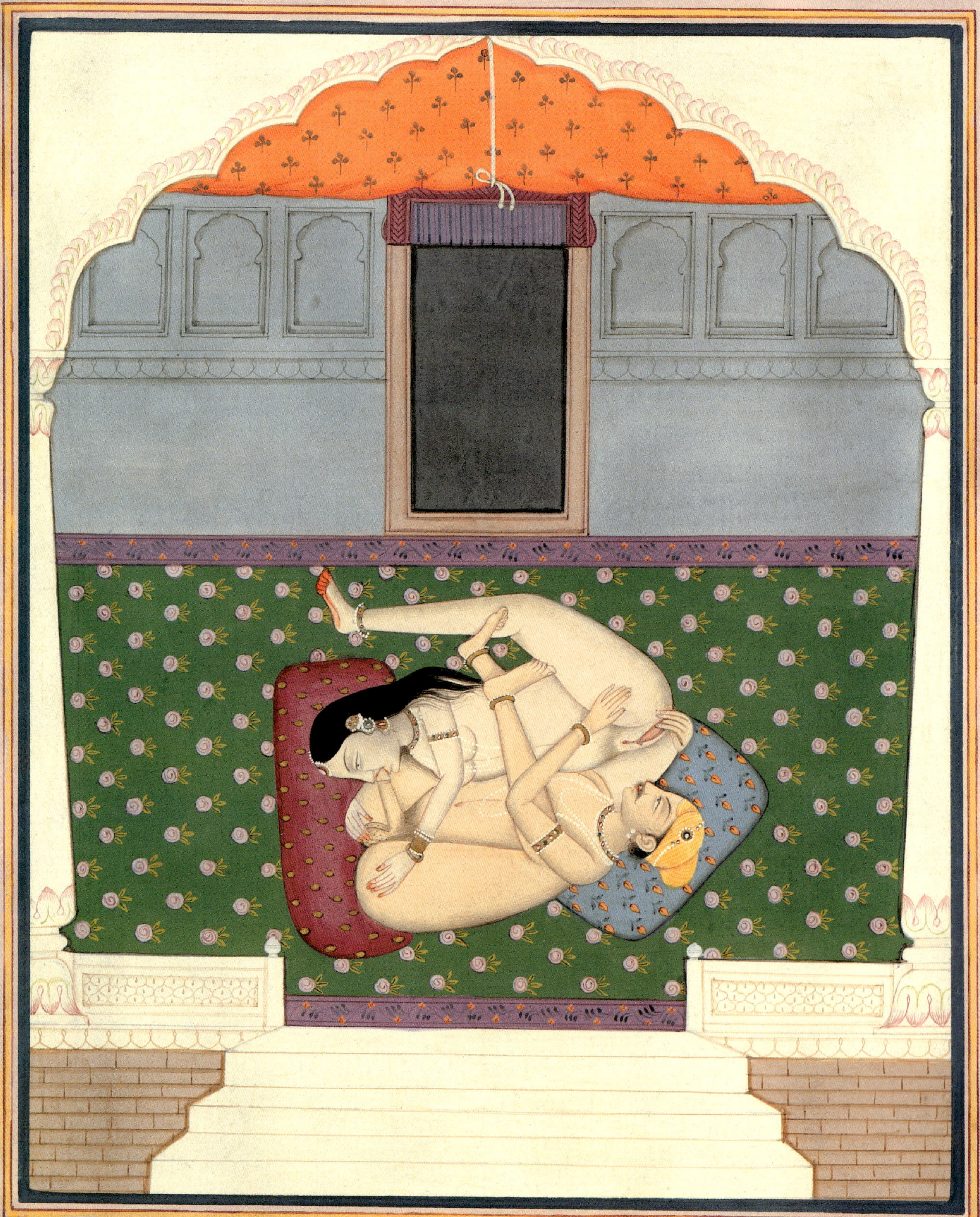

Vom Auparishtaka, dem Oralverkehr

Es gibt zwei Typen von Eunuchen – jene, die sich als Männer verkleiden und aufführen, und jene, die als Frauen daherkommen. Die als Frauen verkleideten Eunuchen tragen entsprechende Kleider, imitieren Sprache, Gesten, Zärtlichkeit, Schüchternheit, Einfachheit, Weichheit und Scheu der Frauen. Was der Mann gewöhnlich am weiblichen Unterleib macht, geschieht nun im Mund des Eunuchen. Dies nennt man *Auparishtaka*. Diese Eunuchen erlangen ihr imaginäres Vergnügen und ihren Lebensunterhalt durch diese Form der Vereinigung. Sie leben das Leben von Kurtisanen. Dies zu den Eunuchen, die sich als Frauen geben.

Als Männer verstellte Eunuchen behalten ihre Wünsche für sich. Wenn sie eine Tätigkeit ausüben, dann bevorzugen sie die des Masseurs. Unter dem Vorwand des Massierens umfasst ein Eunuch dieses Typs die Schenkel des Mannes, den er massiert, zieht sie an sich heran und berührt danach dessen Hüften und den

Gegenüberliegende Seite: Unter den Händen des Geliebten wird der Körper zum willigen Werkzeug der Lust.

mittleren Teil des Körpers. Wenn er bemerkt, dass der *Lingam* des Mannes steht, presst er ihn mit der Hand und reizt ihn weiter.

Wenn der Mann die Absicht des Massierenden erkannt hat und sich nicht dazu äußert, setzt der Eunuch seine Tätigkeit fort und beginnt dann mit dem Verkehr.

Wenn der Mann den Masseur allerdings nachdrücklich zum Weitermachen auffordert, dann sträubt der sich zunächst ein bisschen und gibt erst zum Schluss, scheinbar widerwillig, nach.

Acht Verrichtungen führt der Eunuch dann nacheinander aus: die nominale Vereinigung; die Seiten beißen, außen drücken, innen drücken, küssen, reiben, eine Mangofrucht aussaugen, verschlucken.

Oben: Ein erschöpfter Liebhaber wird aufs Neue erregt, wenn die Partner die Rollen tauschen.

Gegenüberliegende Seite: Oralverkehr war der Ehefrau verboten. So schaut sie verstohlen zu, während sich ihr Mann mit einer Kurtisane zu vergnügen beginnt.

Wenn eine Verrichtung beendet ist, bekundet der Eunuch seinen Wunsch, aufzuhören. Doch wenn der Mann noch eine »Behandlung« verlangt, dann folgt die nächste und danach noch eine usw.

• Wenn der Eunuch den *Lingam* des Mannes in der Hand hält, ihn zwischen seine Lippen nimmt und dann den Mund darüber stülpt, dann heißt das die »nominale Vereinigung«.

• Wenn der Eunuch das Ende des *Lingam* wie eine Blüte zwischen den Fingern hält und die Seiten mit den Lippen drückt, aber auch mit den Zähnen zwickt, dann heißt das »die Seiten beißen«.

• Wenn er zum Weitermachen aufgefordert wird, presst der Eunuch das Ende des *Lingams* kräftig mit den Lippen und küsst ihn, als ob er ihn herausziehen wollte. Das heißt »außen drücken«.

• Bei der nächsten Stufe steckt er sich den *Lingam* noch tiefer in den Mund, presst ihn mit den Lippen und lässt wieder los. Das heißt »innen drücken«.

• Wenn der Eunuch den *Lingam* in seiner Hand hält und so küsst wie den unteren Teil des Gliedes, dann heißt das »küssen«.

• Wenn nach dem Küssen die Zunge über das ganze Glied fährt und dabei sein oberes Ende passiert, dann heißt das »reiben«.

• Wenn auf dieselbe Art der halbe Penis in den Mund genommen, kräftig geküsst und an ihm gesaugt wird, heißt das »eine Mango aussaugen«.

• Wenn der Eunuch mit Einwilligung des Mannes schließlich den ganzen *Lingam* in seinen Mund nimmt und ihn bis zum Ende bearbeitet, dann heißt das »verschlucken«.

Bei dieser Form des Verkehrs mag es auch zum Schlagen und Kratzen kommen.

Der Oralverkehr wird auch von unkeuschen und gewöhnlichen Frauen, von Dienerinnen, Dienstmädchen ausgeführt, also von solchen Frauen, die mit niemandem verheiratet sind, aber vom Massieren leben.

Gegenüberliegende Seite: Die Vereinigung mit dem Mund ist willkommen, wenn beide damit einverstanden sind und sie beiderseitigem Vergnügen dient.

Die *Acharyas* – die ehrenwerten alten Autoren – vertreten die Ansicht, dass dieser Oralverkehr Sache eines Hundes und nicht eines Mannes ist, weil es eine niedere Handlung ist, die den Regeln der Heiligen Schrift widerspricht, und weil der Mann Schaden nimmt, indem er seinen *Lingam* in Kontakt mit dem Mund von Eunuchen und Frauen bringen lässt. Aber Vatsyayana meint, dass die Regeln der Heiligen Schrift für jene nicht gelten, die Kurtisanen besuchen, und das Gesetz nur den Oralverkehr mit verheirateten Frauen verbietet. Was die Verletzung des Mannes betrifft, so kann dem vorgebeugt werden.

Die Diener einiger Personen pflegen den Oralverkehr mit ihren Herren. Auch unter einigen Bürgern, die sich gut kennen, ist er untereinander üblich. Einige Haremsdamen haben Oralverkehr mit ihren Gefährtinnen, wenn sie liebebedürftig sind. Und einige Männer machen es mit Frauen.

Wie man das macht (d.h. die *Yoni* küssen), kennt man vom Küssen des Mundes. Wenn ein Mann und eine Frau beim Oralverkehr Kopf an Fuß liegen, dann heißt das »Vereinigung der Krähe«.

In der Sucht nach *Auparishtaka* verlassen Kurtisanen mitunter Männer, die liberal und versiert sind und die andere guten Eigenschaften besitzen. Die Kurtisanen fühlen sich zu Personen niederer Herkunft hingezogen, wie beispielsweise Sklaven oder Elefantenwärtern, die bereit sind, Oralverkehr mit ihnen zu haben.

Der Oralverkehr sollte niemals von einem Brahmanen, einem Minister mit staatlicher Verantwortung oder von einem Mann mit gutem Ruf ausgeführt werden, weil – obwohl von den *Shastras* erlaubt – es keinen Grund gibt, ihn zu praktizieren. Er sollte nur in besonderen Fällen angewendet werden.

Gegenüberliegende Seite: Die Frauen genießen bei Speisen, Trank und Liebesspiel vielfältige Sinnesfreuden.

Folgende Seiten: Die »pressende Stellung« verwöhnt Mann sowie Frau mit dem erregenden Gefühl intensiver Körperlichkeit.

Wie man Lust weckt

Wenn ein Mann unfähig ist, eine Elefantenfrau *(Hastini)* zu befriedigen, dann sollte er verschiedene Mittel nutzen, ihre Leidenschaft zu wecken. Zu Beginn sollte er mit den Händen und Fingern ihre *Yoni* reiben. Das ist ein Weg, eine Frau sexuell zu reizen. Er kann auch gewisse Apadravyas genannte Hilfsmittel, die dem *Lingam* angelegt werden, verwenden. Sie machen das Glied länger oder dicker. Nach Ansicht von Babhravya sollten diese Hilfsmittel aus Gold, Silber, Kupfer, Eisen, Elfenbein, Büffelhorn, verschiedenen Hölzern, Blech oder Blei sein. Sie müssen weich, kühl, sexuell stimulierend sein und gut sitzen.

Nun zu einigen solcher *Apadravyas:* Der »Armreif« *(Valaya)* sollte die gleiche Größe wie das Glied besitzen. Seine Außenfläche ist rau und mit Noppen besetzt. Das »Paar« *(Sanghati)* besteht aus zwei Armreifen. Die »Armspange« *(Chudaka)* besteht aus drei oder mehr miteinander verbundenen Armreifen, bis sie die erforderliche Länge des Gliedes erreichen. Die »Einzelarm-

Gegenüberliegende Seite: Der erfahrene Liebhaber tut alles dafür, dass seine Partnerin den Höhepunkt zuerst erreicht.

spange« wird geformt durch Umwickeln des *Lingam* mit Draht, dies entsprechend seines Ausmaßes. Das *Kantuka* oder *Jalaka* ist ein an beiden Enden offenes Rohr, außen rau und mit weichen Noppen besetzt, um der Größe der Scheide zu entsprechen. Es wird um die Hüfte gebunden.

Sind solche Hilfsmittel nicht erhältlich, kann es auch eine Röhre aus Holzapfelholz, das Röhrenstück des Flaschenkürbis oder ein dickes, durch Öl und Pflanzenextrakte weich gemachtes Stück Schilfrohr sein. Man befestigt sie mit Schnur an der Hüfte. Die genannten Hilfsmittel können in Verbindung mit oder anstelle des Penis verwendet werden.

Zum Abschluss auch dazu einige Merksätze: »Jener, der mit den wahren Prinzipien dieser Wissenschaft der Liebe vertraut ist, achtet *Dharma*, *Artha*, und *Kama* und berücksichtigt seine Erfahrungen und die Lehren anderer. Er handelt nicht einfach nach dem Diktat seines Verlangens.«

Eine Handlung wird niemals mit Nachsicht bewertet, nur weil sie von der Wissenschaft autorisiert worden ist. Denn es muss daran erinnert werden: Die Absicht der Wissenschaft ist es, dass nach den von ihr aufgestellten Regeln nur in besonderen Fällen verfahren werden sollte. Nach dem Lesen und Studieren der Werke von Babhravya und anderen alten Autoren wurde das *Kamasutra* von Vatsyayana entsprechend den Vorschriften der Heiligen Schrift zusammengestellt, zum Nutzen der Welt, während er das Leben eines religiösen Studenten führte und sich ganz in die Anbetung der Gottheit versenkte.

Dieses Werk beabsichtigt nicht, einzig als eine Anleitung zur Befriedigung unserer Wünsche zu dienen. Eine Person, die die wahren Prinzipien dieser Wissenschaft kennt und die ihr *Dharma*, *Artha* und *Kama* hütet sowie die Bräuche der Menschen achtet, wird mit Gewissheit die Meisterung über ihre Sinne und Gefühle erlangen.

Kurz gesagt, eine intelligente und umsichtige Person, die das *Dharma* und *Artha* sowie *Kama* befolgt, ohne zum Sklaven ihrer Leidenschaften zu werden, erlangt Erfolg in allem, was sie unternehmen mag.

Oben: Die Hirschjagd und das Pferd eines Mannes symbolisieren seine Standhaftigkeit und Ausdauer sowie bei der Frau ihre wilde Zärtlichkeit beim Liebesspiel.

Folgende Seite: Ein verliebtes Paar berauscht sich an Wasserpfeife, Wein und einem sinnlichen Vorspiel.

Teil 2

Über die Verführung

Von den charakteristischen Merkmalen der Männer und der Frauen

Ein Mann kann hinter der Frau eines anderen her sein, sozusagen um sein Leben zu retten, wenn die Intensität seiner Liebe unaufhörlich zunimmt. Es gibt zehn Stufen wachsender Intensität mit diesen Merkmalen: Liebe durch Blickkontakt; Verständnis füreinander bzw. Seelenverwandtschaft; ständiges Denken an sie; Schlaflosigkeit; Abmagern; Abwenden von Vergnügungen; Verlust des Schamgefühls; Irrsinn; Ohnmacht; Tod.

Die älteren Autoren sagen, dass ein Mann von der Form des weiblichen Körpers und von ihren Eigenschaften und Kennzeichen die Einstellung, die Wahrhaftigkeit, Reinheit und den Willen einer jungen Frau ablesen und ebenso die Intensität oder Schwäche ihrer Leidenschaft erkennen sollte. Doch Vatsyayana ist der Ansicht, dass die Formen des Körpers und die Eigenschaften und Kennzeichen auch falsche Aufschlüsse über den Charakter liefern können und dass Frauen nach ihrem Benehmen, der Ausdruckskraft ihrer Gedanken und den Körperbewegungen beurteilt werden sollten.

Gegenüberliegende Seite: Zwei Frauen verbergen hinter einem Sichtschutz das Liebesspiel des Prinzen mit einer anderen, während die erboste Prinzessin von ihren Dienerinnen zurückgehalten wird.

Folgende Seiten: Die Gopis baden und tollen bei Vollmond im Fluss. In ihrer Mitte hält Krishna Radha umschlungen und genießt die Aufmerksamkeit der jungen Frauen.

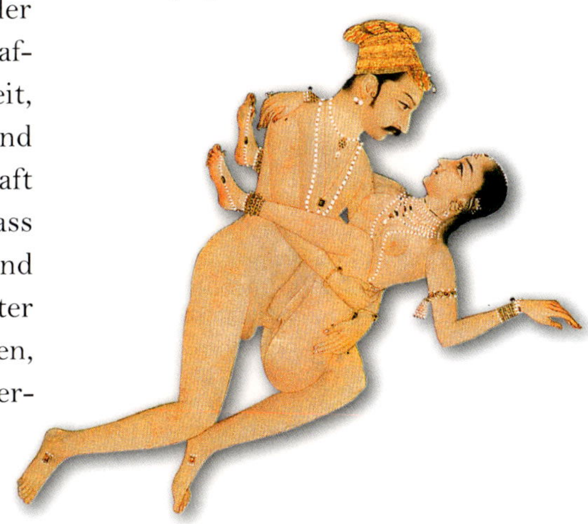

Nun gibt Gonikaputra als generelle Regel an, dass eine Frau sich in jeden hübschen Mann verliebt, den sie sieht, wegen verschiedener Umstände häufig aber keine weiteren Schritte unternimmt. Bei der Liebe treffen auf die Frau folgende Umstände zu: Sie liebt ohne Rücksicht auf Recht oder Unrecht und versucht nicht, den Mann einfach zur Erreichung eines bestimmten Zieles rumzukriegen. Ja, wenn ein Mann zuerst die Initiative ergreift, scheint sie unwillig zu sein, sich mit ihm zu verbinden. Doch wenn die Versuche, sie zu gewinnen, hartnäckig genug wiederholt werden, willigt sie schließlich ein. Andererseits darf die Frau die Versuche nicht aufgeben, den Mann für sich zu gewinnen, der seine Gefühle aus Moral und Klugheit unter Kontrolle hält und ihnen nicht nachgibt, selbst wenn er zu lieben begonnen haben sollte und oft an die Frau denkt. Manchmal unternimmt er einen Anlauf, das Objekt seiner Zuneigung zu bekommen, und wenn das nicht klappt, gibt er auf. Erobert er sie hingegen zu schnell und zu einfach, dann wird er ihrer oft überdrüssig.

Die Gründe dafür, dass Frauen versuchen, Annäherungsversuche von Männern zurückzuweisen, lauten: Zuneigung zu ihrem Gatten; Wunsch nach einem legitimen Kind; Mangel an Gewissheit, da der Mann viel herumreist; Möglichkeit, dass der Mann bereits einer anderen gehört; Angst, dass der Mann seine Absichten nicht für sich behält; Glaube, dass der Mann zu sehr seinen Freunden ergeben ist und ihnen zu viel Aufmerksamkeit widmet; Scheu, da er eine angesehene Persönlichkeit ist; Angst, da er mächtig ist oder – im Fall der Rehfrau – zu ungestüme Leidenschaft besitzt; Schüchternheit angesichts seiner Erfahrenheit; der Gedanke, einst mit ihm nur freundschaftlich verbunden gewesen zu sein; Geringschätzung, da es ihm an Kenntnissen über die Welt mangelt; Misstrauen wegen seines niederen Charakters; Abneigung wegen seiner Unfähigkeit, ihre Liebe für ihn zu begreifen; im Fall einer Elefanten-Frau der Gedanke, dass er ein Hase-Mann ist oder nur schwache Leidenschaft zeigt; Sorge, dass ihm irgend etwas wegen seiner Leidenschaft zustoßen könnte; Verzweiflung über

Gegenüberliegende Seite: Wenn ein Mann ausdauernd seine erotischen Ziele verfolgt, so gelingt es ihm, jede Frau zu erobern, die er will.

خلوت سلطان جهاندار ولد جهانگیر
عمل عبدالحمید

die eigene Unvollkommenheit; Furcht vor der Entdeckung; Illusionslosigkeit angesichts seiner grauen Haare oder seines schäbigen Aussehens; Angst, dass er von ihrem Gatten geschickt sein könnte, um ihre Keuschheit zu prüfen; der Gedanke, er könnte zu viel Wert auf Moral legen.

Welche der genannten Gründe ein Mann auch erfahren mag, er sollte sich von Anfang an bemühen, sie zu beseitigen. So muss er die Scheu, die vielleicht von seiner Bedeutung und seinem Können verursacht wird, beseitigen, indem er der Frau seine starke Liebe und große Zuneigung bekundet. Den Mangel an Gelegenheiten oder seine Unerreichbarkeit sollte er aus der Welt schaffen, indem er ihr einige einfache Wege des Zugangs zu ihm zeigt. Der ausufernde Respekt seitens der Frau ihm gegenüber sollte ausgeräumt werden, indem er sich sehr umgänglich gibt. Die Schwierigkeiten, die daraus entstehen, dass er als schwacher Charakter betrachtet wird, sollte er gegenstandslos machen, indem er seine Tapferkeit und Weisheit demonstriert; und jene, die aus Vernachlässigung stammen, durch verstärkte Aufmerksamkeit und solche, die aus Furcht entstehen, durch geeignete Ermutigung wettmachen.

Folgende Typen von Männern haben gewöhnlich Erfolg bei Frauen: die in der Wissenschaft der Liebe versierten Männer; jene, die talentierte Geschichtenerzähler sind; Männer, die von ihrer Kindheit an mit Frauen vertraut sind; jene, die das Vertrauen von Frauen gewonnen haben; Männer, die gern Geschenke machen; gute Unterhalter; Männer, die das machen, was sie mögen; jene, die zuvor noch keine andere Frau geliebt haben; Männer, die als Botschafter geschickt werden; die ihre Schwachpunkte kennen; Männer, die mit ihren Freundinnen vereint sind; die gut aussehen; Männer, die mit Frauen aufgewachsen sind; Männer, die sich sexuellen Vergnügungen hingeben, selbst wenn es mit den eigenen Dienerinnen ist; die Liebhaber der Töchter ihrer Amme; die spät geheiratet haben; Männer, die Geselligkeit mögen; liberale Männer; jene, die man wegen ihrer Stärke (Bullenmänner) rühmt; tapfere Männer und solche mit Unternehmungsgeist; Männer, die den ei-

Gegenüberliegende Seite: Musik kann während des Liebesaktes der unterhaltsamen Ablenkung dienen, aber auch als Aphrodisiakum wirken.

genen Gatten in Aussehen, in Erfahrung, in guten Eigenschaften und Freizügigkeit ausstechen; Männer, deren Kleidung und Lebensart großartig sind.

Nachfolgend die Frauentypen, die man einfach erobert: Frauen, die an der Haustür stehen; Frauen, die stets auf der Straße Ausschau halten; Frauen, die schwatzend im Haus des Nachbarn sitzen; eine Frau, die die Männer anstarrt; eine Botin; eine Frau, die Männer von der Seite ansieht; eine Frau, die ihren Ehemann hasst oder die keine Kinder hat; eine Frau, deren Familie oder Kaste nicht sehr bekannt sind; eine Frau, deren Kinder gestorben sind; eine nach Gesellschaft süchtige Frau; eine Frau, die scheinbar ihrem Gatten sehr zugetan ist; die Gattin eines Schauspielers; eine Witwe; eine arme Frau; eine Vergnügungssüchtige; eine Eitle; eine Frau, deren Gatte ihr im Rang oder in den Fähigkeiten unterlegen ist; eine Frau, die stolz ist auf ihr künstlerisches Geschick; eine Frau, deren Geist durch Schuld ihres Gatten verwirrt ist; eine Frau, die als Kleinkind mit einem reichen Mann verheiratet wurde und ihn nicht mochte, als sie erwachsen wurde, wünscht einen Mann, der in Gesinnung, Talent und Klugheit zu ihr passt; eine Frau, die grundlos von ihrem Gatten gering geschätzt wird; eine Frau, die von anderen Frauen gleicher Stellung und Schönheit nicht geachtet wird; eine Frau, deren Mann viel reist; die Gattin eines Juweliers; eine eifersüchtige Frau, eine Habsüchtige; eine Unmoralische; eine sterile Frau; eine Faule; eine feige Frau; eine Buckelige; eine Zwergin; eine versehrte Frau; eine vulgäre Frau, eine übelriechende Frau, eine Leidende, eine alte Frau.

Die Merksätze zu diesem Thema: »Verlangen, das der Natur entspringt und das durch die Kunst gesteigert wird und das durch Klugheit alle Gefährlichkeit verliert, wird fest und beständig. Ein kluger Mann, der sich auf seine Fähigkeit verlässt und sorgsam die Ideen und Vorstellungen von Frauen beachtet und der die Gründe dafür beseitige, dass sich Frauen von Männern trennen, wird im Allgemeinen Erfolg bei ihnen haben.«

Gegenüberliegende Seite: Mann und Frau sollten gemeinsame Ausflüge unternehmen, das stärkt ihr Zusammengehörigkeitsgefühl.

Vom Prüfen des Gemüts einer Frau

Wenn ein Mann bemüht ist, eine Frau für sich zu gewinnen, sollte er erst prüfen, was sie denkt und fühlt. Wenn sie ihm zuhört, aber ihm in keiner Weise ihre eigenen Absichten andeutet, sollte er versuchen, einen Vermittler einzuschalten. Wenn sie nach dem ersten Treffen besser gekleidet zum Rendezvous kommt und ihm an einen einsamen Ort folgt, dann kann er gewiss sein, dass er sie mit ein bisschen Druck rumkriegt. Eine Frau, die einem Mann den Kopf verdreht, sich ihm aber selbst nach langer Zeit nicht hingibt, sollte als Tändlerin in der Liebe betrachtet werden. Doch angesichts der Unbeständigkeit des menschlichen Wesens kann auch eine solche Frau erobert werden, wenn man lange genug an einer engen Bekanntschaft festhält.

Wenn eine Frau die Aufmerksamkeit eines Mannes nicht erwidert und aus Respekt vor ihm und aus Eigenstolz ihn nicht treffen oder sich ihm nicht nähern will, kann sie nur unter Schwierigkeiten erobert werden – entweder indem er sich um ein vertrautes Verhältnis bemüht

Gegenüberliegende Seite: Wenn ein Mann seine Partnerin beim Koitus schlägt, soll sie sich wehren – aber nur, um damit seine Erregung umso mehr zu steigern.

oder mit Hilfe eines außerordentlich geschickten Vermittlers. Bandelt ein Mann mit einer Frau an und lässt sie ihn mit harschen Worten abfahren, kann er sie nur mit Geduld und wiederholten Anläufen erobern, etwa folgendermaßen:

Wenn sie in seiner Anwesenheit einschlummert, legt er seinen linken Arm um sie. Er wird, wenn sie erwacht, spüren, ob sie ihn in Wirklichkeit zurückstößt oder ihn nur auf solche Art abweist, als ob sie wünscht, er möge diese Zärtlichkeit wiederholen. Und was er mit dem Arm macht, das kann er auch mit dem Fuß tun. Hat er in diesem Punkt Erfolg verbucht, umfasst er sie nun etwas enger. Wenn sie das nicht mag und aufsteht, sich am nächsten Tag jedoch wie gewöhnlich verhält, dann darf er davon ausgehen, dass sie nicht unwillig ist, sich mit ihm zu vergnügen.

Kommt sie allerdings nicht wieder, muss sich der Mann eines Vermittlers bedienen. Trägt das Früchte und sie erscheint nach längerer Zeit wieder, darf der Mann schlussfolgern, dass sie es nicht ablehnen würde, mit ihm anzubändeln. Wenn eine Frau dem Mann eine Chance bietet und ihre Liebe zu ihm bekundet, muss er darauf zusteuern, sich ihrer zu erfreuen.

Wenn eine Frau den Mann weder ermutigt noch ihn meidet, sich aber an einem abgelegenen Platz versteckt, dann muss der Mann mit Hilfe einer Dienerin, die sie gut kennt, ihrer habhaft werden. Bleibt sie, wo sie ist, nachdem der Mann nach ihr rufen ließ, sollte sie durch Einschaltung eines geschickten Vermittlers überzeugt werden. Lässt sie dem Mann dann immer noch nichts ausrichten, muss er gründlich über sie nachdenken, ehe er neue Versuche beginnt. So endet das Prüfen, wie eine Frau denkt und sich verhält. Ein Mann soll zuerst einer Frau vorgestellt werden und dann eine Unterhaltung mit ihr anfangen. Er darf ihr versteckt seine Liebe andeuten, und wenn er aus ihren Erwiderungen abliest, dass sie seine Hinweise günstig aufnimmt, dann muss er sich ohne Furcht ans Werk machen, sie für sich zu gewinnen. Eine Frau, die ihre Liebe dem Mann gegenüber schon beim ersten Gespräch erken-

Gegenüberliegende Seite: Da ihrem Verlangen keine Grenzen gesetzt sind, können sich Mann und Frau zu jeder Tageszeit lieben.

برید و خون بسیاری جاری شد جوان از کمال شوق

Gegenüberliegende Seite: Inmitten eines üppigen Parks streichelt eine Frau ihren Liebhaber zärtlich mit ihrer Hand und einer Blume.

nen lässt, kann sehr einfach erobert werden. Ebenso kann man damit rechnen, dass eine lüsterne Frau, die man auf liebenswürdige Art anspricht und die darauf ihre Liebe offen wörtlich ausdrückt, sich im Handumdrehen verführen lässt. Es trifft auf alle Frauen zu, ob klug, schlicht oder vertraulich, dass jene, die ihre Liebe offen zeigen, einfach zu gewinnen sind.

Eine junge Frau gibt, wie nachfolgend beschrieben, ihre Liebe stets durch äußere Zeichen und Handlungen zu erkennen: Sie schaut dem Mann niemals ins Gesicht. Sie reagiert schüchtern, wenn er sie betrachtet. Sie sieht ihn heimlich von der Seite an. Sie senkt den Kopf, wenn er sie etwas fragt, und sie antwortet unzusammenhängend und in unvollendeten Sätzen. Sie mag es, lange in seiner Begleitung zu sein. Sie spricht zu ihrem Personal in besonderem Ton und hofft, seine Aufmerksamkeit zu erringen, wenn sie etwas von ihm entfernt steht. Sie sucht diesen oder jenen Vorwand, ihm Geschichten so ausführlich zu erzählen, dass sie damit die Unterhaltung in die Länge ziehen kann. In seiner Anwesenheit küsst und umarmt sie ein Kind auf ihrem Schoß. Sie malt Ornamente auf die Stirn ihrer Dienerinnen. Sie führt sportliche und ästhetische Bewegungen aus, wenn ihr Personal in Anwesenheit des Liebsten mit ihr scherzt. Sie hat Vertrauen zu den Freunden des Liebhabers, achtet sie und gehorcht ihnen. Sie zeigt sich seinen Dienern gegenüber freundlich, spricht mit ihnen und weist sie zu Arbeiten an, als wäre sie die Hausfrau. Und sie hört aufmerksam zu, wenn sie Geschichten über ihren Liebhaber oder irgendjemand anders erzählen. Sie betritt sein Haus, wenn sie dazu von der Tochter ihrer Amme ermutigt wird, und bringt es fertig, mit deren Assistenz mit ihm zu plaudern und zu spielen. Sie vermeidet es, ihrem Liebsten zu begegnen, wenn sie nicht ordentlich gekleidet und geschmückt ist. Eine Freundin beauftragt sie, ihm einen Ohrring, eine Blumengirlande von

Oben: Ein Liebhaber sollte der Frau versichern, dass er ihr gegenüber stets respektvoll und aufmerksam sein wird.

Gegenüberliegende Seite: Ein Mann umwirbt seine Geliebte, indem er als Liebesgott Kamadeva auftritt, der mit Lotuspfeilen die Leidenschaft der Sterblichen entfacht.

ihr zu überbringen, um die er gebeten haben könnte. Sie trägt immer etwas, das er ihr vielleicht geschenkt hat. Sie wird betrübt, wenn ihre Eltern einen anderen Bräutigam erwähnen, und natürlich trifft sie sich nicht mit dessen Leuten.

Auch dazu gibt es wieder einige Merksätze: »Ein Mann, der die Gefühle eines Mädchens für ihn erkannt und verstanden hat und der die Anzeichen und Bandlungen zur Kenntnis genommen hat, in denen sich jene Gefühle äußern, der sollte alles in seiner Macht Stehende veranlassen, eine Verbindung mit dem Mädchen einzugehen. Er sollte ein Mädchen für sich gewinnen durch kindliche Spiele, eine reifere Jungfrau durch seine Fertigkeiten in den Künsten und ein Mädchen, das ihn liebt, indem er andere Personen einspannt, denen es vertraut.«

عمل رشید

Wie man eine Frau für sich gewinnt

Die alten Autoren äußern die Ansicht, dass Mädchen nicht so einfach verführt werden, wenn man eine Botin einschaltet; besser seien die direkten Bemühungen des Mannes. Hingegen kommt man an die Ehefrauen anderer besser mit der Hilfe von Botinnen heran als durch eigene Anstrengungen. Doch Vatsyayana hält fest, dass – wenn immer möglich – ein Mann in diesen Angelegenheiten selbst handeln sollte. Und nur, wenn das unpraktisch oder unmöglich ist, setzt man eine Botin ein. Was die Behauptung betrifft, dass Frauen, die offen und frei sprechen und handeln, durch persönliches Bemühen des Mannes zu erobern seien, während Frauen ohne diese Eigenschaften eher durch Botinnen überzeugt werden könnten, so ist das eben nichts weiter als nur Gerede.

Wenn ein Mann in dieser Sache selbst handelt, dann sollte er vor allem und zuerst auf die folgende Weise Bekanntschaft mit der Frau, die er liebt, schließen:

Erstens arrangiert es der Mann so, dass er dieser Frau bei einer natürlichen oder einer besonderen Gele-

Gegenüberliegende Seite: Die Frau öffnet ihre Beine weit, um ihren Geliebten zu empfangen.

genheit begegnet. Eine natürliche Gelegenheit kann ein Treffen im Hause eines Freundes, eines Angehörigen der gleichen Kaste, eines Ministers oder eines Arztes sein, aber ebenso eine Hochzeit, eine Opferzeremonie, sowie auch Festivals, Gartenfeste oder Bestattungen.

Zweitens macht sich der Mann bei der Begegnung vorsichtig bemerkbar, und zwar derart, dass seine Absichten nicht verborgen bleiben. Er sollte seinen Bart zwirbeln, mit den Fingern knacken, seinen Schmuck klimpern lassen, sich auf die Unterlippe beißen und andere Zeichen dieser Art machen. Schaut sie zu ihm herüber, so spricht er mit Freunden und anderen Frauen über sie. Dabei gibt er ihr seine Weitherzigkeit und seine Freude am Vergnügen zu erkennen. Sitzt er an der Seite einer guten Freundin, sollte er gähnen, sich rekeln und ihr nur lustlos zuhören. Eine Konversation mit Hintersinn könnte er mit einem Kind oder einer anderen Person führen. Das Gespräch bezieht sich angeblich auf eine dritte Person, doch tatsächlich ist die Frau gemeint, die er liebt. Auf diese Art kann seine Liebe unter dem Vorwand gezeigt werden, dass sich seine Konversation auf andere und nicht auf sie bezieht. Er sollte Zeichen setzen, die Bezug zu ihr haben, beispielsweise mit seinen Nägeln oder einem Stock etwas in den Boden kratzen. Das alles muss zur rechten Zeit und am rechten Ort geschehen.

Drittens spielt der Mann mit einem Kind auf ihrem Schoß. Er gibt ihm etwas in die Hand und nimmt es ihm wieder weg. Dann könnte er mit ihr eine Unterhaltung über das Kind beginnen. Allmählich lernen sie sich so kennen, und er führt sich bei ihren Verwandten auf angenehme Art ein. Später kann diese Bekanntschaft zum Vorwand genommen werden, sie häufig in ihrem Haus zu besuchen. Bei diesen Gelegenheiten sollte er in ihrer Abwesenheit über das Thema Liebe reden. Allerdings sollte sie sich dabei in Hörweite befinden. Mit wachsender Intimität kann er ihr nun etwas zum Aufbewahren geben und sich von Zeit zu Zeit davon etwas bei ihr abholen. Er mag ihr einige Duftstoffe oder Betelnüsse zum Aufbewahren

Gegenüberliegende Seite: Zu einer erfüllten Liebe gehören auch der gemeinsame Tanz und Gesang.

Oben: Mann und Frau sind im Akt der Liebe gleichberechtigt und sollten einander in Elan sowie in Enthusiasmus entsprechen.

Gegenüberliegende Seite: Es gibt zahllose Möglichkeiten für das Liebesspiel, so können sich mehrere Frauen gleichzeitig an einem Mann erfreuen.

geben. Danach bemüht er sich, sie mit seiner Ehefrau bekannt zu machen, beide zu vertraulichen Gesprächen zu veranlassen und gemeinsam an einsamen Orten zu verweilen. Um sie häufig zu sehen, arrangiert er, dass die beiden Familien denselben Goldschmied, denselben Korbmacher, denselben Färber und denselben Wäschemann haben. Ganz offen sollte er ihr unter einem Vorwand lange Besuche abstatten und an ihren Geschäften beteiligt sein. So führt ein Geschäft zum nächsten, um die Zweisamkeit zu intensivieren. Sobald sie etwas wünscht, wenn sie Geld braucht oder eine Ausbildung in einer der Künste, soll er sie wissen lassen, dass er willig und fähig ist, alles für sie zu tun, ihr Geld zu geben, sie in einer der Künste zu unterrichten. Das alles liege in seiner Macht und Fähigkeit. Er darf mit ihr in Gesellschaft anderer Leute diskutieren, über Tun und Lassen

anderer Personen reden, verschiedene Gegenstände, wie Edelsteine oder Schmuck, prüfen. Bei solchen Gelegenheiten zeigt er ihr gewisse Dinge mit Wert. Kommt es darüber zu Meinungsverschiedenheiten, so gibt er nach, widerspricht nicht, sondern versichert, dass er ihr in jeder Beziehung zustimmt.

So enden die Möglichkeiten, die Bekanntschaft mit einer begehrten Frau zu arrangieren. Nun, nachdem ein Mädchen mit einem Mann – wie oben beschrieben – bekannt geworden ist und die Liebe zu ihm mittels verschiedener äußerer Zeichen und Körperhaltungen zu erkennen gegeben hat, muss der Mann jede Anstrengung unternehmen, es zu erobern. Da Mädchen aber mit der sexuellen Vereinigung nicht vertraut sind, müssen sie mit der größten Vorsicht behandelt werden. Der Mann muss mit beträchtlicher Behutsamkeit vorgehen, auch wenn das bei Frauen, die an Geschlechtsverkehr gewöhnt sind, nicht nötig ist. Wenn die Absichten des Mädchens bekannt sind und es seine Schüchternheit überwunden hat, sollte der Mann sein Geld ins Spiel bringen, um Kleidung, Ringe und Blumen zu kaufen. Dabei muss er besonders darauf achten, dass seine Geschenke hübsch und wertvoll sind. Hingegen sollte er von dem Mädchen eine Mischung aus Betelnüssen und Betelblättern bekommen. Und auf einer Gesellschaft sollte er um die Blume im Haar oder in der Hand des Mädchens bitten. Blumen, die er ihm schenkt, duften süßlich und sind mit Zeichen seiner Nägel oder Zähne markiert. Mit zunehmender Beharrlichkeit zerstreut er die Ängste des Mädchens und bringt es allmählich dazu, mit ihm an einsame Orte zu gehen. Dort umarmt er es und küsst es. Und wenn dann die Zeit kommt, ihm einige Betelnüsse zu reichen bzw. einige von ihm gereicht zu bekommen, oder beim Austausch von Blumen, berührt und drückt er die intimen Körperpartien des Mädchens und bringt somit seine Bemühungen zu einem befriedigenden Abschluss.

Oben: *Wenn ein Mann zwei Ehefrauen hat, sollte er beiden die gleiche Aufmerksamkeit schenken.*

Bemüht sich ein Mann, eine Frau zu verführen, dann sollte er nicht versuchen, zur gleichen Zeit eine andere Frau zu verführen. Wenn er bei der ersten Erfolg hatte, kann er sich ihre Zuneigung bewahren, indem er ihr Geschenke macht, die ihr gefallen, und sich dann der anderen Frau zuwenden. Wenn ein Mann den Gatten einer Frau zu einem Platz in der Nähe seines Hauses gehen sieht, sollte er sich mit dieser Frau nicht einlassen, selbst wenn sie zu dieser Zeit ganz problemlos zu gewinnen ist. Ein kluger Mann, der auf seinen Ruf hält, denkt nicht an das Verführen einer Frau, die furchtsam und zaghaft ist, der man nicht trauen kann, die gut behütet ist oder Schwiegervater und Schwiegermutter besitzt.

Von der Kunst des Verführens

Wenn ein Mädchen beginnt, die Liebe des Liebhabers durch äußere Zeichen und Bewegungen zu zeigen, muss er versuchen, es mit verschiedenen Mitteln und Methoden vollständig für sich zu gewinnen. Beim Sport und Spiel sollte er absichtlich die Hand des Mädchens halten. Er kann alle Arten der Umarmungen, wie die berührende und andere bereits in den vorigen Kapiteln beschriebene, versuchen.

Beim Schwimmen taucht er in einiger Entfernung von ihm und kommt ganz dicht bei dem Mädchen wieder empor. Er weist es mit Begeisterung auf das frische Grün der Bäume und andere sprießende Zeichen der Natur hin. Er beschreibt ihm den Schmerz, den er wegen seiner Liebe erleidet. Er berichtet von dem wundervollen Traum, den er hatte und in dem andere Frauen auftauchten.

Bei Geselligkeiten und Versammlungen seiner Kaste setzt er sich ganz in die Nähe des Mädchens und nutzt diesen Vorwand zum körperlichen Kontakt. Wenn er seinen Fuß auf den des Mädchens setzt, berührt er ganz

Gegenüberliegende Seite: Die Verbindung von Liebesakt und Bogenschießen verweist auf die vielfachen (Jagd-)Talente, durch die sich ein Kavalier auszeichnen sollte.

Oben: Bei diesem Rollentausch imitiert der Mann den Bogen und die Frau legt den Pfeil an.

vorsichtig erst dessen Zehen und drückt dann die Nagelspitzen. Hat er damit Erfolg, nimmt er den Fuß in seine Hand und wiederholt dasselbe. Bei anderer Gelegenheit klemmt er einen Finger von der Hand des Mädchens zwischen seine Zehen, wenn es dabei ist, seine Füße zu waschen.

Wann immer er dem Mädchen etwas gibt oder etwas von ihm nimmt, beweist er durch sein Verhalten, wie sehr er es liebt.

Ghotakamukha sagt: »Ein Mann mag ein Mädchen noch so sehr lieben, er hat dennoch keinen Erfolg, ein Mädchen für sich zu gewinnen, wenn er nicht eine Menge erzählt.»

Am Ende, wenn der Mann das Mädchen als vollständig erobert betrachtet, mag er beginnen, sich ihm intim zu nähern. Was die Ansicht betrifft, dass Frauen abends und im Dunkeln gewöhnlich weniger zurückhaltend sind und sich den Männern nicht widersetzen und man deshalb zu dieser Zeit Spaß mit ihnen haben sollte, das ist nichts weiter als Gerede.

Ist es dem Mann unmöglich, seine Bemühungen allein fortzusetzen, dann kann er die Tochter der Amme der jungen Frau oder eine Freundin einspannen, der sie vertraut, damit sie zu ihm geleitet wird, ohne dass sie seine Absichten durchschaut. Er sollte dann wie oben beschrieben vorgehen. Er könnte am Anfang auch sein Dienstmädchen zu der jungen Frau schicken, damit sich beide anfreunden, und noch andere Mittel einsetzen, um sie zu erobern.

Schließlich, wenn er ihre Gefühle durch ihr äußeres Verhalten und Benehmen ihm gegenüber bei religiösen Zeremonien, Hochzeitsfeiern, Messen, Festen, Theateraufführungen, öffentlichen Versammlungen und bei anderen Anlässen erkannt hat, sollte er beginnen, sich ihrer zu erfreuen, wenn sie allein sind. Denn Vatsyayana hält fest, dass Frauen, wenn man sie zur richtigen Zeit und am rechten Ort bedrängt, sich nicht von ihren Liebhabern abwenden.

Wenn ein ordentlich erzogenes Mädchen mit guten Eigenschaften, obwohl in einfacher Familie geboren oder nicht vermögend und deshalb von ihresgleichen nicht begehrt oder ein Waisenmädchen oder von den Eltern verlassen, dennoch die Regeln der Familie und der Kaste beachtend, wenn ein solches Mädchen bei entsprechendem Alter in den Stand der Ehe treten möchte, dann muss es versuchen, einen starken und hübschen jungen Mann für sich einzunehmen oder eine Person, von der es glaubt, sie wäre wegen Gedankenschwäche und auch ohne Zustimmung der Eltern bereit, es zu heiraten. Es sollte zu solchen Mitteln greifen, die es bei besagter Person liebenswert machen.

Es sollte den begehrten Mann häufig sehen und besuchen. Die Mutter des Mädchens sollte ebenfalls für häufige Begegnungen der beiden sorgen und eventuell eine Freundin und die Tochter der Amme einschalten. Das Mädchen sollte versuchen, sich mit dem Geliebten heimlich an einem einsamen Ort zu treffen.

Doch die alten Autoren meinen, selbst wenn ein Mädchen den Mann noch so sehr liebt, darf es sich nicht anbieten und die ersten Anspielungen machen, denn ein Mädchen verliert damit seine Würde und läuft Gefahr, verachtet und abgewiesen zu werden. Zeigt der Mann aber den Wunsch, sich des Mädchens zu erfreuen, darf es sich ihm gegenüber freundlich und offen verhalten und keinen Wandel in ihrem Betragen erkennen lassen, wenn er es umarmt, und alle Bekundungen seiner Liebe entgegennehmen.

Aber wenn er versucht, das Mädchen zu küssen, dann sollte es sich widersetzen. Bittet er um die Erlaubnis, mit ihm Geschlechtsverkehr zu haben, darf das Mädchen nach beträchtlichem Widerstand und Zögern nur erlauben, dass er die Intimstellen berührt. So von ihm bedrängt, darf es sich ihm nicht hingeben, als ob es der eigene Wunsch wäre, sondern es muss sich seinem Drängen, es sich zu nehmen, widersetzen. Nur wenn das Mädchen Gewissheit hat, dass er es wirklich liebt und dass der Liebhaber es wirklich anbetet und seinen Sinn nicht ändern wird, nur dann sollte es sich ihm hingeben und ihn von einer schnellen Hochzeit überzeugen. Nachdem das Mädchen seine Jungfernschaft verloren hat, muss es guten Freundinnen davon erzählen.

Die Merksätze zum Thema lauten folgendermaßen: »Ein sehr begehrtes Mädchen sollte den Mann heiraten, den es mag und von dem es glaubt, er würde ihr folgen und in der Lage sein, ihr Vergnügen zu berei-

Gegenüberliegende Seite: Ihre Freundinnen versuchen, eine Frau zu unterhalten, die sich nach ihrem Liebhaber sehnt.

Unten: Eine Frau gerät in Ekstase, als sie ihren Fuß auf der Brust ihres Liebhabers abstellt.

ten. Doch wird das Mädchen von seinen Eltern aus dem Streben nach Reichtum an einen reichen Mann verheiratet, ohne den Charakter oder das Aussehen des Bräutigams in Betracht zu ziehen, oder wenn es einem Mann gegeben wird, der mehrere Frauen hat, so wird es sich niemals zu diesem Mann hingezogen fühlen, selbst wenn er über gute Eigenschaften verfügt, ihren Wünschen nachgibt, aktiv, stark und gesund ist und sich auf jede Art bemüht, dem Mädchen zu gefallen.

Ein Gatte, der folgsam und dennoch sein eigener Herr ist, mag er auch arm sein und nicht gut aussehen, ist besser als einer, der hübsch und attraktiv ist, aber zu vielen Frauen Beziehungen unterhält.

Die Ehefrauen von reichen Männern, wenn es deren viele gibt, sind im Allgemeinen ihren Gatten gegenüber nicht besonders verbunden, nicht sehr vertraulich, und sie nehmen Zuflucht zu anderen Männern, auch wenn sie alle äußeren Freuden des Lebens genießen können.

Ein Mann von niederer Gesinnung verdient nicht, verheiratet zu sein; ebenso trifft das auf einen Mann zu, der viele Frauen und Kinder hat, dem Sport sowie dem Spiel verfallen ist und nur zu seiner Frau kommt, wenn es ihm beliebt.

Von allen Liebhabern eines Mädchens eignet sich nur jener zum wahren Gatten, der die Eigenschaften besitzt, die das Mädchen mag. Und nur ein solcher Gatte erfreut sich wirklicher Überlegenheit über das Mädchen, weil er der Gatte aus Liebe ist.«

Gegenüberliegende Seite: Ein Mann sollte auf sein Äußeres achten, wenn er einer Frau den Hof macht.

Folgende Seite: Diese animalische Stellung stimuliert die sensibelsten Punkte der Frau und bereitet ihr höchste Lust.

Teil 3
Über die Heirat

Wie man die richtige Frau wählt

Wird ein jungfräuliches Mädchen derselben Kaste in Übereinstimmung mit den Regeln der Heiligen Schrift verheiratet, so ergeben sich aus dieser Verbindung: das Erlangen von *Dharma* und *Artha*, Nachkommenschaft, Anhänglichkeit, Erweiterung des Freundeskreises und ungetrübte Liebe. Aus diesem Grunde sollte ein Mann seine Zuneigung einem Mädchen schenken, das aus guter Familie kommt, dessen Eltern noch leben und das drei oder mehr Jahre jünger ist als er. Es sollte aus einer sehr angesehenen Familie stammen, die reich ist, über gute Beziehungen verfügt, viele Verwandte und Freunde hat. Es sollte auch schön sein, von guter Verfassung, mit Glücksmalen am Körper, schönen Haaren, Nägeln, Zähnen, Ohren, Augen sowie Brüsten, wie man sie sich vorstellt, und es darf keine Mängel oder gesundheitliche Probleme haben. Selbstverständlich muss der Mann ebensolche Qualitäten besitzen. Aber, so sagt Ghotakamukha, ein Mädchen, das schon mit anderen geschlafen hat, d.h. keine Jungfer mehr ist, sollte nicht

Gegenüberliegende Seite: Der Mann umfasst zärtlich das Haar der Frau. Er dringt nur wenig in sie ein, um die beiderseitige Lust zu verstärken.

Oben: Sich nach dem Mann umzusehen, der von hinten eindringt, wirkt auf ihn stimulierend.

Gegenüberliegende Seite: Das Schönheitsideal des Kamasutra: eine Frau soll ein volles, strahlendes Gesicht (wie der Mond), schwere Brüste, breite Hüften und runde, stämmige Schenkel haben.

geliebt werden, weil es erneut anfällig dafür werden würde. Eine Hochzeit mit einem Mädchen auszurichten, wie eingangs beschrieben, kostet die Eltern und Verwandten des Mannes Mühe. Wenn beide Seiten es wünschen, dürfen auch Freunde in die Angelegenheit einbezogen werden. Diese Freunde sollten den Eltern des Mädchens von allen Schwächen berichten, die andere Heiratskandidaten gegenwärtig oder künftig haben. Gleichzeitig sollten sie alle Vorzüge ihres Freundes, auch die der Vorfahren der Familie, schildern und sogar übertrieben darstellen, um ihn im besten Licht zu zeigen und damit besonderen Eindruck auf die Mutter des Mädchens zu machen. Einer der Freunde könnte sich als Astrologe ausgeben und eine Zukunft in Glück und Wohlstand für seinen Freund voraussagen, indem er die günstige Konstellation der Sterne deutet, glückverheißende Omen und Zeichen zeigt, den vorteilhaften Eintritt der Sonne in das Zeichen des Tierkreises sowie Glücksmale am Körper des Freundes erwähnt. Andere wiederum könnten die Eifersucht der Mutter wecken, indem sie erzählen, dass ihr Freund die Möglichkeit hätte, von anderer Seite ein noch besseres Mädchen als ihre Tochter zu bekommen.

Ein Mädchen nimmt man dann zur Frau, wenn Fortuna lächelt, Zeichen, Omen und die Worte anderer günstig sind. Denn Ghotakamukha meint, ein Mann darf nicht zu beliebiger Zeit heiraten, wenn es ihm gefällt. Ein Mädchen, das schläfrig ist, weint oder weggelaufen ist, als man um seine Hand anhielt, oder mit einem anderen verlobt ist, sollte nicht geheiratet werden. Folgende sollte man gleichfalls meiden: eine, die verborgen gehalten wird; die einen schlecht klingenden Namen trägt; eine mit flacher Nase; eine mit nach oben gewölbten Nasenlöchern; eine, die wie ein Mann aussieht; eine, die gebückt geht; eine mit O-Beinen, eine mit vorstehender Stirn; eine Glatzköpfige; eine, die nichts von Reinlichkeit

hält; eine, die von jemand anderem befleckt worden ist; eine an *Gulma* Leidende; eine, die verunstaltet ist; eine, die noch nicht ihre Pubertät erreicht hat; eine Freundin; eine, die eine jüngere Schwester ist, sowie eine *Varshakari*.

Doch einige Autoren sagen, dass man Prosperität nur durch die Heirat des Mädchens erlangt, zu dem man sich hingezogen fühlt, und dass deshalb kein anderes Mädchen als das geliebte geheiratet werden sollte.

Wenn ein Mädchen heiratsfähig wird, sollten es die Eltern hübsch kleiden und so platzieren, dass es von allen gut gesehen werden kann. Jeden Nachmittag, nachdem sie es nett angezogen und geschmückt haben, schicken sie es mit ihren Begleiterinnen zu Sport und Spiel, zu Opferfesten und Hochzeitszeremonien, um so der Gesellschaft die Vorteile des Mädchens zu zeigen, denn es ist eine Art Ware. Mit freundlichen Worten und Gesten sollten sie jene empfangen, die vielversprechend aussehen, von ihren Freunden und Verwandten begleitet zu Besuch kommen, um ihr Interesse an der Tochter zu bekunden. Nachdem diese passend gekleidet wurde, sollte sie ihnen präsentiert werden.

Danach hat man auf das Glück zu warten und kann einen späteren Termin vorschlagen, um dann die Hochzeit der Tochter festzulegen. Bei dieser Gelegenheit, wenn die entsprechenden Personen eingetroffen sind, empfehlen ihnen die Eltern des Mädchens, zunächst ein Bad zu nehmen, dann zu speisen, und danach erklären sie: »Alles zu seiner Zeit.« Möglichem Drängen geben sie nicht nach, sondern verschieben die eigentliche Angelegenheit auf später im Verlauf des Besuchs.

Hat der Mann sich für das Mädchen entschieden, dann heiratet er es gemäß dem Brauch des Landes oder entsprechend seinem eigenen Wunsch, in Übereinstimmung mit den Regeln der Heiligen Schrift und entsprechend einer der vier Arten der Heirat.

Gegenüberliegende Seite: Bei der »Spitze«, auch »Kreisel« genannt, dreht sich die Frau während des Koitus auf dem Schoß des Mannes.

Vergnügungen in Gesellschaft anderer, beispielsweise Verse vollenden, die ein anderer begonnen hat, Hochzeitsfeiern und andere Zeremonien, sollen nicht zusammen mit Vorgesetzten oder Untergebenen gepflegt

Oben: Eine Variation der »Zange«: die Frau presst den Lingam mit ihrer Yoni. Die Penetration ist tief.

Gegenüberliegende Seite: Mit seinen kontrollierten Stößen kann der Mann bei dieser Variante der »weit geöffneten Stellung« seine Partnerin optimal stimulieren.

werden, sondern nur mit Ebenbürtigen. Als eine hohe Verbindung gilt, wenn ein Mann nach der Hochzeit seine Gattin und deren Verwandte wie ein Hausangestellter bedienen muss. Von den Weisen wird eine solche Verbindung getadelt. Andererseits sprechen die Weisen von niederer Verbindung, wenn ein Mann mit seinen Verwandten über seine Gattin herrscht. Doch wenn Mann und Frau sich gegenseitig Respekt erweisen und Vergnügen bereiten und den Verwandten beider Seiten ebenso, dann nennt man das eine Verbindung im eigentlichen Sinne des Wortes. Deshalb sollte ein Mann sich weder auf eine Verbindung einlassen, durch die er verpflichtet wird, sich später vor seinen Angehörigen zu beugen, noch auf eine niedere Verbindung, die weltweit von allen getadelt wird.

عمل منوهر

Wie man das Vertrauen eines Mädchens gewinnt

Während der ersten drei Tage nach der Hochzeit sollten Mann und Frau auf dem Boden schlafen, sich sexuellen Vergnügens enthalten und ihre Mahlzeiten ungewürzt zu sich nehmen. Während der folgenden sieben Tage sollten sie zum Klang angenehmer Musik baden, sich schmücken, zusammen speisen und ihren Verwandten sowie jenen, die als Trauzeugen gekommen sind, Aufmerksamkeit erweisen. Das gilt für Angehörige aller Kasten. In der Nacht des zehnten Tages beginnt der Mann, mit schmeichelnder Stimme zu sprechen und so das Vertrauen der Frau zu gewinnen. Einige Autoren sagen, dass er drei Tage nicht mit ihr sprechen sollte, damit sie sich an ihn gewöhnt. Babhravyas Anhänger jedoch sind der Meinung, dass, wenn der Mann drei Tage lang nicht zu ihr spricht, sie entmutigt werden, ihn als geistlos wie eine Säule betrachten und sich zurückgestoßen fühlen könnte. Sie mag in ihm sogar einen Eunuchen vermuten. Vatsyayana sagt, dass der Mann beginnen sollte, ihr Vertrauen zu gewinnen, aber zunächst Abstand nimmt von sexuel-

Gegenüberliegende Seite: Unerfahrenen Frauen soll sich der Mann mit Geduld nähern und Schritt für Schritt ihr Vertrauen erlangen.

len Annäherungsversuchen. Da Frauen von zarter Natur sind, möchten sie einen zärtlichen Anfang. Wenn sie gewaltsam von einem Mann genommen werden, mit dem sie gerade erst bekannt geworden sind, so können sie plötzlich zu Hassern von sexuellen Beziehungen werden und manchmal selbst zu Hassern des männlichen Geschlechts.

Der Mann sollte sich deshalb der Frau in einer Weise nähern, die sie mag, und er bedient sich dabei am besten solcher Mittel, mit denen er mehr und mehr ihr Vertrauen gewinnt.

Wenn sie seine Umarmung duldet, schiebt er ihr eine *Tambula*, ein Tütchen aus Betelblatt mit Betelnuss gefüllt, in den Mund. Sollte sie das nicht mögen, so muss er sie mit Überredung, mit Flehen und Schwüren zu ihren Füßen kniend dazu bewegen, denn es ist eine universelle Regel, dass eine Frau, mag sie noch so scheu oder ängstlich sein, niemals einen zu ihren Füßen knienden Mann abweist. Wenn er ihr diese *Tambula* gibt, sollte er sie zärtlich und weich auf den Mund küssen, ohne einen Laut von sich zu geben. Willigt sie in dieser Richtung ein, dann muss er sie zum Sprechen bringen. Gelingt ihm das, stellt er ihr Fragen über Themen, von denen er vorgibt, nichts zu verstehen, und die in ein paar Worten beantwortet werden können. Spricht sie nicht, sollte er sie nicht ängstigen, aber wieder und wieder in versöhnlicher Art dieselben Fragen stellen. Antwortet sie immer noch nicht, dann drängt er sie zu einer Erwiderung. Denn Ghotakamukhta sagt: »Alle Mädchen hören alles, was ihnen Männer sagen, während sie selbst manchmal kein Wort äußern.« So bedrängt, kann sie mit dem Schütteln ihres Kopfes reagieren. Doch ist sie immer noch zu sehr beunruhigt, dann macht sie auch das nicht. Wird sie von dem Mann gefragt, ob sie ihn mag, schweigt sie zunächst lange. Erst wenn sie zur Antwort gedrängt wird, signalisiert sie durch Kopfnicken ihre Bejahung. Kannte der Mann die Frau schon vorher, könnte er auch eine Freundin einschalten, die das Vertrauen beider besitzt und die Konversation zwischen beiden zu fördern vermag. In sol-

Gegenüberliegende Seite: Die Stellung, bei der die Frau, auf dem Rücken liegend, abwechselnd ihre Beine nach oben streckt, nennt man »den Bambus spalten«.

chem Fall hört die Frau gesenkten Kopfes und lächelnd zu. Doch wenn die vermittelnde Freundin ihrerseits mehr sagt, als gewünscht wird, sollte die Frau mit ihr schimpfen. Die Freundin könnte im Scherz etwas sagen, was die Frau gar nicht geäußert hat, und noch hinzufügen: »So hat sie es gesagt.« Darauf kann die Frau undeutlich und verschmitzt ausrufen: »O nein! Das habe ich nicht gesagt!« Dabei sollte sie lächeln und einen verstohlenen Blick auf ihren Gatten werfen.

Wenn die Frau mit dem Mann vertraut ist, legt sie die *Tambula*, den Balsam oder die Girlande, um die er vielleicht gebeten hat, dicht vor ihn oder steckt es gar oben in seine Kleidung. Während sie das tut, könnte er ihre jungen Brüste berühren, indem er leicht mit den Fingernägeln darüber fährt. Will sie ihn daran hindern, entgegnet er: »Ich mache es nicht wieder, wenn du mich umarmst.« Er sollte sie dazu bringen, dass sie ihn umarmt. Während sie das tut, streicht er ihr mit seiner Hand wiederholt über den Körper. Allmählich sollte er sie auf seinen Schoß ziehen und sich bemühen, ihre Einwilligung zu erhalten. Wenn sie ihm nicht nachgibt, kann er ihr drohen: »Mit meinen Zähnen und Nägeln werde ich deine Lippen und Brüste markieren und Ähnliches auch an meinem Körper machen und es meinen Freunden zeigen und erzählen, dass du das getan hast. Was wirst du dann sagen?« Auf diese Art, so wie man dem Gemüt eines Kindes Angst und Vertrauen einflößt, macht der Mann sie langsam seinen Wünschen gefügig.

In der zweiten und dritten Nacht, nachdem ihre Zutraulichkeit zugenommen hat, darf er sie mit seinen Händen am ganzen Körper abtasten und sie überall küssen. Er sollte seine Hände auf ihre Schenkel legen und sie massie-

Gegenüberliegende Seite: Eine Dienerin hilft ihrer Herrin in die Kleider, während deren Liebhaber einen Blick auf sie erhascht.

ren. Hat er Erfolg, dann reibt er zärtlich ihre Gelenke. Versucht sie, das zu verhindern, könnte er entgegnen: »Wem schadet es, wenn ich das tue?« Hat er diesen Punkt erreicht, streichelt er ihren Intimbereich, löst Gürtel und Knoten ihrer Kleidung, schlägt ihr Untergewand hoch und massiert die nackten Schenkel. Für das alles nennt er Vorwände, beginnt aber noch nicht mit dem eigentlichen Geschlechtsakt. Er könnte von den vierundsechzig Arten sprechen, ihr seine große Liebe beteuern und von seinen Hoffnungen und Vorstellungen schwärmen, die er seit langem in Bezug auf sie hegt. Er verspricht ihr Treue für die Zukunft, zerstreut alle ihre Befürchtungen hinsichtlich Rivalinnen. Und zum Schluss, nachdem sie ihre Scheu ganz abgelegt hat, beginnt er, sie auf solche Art zu begatten, dass sie sich nicht fürchtet. Das zum Thema, wie man das Vertrauen des Mädchens gewinnt. Die Merksätze dazu lauten:

»Ein Mann, der nach den Neigungen der Frau handelt, sollte versuchen, sie so zu beeindrucken, dass sie ihn liebt und ihr volles Vertrauen in ihn setzt. Ein Mann kommt weder zum Erfolg, indem er genau ihren Neigungen Folge leistet, noch indem er vollständig dagegen handelt. Er muss einen Mittelweg finden.

Ein Mann, der weiß, wie er Frauen dazu bringt, dass sie ihn lieben, wie auch, ihnen Ehre zuerweisen und ihr Vertrauen zu gewinnen, der wird ein Objekt ihrer Liebe. Doch jener, der ein Mädchen vernachlässigt, weil er es als zu schüchtern betrachtet, der wird von ihm verachtet als Rohling, der keine Ahnung vom Wirken des weiblichen Gemüts hat. Außerdem: Ein Mädchen, das gewaltsam von jemandem genommen wird, der die Herzen der Mädchen nicht versteht, wird nervös, ängstlich und deprimiert. Und plötzlich beginnt es, den Mann zu hassen, der ihm das angetan hat. Wenn die Liebe des Mädchens nicht verstanden und erwidert wird, gerät es in Verzweiflung und wird entweder ein Hasser der ganzen Männerwelt oder, während es den eigenen Mann hasst, sucht es schließlich Zuflucht bei anderen Männern.«

Gegenüberliegende Seite: Körperbeherrschung und Beweglichkeit sind für Mann und Frau Voraussetzung, um die besonderen Genüsse der Liebe zu erfahren.

Folgende Seiten: Stellungen, bei denen der Mann die Frau trägt, sind schwierig, aber lustvoll, weil die eng umklammerten Genitalien für besondere Reize sorgen.

خلوت شهزاده شهریار ولد جهانگیر
عمل هونهار

Vom Leben als sittsame Gattin

Eine sittsame Frau, die ihrem Mann zugetan ist, sollte im Einklang mit seinen Wünschen handeln, als ob er ein göttliches Wesen wäre. Und mit seiner Einwilligung sollte sie es übernehmen, sich um seine Familie zu kümmern. Sie hat das Haus sauber zu halten, es an verschiedenen Stellen mit Blumen zu dekorieren, den Fußboden eben und rein zu halten, so dass alles nett und ordentlich aussieht. Um das Haus legt sie einen Garten an, der alles für die morgendlichen, mittäglichen und abendlichen Opferzeremonien Erforderliche liefert. Außerdem kümmert sie sich um den Altar der Hausgötter. Denn Gonardiya sagt: »Nichts erfreut das Herz des Hausherrn mehr, als wenn seine Gattin sorgfältig all die Aufgaben erfüllt, die eben erwähnt wurden.«

Gegenüber den Eltern, Verwandten, Freunden, Schwestern und Bediensteten des Gatten verhält sie sich so, wie es diese verdienen. Im Garten pflanzt sie Gemüse, Fenchel und *Xanthochymus pictorius.* Sie legt Beete an mit verschiedenen Blumen, beispielsweise *Tra-*

Gegenüberliegende Seite: Der Ehemann übt sich im Bogenschießen, während seine Frau neben ihm liegt und träumt.

Folgende Seiten: Der Ehemann sollte seine Frau stets an seiner Seite haben, auch wenn er sich der Gesellschaft von Kurtisanen erfreut.

pa bispinosa, Jasmin, *Gasminum grandiflorum*, Gelbes Tausendschön, Wildjasmin, *Tabernamontana coronaria*, Nadyawort und Chinarose, dazu das duftenden Gras *Andropogon miricatus*. Sie sorgt auch für das Aufstellen von Bänken und Lauben. Und in die Mitte des Gartens könnte sie einen Brunnen oder auch ein Wasserbecken setzen lassen.

Die Gattin sollte stets die Begleitung von Bettlern und Bettelmönchen, unzüchtigen und schurkischen Frauen, weiblichen Wahrsagern und Zauberern meiden. Bezüglich der Speisen behält sie ständig im Auge, was ihr Gatte mag und was nicht und welche Dinge gut und gesund sind für ihn und welche nicht. Hört sie ihn heimkommen, so erhebt sie sich sofort und zeigt sich bereit, alles auszuführen, was er anordnet. Entweder befiehlt sie den Dienern, seine Füße zu waschen, oder sie tut das selbst. Geht sie mit ihm aus, legt sie ihren Schmuck an. Ohne seine Einwilligung darf sie keine Einladungen verschicken und auch keine annehmen, keine Hochzeitsfeste oder Opferrituale besuchen, nicht in Begleitung von Freundinnen sitzen oder die Gotteshäuser besuchen. Wenn sie sich an Sport und Spiel beteiligen will, dann ohne gegen seinen Willen zu verstoßen. Sie setzt sich immer nach ihm hin und steht vor ihm auf. Sie weckt ihn nicht, wenn er schläft. Die Küche sollte sich in einem ruhigen, abgelegenen Winkel des Hauses befinden, der Fremden nicht zugänglich ist. Sie muss stets rein aussehen.

Im Fall eines Fehlverhaltens ihres Gatten schimpft sie nicht sehr, sondern darf ein bisschen verärgert sein. Sie darf ihn nicht mit Kraftausdrücken belegen, sondern tadelt ihn mit versöhnlichen Bemerkungen, egal ob er allein oder in Begleitung von Freunden ist. Außerdem darf sie kein zänkisches Weib sein. Denn Gonardiya sagt: »Es gibt für einen Gatten keinen größeren Grund für Missfallen als diese Unart von Frauen.« Schließlich vermeidet sie schlechte Ausdrücke und mürrische Miene und ebenso, beiseite zu sprechen, in der Tür zu stehen

Gegenüberliegende Seite: So wie die Ehefrau den Wünschen des Ehemannes folgt, sollte er ihre Sehnsüchte erfüllen sowie ihren Erfahrungsschatz erweitern.

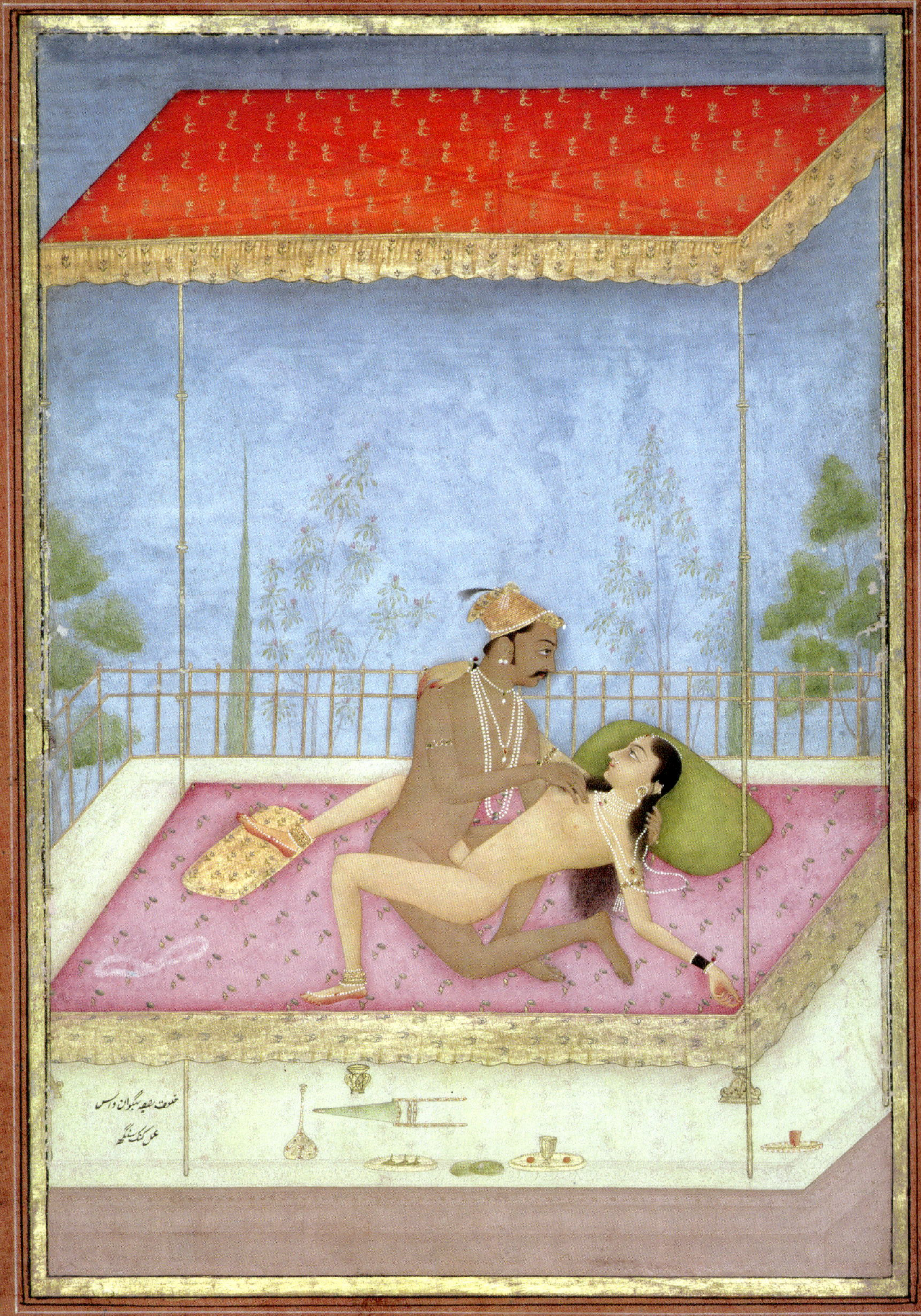
عمل کنک سنگه

und auf Passanten zu schauen, im Vergnügungspark zu plaudern, für längere Zeit an einem einsamen Ort zu verweilen. Selbstverständlich hält sie ständig ihren Körper, ihre Zähne, ihr Haar und alles, was zu ihr gehört, sauber und in ordentlichem Zustand.

Möchte sich die Frau ihrem Gatten privat nähern, so zieht sie an Ornamenten reiche Kleidung an, zu der auch Blumen und mehrfarbiger Schmuck gehören. Und sie trägt süßlich duftendes Parfüm auf. Hingegen sollte ihre Kleidung für den normalen Tag aus einem dünnen, eng gewebten Stoff, ein paar Ornamenten und Blumen bestehen, und sie verwendet nur ein bisschen Parfüm. Hält sie das Fasten und die Gelübde ihres Gatten ein und versucht er, sie davon abzubringen, so hat sie ihn zu überzeugen, dass er es ihr doch gestattet.

Zur geeigneten Jahreszeit, auch wenn sie billig sind, kauft sie Erde, Bambus, Feuerholz, Felle und Eisentöpfe sowie Salz und Öl ein. Wenn erforderlich, kauft sie auch Duftstoffe, Behälter aus der Pflanze *Wrightea antidysenterica* oder ovalblätterige *Wrigthea*, Arzneien und andere ständig gebrauchte Dinge und verwahrt sie an einem sicheren Platz im Haus. Die Saat von Rettich, Kartoffel, Runkelrübe, Indischem Wermut, Mango, Gurke, Aubergine, *Kushmanda*, Flaschenkürbis, *Suvana*, *Bigonia indica*, *Premna spinosa*, Sandelholz, Knoblauch, Zwiebel und verschiedenem Gemüse kauft sie so, dass sie zur rechten Zeit in den Boden gebracht werden kann.

Fremden darf die Ehefrau nichts vom Ausmaß des Reichtums berichten und auch keine Geheimnisse verraten, die ihr ihr Mann anvertraut hat. Sie hat alle Frauen ihres Ranges bezüglich Geschick, Erscheinung und Aussehen, Stolz, Kochkunst und der Art, ihrem Mann zu dienen, zu übertreffen. Die Jahresausgaben sollten im Einklang mit den Einnahmen stehen. Aus restlicher Milch kann man Butterfett machen, Öl und Zucker zu Hause zubereiten. Dort kann man auch Spinnen und Weben, aus Baumrinde Seile und Schnüre anfertigen. Die Ehefrau befasst sich auch mit dem Reinigen und

Gegenüberliegende Seite: Um ihrem Mann zu zeigen, dass sie Lust auf Sex hat, soll die Frau prächtige Gewänder, auffälligen Schmuck und süßlich duftendes Parfüm tragen.

Zerstampfen von Reis und sorgt für die Verwendung der kleinen Körner und der Spreu. Sie ist verantwortlich für das Zahlen der Löhne an das Dienstpersonal, die Beaufsichtigung der Feldarbeiten sowie für die Widder, Hähne, Wachteln, Papageien, Stare, Kuckucke, Pfaue, Affen und Rehe. Schließlich muss sie die Einnahmen und Ausgaben des Tages vergleichen. Abgetragene Kleidung sollte den Hausangestellten geschenkt werden, die gute Arbeit verrichteten, um ihnen zu zeigen, dass ihr Dienst Anerkennung findet, oder sie sollte andere Verwendung finden. Besondere Aufmerksamkeit hat den Gefäßen zu gelten, in denen Wein zubereitet und aufbewahrt wird. Alle Käufe und Verkäufe müssen sorgfältig vorgenommen werden. Freunde des Gatten muss die Ehefrau willkommen heißen, indem sie sie mit Blumen, Balsam, Duftstäbchen, Betelblättern und Betelnüssen beschenkt. Ihre Schwiegereltern muss sie gebührlich behandeln und ihnen stets gehorchen. Nie darf sie ihnen widersprechen oder ihnen kurz angebunden oder in harschen Worten antworten. Sie darf in deren Gegenwart auch nicht laut lachen. Die Freunde und Feinde der Schwiegereltern muss sie wie ihre eigenen behandeln. Außerdem sollte sie nicht eitel oder zu sehr auf Vergnügungen aus sein. Sie sollte sich dem Dienstpersonal gegenüber liberal verhalten, es an Feiertagen und Festen auszeichnen, aber nichts weggeben, ohne zuvor den Gatten davon in Kenntnis gesetzt zu haben.

Dies zum Thema, wie man das Leben einer sittsamen Gattin führt.

Während längerer Abwesenheit ihres Mannes trägt die sittsame Ehefrau nur ihre Amulette und Glücksbringer und hält das Fasten zu Ehren der Götter ein. Während sie sehnsüchtig auf Neuigkeiten von ihrem Gatten wartet, fährt sie mit den Haushaltspflichten fort. Sie sollte in der Nähe der älteren Frauen im Haus schlafen und ihnen behilflich sein. Sie muss sich um die Pflege der Sachen kümmern, an denen ihr Gatte hängt, und die Arbeiten fortsetzen, die er begonnen hat. Sie darf nicht

Gegenüberliegende Seite: Wenn der Mann erregt ist, muss er auch seine Frau in Stimmung bringen, indem er sie zärtlich an ihren erogenen Zonen streichelt.

Gegenüberliegende Seite: Haltungen im Stehen verlangen Kraft und Kontrollvermögen.

Folgende Seiten: Rhada hat das Liebeslager vorbereitet und wartet sehnsüchtig darauf, dass Krishna ihr seine Aufmerksamkeit schenkt.

Zuflucht suchen bei Verwandten, außer bei freudigen oder traurigen Anlässen; dann sollte sie in ihrer üblichen Reisekleidung zu ihnen gehen, begleitet von Bediensteten ihres Gatten, und dort nicht zu lange verweilen. Das Fasten und die Feste sollten in Übereinstimmung mit den Ältesten des Hauses befolgt werden. Das Vermögen sollte durch Käufe und Verkäufe gemäß den Regeln der Händler sowie durch Mithilfe ehrlicher, von ihr überwachter Diener vermehrt werden. Die Einnahmen sollten gesteigert und die Ausgaben so weit wie möglich gesenkt werden. Kommt der Ehemann von seiner Reise zurück, empfängt seine Ehefrau ihn zunächst in ihrer Alltagskleidung, damit er gleich erkennt, womit sie sich in der Zeit seiner Abwesenheit beschäftigt hat, und übergibt ihm ein paar nette Geschenke sowie die notwendigen Utensilien zum Anbeten der Götteridole.

Dies zum Verhalten der Frau während längerer Abwesenheit des Gatten. Die Merksätze zum Thema sind: »Die Gattin, sei sie aus nobler Familie, eine wiederverheiratete jungfräuliche Witwe oder eine Konkubine, muss ein züchtiges Leben führen, ihrem Gatten ergeben sein und alles für sein Wohlergehen tun. So handelnde Frauen erwerben *Dharma*, *Artha* und *Kama* sowie eine hohe Stellung in der Gesellschaft, und sie bewirken damit im Allgemeinen, dass der Gatte ihnen gewogen bleibt.«

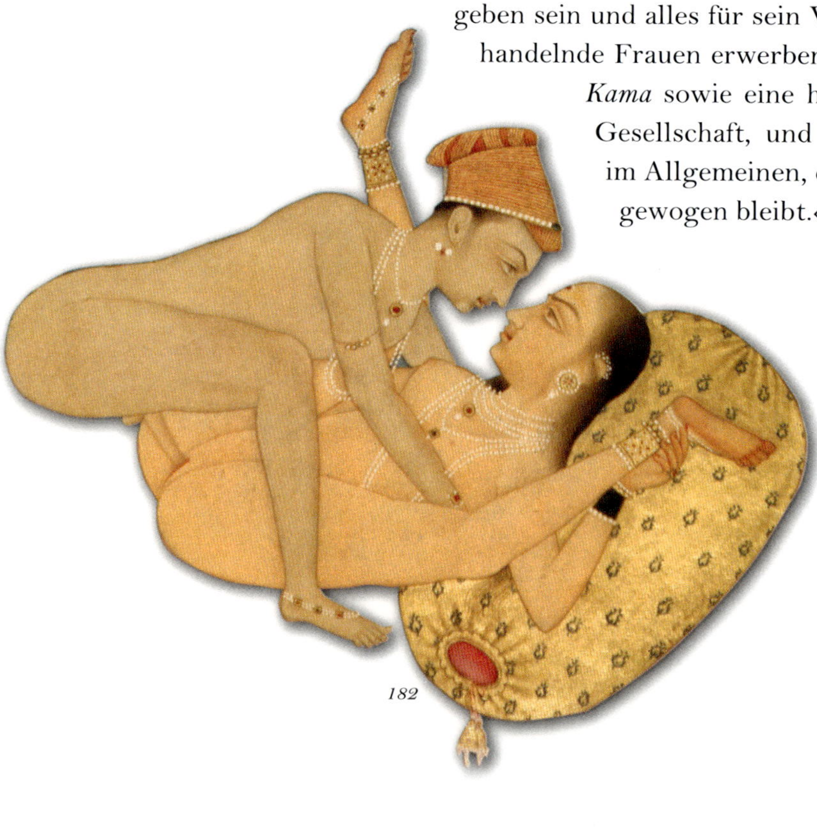

Vom Benehmen der Ehemänner und der Ehefrauen

Die Gründe für zusätzliche Heiraten sind: Torheit oder Jähzorn der Gattin; der Gatte mag sie nicht; keine Nachkommen; fortgesetzte Geburt von Töchtern; Unmäßigkeit des Gatten.

Von Anfang an sollte eine Ehefrau sich bemühen, das Herz ihres Gatten zu gewinnen, indem sie ihm ständig ihre Hingabe, ihren guten Charakter und ihr Wissen beweist. Bekommt sie allerdings keine Kinder, dann empfiehlt sie ihrem Mann selbst, eine andere zu heiraten. Und wenn er die zweite Frau geehelicht hat und ins Haus bringt, dann hat die erste Gattin ihr eine höhere Position einzuräumen und sie als Schwester zu betrachten. Morgens sollte die ältere Gattin die jüngere dazu zwingen, sich in Gegenwart ihres Gatten zu schmücken, und nichts dagegen einwenden, wenn der Gatte der jüngeren Frau alle Gunst erweist. Macht die jüngere Ehefrau etwas, was dem Gatten missfällt, darf die ältere das nicht durchgehen lassen, sondern sie muss stets bereit sein, sorgfältig Rat zu geben. Sie muss die jüngere im

Gegenüberliegende Seite: Ein Mann, der mehrere Ehefrauen hat, muss seine erotische Gunst auf alle gerecht verteilen.

Beisein des Gatten verschiedene Dinge lehren. Deren Kinder muss sie wie eigene behandeln. Deren Dienstpersonal muss sie sich noch aufmerksamer als ihrem eigenen widmen. Deren Freundinnen muss sie mit Liebe und Freundlichkeit überschütten und deren Verwandte mit großer Ehrerbietung.

Gibt es noch mehr Ehefrauen außer ihr, dann muss sich die ältere Gattin mit der verbünden, die ihr im Rang und Alter am nächsten steht. Und sie sollte Streit inszenieren zwischen der Gattin, die zuletzt in der Gunst des Ehemannes stand, und der jetzigen Favoritin. Dann sollte sie mit der ersten sympathisieren. Und nachdem sich alle anderen Frauen versammelt haben, sollte sie die veranlassen, die Favoritin eine Intrigantin und Sünderin zu schelten, ohne selbst daran beteiligt zu sein. Wenn die Favoritin mit dem Gatten streitet, sollte die ältere Ehefrau sich einmischen, ihr falsche Ermutigung geben und damit den Zank noch intensivieren. Gibt es nur eine kleinere Meinungsverschiedenheit zwischen beiden, dann sollte die ältere Gattin alles tun, damit daraus ein ernster Streit wird. Bemerkt sie, dass auch danach der Gatte an der Favoritin festhält, muss sie ihre Taktik ändern und nun versuchen, eine Versöhnung zwischen beiden zu arrangieren, damit sie sich nicht das Missfallen des Gatten zuzieht. Damit endet der Abschnitt über das Benehmen der älteren Ehefrau.

Die jüngere Gattin sollte die ältere als ihre Mutter betrachten. Sie darf ohne Wissen der Älteren nichts verschenken, auch nicht an ihre Verwandten. Sie muss ihr alles über sich selbst erzählen. Und sie darf sich ihrem Gatten nicht ohne Erlaubnis der Älteren nähern. Was auch immer ihr die ältere Ehefrau berichtet, darf sie anderen nicht mitteilen. Um die Kinder der älteren Frau sollte sie sich noch mehr als um die eigenen kümmern. Ist sie allein mit ihrem Gatten, hat sie ihn zuvorkommend zu bedienen. Aber sie darf ihm nichts von dem Schmerz erzählen, den sie durch eine Rivalin unter den Ehefrauen erleidet. Heimlich mag sie von ihrem Gatten

Gegenüberliegende Seite: Die Ehefrau sollte sich für ihren Mann pflegen und hübsch zurechtmachen.

Folgende Seiten: Eine Frau kann ihren Mann mit außergewöhnlichen sexuellen Genüssen verwöhnen, um ihre Konkurrentinnen auszustechen.

auch ein paar Hinweise erhalten, warum er sie so besonders mag. Und sie kann ihm beteuern, dass sie nur für ihn lebt und für die Zuneigung, die er ihr erweist. Niemals darf sie anderen Personen ihre Liebe zu ihrem Gatten oder dessen Liebe zu ihr enthüllen – weder aus Stolz noch aus Ärger, denn eine Ehefrau, die Geheimnisse ihres Mannes ausplaudert, wird von ihm verachtet. Um einen Gunstbeweis vom eigenen Gatten, sagt Gonardiya, sollte man aus Furcht vor der älteren Ehefrau stets nur unter vier Augen ersuchen. Wird die ältere Ehefrau von dem Gatten nicht gemocht oder ist sie kinderlos, sollte sie mit ihr sympathisieren und dem Gatten dasselbe empfehlen. Doch in der Lebensführung als züchtige Frau muss sie sie übertreffen. Damit endet das Verhalten der jüngeren gegenüber der älteren Gattin.

Eine Witwe in armen Verhältnissen oder eine Witwe von schwachem Wesen, die sich wieder mit einem Mann verbindet, wird eine wiederverheiratete Witwe genannt. Die Anhänger Babhravyas sagen, dass eine jungfräuliche Witwe keinen Mann heiraten soll, den sie wegen schlechten Charakters oder seiner mangelnden guten Eigenschaften ohnehin wieder verlassen wird. Sie soll sich deshalb lieber einem anderen Mann zuwenden. Gonardiya glaubt, dass es besser ist, einen Mann mit ausgezeichneten Eigenschaften zu besitzen, da der Grund für die Wiederheirat einer Witwe ihr Wunsch nach Glück ist, und das – verbunden mit Liebe und Beglückung – kann nur ein Mann mit solchen Eigenschaften. Vatsyayana dagegen denkt, dass eine Witwe jeden Mann heiraten mag, der ihr gefällt und von dem sie glaubt, dass er zu ihr passt.

Zur Hochzeit sollte die Witwe Geld von ihrem künftigen Gatten bekommen, um die Kosten für die Feiern und Picknicks mit ihren Verwandten zu bezahlen und ihnen und ihren Freunden nette Geschenke zu machen. Sie darf das auch auf eigene Kosten machen, wenn sie es wünscht. Ebenso kann sie den eigenen oder den vom Gatten besorgten Schmuck tragen. Keine festen Regeln gibt es über den Austausch von Liebesgeschenken zwischen

Gegenüberliegende Seite: Die Stellungen mit vertauschten Rollen können für den Mann besonders erregend sein – vor allem, wenn die Frau dabei seinen Lingam massiert.

ihr und dem Gatten. Verlässt sie auf eigenes Verlangen nach der Hochzeit ihren Gatten, dann muss sie ihm alles zurückgeben, was sie von ihm erhalten hat, mit Ausnahme der gegenseitigen Geschenke. Wird sie allerdings von ihrem Ehemann zum Verlassen des Hauses gezwungen, so muss sie ihm nichts zurückgeben.

Nach der Heirat lebt sie im Haus des Mannes so wie eines der Hauptmitglieder der Familie. Aber die anderen Damen der Familie behandelt sie mit Freundlichkeit, die Diener mit Großzügigkeit und alle Freunde des Hauses zuvorkommend und mit Geselligkeit. Sie zeigt, dass sie besser mit den vierundsechzig Arten der Liebe vertraut ist als alle anderen Frauen des Hauses. Im Fall eines Streits mit ihrem Gatten darf sie ihn nicht scharf tadeln. Privat muss sie alles machen, was er will. Sie darf die vierundsechzig Arten des sexuellen Genusses anwenden. Anderen Ehefrauen ihres Gatten hat sie zu gehorchen, deren Kindern Geschenke zu geben, sich als Lehrerin zu betätigen und Schmuckgegenstände und Spielzeug für sie zu basteln. Den Freunden und Angestellten ihres Gatten sollte sie mehr vertrauen als den anderen Frauen. Schließlich sollte sie Gefallen haben am Besuch von Gesellschaften, Picknicks, Festen und Festivals sowie für alle Arten von Sport, Spiel und Unterhaltung. Dies zum Benehmen einer jungfräulichen Witwe, die wiederverheiratet wurde.

Eine Frau, die von ihrem Mann nicht geliebt und von den anderen Frauen behelligt und geärgert wird, muss sich mit der Frau verbünden, die am meisten von dem Ehemann geliebt wird und die ihn mehr als die anderen bedient. Der sollte sie alle Künste, mit denen sie vertraut ist, beibringen. Sie sollte zu den Kindern des Gatten wie eine Amme sein. Und nachdem sie seine Freunde für sich eingenommen hat, können diese ihm von ihrer Hingabe berichten. Bei religiösen Zeremonien ist sie der Vorstand, ebenso bei Gelübden und beim Fasten. Von sich selbst darf sie keine zu hohe Meinung haben. Liegt ihr Gatte auf dem Bett, nähert sie sich ihm nur, wenn er das wünscht. Sie darf ihn nicht tadeln oder sich ihm gegenüber irgendwie auf-

Gegenüberliegende Seite: Wenn beide es wünschen, kann sich eine verheiratete Frau zugleich mit ihrem Gatten und einem weiteren Mann vereinigen.

Gegenüberliegende Seite: Erlaubt ist, was beiden gefällt – auch der eigentlich »unsittliche« Oralverkehr.

sässig zeigen. Streitet sich ihr Gatte mit einer seiner Frauen, muss sie sie wieder versöhnen. Wünscht er, eine seiner Frauen heimlich zu treffen, arrangiert sie das. Sie nimmt die Schwachpunkte ihres Gatten zur Kenntnis, aber behält das für sich. Sie muss sich so benehmen, dass dies dazu führt, dass er in ihr eine gute und hingebungsvolle Gattin erblickt. Dies zum Verhalten einer Ehefrau, die von ihrem Gatten nicht geliebt wird.

Ein Mann, der mit vielen Frauen verheiratet ist, muss alle fair behandeln. Er darf keine missachten oder übergehen und keiner die Liebe, Leidenschaft, körperlichen Makel und intimen Besonderheiten einer anderen enthüllen. Keine darf eine Gelegenheit erhalten, zu ihm über ihre Rivalinnen zu sprechen. Beginnt doch eine, schlecht über eine andere zu reden, muss er sie zurechtweisen und ihr sagen, dass sie genau denselben Makel in ihrem Charakter hat. Der einen sollte er durch geheime Vertraulichkeit Gunst erweisen, einer anderen durch geheime Achtung, noch einer anderen durch geheime Schmeichelei. Er sollte sie alle erfreuen, indem er mit ihnen durch die Gärten spaziert, durch Amüsement, Geschenke, indem er ihre Verwandten ehrt, ihnen Geheimnisse mitteilt und schließlich durch die Liebesakte. Eine junge Frau von gutem Wesen, die sich entsprechend den Regeln der Heiligen Schrift aufführt, gewinnt die Anhänglichkeit ihres Gatten und die Oberhand über ihre Rivalinnen.

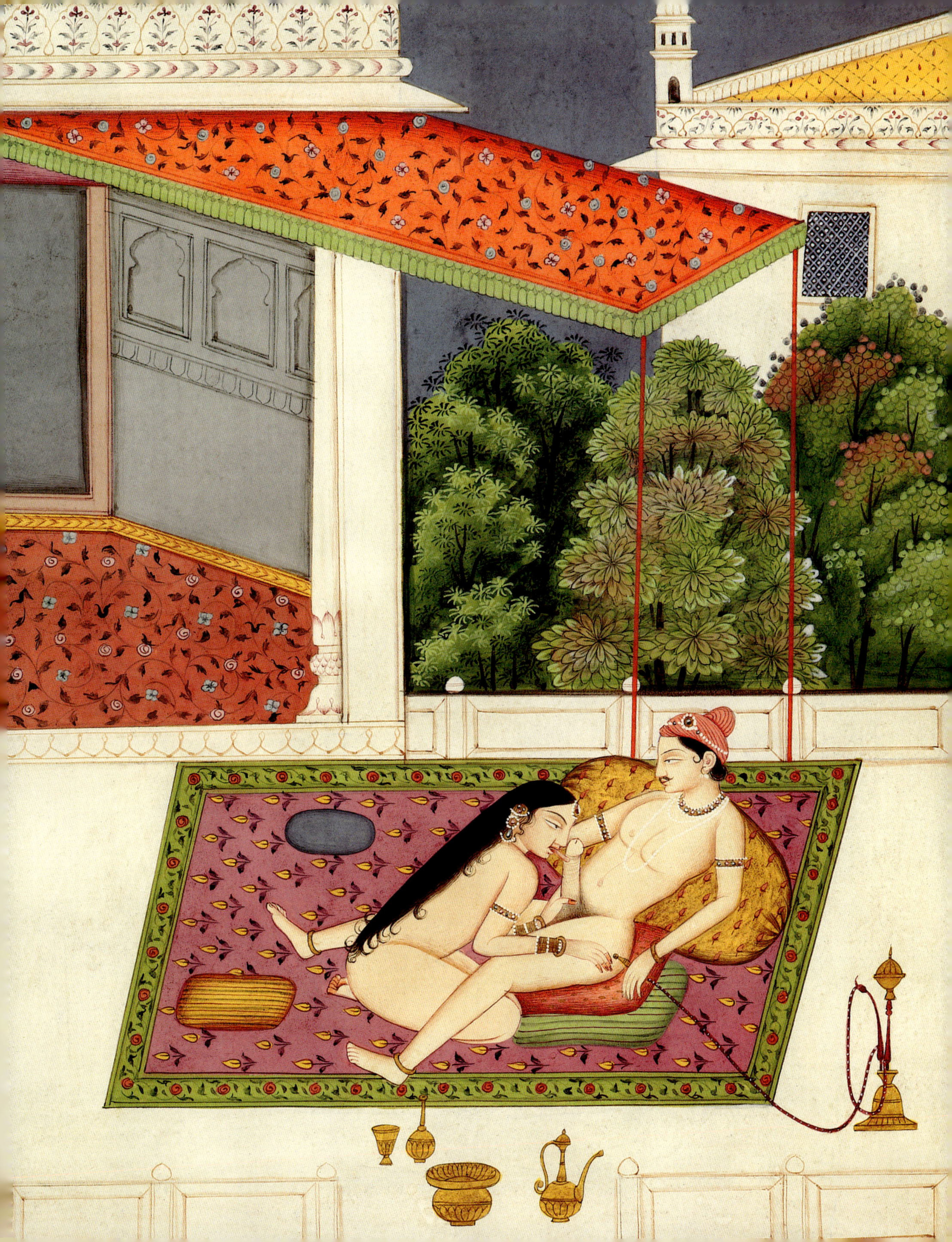

Wie man Gefühle durch äußere Zeichen und Taten bekundet

Ein armer Mann mit guten Eigenschaften, ein Mann aus einer niederen Familie mit mittelmäßigen Eigenschaften, ein Nachbar mit Reichtum und einer, der unter der Kontrolle seines Vaters, seiner Mutter oder seiner Brüder steht, sollte nicht heiraten, ohne versucht zu haben, ein Mädchen für sich zu gewinnen, das er seit dessen Kindheit liebt und schätzt.

So sollte ein Junge, der von seinen Eltern getrennt im Hause seines Onkels lebt, den Versuch machen, die Tochter des Onkels oder ein anderes Mädchen für sich zu gewinnen, selbst wenn dieses vorher bereits mit einem anderen verlobt wurde.

Hat ein Junge auf diese Art begonnen, ein Mädchen, das er liebt, zu betören, dann muss er seine Zeit mit ihm verbringen, es mit verschiedenen Spielen und anderen Dingen unterhalten, die zum Alter des Mädchens passen, beispielsweise Blumen pflücken, Girlanden aus Blumen flechten, Rollen von Mitgliedern einer fiktiven Familie spielen, Essen zubereiten, Spiel mit Würfeln und Karten,

Gegenüberliegende Seite: Wer eine Frau verführen will, sollte ihrer Vertrauten von den eigenen Talenten als Liebhaber berichten, denn es ist davon auszugehen, dass diese der Angebeteten davon erzählt.

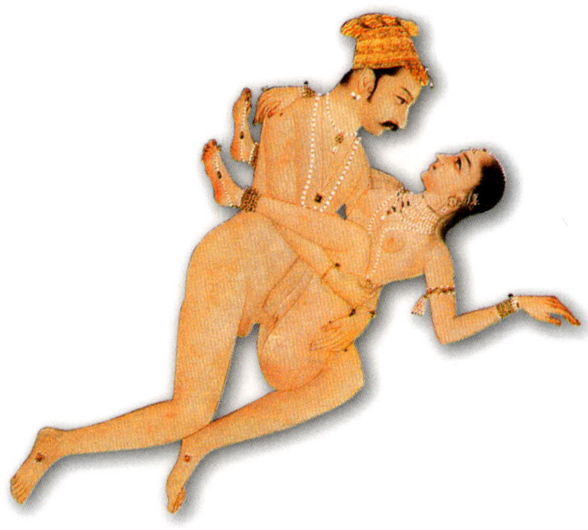

das Spiel der Ungleichen und Gleichen, das Spiel vom Suchen des Mittelfingers, das Spiel von den sechs Steinen und andere, die im Lande üblich sind und der Verfassung des Mädchens entsprechen. Zusätzlich sollte er andere Spiele einführen, bei denen mehrere Personen, z. B. Freunde, weibliches Dienstpersonal, mitwirken. Das könnten Verstecken, Blinde Kuh aber auch gymnastische Übungen sein.

Der Junge sollte stets jeder Frau, dem das Mädchen vertraut, größte Freundlichkeit erweisen bzw. Bekanntschaft mit ihnen schließen. Vor allem sollte er durch Artigkeiten und kleine Dienste die Tochter der Amme des Mädchens an sich binden, denn wenn die gewonnen wird, legt sie seinen Absichten, selbst wenn sie die durchschaut, nichts in den Weg und ist manchmal in der Lage, eine Verbindung zwischen ihm und dem Mädchen zu arrangieren. Obwohl sie den wahren mangelhaften Charakter des Mannes kennt, schildert sie seine vielen exzellenten Eigenschaften gegenüber den Eltern und Verwandten des Mädchens, auch wenn sie von ihm damit nicht beauftragt wurde.

Als nächsten Schritt bringt er das Mädchen dazu, dass es ihn privat trifft. Dabei erklärt er, dass er ihm heimlich die Geschenke übergibt, weil er Angst hat, den Eltern beider könnte das missfallen. Er könnte hinzufügen, dass die Geschenke, die er ihr gemacht hat, von anderen sehr begehrt sind.

Nimmt die Liebe des Mädchens spürbar zu, könnte er ihm, wenn es das mag, nette Geschichten erzählen. Wenn dem Mädchen Taschenspielerei gefällt, sollte er es mit der Vorführung einiger Tricks vergnügen. Oder wenn es neugierig ist, künstlerischen Aufführungen zuzusehen, sollte er eine Kostprobe eigenen Talents geben. Wenn es Gefallen an Musik findet, kann er es damit unterhalten.

Bevor es nach Hause zurückkehrt, überreicht er dem Mädchen Blumensträuße, Kränze fürs Haar, Ohrgehänge und Ringe, denn das sind die richtigen Gelegenheiten für solche Aufmerksamkeiten.

Gegenüberliegende Seite: Einer im Kamasutra erfahrenen Frau gelingt es leicht, den müden Liebhaber wieder auf Trab zu bringen.

Die Tochter der Amme des Mädchens sollte er in den vierundsechzig Arten des von Männern ausgeübten Vergnügens unterweisen und sie unter diesem Vorwand auch von seinen großen Fertigkeiten in der Kunst der sexuellen Freuden in Kenntnis setzen.

Stets sollte er feine Kleidung tragen und so gut wie nur möglich aussehen, denn junge Frauen lieben Männer, die nett aussehen und adrett gekleidet sind. Was die Ansicht anlangt, dass Frauen, selbst wenn sie sich verlieben, von sich aus keine Anstrengungen machen, sich dem Objekt ihrer Zuneigung zu nähern, so ist das eben nur Gerede.

Gegenüberliegende Seite: Der Akt ist eine vergnügliche Leibesübung, deshalb ermuntert Vatsyayana dazu, alle Körperteile einzubeziehen.

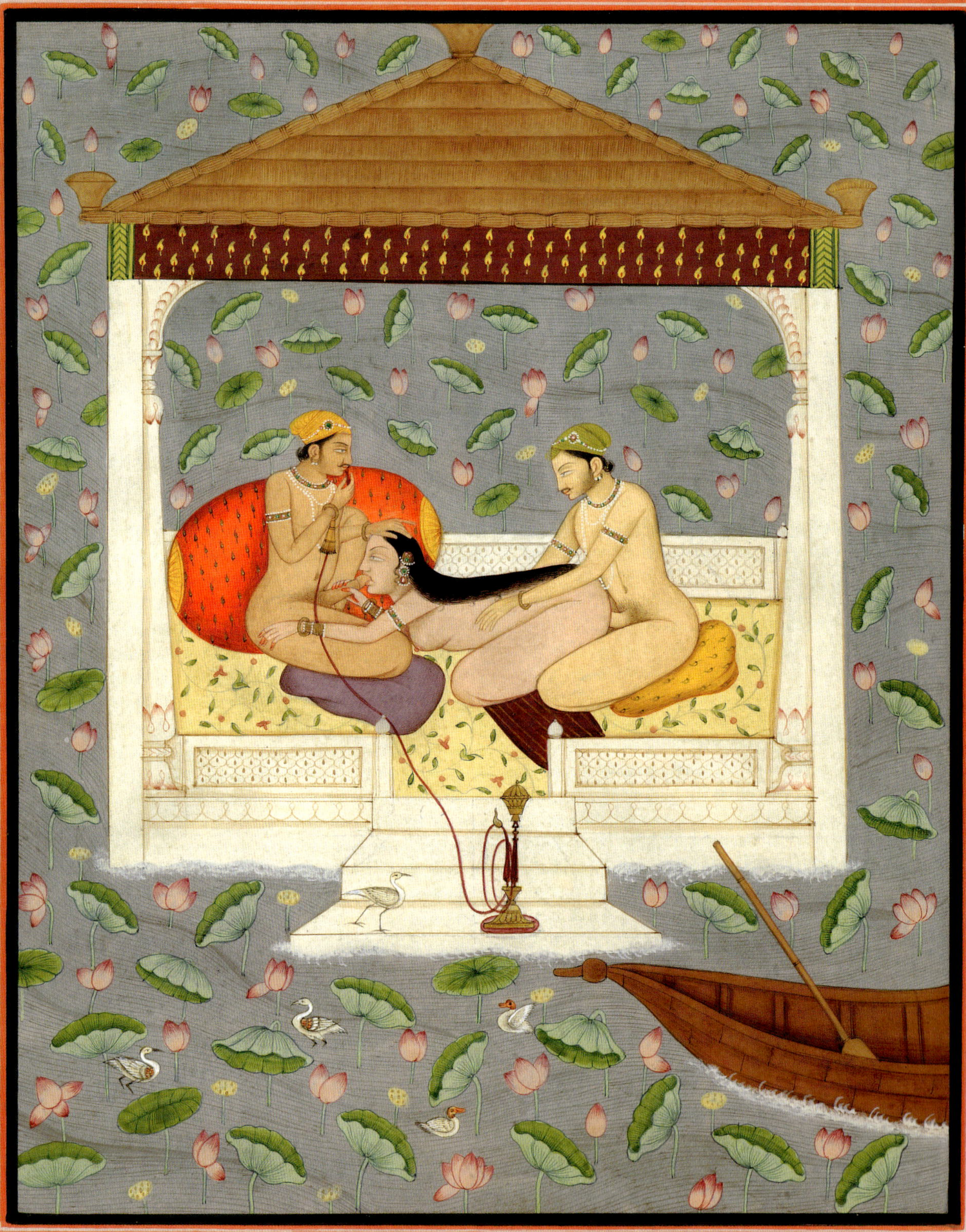

Literaturhinweise

Kamasutra für jeden Tag

(Dorling Kindersley 2022)
Benötigt die neue Partnerschaft mehr Feuer oder möchten Sie die Intimität in der bestehenden Beziehung auffrischen? Dieser Leitfaden bietet sinnlich und lustvoll 365 Möglichkeiten für ein frisches Liebesleben! Angeregt von den Klassikern der erotischen Literatur, wie dem Kamasutra, vereint dieses Buch Leidenschaft und sexuelle Kreativität auf moderne Art und Weise.

Kamasutra Workout

(Dorling Kindersley 2018)
Kamasutra meets Workout: Dieses originelle Buch im kompakten Format ist eine Verbindung aus Fitness- und Sex-Ratgeber. Hier erwarten Sie 300 illustrierte Kamasutra-Stellungen von sinnlich bis akrobatisch, die Ihnen zeigen welche Muskeln beansprucht, wieviel Energie beim Bettsport verbrannt wird, wie beweglich beide Partner sein müssen und wie lange die Stellung gehalten werden sollte. Bei dieser sportlichen Variante der klassischen Sexpraktik bekommt jeder sofort Lust aufs Training: Spaß im Bett haben, gleichzeitig Kalorien verbrennen und Muskeln aufbauen. „Sexercise" in Perfektion!

Gegenüberliegende Seite: Ein abgelegener Pavillon, umgeben von Lotusblüten, bietet das perfekte Ambiente für aufregenden Sex zu dritt. Der Lotus ist das Sinnbild der erotischen Liebe.

Folgende Seiten: Ein Mann muss seine Liebste mit Geschenken und spontanen Besuchen umwerben, ehe sie dem Liebesakt zustimmt.